THE STRUCTURES OF THE LIFE-WORLD

Northwestern University
Studies in Phenomenology
and
Existential Philosophy

Translated by

Richard M. Zaner

and

David J. Parent

THE
STRUCTURES
OF THE
LIFE-WORLD

Volume II

Alfred Schutz
and
Thomas Luckmann

Northwestern University Press
Evanston, Illinois 60201

Printed in the United States of America

Library of Congress Cataloging-in-Publication Data
(Revised for vol. 2)

Schutz, Alfred, 1899-1959.
  The structures of the life-world.

  (Northwestern University studies in phenomenology
& existential philosophy)
  Translation of Strukturen der Lebenswelt.
  Series statement in v. 2: Northwestern University
studies in phenomenology and existential philosophy.
  Includes bibliographical references.
  1. Life. 2. Knowledge, Sociology of. 3. Phenomenology.
I. Luckmann, Thomas, joint author. II. Title.
BD431.S284913   110   72-85708
ISBN 0-8101-0395-8 (v. 1)
ISBN 0-8101-0832-1 (v. 2)
ISBN 0-8101-0833-X (pbk. : v. 2)

Contents

Translators' Preface

It has been fifteen years since the first volume of this seminal study was published.[1] That volume quickly won wide critical acclaim, and has had substantial influence among social and human scientists and philosophers. The second volume will, we believe, be similarly received.

As those who have read the first volume know, there were only a few tantalizing hints about the contents of the second. Professor Luckmann indicated in his preface to the former that he had decided to remove several of its sections. One, on the boundaries of the social world, led Luckmann to conclusions with which, as Aron Gurwitsch pointed out to him, Schutz would have been unlikely to agree.[2] Another dealt with language in everyday life. Luckmann noted that although it was intended as a key part of the analysis of the connection between various finite provinces of meaning in chapter 2, "it grew out of all proportion and developed into an analysis of the constitution of language in everyday life."[3] Luckmann thus decided to incorporate it into chapter 6, and it is included here.[4]

As he also noted, another major change in Schutz's original plan had to be made: the projected chapter on the methodology of the social sciences was abandoned entirely. Not only did Schutz's plan not go much beyond what he had already accomplished in his earlier work,[5] but he did not give enough detail on how he had intended to proceed and what he intended to say beyond what had already been accomplished.[6]

Students of Schutz will also recall the unusual circumstances that led to this last study: that he had for some years planned to write this book, and that he had begun intensive preliminary work during the summer and fall of 1958, the year before his death in the spring of 1959. That preparatory work included a general outline, numerous references to his published work along with suggestions for its integration into the book, and drafts and *aide-mémoires* for analyses still to be carried out.

At Schutz's request, these materials were handed over to Luckmann by his widow, Ilse Schutz, with whom he also discussed the project. Realizing that although the study would surely have been the *magnum opus* of Schutz's prolific scholarly life, Luckmann was also acutely aware that, however faithfully he sought to adhere to Schutz's intentions,

> This book cannot be the book as Schutz would have written it. It is not even the book *I think* he would have written: a complete submersion of my own thought and work in his plan was neither possible nor, I am sure, was it something that Schutz would have wished under the circumstances.[7]

Even so, Luckmann's part in bringing out this remarkable study is both substantial and commendable. Working on these volumes, he noted, occupied "the major part" of his adult life,[8] a point of scholarly and personal devotion that should not go unrecognized or unappreciated. It should as well be noted, to Luckmann's great credit, that he has succeeded in this very difficult task with impressive skill and discipline. Even though he could not completely submerge his own thinking, he became so immersed in this project that it is in a sense true, as he says, that there are "whole areas of my thinking . . . where I find it most difficult to say with certainty what is *not* his."[9] His strong sense of scholarly integrity, however, should also be emphasized, as is evident in his own words:

> In a sense this book is the *Summa* of Schutz's life, and as such it is his book alone. In another sense it is the culmination of the work of many authors, among whom Schutz is the most important and I am merely the last. The analysis of the

structures of everyday life, however, is not completed in this book. It is an unending task of a *philosophia perennis* and of a historical theory of society.[10]

Indeed, in a discipline that has long prized the work of the individual, *The Structures of the Life-World* is a unique achievement, the product of a rare and wholly praiseworthy labor of genuine love, the single and singular work of two gifted scholars.

Like the first volume, the second presents remarkably detailed and incisive analyses of significant features of the life-world. Unlike the first, the second contains only two (albeit quite lengthy) chapters, which complete the plan of the first. In Volume I, Schutz and Luckmann had proceeded step by step with a phenomenological explication of the everyday life-world: its spatio-temporal stratification; horizons and zones of operation; the formation and articulation of the stock of knowledge; relevance systems and typicality; and the complex interrelations of knowledge acquisition and distribution via language, objectivations of the relative-natural worldview, subjectivity and society.

In Volume II, the authors cap these systematic explications with a detailed description of "The Life-World as the Province of Practice" (chapter 5) and "The Boundaries of Experience and Boundary Crossings: Communication in the Life-World" (chapter 6). Both chapters are built solidly on the foundations laid in the first volume. Chapter 5 explicates the structures of human action from encounter, experience, and thought to action, choice, project, and social interaction. Chapter 6 examines the ways by which the boundaries set by life itself are variously transcended: the "small" transcendencies that constitute the objective world; the "medium" transcendencies that appresent the fellowman through different experiences and co-experiences; and the "great" transcendencies that arise from encounters with other states of consciousness and situations (sleep, dream, ecstasy, crisis, death) that give glimpses of "other realities" beyond the everyday life-world in and through artistic or literary creation and religious and theoretical concerns. The chapter includes a section devoted to semiotic analysis of the various vehicles of appresentation: indications, marks, signs, and symbols. It concludes with a section on language, its constitution as a system of social meaning, its connection with the social structure, and its subjective correlatives.

The entire body of Schutz's materials from which Luckmann actually worked is included in an appendix. With Luckmann, we believe these materials will have substantial scholarly interest, for they provide a valuable research tool for viewing Schutz's earlier work and how he intended to reorganize it within this last *oeuvre*, as well as for other scholarly tasks. The core of the appended materials consists of Schutz's notebooks, written originally in German, that bring together and rearrange articles and essays he had originally published in English. The version of these notebooks we present here has been translated from the published German edition by Professor Luckmann. We have also included Schutz's file cards and tentative outline of the project, along with Luckmann's explanatory preface, summary of the contents, and list of abbreviations.

We are convinced that these two volumes constitute a truly seminal achievement, unmatched in their significance for the social and human sciences and for philosophy. The phenomenological explication of the life-world was Schutz's lifelong preoccupation. Thanks in large part to his comprehensive and original efforts, this theme has since come to be generally recognized as of critical importance for every disciplined study of human life and the nature of social reality.

Translators' Note

Recognizing the place Luckmann justifiably occupies in both volumes—perhaps even more evident here than in the first—we have nevertheless sought to render this volume into language commensurate with Schutz's own well-known terms and phraseology, and at all times in terms that cohere with the first volume.

As in Volume I, for instance, *Erfahrung* has been translated at times as "encounter" and at times as "experience," the context serving to provide the appropriate sense. As usage in German and English is similar about capitalizing or not capitalizing "Other" and "other people," the translators have generally followed the lead of the German text and have capitalized only when there was an explicit intention to highlight the transcendency of the fellowman. Philosophical translation poses special problems. The guideline we have followed is to use, as far as possible, idiomatic language that accords with the educated general reader's sense of usage, while abiding with the conventions of technical accuracy and current philosophical terminology. The result cannot, of course, be a code for word-for-word rendition of the German original—such a task is not generally the purpose of translation. We hope that the text is readable, clear, and accurate and will enable the reader to follow the authors' thought with ease, understanding, and enjoyment.

Special thanks go to the National Endowment for the Humanities for funding received by David J. Parent in the summer of 1988 to participate in the Second Literary Translation Institute at the University of California, Santa Cruz, directed by Gabriel Berns and Joanna Bankier. In addition to the stimulating group program at the institute, time and facilities were provided to work on individual projects, for which Professor Parent is most grateful. We wish to give special acknowledgment as well to Mrs. Ilse Schutz, whose enduring encouragement, support, and patience over the years have been crucial to this and many other projects to make Alfred Schutz's seminal endeavors available to the scholarly community.

5

The Life-World
as the
Province of Practice

A. Action and the Understanding of Action as a Performance of Consciousness

1. Life, Experience, Action

The life-world is the quintessence of a reality that is lived, experienced, and endured. It is, however, also a reality that is mastered by action and the reality in which—and on which—our action fails. Especially for the everyday life-world, it holds good that we engage in it by acting and change it by our actions. Everyday life is that province of reality in which we encounter directly, as the condition of our life, natural and social givens as pregiven realities with which we must try to cope. We must act in the everyday life-world, if we wish to keep ourselves alive. We experience everyday life essentially as the province of human practice.

Everywhere, in the most varied societies and language communities, a distinction is made between what we do and what we leave undone, and probably everyone can in most cases distinguish whether he acts or not, and whether others act or not. What is it, however, that separates action from inaction? And how does a person, more precisely, experience his own action and that of others?

To start from the beginning again, reaching back to previous analyses: processes of consciousness consist of multiply interconnected syntheses.[1] From an Ego-pole, as Husserl showed in his investigations, intentional performances are directed at something that discloses itself in its universal structure, whether it happens to be a perceiving or a fictional presentation, memory, judgments, etc. On the basis of the analyses of this structure carried on diligently by Aron Gurwitsch,[2] we distinguish between a thematic kernel, the thematic field in which a kernel is imbedded, and an open horizon in which the thematic field stands. How one particular thematic kernel and not another happens to come into relief in the stream of consciousness at any given time, how a theme happens to be experienced routinely or explicated as a problem, was described in the analyses of the relevance-systems.[3] Summing up these findings without going into details again, we can say that experiences are constituted as thematic kernels within the syntheses of consciousness; in the constitution of experiences, interconnected thematic, interpretative, and motival relevances work together systematically.

Along with the kernels of current phases of lived experiences, thematic components are also represented.[4] The lived experience of a visual object of perception includes, for example, not just the view of the front side, given impressionally and currently in direct evidence, but also its hind side, which is appresented simultaneously—though not in original evidence. With all lived experiences, which belong to the everyday life-world, "their" type—i.e., the one with which they are endowed on the basis of prior experience—is automatically appresented as the total context of characteristic thematic elements. Even before overlaying by objectivations (mainly semantic classifications) which are socially mediated and deposited linguistically in the subjective stock of knowledge, a schematic context of tactile, olfactory, and utilitarian qualities is (in our example of a seen object) fused through passive syntheses with the actually grasped visual form. All these syntheses, including the appresentations of the type subjectively relevant in each case, produce the unity of everyday objects, qualities, and events taken for granted in the natural attitude. They cause the apparently simple occurrence of these objects, qualities, and events in the course of lived experience.

The Ego focuses its attention on some lived experiences. How this happens has also been described in Volume I, in the analysis of the relevancy systems. Lived experiences adverted to an attentive Ego are characterized by a higher degree of determinacy and distinctness of the lived experiential core and greater thematic consistency of the experiential flow. Such lived experiences (*Erlebnisse*), in which the Ego is, so to speak, firmly engaged, we will call encounters (*Erfahrungen*). In short, lived experiences stand in relief in the stream of consciousness; encounters are lived experiences that are singled out by attention.

As actually present consciousness processes, encounters still have, of themselves, no real meaning. They obtain meaning only in reflexive, subsequent performances of consciousness. As long as I am caught up in my lived experiences, it is the objects of these lived experiences that occupy me. Only when I grasp well-circumscribed lived experiences—i.e., encounters—reflexively, beyond their current actuality, do they become memorable, open to inquiry as to their constitution, and meaningful. When the Ego looks at, or more precisely looks back at, its own encounters, it lifts them out of the simple actuality of the original flow of experience and puts them in a broader context. This context necessarily points beyond the Ego's simple engagement in its experiences. It is a context of meaning; meaning is a relational magnitude established in consciousness, *not* a particular experience or a quality ascribable to experience itself. It concerns, rather, the relation between an experience and something else. In the simplest case this something else is an experience other than the present one, e.g., a remembered experience. The just-past experience, whose lived experiential evidence still resonates, is grasped in relation to the merely remembered one as identical, similar, opposite, etc. The other point of reference can, however, also be something more complicated than a single experience: it can be a pattern of experience, a higher-level typification, the solution of a problem or the justification of an action. Let it be pointed out at once that social meaning-systems are comprised of subjective positings of meaning. In all societies, stylistic units of meaning are objectivated as communicative genres and form traditions of meaning-positing. In literate cultures, moreover, literary genres, which can unburden the individual still more strongly from positing and discovering meanings by his own resources, are "made available." Communicative genres extend from everyday proverbs to fables, from conventions of cursing and scolding to legends of the saints.

Why a person focuses on particular encounters—and how he does so—depends not only on the respective present situation, but also, as we have seen,[5] on a subjective, although socially stamped relevance-system—and finally purely and simply on his own subjective stock of knowledge. In sum, lived experiences are set in relief in the stream of consciousness; encounters are lived experiences that are singled out by attention; some experiences become meaningful through reflected performances of consciousness that relate experience to something else.

Some experiences, however, have a peculiar time-structure, and accordingly a unique meaning-dimension that distinguishes them from all other experiences. When experiences are not simply reeled off, when they are made meaningful not only after the fact, but follow a project or plan, they receive their essential—we can even say, actually present—meaning from their relation to the project. Of course, this relation can be one of a practically complete fulfillment of the project, of merely partial fulfillment and partial nonfulfillment, or even of total failure. Experiences that derive their meaning from their relation to a human project are called acts.

Acts are flows of experience that are seen not just in themselves but from my vantage point. They are motivated. The driving motive of an act is the attainment of a goal that is projected in advance by the one who acts. More precise statements will be made below on the motive, project, and time-structure of action and on the meaning of acts.

2. The Subjective and the Objective Meaning of Action

a. Action and Accountability

Action is clearly a component of everyone's everyday world. In the natural attitude, everyone takes it for granted that other people live in the world, experience it, and act in it "exactly as I do." Why is this so? At first sight, I seem able to talk with certainty only about myself, when I act and when something merely happens to me. Of my fellowmen, on the contrary, I can by no means always say with certainty whether or not they aim at a goal, much less if that goal is determinate.

No doubt only the agent himself, and no one else, can decide with ultimate certainty whether he had planned something that is now happening thus or otherwise, or whether the events in question are taking place without being planned by him. He, the actor, is the ultimate authority who must be consulted to determine whether or not an act is occurring in a given case. He alone knows the purpose— if any—for which the occurrence was planned. But it must quickly be added that although in principle—i.e., both theoretically and morally—the agent has the ultimate authority in this regard, however, in practice, namely in everyday reality, what matters is the appearance of action or inaction (though not a deceptive appearance but rather one that is on the average reliable). For the actor does not live all by himself, but rather in a social world. Both his action and his inaction have perceptible effects on other people, just as others' action or inaction has considerable effects for the agent. Action, a subjective performance of consciousness, is at the same time *the* precondition for the construction of the social world. Action and related concepts belong to the semantic and basic syntactic categories of a language, in some languages more markedly than others. There are rules of application for these concepts, criteria for language usage that such linguistic categories realize in concrete speech acts. Semantics, syntax, and pragmatics together determine whether and how members—as well as types and groups of members—of a society are assigned responsibility for their actions and inactions.

The forms of social responsibility objectivated in the language system and in procedural rules differ from society to society and from epoch to epoch. The question whether these distinctions are fundamental or only superficial cannot be answered at all without determining precisely what one means by fundamental or superficial—and probably only with difficulty even after such a determination (e.g., by reference to universal structures of consciousness, reciprocity of perspectives, anthropological principles of personal identity, etc.). Certainly, the concept of action does not everywhere coincide with the use that has developed in modern Indo-European languages—a group of languages that already exhibit significant differences from one another and have undergone remarkable changes in just a few centuries. Nor is the "unit" of accountability—i.e., what is considered to be the socially significant bearer of responsibility—everywhere and at all times so clearly and simply the individual man as might be assumed in a self-styled individualistic age. The boundaries between action and inaction are not everywhere the same, nor are they always drawn with equal sharpness. Simply consider the principle of clan liability (*Sippenhaft*) in tribes that practice blood vengeance; moral casuistry based on dream-"deeds" (e.g., concerning ejaculation in sleep); the more recent juridical, psychiatric, and moral-philosophical discussions of responsibility before the law ("crimes of passion," or under the influence of drugs, etc.) and human accountability in general, especially pronounced in American legal practice under the influence of a remarkable sociologism in the post-McNaughton period.

In any case, despite the most varied magical, religious, and scientific ideas about man's lack of freedom, his "being possessed" by outside forces, the governance of his deeds by the gods, his "genetic" or his "social" determination, and the like, all human societies are based on a fundamentally identical assumption: namely, that people can either do something or leave it undone. As stated above and as is generally known today anyway, the general principle of human accountability is not explicated in the same fashion everywhere. Sometimes it is restricted to certain classes of persons, e.g., adults, males, freemen; in some cultures even the category "man" was not understood in our sense. This becomes particularly clear when the principle of accountability is extended to other living creatures, e.g., dogs, pigs, trees, sweet potatoes. In any case, such restrictions and expansions of the concept can be detected in the "official" worldviews influenced by determinable ruling interests; it is uncertain, however, how deeply such "official" worldviews reach into the everyday prag-matic orientations of ordinary people. But it can be suspected with great probability that the stratified, historically practiced "anthropol-ogies" and ideas of normalcy (for they are at issue here) are deter-minative for everyday life at least by means of legal systems, if not by religion. For all expansions and narrowings of the concept of man and his action, the basic principle remains the same: *some* form or other of accountability is necessarily presupposed in the construction of historical social worlds. This principle constitutes the life-world, especially everyday reality, as the province of practice.

We have up to this point determined two things: on the one hand, action is a social category of paramount practical significance, since accountability as the foundation of social orders ultimately re-fers to action; on the other hand, no external human authority can decide with absolute certainty whether someone has acted or not. How are these two statements interrelated?

b. Action and Conduct

That the agent is the final authority in regard to his own action means primarily that action is a performance of consciousness and not an objective category of the natural world. It does not mean that the performance of consciousness cannot be *socially* objectivated. We will not here go into the fact that it is indeed possible to report and ne-gotiate *about* action. Some, indeed much, important action is also ac-cessible as such to other people—not directly, however, but mediately. What mediates action is conduct, a physical occurrence in space and time that can inform others who observe a person's action or inaction, just as it also gives the actor himself information about the course of the action. Of course, conduct does not appear in the same perspective to the actors and to the observers. Moreover, the actor himself does not always, much less absolutely, need mediated information about his behavior, for he can apprehend it directly from his own project and he has it under control in his inner perception of the course of action. But the actor is at the same time the observer of other people's actions; every person acts, and every person experiences the action of others. The perspectives under which conduct is seen as action, indeed by both actors and observers, are interrelated systematically as nuances of meaning of typically similar or identical processes; they are, in principle, interchangeable. In the natural attitude of everyday life, everyone is, precisely from his dual role as actor and observer prior to any theoretical reflection, perfectly well aware that although in principle conduct embodies action only very imperfectly, in practice it points to action in an extremely useful way.

Thus a complex but inseparable connection exists between action, as a course of experience subjectively projected in advance, and conduct, which can be grasped by one's fellowman as the embodiment of action. According to the principle of the reciprocity of perspectives, a man "sees" that others act just as he does, just as he also "sees" that others treat him as an actor. He remains in his own eyes (and so not just within an intentional ethics but also in an analysis of consciousness) the ultimate authority to decide whether or not he has acted in a given case; but it is the others, his fellowmen, who (on the basis of socially objectivated rules of typical, observable courses of conduct deposited in the stock of knowledge) ascribe the typical presence or nonpresence of a goal, a plan of action. As the authority that is valid in practice, the others decide whether something was an action or not. But in a certain sense one is oneself "the others," though not in the individual case of a detached action, but rather in the total context of the manner of living. For, after all, one applies, just as other people in the last analysis also apply, the socially constructed rules that ascribe certain types of action to certain norms of conduct.

One's conduct is not, therefore, merely incidentally correlated with one's action. This relation is grasped consciously and manages, to a certain degree, to control one's conduct as a significant expression of one's action for other people to see. Where it matters, one gears one's behavior to interpretation by others. This is not so much a matter of intentional deception—though of course that possibility also exists. As will be shown below,[6] two other consequences are more important. First, steering one's own behavior toward anticipated interpretation by others is a basic presupposition of communicative action. Secondly, this teaches us that the behavior of others is not only naturally an imperfect embodiment of their action, but that it also artificially by human intention partly expresses and partly conceals, or possibly even just simulates their action. This knowledge is of great importance for everyday practice: one learns both to "adjust" one's own conduct appropriately to the goal of action and also to improve one's interpretations of the conduct of others.

At the conclusion of these remarks, surely it is hardly necessary to point out that of course not only action but also experience that is not preplanned is at least in part detectable from conduct. When a person in a dangerous situation turns pale and does nothing, it is an obvious conclusion that he is at least startled. The conduct of others enables us to draw conclusions not only about their action but also about how they internally experience what is happening to them.

3. Thinking and Operation

Action is experience planned in advance: the person who acts knows that he acts. As an outside observer, a fellowman, since he himself is also an acting person, can usually tell from another's conduct whether or not that person acts. This holds good in any case for most situations of everyday life and for most practical purposes. Even without knowing why he is running and where he is running to, it should not be difficult to tell that a running man is acting. Nor should it present a particular problem to decide that a person who is lying down with a relaxed facial expression and breathing regularly is asleep and not acting—at least not in the everyday sense of the word. Of course, now and then one can be mistaken. In any case, we are not speaking here primarily of reliable recognition of another person's specific motives and goals in a concrete situation. What we are discussing is the fact that typical sequences of behavior can be apprehended and learned as the typical embodiments or signs of typical action.

But let us now reflect on whether this holds true in the same fashion for all kinds of behavior. Assume that I am sitting by the seashore and a flock of wild ducks flies past. If I have fallen asleep while sitting there, for me these wild ducks did not fly past. Things are different if I am awake but preoccupied with an inner problem: then I will indeed see but not experience the wild ducks; they will not have been thematized in my consciousness and I will not have become aware of them even though I saw them. It is again different if I turn my attention to the wild ducks: I enjoy their beauty as they fly by. Finally, I can count the ducks, even separately by sex insofar as they are sexually dimorphous birds, e.g., mallards. From my point of view these are all very different things. For a passerby, however, only one thing is actually given: he sees me sitting there, and he sees the wild ducks flying by. To be sure, even for him, what are for me completely different things do not thereby vanish. Observing the situation in which he finds me and the wild ducks, he will apply his knowledge and consider the various possibilities. If I am asleep he will notice by my physical posture, my snoring, and the like, that the wild ducks he sees are not on hand for me at the moment. In case there are no sufficient indications of the like, however, he will not be able to assume this without further ado. On the contrary, if he sees that I turn my head toward the flock of ducks, he will rightly assume that I am watching them. If he notices, in addition, that I am moving my lips he will probably assume that I am counting the ducks to myself— unless, appraising my bodily posture and facial expression, he suspects that I am praying in an ecstasy of nature worship. If the passerby is not a stranger but an old friend, many of his suspicions will have a greater degree of credibility. But although he knows that I am an amateur ornithologist, his suspicions will be almost purely speculative if my conduct (physical posture, lip-movements, etc.) allows for no classification under a type of experience or action. He can choose among many possibilities, but his choice will then be supported by no clue to my conduct.

This example has, of course, merely clarified graphically that not all action is detectable from conduct, although it may frequently even then be surmisable based on typical understandings of a situation and specific knowledge of people. Without doing too much violence to the colloquial meaning of the word, this kind of action could be called thought. Consequently, thought would be action that is not detectable from conduct.

Up to this point we have, for good reasons, defined action from the standpoint of the actor, although naturally we then also tried to illuminate it from the observer's standpoint. It is not easy to see why we should suddenly change standpoint now, when we want to bracket out a certain kind of action. Let us therefore try to establish how this still not well defined kind of action looks from the actor's viewpoint.

Naturally, I know that other people recognize and interpret some of my acts by my conduct, a knowledge that is often of great practical significance from my viewpoint, but not always. But it does not seem to me at all imperative to find essential differences in my actions on this basis. For I am still performing mere operation of thought. Whether or not I move my lips in doing so is irrelevant, just as is the circumstance that someone may perhaps be observing me. In contrast, the distinction between actions by which I engage in the surrounding world, and actions to which that does not apply, is, for me as agent, by no means based on incidentals. If someone were to remind me of my lip-movements in counting and to say that I am thereby somehow "engaging" in the surrounding world, I would simply have to be more precise and distinguish between actions that reach into the surrounding world only accidentally (because, through my body, I happen to be a component of the world), and actions that do so necessarily. Whether I move my lips when counting ducks or even record the number of ducks with checkmarks on a piece of paper is, from my point of view, just as incidental for counting itself as the fact that I turn pale when startled. For the observer, that is naturally a different matter, for these are all useful indications.

Accordingly we want to view *thinking* as an act that, in its execution and plan of action, does not necessarily engage in the surrounding world. No one will deny that the effects of thinking can change the world. But this happens only when thought is translated into a different kind of action.

This other kind of action can be called *operation* (*Wirken*). Operation is action that in its design necessarily engages in the surrounding world. The actor engages in the world by means of his body, not merely because the body is "there" but by controlled changes of posture, movements, speech, etc. This is the essential difference between thinking and operating. Yet it must not be forgotten that the same performances of consciousness are presupposed in operating as in thinking. Moreover, thinking and operating also have a very similar time-structure, though it differs in one respect. This will be treated in more detail below.[7]

As was already mentioned, whether he thinks or operates, the actor is always in the world by means of his body. For the observer, a fellowman's body is always a field of expression: for his thinking, for his experiences, even for his lived experiences—indeed, under some circumstances even for states that are not at all within his conscious grasp, such as certain symptoms of sickness (which the specialist does apprehend). Man, as the observer of other men, learns the indications in conduct for "thinking" and for "operating." These are useful for him as a social actor. As we have seen, such indications in conduct are not selective enough for the actor himself to grasp his action adequately. On the whole, however, the delimitations of thinking and operating will coincide for actor and observer alike: actors are observers, and observers are actors. Indications of action contained in conduct—which are immediate for operation, circumstantial for thought—are typified appropriately and graphically, insofar as generally significant kinds of operating and thinking are concerned, and deposited in the social stock of knowledge. There are of course limiting cases: it is not, e.g., completely inaccurate to say that some people "think aloud." But in general and for the most part, thinking is both action that does not engage in the surrounding world (as the actor sees it) and action that is not detectable from conduct (as the other person sees it). Incidentally, a theory of action that is organized in terms of observer categories (not just methodologically or for research practice, but also dogmatically in its ontology or theory of science) must miss its object.

4. Work

Among the many different kinds of operation, one especially merits closer examination. All operation, as controlled corporeal conduct, in some way engages in the world. But not every operation changes the surrounding world in a way that is significant for the practical objectives of everyday life. On this point we should not be misled by the metaphysical question—which is not pertinent for everyday practice—whether every action, indeed every event, be it "inner" or "outer," does not change reality. If after merely accidental "thinking aloud" I happen to frame my train of thought intentionally in words, I have gone over from thinking to operating: something has changed essentially in the mode of action. But in the surrounding world nothing has noticeably changed, and in myself hardly anything noticeable.

Now assume that I clothe my train of thought in words for someone else and ask him to cut down a tree. When he does cut it down, I have then engaged in the surrounding world in a manner that changes it, although I myself have not lifted a finger. The effect resembles what I would have achieved if I had personally cut down the tree. Add a somewhat less simple example: In a no-smoking compartment I ask a smoker to stop smoking. If he does not heed my request and I remove his cigarette from his mouth and throw it out the window, the result is in a certain sense also the same: he is no longer smoking. The social situation, however, has changed much more drastically than in the example of chopping down the tree one-self or asking someone else to do it. Yet all these examples have one thing in common. Some determinate effect, a change in the natural and social world, was achieved by a plan of action. It is, moreover, quite clear that man's surrounding worlds are not merely part of nature, but are also always social. We will not at this point go into the difficult problem of the flexible and historically variable boundaries of the social world.[8]

One can dream about cutting down trees, one can observe it, think about it, talk about it, convince others to do it, or do it oneself. This shows that, despite all unclear transitions in individual cases, it is meaningful to stress the kind of operation that changes the sur-rounding world according to the plan of action. Change is thus not a purely accidental effect of action. It must rather be intended and inserted in the plan of action, whether or not the performance of the act succeeds. Leaving tracks behind in the snow is not part of the project, but stomping out a path in the snow surely is. This shows that even this kind of operation cannot be unambiguously attached to criteria of conduct, but rather must be understood from its mean-ing to the actor. Let us call it *work*.

This conception of what work means does no great violence to the colloquial usage of the word. But clearly the precise delineation suggested does not correspond to the concept's blurred connotations in modern industrial societies, not to mention that no such concept existed in earlier tribal societies. Remnants of early Christian, Calvin-ist, and Lutheran history of ideas are still contained in the capitalist and Marxist versions of the concept of work in the modern world, where there is little sign of a unified conception of it—quite apart from its valuation. The functionalist orientation of most social science concepts of work is useful for certain ends, but has its own difficulties, as professional sociology, for example, shows. This holds especially for historical and intercultural comparative analyses, since the con-cept of work—so central to social organizations of everyday reality and their ideological corroboration—is subject to historical contrac-tions and expansions. In this context, too, a broad but precise defi-nition of work as a particular kind of life-worldly operation may be useful.

This definition, of course, includes productive activities in an economic sense, but it also includes all those forms of social action by which a change is made in the social world: declarations of love, marriages, baptism, court deliberations, the sale or even the collecting of postage stamps, revolutions and counterrevolutions.

Let me stress once more that work must be understood in terms of the project. The actor works when he wants to achieve something definite in the surrounding world. This can be something natural or social, as "social" and "natural" happen to be understood in a society. For a physicist, of course, speech is obviously a physically measurable event. In the practical everyday attitude, however, one speaks in order to influence people and knows that it is also possible to cut down trees indirectly by speaking. Therefore, at least on the level of the constitution of the meaning of everyday action, a distinction between work and communication is out of place. There are of course very important differences between simpler forms of operation and communicative acts—these will be analyzed more precisely in the investigation of signs, symbols, and language.[9] But the line of separation cuts right across the category of work. Work is not just simple operation; communication is not just idle talk.

One more point I want to make concerns the specific meaning of work. Work was distinguished from other kinds of operation by the fact that in its project it aims for a *particular* change of the surrounding world, the specific motive of which is irrelevant in this context. Whether one cuts down a tree for firewood or to earn money, for training and conditioning, or as a counterbalance for "mental" work, or for any other reasons, is important both for the individual and for the social organization of work—but in all cases it is work.

And finally: no one will call me to account for what I think. If I "think aloud" it is surely harder to "talk my way out" as not having meant it literally. But I am in any case responsible for trees chopped down and for cigarettes removed from someone's mouth. As work was defined, therefore, it forms the fundamental category of *social* attribution of responsibility.

In some societies and under certain circumstances, punishment is dealt out even for thinking, if one is caught—and since thinking can also have unintended effects in conduct, being caught is not absolutely out of the question. All the more so can one be called to account for one's operation, i.e., for an act that by its very project engages in the surrounding world, even if the effects in question were not subjectively intended (at least when such effects are typically foreseeable by normal actors). The attribution of responsibility is governed in this case by what we have defined as work: if definite effects of an operation are foreseeable, one *should* orient oneself by them; whether in a concrete case one actually did so or not can be left out of consideration. The social varieties of attribution of responsibility

certainly differ greatly on this very point: they reach from tribal liability to pure attitudinal ethics.

5. The Time Structure of Action

For an act to occur, someone must act. For someone to act, an act
must be projected. Expressed so simply, the time structure of action
appears to be relatively simple. Without wanting to complicate things
unnecessarily, however, we must examine the time perspective of action and of the act somewhat more closely. By action we designate
primarily the step-by-step performance of an act; by act, however, we
mean the finished chain of the action-history, the completed act.

Every action, as was said, is preceded by a project. Three things
are of such importance for the relation between action and act that
they should be investigated separately: first, the relation of the individual project to superimposed plans and hierarchies of plans; second, the careful consideration of the practicability of the projects;
and third, the choice between competing goals of action.[10] Let us
therefore here restrict ourselves to the time perspective of the project,
insofar as this restriction can be maintained. In the project, the goal
of action, the completed act, is first imagined. This imagining is a
fantasying: neither is actual experience grasped in self-givenness, nor
does one remember something or make an abstract judgment. It
involves, rather, a reaching-forward (*Vorgriff*) into the future. This
reaching-forward is quite concrete; the future is determinate, predetermined by me as future, but it is Utopian: it concerns something
that has not yet happened. What has not yet happened, although it
will happen if it depends on me, is now at present only imagined.
The time perspective of this representation can be designated most
graphically by the term *futurum exactum* borrowed from Scholastic
grammar.

The action imagined *modo futuri exacti* can be aimed for only
according to its general type, i.e., as relatively empty (but of course
not *completely* empty), or it can be determined extensively and in detail
(i.e., absolutely full of content). It naturally makes a difference whether
I want to marry my longtime girlfriend in a particular church at a
particular hour on a particular day before a clergyman with whom
I am acquainted, or advertise for a bride, "as is no longer uncusto-
mary." But in both cases I have projected something that is identical
in one of the anticipated points of the definition ("marriage")—namely,
in the one that is in many ways most important. Incidentally, this

example can be used to illustrate two additional, interrelated, and important aspects of the project. What was said in general about the constitution of types[11] holds good, of course, also for typifications of goals of action. First, it is among other things clear that the typifications are made routinely available to the members of a society in the semantic categories of a given language, and hence as socially distributed contents of a societal stock of knowledge. Second, if a label for the act exists "objectively" in this way, if action of this type has often been done and the steps of action leading to the goal are "subjectively" unproblematic, then the project planning is, in a given situation, simply called off. In this case the planning is little more than the singling out of a fully constructed theme in the flow of experience.

But things are somewhat different when various components of the imagined act are uncertain and the steps that are supposed to lead to the goal are problematic for the actor. Although it is still not a question of choosing between various competing projects (this case will be described more precisely later on), still here too the project clearly stems from planning, from an interpretative act, and is not merely at hand. What consciousness grasps is either uncertain aspects of the action pictured *modo futuri exacti,* or the sequence of individual steps leading to the goal of action, or open aspects of the individual steps. Not just actions as such, but also the individual steps of an action can be singled out from the imagined course of action, thematicized, and grasped *modo futuri exacti.*

Action does not follow quasi-automatically from the project. A decision is still needed to translate the project into deed. For the project can have turned out to be unfeasible or to be implementable only at too high a price; something more urgent may have intervened so that I must postpone the project, and more of the like. But once a decision is added to the project, action begins. Apart from a few particularities of operation that will have to be described below, it can be said in general that the actor takes it for granted that the individual steps in the performance of an act are oriented by the project. If he has estimated the feasibility of the project correctly and no unexpected obstacles arise (the case of social action is especially complicated in regard to these two points), then individual steps unfold almost of themselves. In its meaning, action is then indeed still based on the past project that reached forward into the future (*modo futuri exacti*)—at the time when the project actually had been planned (the project thus remains contained in the thematic field of the flow of experience by this peculiar temporal note). But the kernels of experience of the individually realized (or more accurately, now being realized) stages of an act are presented as essentially present.

Under certain circumstances, as was said, the stages of an act "unreel" quasi-automatically and the actor takes it for granted that they are oriented by the project. This means that in performing the act he does not have to be reflexively cognizant of the individual steps. This holds good as long as the steps remain unproblematic (i.e., for example, when they are completely routinized) and meet no unexpected resistance. However, if the steps themselves contain component acts that have a more or less problematic character, as for example in all more complicated and nonroutinized acts of thought, then the steps themselves are thematized consciously as such. The action then does not "unreel" but rather takes, so to speak, the form of a chain in which each link must be forged to the next.

Finally, a few particularities of the time-structure of operation must be pointed out. These can be explained by the fact that operation, as was already explained, is an action that in its inherent project necessarily engages in the outside world. The actor can, however, engage in the surrounding world only if he acts with and by means of his body. He does so by changing the location of his body as a whole by means of his limbs, or by moving his limbs singly or together, wholly or in part, or by moving his fingers, eyebrows, vocal cords, etc.

Obviously, not all body movements can be controlled, i.e., are actions, just as on the other hand not all acts are based on body movements. In reality the boundaries between controlled and uncontrolled body movements are certainly not sharp and unambiguous. Moreover, they do not proceed exactly the same in all societies for all men. Even "pure" thought, as was stated above, definitely can happen with "corporeal participation" (such as counting on the fingers). On the other hand, completely unintended body movements—which are thus not examples of operation—can cause changes in the surrounding natural and social world. Yet obviously, operation is not just an analytical construct; rather, *for* social relations it is the most important, and *in* social relations it is normally also the most easily recognizable case in which action and body movements appear in unison.

We become conscious of operating, of acting by means of our animate organism, on two different levels. First, we experience the movements of our body from within, as our own movement, as changes in the relation of body and world that are under our control. In corporeal movements our will is realized little by little, in time. The movements we experience belong to our stream of consciousness. For I experience my operation—as naturally also every other action—in self-givenness, namely in the actually present phase of inner time, but in constant fusion both with the just-now-beginning future phase of consciousness and with the still-resonant phase that was actually present just a moment ago. In addition to this constant protentive and retentive synthesizing of operation in the stream of my time, I am moreover from case to case linked with the future through expectations and with the past through memories in active grasps (*Zugriffe*) of consciousness.[12] In short, the movements experienced by us always belong to duration (*durée* in Bergson's sense) and sometimes also to the time of our *performances* of consciousness.

Second, we experience the movements of our animate organism, as distinguished from "mere" thinking, as a sequence of events in the outside world. Our body moves in a space in which it meets resistances, in a space in which other things and other people always stand and often move. Our movements occur at the same time as other movements do. Within certain limits, which were described in detail above,[13] we can perceive our movements just as we perceive the movements of others. We notice that others observe our movements, just as we do theirs. One's own movements can be registered just as those of other people are; distances we cross can be measured just as those that others have crossed are. In a retentive or protentive grasp of thought I can insert my own or other people's movements into my plans of action by means of calculations on the distances covered. I can include these distances in my stages of action; I can double these distances, or combine them (e.g., in a relay race). I can establish firm relations between distance and time spent. The dimension in which my movements take place is not just the social time in which I orient myself with and by others "like myself"; it is, rather, a spatio-temporal coordinate-system in which stands everything I experience *concretely* in this time, including my operative self.

Our operation belongs "at once" to two times, not "first" to one time (e.g., prereflexively, to inner time) and "then" to the other (e.g., reflexively, to world-time). Our movements are at the same time an event of consciousness and a sequence of events in the outside world. Certainly, the indivisible, nonspatial, flowing inner time is not everyone's time; it is only my time—and yours, insofar as I experience myself in the living presence of a we-relation. And the homogeneous, anonymous, objective world-time is just as certainly not simply my time, but precisely *also* mine. But without question I find myself at a concrete intersection of the two times, the one that is *only* mine and the one that is *also* mine. As was said above: at this intersection of consciousness and world in the living present it is also possible for me to experience others "like myself."

Inner time and world-time are both irreversible. But thinking, an action located exclusively in inner time, is revocable in a way that does not hold true for operation. Operation engages in the outside world and takes place in world-time: what has happened, has happened. Although I can try to remove the effects of my operation, even that is possible only to a limited extent; social time, world-time has gone by. Although I can give back the cigarette I removed from the lips of the man sitting opposite me in the no-smoking compartment and apologize, the fact itself cannot be removed from the world. And if I have moved a boundary stone on a dark, foggy night, I can put it back because of qualms of conscience—if no one noticed what I have done. But in principle the crime is reconstructible. And once I have cut down a tree I cannot put it back. Wherever it is a matter of life and death (of humans or trees), the irrevocability of operation is clear: it is, of course, final.

Indeed in a certain sense I cannot make even what I have thought (and what I have not thought) as if it had never happened. Even lived experiences that take place only in internal time are irrevocable. But I can make up for every thought in a manner that does not apply to operation. Naturally, there can be important differences even there, but in general it is not of great significance whether I find the solution to a mathematical problem yesterday or not until tomorrow, whether I come to the end of my daydream that I am the Emperor of China somewhat earlier or somewhat later, etc. But it does make an essential difference whether I planted the oak in front of my house yesterday or ten years ago; I cannot make up today for what I neglected to do ten years ago. I can choose between doing and not doing and I can choose what I intend to do, but I cannot choose what I have already done. Certainly something similar can also be said about thought: I can choose between thinking and not thinking, I can decide to reflect about some particular thing tomorrow, but I cannot choose not to have thought something that I have thought. I can at most try to forget it. That is where the difference lies: Whether I forget it or not concerns only me, for something has occurred only in inner time, but not "objectively."

6. Projects and Attitudes (Action in the In-order-to and the Because-Motives)

Action, let it be stressed once again, gets its meaning—or more precisely its actual meaning as action—from the project. In the project the goal of the act is envisioned in advance (*Vorstellung*); the individual steps of the act relate to this goal. In terms of the project every step should lead closer to the goal; every step is taken in order to reach the goal—step by step. But even the project has a prior history. Many acts are, precisely speaking, only partial acts; many goals of acts stand in immediate connection with other goals. Projects of such acts thus originate from pre-, co-, and especially super-ordinated projects. But there are also projects that result from previous acts without being co- or even sub-ordinated to their goals. Most notable perhaps is that case (we will have to investigate it more closely below) in which one determinate project among others is consciously sought out among the other competing projects; indeed, even the choice of project is then itself an act, namely an act of thought. Projects can, however, also be direct answers to the elements of a concrete, actual situation imposed on the actor. And finally a project can ensue from the sedimentations of past encounters and lived experiences without having been forcibly provoked by the situation. Projects can be said quite generally to be conditioned by the entire biography, but here something else is meant: namely, that some projects are triggered by specific sediments of encounters and lived experiences. Whereas other lines of the project's genesis can be explained by the structure of the action, the specifically biographical conditioning of the projects we have discussed under the concept of orientation[14] belongs to the total context of the origin of the self, of a personal identity, in the life-world.

In the analysis of the relevancy structure as motivation in the in-order-to context and motivation in the "because"-context, we examined the project and the biographical conditioning of action at some length.[15] The analyses were illustrated extensively using Carneades' example, and the close interdependence of motivation with the other dimensions of relevance, namely thematic and interpretative relevance, was shown. We can therefore be satisfied here with repeating the results of those investigations, especially such as are most important for clarifying the structure of action.

It was shown, first, that the goal of an act motivates action and hence, of course, also the individual steps of action, and second, that the—conscious or habitual—choice of goals of an act is motivated by attitudes, by sedimentations of specific encounters and lived experiences relevant to the act.

When we say that the goal of the act motivates action, this has different but basically equivalent meanings depending on the mode of consideration. Let us first go back to the time preceding the completion of the action. In this case the steps leading to the goal are, as it were, rolled up backwards: the still-unattained goal of the act is given to the actor from the beginning *modo futuri exacti* so long as the actor keeps it in sight. This envisioned goal (envisioned as attained) leads us in the opposite direction, toward the beginning. We take the last step in order to be able to reach the goal; we take the next to the last one in order to take the last one, and so on, back to the first step, which we do in order to be able to reach the goal by way of the many intermediate steps. This in-order-to motivation-chain in which one step of the act is added to the other, accordingly, does not become "actual" "from behind," but rather it is just rolled up in idea and statement; for the "behind," the goal of the act, is really motivated "from the front."

In contrast, when we turn back to the end of the action, we have an overall view of its process as a completed act. The same motivation-chain now appears in a new time-perspective. What in the action itself seemed goal-oriented as a "teleological" motivation turns out after the fact to be a causal chain, a series of because-motives. What was once formulated as an "in-order-to" sentence can then be transformed into a "because"-statement. Certainly, these changes of sentence-form lead to no change of content, but merely to a different formulation of the same state of affairs, something that could thus be designated as "counterfeit" because-sentences.[16] Moreover, what has just been said about the completed act also holds true for retrospection to a not-yet-completed course of an act, since in this case, too, the real action is interrupted and the actor already has behind him the previously taken steps of the act.

The situation is different with "genuine" because-sentences. These apply to an irreversible state of affairs. They explain the choice of project and the choice of individual steps leading from the project to the goal—the completed act—by a one-sided sequence of causes. Here nothing future (the goal of the act) can explain something present (the current action), but rather only the long since past explains the recent past and the recent past explains what was present just a moment ago. The causes of action are sought not in projects, but in what is already given. The pregiven consists, however, of lived experiences and encounters that have sedimented into attitudes; these now motivate the inclination to act thus and so, and not otherwise.

Attitudes themselves are not motivated, at least not in the genuine sense of the word. For one does not plan one's attitudes: one plans action, not one's inclinations to act. One does not decide to be afraid of snakes; rather this fear stems from specific lived experiences, e.g., from a childhood trauma. Still less does one fear snakes in order to avoid them; one avoids them because one fears them. Of course, a person can try to influence his own attitudes by setting out, like the fairy tale character, "to learn fear"; he can decide to fight down his fear of snakes. So quite strictly speaking, attitudes are not just sediments of encounters and lived experiences but can, though perhaps only slightly, be stamped by the results of an act. For this reason alone, attitudes could perhaps be said to be somehow "motivated."

But that would be a rather misleading way of speaking. On the contrary, attitudes themselves obviously have a motivating effect. A person who is afraid of snakes acts differently in their vicinity from one who is not. An attitude consists in the readiness (under certain conditions that are evocable in the typological system of the subjective stock of knowledge) to steer toward particular goals and to set in motion certain modes of conduct (the close connection of thematic, interpretative, and motivational relevance has repeatedly been pointed out in Volume I!). Naturally this also means: to start with the first "in-order-to" of an in-order-to motivation-chain.

Thus attitudes, like projects, have their prior history. Whereas normally the prior history of the project can easily be reconstructed by the actor, that does not hold true for the prior history of attitudes. The actor is clearly conscious of his attitudes only in part, if at all; insofar as they happen to consist of the results of an act, they can be lifted back up to consciousness. Beyond that the actor will find it difficult, if not impossible, to reconstruct the genesis—and thus an essential part of the meaning—of his attitudes in the fullness of all the sediments of lived experience they contain and to understand them in their context.

B. The Project: Possibilities, Plans, and Choice

1. Fantasying and Projecting

We have designated action as projected encounter or projected conduct and demonstrated that in the project the goal of an act is envisaged *modo futuri exacti*. Something future thus motivates something present—to be sure, a future that is anticipated *now* but has not yet occurred.

Projects are Utopian: in a performance of the fantasying consciousness I envision a condition that has not yet occurred. But there are different kinds of Utopias: Utopias as projects and Utopias as apparent projects. What and how I fantasy is stamped by the past through overlayings of my lived experiences and encounters. I can fantasy something that I know with certainty (or assume with the utmost probability) will never happen (even if I wanted it to—and when I fantasy something, this is far from saying that I really want it to happen). Moreover, I can in fantasy anticipate something that I expressly do not want, but rather whose occurrence I fear.

Unlike daydreaming, the project of an act is characterized above all by my assumption at the moment of projection that the project will be realizable. Naturally, I thereby tacitly make the additional assumption that there will be no fundamental change in the prevailing circumstances—including myself. I imagine that five hundred years ago as Madame President of China I ordered a payment of white, green, and yellow striped dragons by ten blind men. I do not find it hard to picture the details exactly (e.g., the vivid colors, the age and sex of the blind persons), although I know that I cannot go back five hundred years, that five hundred years ago China was an empire and not a republic, that there is no such thing as dragons, and if there were, they would probably not be striped with those colors, and finally that blind men would in any case not be able to see the stripes. In short, it is not hard to determine that this fantasy is not a Utopia and that it has nothing to do with a project of action, that it is not even an apparent project.

But what about envisioning the following? I imagine that in one hundred years, dressed in shirt and trousers and tennis shoes, I will climb the Triglav in winter by its north face. Now, it is virtually impossible that I will still be alive in one hundred years, and even if by some miracle that should happen I could not survive a winter climb in shirt and trousers of even the Salzburg Castle Mountain. So this is not a feasible project! Nor is it pure fantasy: some people even now reach an age far above a hundred years; the winter climate could change abruptly; mountain guides could hoist me up on a cable; etc. All this is highly improbable, for a few basic circumstances would have to be changed—but it is not absolutely impossible.

Next, I envision that next year, after intensive training and conditioning and successful climbing lessons with experienced alpinists, I will climb the north face of the Triglav in summer. A feasible project, although naturally I could break a leg or even my neck on my way to the bathroom the eve of the undertaking. What is improbable about the whole matter is just that I will decide to transpose it into fact: I do not in any case want to climb the Triglav via the north face, nor are climbing lessons absolutely recommendable at my age. But to go to the top of the Triglav comfortably in two days, staying overnight in the Kredarica chalet, by the usually safe route, *that* is an idea that is easily practicable not only as a project, but I am even already toying with the idea of making it into a decision.

Now the Alps are always ready to demonstrate to flatland tourists the finer distinctions between such ideas. Everyone will probably acknowledge that people over a hundred years old cannot climb mountain faces in winter in shirt-sleeves. To decide on the practicability of other ideas, one must however already know somewhat more about mountains in general, about the Julian Alps in particular, and especially about one's own abilities. Before it can be decided whether we are dealing with practicable or empty Utopias, various questions must be answered: where one is (if a person is in San Francisco, he will not be able to "climb" the Salzburg Castle Mountain in the next few hours); who and how one is (is one lying in a plaster cast?); what one can do (mountain-climbing at advanced stages of difficulty), and what one knows (some people, children and adults, intelligent and stupid, make impracticable projects without realizing that the projects are impracticable). And even practical, feasible projects, of course, do not always lead to success. More about this below.

Despite all differences, these examples do have one thing in common: they can be envisioned, they are composed of typical elements of a subjective stock of knowledge. The first example shows that such elements of knowledge could be applied contrary to the facts, in total, envisioned concreteness but with complete awareness that the fantasies could never become reality. The variations in the following examples show that the probability of occurrence of the conditions necessary to carry out the project—the various means to the end, the individual steps of the act, etc.—is estimated based on the actor's knowledge. A scale of gradation extends from impossibility (which, as was shown, does not necessarily mean absurdity) to possibility—and there, from extremely slight to very high probability; and the distance from one degree to the next is sometimes farther, sometimes closer. The issue here is always probability for the actor: subjective probability is always determined by the current state of the actor's subjective stock of knowledge. Yet generally the actor is not distinctly conscious of a gradation-scale of probability values. One exception is the case of rational action, which will have to be looked at more closely below, since in that case the weighing of the various

possibilities is performed consciously and thus made accessible to reflexive systematization.

All the examples, moreover, have one more thing in common:
the nonrealization of impossible fantasies is indeed certain, but the
realization of possible projects can by no means be predicted with
absolute certainty. I can say with certainty that I will not be Madame
President of China five hundred years ago, because that is impossible
for a variety of reasons. Other things being equal, I can say with
almost as much certainty that I will not go walking on the Salzburg
Castle Mountain tomorrow. First, I have no desire to do so; and second, I have decided firmly not to do it. Whatever else may yet happen
besides my firm decision to make this walk impossible (that I break
a leg, that the Castle Mountain is blocked off by the police, etc.) does
not at all change the certainty of the prediction that I will not do
something. In contrast, all possible circumstances can prevent the
execution of a totally practicable project. For I can project my action
only according to its type and with typical probability of success, not
however with certainty as to the individual case. This also means that
fantasying projection suffers from the uncertainty of the future and
that the "other things being equal" stipulation applies nonsymmetri-
cally: weakly for projects not to do something (there it affects essentially only my own self and fluctuations of my will), strongly for projects
to do something, especially for operation and work (where it concerns
the whole world in its "objective" constitution).

It is a matter of fastening onto the essential difference between
mere fantasying and planning. Planning is fantasying in the framework of open possibilities, a thinking *modo potentiali*. Mere fantasying,
on the contrary, is not bound to stay within the limits of the possible
as these are inscribed in the subjective stock of knowledge.

2. Practicabilities and Reach

Projecting is thus anything but a free fantasying. It is, rather, the
envisioning of a future condition within certain uncrossable boundaries. These boundaries are the limits of the possible—the word "possible" understood in its everyday meaning. Since we will, however, use
the (Husserlian) distinction between open and problematic possibilities for the following more precise description of the choice between
projects that are "possible"—in the everyday sense—it would be better to speak here of a fantasying within the framework of the *practicable*.

Obviously, nothing is either practicable or impracticable as such. To begin with, the practicable is divided along the boundaries of the provinces of reality of a finite meaning-structure. Projects for complex daydreams, plans to write a novel, and projects to fell a forest move in different provinces of the practicable. Here we are interested mainly in the everyday world; but even in this province of reality, there are various planes of practicability depending on whether we are concerned with "mere" thinking, or an operation in nature, or one in the social world.

Independently of the concrete peculiarities of the various provinces of reality, the term "practicability" always refers simultaneously to two interconnected presuppositions for the realization of a project: first, the estimation on the part of the would-be actor that the objective conditions for reaching his goal, conditions that apply to the respective province of reality, are given; and second, the conviction that his own "capacities" are sufficient to make the performance of the steps of the act practicable. In short, a project seems practicable when the actor assumes in the mode of hypothetical relevance (if ... then ...)[17] that he could transpose what he happens to be fantasying into reality. The estimation of the practicability of a determinate project is necessarily based on general assumptions. Every concrete projecting is based on the usually tacit assumption that I could also do today and tomorrow what I did yesterday—insofar as the circumstances do not cogently prove the contrary. This presupposition is, in its turn, connected with the assumption that today is essentially the same as yesterday and that there will be a tomorrow like today—of course, taking into consideration concrete individual changes. In our description of the subjective stock of knowledge, these assumptions were already seen to be among its basic elements and were analyzed with the help of the Husserlian categories of "I can always do it again" and "And so forth."[18] "I can always do it again" of course only as long as there is an "And so forth"; but I know that there will be an "And so forth" long after I will no longer be able to do anything.

In other words, "I can always do it again" has a biographical dimension. A part of the experience of getting older is mainly that one notices how the limits of "capability" shift. At first the limits broaden by leaps and bounds; then, they stay at a certain level without substantial change; sooner or later they begin to shrink. With increasing age one begins to notice that many "other things being equal" (ceteris paribus) provisos, to which formerly one did not have to pay much attention in one's projects and actions, suddenly need to be thought over carefully. Yet it must be remembered, too, that each course of life is imbedded in a history and that this history has a technological stratum that is significant for life and action. Of course, it makes a difference for the construction of the projects of action whether or not a declining memory can be assisted by written notes, whether eyeglasses are available to compensate for the weakening sense of sight or one must submit to the fate of a worsening eyesight—and other things of this sort.

Moreover, knowledge of the age-conditioned changes of "capability" need not be acquired exclusively through one's own experience. It can be noticed in other people, e.g., one's own children, that they can do many things today that were not possible for them yesterday, and it can be seen in one's own parents that their powers are subsiding. But knowledge of periodizations of "capability" is part of the basic contents of the social stock of knowledge. As such, it is socially mediated. Without such knowledge—which certainly need not be formulated into fixed tenets in all societies and which can be imbedded in very different explanatory systems—mothers would hardly be capable of raising their children.

Every project is necessarily composed of typical components. This is most obviously true of projects involving repetitions of courses of action that have long since become habitual. But in principle it holds good no less for new projects. For it is clear that, strictly speaking, the same act can never be repeated; in this sense, every act is "new," and what is repeated is "only" what is typical of the act. But in many acts, in everyday life even in very many acts, precisely the typical and its successful repetition are what matters. Accordingly, the project corresponding to such acts is directed at the typical. On the other hand, there are also projects in which precisely not repetition but innovation is what matters. But even with such acts it is clear that the essential components of project-construction, e.g., the individual steps for reaching the goal, are of a typical kind.

Therefore, in estimating the practicability of a certain project, *general* assumptions of the continued existence of the world as I know it, and of my continued existence in it as I know myself, play a role. Knowledge of the type of objects and events, which stems from other provinces of the subjective stock of knowledge, is also applied. Obviously of great significance in this is *habitual knowledge,* whose "function" consists mainly in simplifying everyday types.[19] Among the various kinds of habitual knowledge, skills must be stressed—and among the skills, mainly the habitual functional units of bodily movement. But even habitual knowledge—in which pregiven goals of acts

are fused with the means for their attainment into proven, unquestioned unities—promotes the routinization of projecting: the practicability of the project no longer needs to be estimated in the individual
case, since it is taken for granted. And finally, knowledge of recipes,
which applies entire "building blocks" of courses of conduct to solving
typical problems (attesting to the practicability of the corresponding
projects by tradition, as it were), should also be mentioned.

Beyond habitual knowledge, *specific elements of knowledge* are
project-relevant for the actor, especially his knowledge of the concrete
limits of his reach and capacity to operate. As was seen above, specific
elements of knowledge are arranged according to types and thus
deposited in the stock of knowledge. However it is a matter here of
case-by-case activation of such knowledge under the basic pragmatic
motive of everyday life: namely, everything in the world that is at
hand or at least on hand for *my* action. The person hoping to act, in
contrast with one who merely fantasizes, uses only such (envisioned)
means to achieve his goal (envisioned *modo futuri exacti*) as lie within
his actual or potential reach. In the analysis of reach it was shown
that besides an obviously spatial dimension, reach has an essentially
temporal and an important social dimension.[20] In this analysis and in
the comments on the primary and secondary zone of operation,[21] the
most necessary things have been said about the structure of act-relevant knowledge from the vantage point of reach and need not be
repeated here.

3. Doubt and Interests

a. Doubt

Many of our everyday actions become habits. They are considerably
routinized not just in their process, but even in their project. The
meaning of such actions has its place in habitual knowledge. As we
have just seen above, there are all kinds of acts whose goals are assumed to be attainable, whose projects seem self-evidently implementable and whose individual steps follow one another quasi-
automatically. But it must not be forgotten that this is not a matter
of mere behavior, but rather of genuine acts. Such acts are, however,
so polished and smooth that they seem to unreel almost without the
actor's participation and conscious planning. Nevertheless, they do
not have the time structure of simple encounters; rather, actually pres-

ent phases of encounter are meaningfully connected with projected ones, with envisioned goals. At one time these goals were not unquestioned but problematic, the projects did not begin by themselves but had to be consciously thematized, and the steps of the act were not taken for granted as following one another but had each to be pondered.

In the natural, pragmatic attitude of everyday life, we have no occasion to want to look behind the appearance of completely routine acts. We could believe that they are in principle constituted differently from acts in which we first pondered carefully whether we should aim for one goal or for another, then consulted our prior knowledge in order to decide what means would be best suited to reach the goal, and finally kept the steps of the act under precise control so that they really brought us closer to the goal. But when circumstances have changed and the "other things being equal" stipulations, inserted almost automatically in our habitual action, fail, we discover that the action that has now become habitual once originated in action that was problematic. After not having gone ice-skating for a long time, we fall down on the first attempt to do it again; after having been bedridden for a long period, we have to learn how to walk again; after having read no Greek for thirty years, we understand little of the text and have to consult our dictionary and grammar. Moreover, we also see in simultaneous comparison with other people that habitual action had its origin in action that was anything but routine. Observing the same type of activity in different people's performances, we see that one person plays a piano sonata like a virtuoso, while another painfully works at it, and a third can do absolutely nothing at the piano except tap out little tunes with two fingers.

Every act, or more accurately every action, is constructed step by step, as has become clear. Polythetic constitution is an essential property of all action. So, in principle, this must hold true even for habitual action—as it was originally constituted. But as we become increasingly accustomed to the individual steps and the transitions between them, slowly the consciousness of the step-by-step construction of the performance of the act is forgotten; it sinks into the secondary passivity of consciousness. The goal, of course, still remains in sight, but monothetically and normally with slight tension of consciousness. The individual steps whereby the action was originally consciously performed move to the edge of the thematic field. This need not be treated more at length here, since the general processes of routinization were already treated in the analysis of the origin of habitual knowledge.[22]

We can say, in any case, that all action begins, or originally began, in problematic situations. Originally the goal did not occur by itself, but had to be chosen; the project first had to be thematized with a certain clarity and distinctness, the practicability considered, and the steps of action measured off. In short, at the beginning of action stood a wish accompanied by doubt. Action begins when one wants something and it does not happen by itself. Doubt, too, begins at that point. Could anything, then, be done so that the wish may yet be fulfilled? And if so, should it be done or not? Are we sure we still really want to abide by our original desire, including all the consequences that its realization could entail? And are we fully convinced that we would not prefer something else, something different that could be thwarted by the fulfillment of the original wish?

These questions illustrate what was established above, namely, that doubt stands at the beginning of action. But the meaning of this must be explained more precisely. Strictly speaking, this sentence stands for a whole chain of statements: first, that action is a projected encounter and not simply something going on of its own accord; second, that projects do not occur by themselves but must be chosen; and third, that the choice of project stems from a situation in which several projects are available for choice. What state of affairs the first of these statements applies to was shown adequately in the above reflections. But the questions that the two other statements raise must be treated below. How do projects occur, if not by themselves? And what does it mean that several projects are available for choice?

b. Interests

Every project stems from a clearly determined interest, namely interest in a future that is formed thus and so and not otherwise. We know that we can influence what will happen tomorrow only to a certain, perhaps very slight, degree, and that much will happen independently of our action or inaction. But in the natural attitude of everyday life, precisely this "actionable" part of the future is of overriding concern for us. The realm of necessity imposed by the given conditions of the world, naturally, always presents a fixed framework within which we wish our future to be so and not otherwise on this or that point. If, based on our knowledge, we can assume that in the future certain events we wish for will happen by themselves, naturally we need do nothing; on the contrary, we must be careful not to undertake anything that could endanger the occurrence of the event. If, however, we assume that certain undesired events could happen, we must reflect on whether we could do something to ward them off. And finally, if we believe that a certain determinate future that we want can be achieved only by our action, nothing except our own action is of any help.

All this has already been said in another form. Nor need it be described in detail again how our knowledge of the world enters into such considerations. How one envisions a certain future and how one then forges plans for this future depend on the respective state of our subjective stock of knowledge.[23] Here a different point should be stressed; namely, that the projection of a plan for a certain event in the future—stemming from our interest in this event—does not occur without relation to the idea of other events in the future in which we also have a stronger or weaker interest. Although interest in a certain event in the future is behind every particular project, our interests in the most varied events in the future certainly do not occur completely unconnected, case after case. Rather, our various interests stand in multiple relations to one another, relations of which we are more or less clearly cognizant.

The reason for this consists simply in the fact that our interests have a prior history. In our life, certain interests have motivated our action toward certain goals—naturally still in the future—goals that were meanwhile achieved (or failed to be) and now belong to the past. How certain acts could satisfy or not satisfy certain interests, how they collided with other interests, and how the collision finally ended are now deposited in our stock of knowledge and in our relevance system. This prior history of interests, projects, and acts has led to the formation of certain attitudes that in given situations "motivate" typical projects on the basis of typical interests.[24] Every person must repeatedly choose between one future or another; every person once gave in to one interest and resisted another. Many projects that seemed practicable at the time and actually were accomplished—projects, let us repeat, that originated from interest in a particular future—now and then led to a future that did not satisfy the original interest ("That is not how I imagined it!") or impaired other interests ("The price was too high!"). In other words, interests have not only a prior history as individual interests in particular occurrences and states of affairs, but also a common history as *our* personal interests.

This means that interests are combined into something like contexts. Plan-hierarchies correspond to such contexts. Projects are "bundled together" if they are compatible. When the goal of a given project is just an intermediate station on the way to a goal that lies beyond, they are brought into a means-end relation. When interests conflict, compromises are made and priorities established. In contrast, it must not be assumed that always and for everyone all interests are ranked in a single, clearly defined, and fully integrated system. There probably is scarcely a person in whose life all interests could be interconnected smoothly and who could completely eliminate all conflicts of interest that occur in him. Certainly, we do make daily plans, with whose help the habitual daily interests can be satisfied. Just as certainly, these daily plans are to a certain degree derived from overarching longer-term plans, indeed even lifetime plans. Nevertheless, a person who seeks to regulate his future down to the last detail according to a rigid plan-hierarchy is hard to imagine; even more so, however, a person whose interests are in complete harmony. For most of us, some interests stand side by side, unmediated and detached, without being intertwined in greater interest-contexts. If at a given time they clash, we must make a decision that cannot be guided by an established system of interests. Certainly individual and cultural differences exist, but these move between the extremes of complete disconnectedness between interests and total integration—without ever reaching the latter.

The biographical development of interests was discussed, as noted above, in the analysis of subjective relevance-systems and especially in the investigations of motivational relevance.[25] Act-projects were there considered from the vantage point of motivation and projects—i.e., motives in the in-order-to context—were seen to stem from attitudes—i.e., motives in the because-context. Attitudes, in their turn, are sedimentations of past experiences, hence naturally also of experiences of acts. These findings do not mean exactly the same as the above statement that projects stem from interests, but unmistakably they are related in meaning. With the analysis of because-motivation we tried essentially to understand attitude as a biographical sediment. What has been said about interests should now cast a new light on this. When we speak of interests, we do not mean just one's own past as it continues to affect action, but also the essential future-orientation of this past. The project is by nature oriented to something future, but even its genesis—from interests—has a complicated time-structure. Interest is, indeed, a sediment of the past. However it is oriented by a future that is relevant for the actor.

4. Choice

a. Open and Problematic Possibilities

We have seen that envisionings of the future are projected from interest in a certain occurrence and are checked for their possibilities of realization with the help of the subjective stock of knowledge, which must decide the practicability of the project. Now, we are left with the last of the questions important for understanding the project of an act: What does it mean that several projects are on hand before an action? How does the actor manage to *choose* one project?

It has just been shown how the actor develops interest in a particular future event or condition. Now, it is certainly quite usual for one not to be interested in several future possibilities at once. In a certain situation and at a given point in time, it often happens that just one single, clearly delineated interest emerges from the interest-context prevailing in the situation. This is the case mainly when the demands of the situation arouse immediate interest in one clearly determinable and highly predictable occurrence. Interest in the urgent bringing about or avoidance of this occurrence ("to avoid crashing with a speeding car") does not allow other ideas of the future to arise at all. Incidentally, we have already described this case in its basic features in the analysis of imposed relevances.[26]

The case of the routine delimitation of interest and project is otherwise different, but it is similar on the point that is significant here. If a certain interest is usually announced at a determinate time, it can be routinely met on the basis of the daily plan that serves for an orderly coverage of recurrent interests ("Lunch at one o'clock"). In neither of these two cases is there a choice between projects that differ in content, clearly conscious to the actor and normally graspable again in memory. In both cases, the actor at first has only the choice between the act that is begun quasi-automatically, and its repression. Generally it is not the act but its repression that would *not* come by itself but would have to be guided by the Self. In this basic sense, namely of being able to do or not do it, all action is voluntary action. However, what interests us here are those forms of action that stem from a choice between projects in a more urgent manner than this basic one. How does a supply of projects having different contents (i.e., x or y, not just x or non-x) come about?

Two groups of conditions under which contentually different projects are offered to the actor can be distinguished. In the first case, two different interests that do not stand in an orderly (e.g., hierarchical or "bundled") connection in a situation are aroused. These interests motivate two different projects, in which two mutually exclusive goals are aimed for ("to go to church or to drive in the mountains"). In the second case, a single interest in achieving a certain goal is predominant ("to drive in the mountains"), but it is accompanied by uncertainty about the suitable steps that could lead to the goal ("the longer superhighway route or the shorter route on a country road"). Thus it is not that two different goals are presented, but rather two (or more) different ways of reaching a single goal. The difference between these two cases is obvious: in the first case it results from the prevailing state of interests, in the second from the respective state of knowledge. Nevertheless, the similarity of the two cases is considerable. A certain inner relationship results from the very fact that all goals that stand somehow or other in the context of interests can be considered intermediate goals, stations on the way to more remote goals. At any rate, many examples that at first sight could be regarded as cases of conflict of interests, could on closer examination be reinterpreted as "means-ends" problems or problems of knowledge.

Whatever the case may be, another, much closer common feature is more important here. In both cases a choice between two possible projects is pondered more or less clearly (more clearly in most cases involving action or inaction); and sooner or later different weights are assigned to the various projects. Let us recall that we discussed the weighing of different possibilities in another context above.[27] The results of the precise Husserlian analyses of open and problematic possibilities[28] were used to describe the constitution of processes of perception and interpretation, and were illustrated by Carneades' example. Here these findings must be transposed to describe the choice between projects.

An envisioning of the future is grasped by consciousness as a possible project of an act only once it aims at a future that to some extent seriously comes into question for the actor. If, on the contrary, it merely points to one of the almost infinite number of states that are somehow conceivable for the future, then it remains on the horizon of consciousness until further notice. What seriously comes in question for an actor is determined by a context of interests that is pregiven to him biographically: however, envisionings of the future that emerge in the actor's consciousness in a given situation need not therefore be immediately assignable to a sharply delineated individual interest. As possible projects of acts, envisionings of the future thus bring along into the situation on their own a certain, still not precisely defined weight. Except for what is already routinely settled ("Tea with milk, but without sugar"), it would be unusual for an envisioning of the future to bring along an exactly measured weight.

Generally, the exact measurement of the weight of such an envisioning of the future as the project of an act first takes place only in the actual process of choice itself. Some decision-situations may have absolute weights for projected acts ("Whatever happens, I will not retreat one step"). In most everyday situations, however, the weight of projected acts is relative: they are determined by comparing one act-project that seriously comes in question with other projects that also come in question. It is thus a matter of tracing the envisionings of the future derived from various interest-contexts back to these interest-contexts. If these latter stand in an overarching or subordinate relation to one another, this clarification already is enough to decide on the relative weight of the competing envisionings of the future. If that is not the case, the considering must be done step by step. Only envisionings of the future that can be taken seriously are, as was said, included in the comparison. Those that are somehow merely imagined unpurposefully are left out of the picture. They carry absolutely no weight, not even an imprecisely defined one. They do not stem from interest-contexts, and nothing speaks for or against them one way or another. More precisely, what speaks against them is only that nothing speaks for them.

Here we were speaking about action and projecting in the natural attitude of everyday life. With certain modifications—for the resistances that action encounters differ according to the various provinces of reality—something similar also holds true of other provinces of reality with finite meaning-structure. There, too, open possibilities become problematic possibilities, except that the transformation is not founded on the interest-contexts of everyday life that are governed by the basic pragmatic motive, but on relevances governing dreams, wishful thinking, and artistic creation. Even an author narrows down the open possibilities under which the future of his characters stands to problematic possibilities. Naturally, he does not do this under the pressure of his own interests; the practicability of his characters' projects is not restricted to the framework of practicability that applies to him and his own everyday reality. The narrowing of possibilities takes place under different criteria: the aesthetic-communicative criteria of a written or oral genre of art. In animal fables, animals can speak, but they have something particular to say. In classical drama the three unities impose narrow spatial and temporal limits on the project-possibilities of the actors, whereas the canon of the naturalistic novel demands that the practicability of the novel-characters' projects must be located within the framework of their everyday world.

The framework of open possibilities always comprises the actor's historically and biographically determinate world—which he takes for granted without question. Open possibilities become problematic for him when it turns out in a concrete situation—which calls for a decision—that they could be of interest for his future. Thus the framework of the problematic possibilities is comprised of a hierarchical plan that is interest-determined. If a future possibility presents itself to the actor as worth striving for or avoiding and a project of an act aiming for it seems practicable, the actor must decide: yes or no— or if as a result nothing essential is changed in the practicability of the project, he must decide whether to postpone the decision. Otherwise the postponement would be just another form of negative decision. And when, in addition to the one future possibility that is worth striving for or avoiding, a second or third one immediately comes to mind as worth striving for or avoiding, the actor must deliberate as to *how* desirable or avoidable the first one is compared with the second, the third, etc.

Open possibilities do not stand in conflict with one another since as little speaks for the one as for the other. However, a conscious advertence of the actor to a determinate future or respectively to a few future possibilities (an advertence motivated in a given situation by corresponding interest-contexts) again creates a doubtful situation. The possibilities compete with one another; value stands against value, interest against interest. But the weights are still not determined exactly and therefore are not comparable; the interrelations of the interests on which future envisionings are based have not yet been clarified. A decision therefore still cannot be made without further ado.

b. Choosing

The actor must decide to which of the problematic possibilities that come in question he should assign the greater weight for his future under the circumstances and in the situation. *He* must decide for a particular future for *himself*, which future—if it should come about— will have the characteristic of having been wanted by *him*. It need hardly be said explicitly that the process of decision itself, the actual choosing, is a process within the actor's inner duration. Although the choice takes place in the fleeting present, it is of course, like all experience and all action, stamped by the past. However, in its meaning, it is obviously and essentially future-oriented.

The past acts upon the process of choice through the experiences that are deposited in the actor's stock of knowledge and have shaped concrete motivation-contexts in his subjective stock of knowledge. In the flowing present of choosing, knowledge and relevance occur in the form of estimates of practicability and interests in certain future possibilities. Strictly speaking, the future is not, for its part, operative, since it "exists" in the present only as something envisioned; figuratively speaking, it affects the anticipatory envisionings of possible future occurrences. In this way past and future together determine the values of the weights that are apprehended in the actually present phases of the stream of consciousness, in which the weighing takes place. Apprehended and not more; for the values of the weights have already been set before the process of choosing between projects begins.

The projecting of a future condition or of an occurrence as a series of conditions takes place step by step. But once the project is finished, the occurrence that has just now (or perhaps a while ago, earlier, a long time ago) been envisioned as completed in the future is held in the consciousness as a (for the time being) finished project. While it remains in grasp, it can gradually be traced back to its interest and checked for the chances of its practicability. Thus even the weighing of a future envisioned as the project for an act takes place polythetically. But once the weight of the project has been established, it can be monothetically grasped, retained, or later called to memory. So it can be used as one relative magnitude compared with the weight of other projects, which are likewise polythetically constituted and monothetically graspable. Since projects for an act cannot be sketched simultaneously but must emerge in the consciousness one after the other, only such a simple retentive grasp reaching back to valuations that were done gradually makes possible the process of choice.

What has been said applies both to provisional and to more or less final weighings. Their difference consists in something else. With the first project that seriously comes into question there are, of course, still no competing projects, no other weights as comparative magnitudes. The provisional weighing of the first project comes about in a clarification of the corresponding interest, of the degree of urgency and the chances of practicability grasped in isolation. That is why the weight thus established also bears from the first the marks of the provisional. However, in all further weighings one can already refer to a comparative magnitude—though one that is under the circumstances determined only imprecisely.

Precisely speaking, the weighing thus proceeds as follows. On the basis of a more or less distinct current interest in a fantasying act of consciousness, an occurrence envisioned as future ("having lunch") occurs in the flux of consciousness. In the further sequence of actually present phases of consciousness, the envisioned future is weighed in the already described manner as project for an act. It is traced back to a somewhat distinctly grasped interest and thus grasped in its be-cause-motive ("hungry"). It is, furthermore, evaluated ("very") on a scale of urgency that is arranged roughly or exactly, clearly or vaguely. The weight ("very much like to go to lunch right away") is ascribed to the envisioned future and can then be called to memory as a component part of the project for the act, without any need to run through the process of weighing again. The weight of the first project is provisional from the start: It has the "other things being equal" stipulation: *if* nothing else seriously tells against it, *then* (I would very much like to) go to lunch (right away).

In the subsequent phases of consciousness, the actor turns his attention to the projects addressed in this formula, motivated by other interests that seriously come into question. In our example, incidentally, the rejection of the project is not as such a serious counter-project: if I am very hungry, I do not "just happen" *not* to go to lunch. Other interests would have to tell for the counter-project: e.g., medical diet, weight loss out of vanity or for reasons of health, religiously motivated fasting, and the like. A content-filled counter-project ("instead of going to lunch I will do something else") could in turn have different reasons (e.g., "to take care of an urgent job"). The weighing of these further projects of course also takes place gradually, but now already with an eye on the weight of the first project (or of the first and the second, etc.). While the first project in its thematic field ("my possible future this-afternoon") still contained no alternatives (for the more or less empty future possibilities contained within its horizon carry no weight compared with the idea of "going to lunch" that was first evoked by a concrete interest as such), the second project carries in its thematic field (again: "my possible future this-afternoon") a highly relevant memory, namely the memory of an occurrence ("very much liking to go to lunch") envisioned as future in the just-previous phase of consciousness and provided with a provisional but effective weight for its desirability and urgency. The full meaning of the second project is also already constituted thereby as that of an *alternative* future. The actor is now confronted with a vital problem: the problem of choice.

Enriched by knowledge that has been contentually determined—that there are serious alternatives to the first project—the actor now goes back to this project. When the project had originally been examined in isolation, there had been no doubt of its practicability and desirability. It is still taken for granted as feasible. Now, however, the question arises for the actor concerning *how* desirable and urgent this first project is compared with the weight of the alternative. The first project is no longer the way it was. The same future is envisioned ("this afternoon"), the same possibility is regarded ("to eat"), but in a fundamentally new perspective ("to eat *or* to finish the job"). What is new about what is envisioned is not the knowledge that in principle any other future whatever could be foreseen, but that a certain other future could be seriously considered. Thus the actor's problem of deciding results in a problem of interpretation: how desirable is one future possibility compared with the other?

The actor now inspects[29] this first project more carefully than the first time. Now he also has every reason to do so, for he must now measure the importance and urgency of his interest in a particular future with the full consciousness of the fact that he is not himself seriously interested in a different future. The provisional weighing of the first project can now be confirmed or modified in comparison with the weights of other projects seriously coming into question and previously also considered. The project and the interest from which the project arose are now grasped no longer in isolation, no longer by themselves and in their connection with one another, but in the broader context. Project still stands against project—but no longer without mediation. Rather, the interests on which the competing projects are based are now located in superimposed motivational contexts (superimposed, namely, on *individual* interests). The projects themselves can now be arranged in biographically anchored plan-hierarchies that precede the partial plans somewhat bindingly.

Often the decision is already made without further ado. For it may turn out that one of the projects under consideration is clearly superior to the other (or respectively to all others that come in question, if there were several). The actor sees one of the projects as doubtless more important according to a plan-hierarchy that must be cogently applied in this situation and the interest in its realization as more urgent under the spatially and temporally prevailing conditions. Afterward the actor will perceive the just described case as if the process of choice that he had just undergone had really been superfluous. He will seem to have somehow forgotten or not immediately recognized what the situation was with the weighing of the competing projects. In any case, all doubt is removed after this first comparison. He need only make his decision to begin carrying out the project.

In this case, too, we certainly have been dealing with a genuine act of choice. Everything began with doubt in a situation of pressure to act, then problematic possibilities emerged, and the continuation consisted of a step-by-step weighing and considering of the projects. Otherwise the decision came remarkably easily. The actor did not suffer the agony of choice. The proximity of this case to habitual action is therefore unmistakable. Certainly in the former the weights of the alternatives have long since been assigned and the decision between the competing projects is unshakably anchored in memory. The projects themselves are thus no longer considered; they appear in consciousness at most just briefly, and immediately fade out again. In our case, however, the competing projects are at first taken firmly into the grip of consciousness. But the decision is made, so to speak, in the first round of selection: the actor merely has to "remember" the assigned weights again. In similar situations in the future he will then need just to remember the decision and no longer the competing projects, and after a few repetitions this act will actually become routine.

Things are different when a first comparison produces no clear decision. Very different reasons can be responsible for this, which can be categorized into roughly three groups of conditions. First, in the initial round, the weights of the competing projects may not have been established with sufficient precision. Second, the actor may not have succeeded in inserting the projects into a single plan-hierarchy with jurisdiction over both (or respectively, all) of them. And finally, the interests on which the projects are based may be in an irreconcilable conflict. Let us examine each of these three possibilities in the given sequence.

The processes of choosing can be located on the most diverse levels of clarity and determinacy of knowledge.[30] Therefore sometimes a comparison between relatively inexact weighings is enough. If one project unmistakably predominates, the actor will seldom care to determine whether it predominates a little more or a little less. If I like neither pork nor cornbread I will decide quickly for beef and potatoes, if I have the choice. But if I am offered pork with potatoes and beef with cornbread, I will have difficulty, and will have to take the trouble to weigh more precisely. Only when one project does not predominate must a second round be sought. With a clearer location of the interests within a relevant motivational context and a more convincing insertion of the projects into a plan-hierarchy, generally in this second round the weights can then be grasped so precisely that their comparison brings a decision. In contrast to the first of the described cases, here clearer reflection and more exact deliberation are necessary. The distance from habitual action is notably greater. Nevertheless, the nature of the choice is the same in both cases. The difference consists in the degree of precision with which the weights have been determined, and in the effort of considering. Instead of being made in the first round, the decision is made in the second or third rounds, or later: there are procrastinators everywhere, and under certain conditions anyone can become one.

But it can also happen that already in the first round the actor determines that he cannot fit the competing projects into any plan-hierarchy that has equal jurisdiction over all of them. Even were he to think it over for hours, one project seems to fall under the jurisdiction of one plan-hierarchy, the other under a different one. As we have already seen in the examples about eating: the choice between beef and pork poses no problem of incompatible standards. If one had to choose between beef and sherbet, however, one would, in the culinary culture with which we are familiar, be exceeding the boundaries between two closer provinces of comparison. Customarily one first selects between main courses and then between dessert offerings. Nevertheless these two (historical and historically developed) categories of experience unquestionably lie on the same plane. Preferences ("Which taste do I like better?") and calculations ("Which one is more nutritious? Cheaper?" etc.) can be compared to one another without particular difficulty. It is much rather a question of the comparability of standards when one is placed before the choice between a meal (let us stay with beef) and a pipe (let us say, filled with burley tobacco). But even there, after all, a reference to overarching points of view should be possible, e.g., to pleasure versus health. According to what standards, however, should one choose between beef and a girl's smile? What are the overarching value-references? What is immediately urgent or possibly subject to postponement? Does one choose a hundred tons of beef for a starving population, if one would have to betray a man to his death for it?

It need hardly be stressed that in situations calling for decisions of this kind it is not a question of more precise determination of weights, a more univocal reference to established hierarchical plans. It is rather a question of deciding about the very standards according to which the comparison and decision will be made. This problem is, of course, posed to the actor only when what he must decide for or against seems important from the first. Even if he could not decide between beef and a pipe for solid reasons, a normal person under normal conditions will waste no further thoughts on the subject. He decides blindly by flipping a coin. (With some imagination, of course, conditions under which such a decision would be vital can always be pulled from one's hat.)

Things are different when from the first something important is concerned, when a certain pressure to act exists yet time is available to make a decision and the actor was able to reach no decision in the first round. He will try the second round no longer under the same presupposition with which he entered the first. He must, however, now turn to the standards themselves: he no longer lives "in" the relevances, but rather tries reflexively to grasp the structure of his subjective relevancy system itself. Perhaps he manages, after all, to "discover" an overarching context for the two apparently incompatible hierarchies of plans called forth in the first round. But if he can relate the individual plans that come in question neither to one another nor to something like a life-plan—and thus via this life-plan then again to one another—he will set out to construct step by step a system into which the previously incompatible hierarchies of plans can be inserted. He must then rethink his interests, recalculating the practicabilities of competing projects. Above all, he will have to assess carefully the possible consequences of realizing these projects, both for himself and for the people who are more or less dear to him, in the short and the long run. If then he can, on the basis of such a clarification, fit into a system the hierarchies of plans that occur in the decision-situation and at first seemed incompatible, the weights of the original projects can at last be re-established and compared. The outcome is a founded decision.

The actor may, however, also determine that the interests to which he has traced back the projects stand in an insurmountable conflict and can be placed in no overarching motivational contexts; the projects can be inserted into no system of plans, and still less into a life-plan. Once again he will have to make a "blind" decision. But if he tosses a coin or uses one of the many other possibilities widespread in the most varied societies and at all times to let fate or chance guide the decision, he is now involved in a completely different manner than when he does the same thing for trivial reasons. If it is not so important to him anyway whether he goes in one direction or another, it simply is not worth the effort of seeking further for a grounded decision. In the present case, on the contrary, the actor has to see at long last that in the imposed situation he *cannot* himself, according to his best knowledge and conscience, make a founded decision. This case is apparently very far removed from habitual action: the actor has thought things over, carefully weighing various possibilities, and now he awaits the outcome with full tension of consciousness. On the other hand, on one important point this case does not resemble the everyday opposite of habitual action, namely, the founded act of choice.[31] The decision is not autonomous. For the decisions in which everyday reason fails also mainly concern crises of everyday life and encroachments of other provinces of reality into everyday reality. Faced with such decisions and without convincing reasons for one of the alternatives, the actor can often think of no other solution than to seek clues and signs from other provinces. He interprets dreams and consults oracles.

c. Social Conditions of Choice

Finally, a few remarks on how far and in what way the choice between projects is socially conditioned. The events in which subjective performances of consciousness in general and the subjective acquisition of knowledge as well as subjective knowledge already on hand are socially objectivated have already been examined extensively.[32] Events leading in the opposite direction, in which elements of subjective knowledge are derived from social stocks of knowledge, have also already been described with some precision.[33] It may nonetheless be useful to clarify how the results of those analyses are to be applied in broad lines to the problem of choice.

It is self-evident that choice is a process within the inner duration of the chooser. Where else could it take place? But it is noteworthy that choice concerns something that does not have the objectivity of the outside world. Future expectations are a particular kind of performance of consciousness. Consciousness grasps in them neither something that is perceptible here and now in self-givenness, nor something that had been perceived earlier and is now made present in memory. The performance of consciousness consists rather of the fantasying presentation (*Darstellung*) of something that is not and never has been on hand. The actor thus does not have to choose between larger and smaller apples that he inspects visually, weighs in his hand, and bites into, but between prospective ideas that are not *immediately* comparable. Certainly, the ideas may concern future apples and have been constructed from encounters with apples recently seen or long ago eaten. Yet the actor has no evidence to go by that could be compared subjectively in present evidence and be calibrated intersubjectively without further ado through a simple indication. It is certainly no accident that in the absence of evidence that refers directly to perception, social processes of various kinds play an essential role in the comparison of something that at first seemed incomparable. It is above all social objectivations built up and preserved over many generations and passed on to children as binding that create comparative standards—if necessary, out of nothing, so to speak.

To be sure, projects (or, more broadly formulated, processes in inner duration generally) seem incomparable only in a theoretical distancing from everyday reality. In the natural attitude of everyday life, nothing prevents a normal, hence socialized adult from proceeding as if in his decisions he were dealing usually, though perhaps not always, with comparable items. He sees no reason to distinguish in this respect between earlier, present, and future apples. In most situations he encounters in daily life he will be able to say what he wants and what he does not want—indeed, he will generally also be able to say how much he wants something or seeks to avoid it. The normal person does not always need to compare all over again. Above all, he does not need to compare everything with everything. Usually he can, as was already stated, keep his deliberations within narrower or broader provinces of experience. Yet he can rely on biographically anchored standards—or at least comparative values—and does not need to resort to a single, uniquely valid general standard. Spinach is preferable to salad; it is better to work in long shifts (though strenuously) than regularly (and moderately); a week (of skiing) in the mountains is better than a week in the city (with leisure for concerts and museums). Accordingly, he will weigh and evaluate the various possibilities that present themselves to him in a certain situation in life for his possibilities of eating, working, and going on a vacation.

It is clear that a normal adult has acquired his own interests and preferences, a more or less clearly hierarchical arrangement of his daily and lifetime plans, and the reasons that he presents to himself and others to justify his decisions, not as an unhistorical individual person, but as a member of a historical society. And it need hardly be emphasized that this acquisition took place only to a slight extent alone and independently, and to a greater extent in intersubjective processes. It would be superfluous to enumerate once again the social conditions for the origin of subjective relevance systems.[34] It is enough to point out that interests and preferences were mostly built up as subjective attitudes and because-motives in sedimentations of intersubjective experience; that plans, calculations of practicability, and grounds for a decision, as components of a subjective repertory of action in socially binding learning processes, were taken from the social stock of knowledge; that justifications for a decision, as essential components of a rhetoric of action (and structurally, of a morality of society), occur relatively early in the learning of a language and of binding language-use on the child's part.

Without detailed investigations—for which this is not the right place—it is hard to say exactly how the conditional relations of linguistically formulated justifications, grounds for a decision, and concrete decisions are involved in the choice between projects. We must be satisfied with remembering in general that interests and preferences, plans and grounds for a decision, and naturally even more so the justifications for an act, can be communicated and shared—unless we prefer to say, are shared and communicated. For whereas some things can only be communicated when they were, in a certain sense, already shared, some can only be shared once they have been communicated.

Language is in many respects the most important of the social objectivations. Here we are interested only in the circumstance that it is a comprehensive subjective system of marks and an intersubjective indication system, and thus makes comparisons between projects possible, credible, and binding. Moreover, we need not anticipate too much an analysis of language as a quasi-ideal system of signs.[35] It suffices to recall that a language is a system of meanings, that the meanings objectivate a sense produced in communicative processes, and that this sense points back to the original subjective meaning of encounters—of course, without being identical with it. In any case, a language provides words and combinations of words for typical experiences within well-circumscribed provinces, in finely or roughly connected, simple or multistratified fields of meaning. It is a very familiar fact that different languages undertake very different divisions of reality. It is also known that linguistic categories stamp both experiences and the arrangement of their provinces—sometimes to a stronger extent, sometimes to a lesser extent—and that under certain circumstances they even constitute them as such.

Since, compared with projects, the linguistically composed valuations act as pre-weightings, we are in the present context interested mainly in the fact that linguistic fields of meaning (and hence provinces of experience) are assigned evaluative dimensions. Especially striking in a language are, in the first place, those language-forms that are expressly used for evaluations of any kind. Perhaps the simplest are those that calibrate the perceived qualities of objects in the outside world along a single dimension of meaning. But even these have gone through a long and by no means simple evolution, as is shown by the (conceptual) history of weights, lengths, volumes, distances, etc., not to mention the more complex case of the measurement of time. Beyond this, languages contain word-meaning fields that serve for the systematic evaluation of taste, smell, movement, but also of the (social) correctness of conduct, intensity of feeling, etc. To deal with evaluations, different languages use both semantic and syntactic means to a different extent. Many languages form comparatives and superlatives with adjectives, some do so also with other grammatical categories. All have a repertory of separate evaluative terms. Moreover, they have laudatory and pejorative words (which play a significant role in the socialization of the child), graduated expressions of horror and ecstasy, curse words and scolding words, pejoratives, and the like.

Besides explicit evaluations, however, all languages also have evaluative dimensions that are firmly fused into the fields of meaning. Consequently even without explicit (semantic or syntactic) evaluation in the context of statements, individual words have evaluative connotations from such fields of meaning. These are actualized intralinguistically and subjectively as well as intersubjectively in communicative processes of the most varied kinds. Moreover, the evaluative dimensions of individual meaning-fields can be almost neutral and only barely influence the actor for or against something, or stimulate him to take a decisive stance. Further, they can be constructed in multiple strata or be quite simple (as it were, on a one-dimensional scale). And finally, it should be noted that although such evaluative dimensions are specific to individual fields of meaning (and the provinces of experience they cover), they can be expanded metaphorically to other provinces.

Linguistically composed evaluations, whether explicit or fused with other language-forms, are used, of course, not just to compare projects. They are important wherever language, according to its basic function, is used intersubjectively: in conversation and narrative, quarreling and agreement, command and request. But since evaluation is inherent in linguistic formulations of types of experience (relatively independently of the time- and reality-character of the experiences), language, in the form of inner language (sometimes stylized into a monologue) plays an especially important role precisely in the step-by-step consideration of envisionings of the future.

A language, thus, makes a general contribution to the choice between projects by objectivating the subjective and by making the non-present and the future present; it makes a particular one by already completed weighings. It provides rememberable and intersubjectively credible standards for objects of the outside world. It repeatedly provides applicable weighings for constructs of fantasy, in comparison with the non-present. And, of course, language helps to formulate the symbolic indications and interpretative systems for dreams and oracles—and nowadays for the psychological sciences—i.e., in cases where an independently founded choice is no longer possible.

c. Action

1. The Decision

Projects can be designed. This does not refer to the self-evident fact that projects come about in conscious processes, but rather that the act that is envisioned *modo futuri exacti* has the character of a project and not, for example, of a physical performance, a speech, the solution of a mathematical problem, etc. It is not hard to envision someone who would like to design plans of action for the various situations that could confront him, to keep them in store as a precautionary measure. He focuses on the project of mentally practicing various sorts of conduct in case of earthquake, flood, and conflagration. Or think of the grandmother, experienced in life, who is ready with well-considered advice to help her grandson who has gotten into difficulties. It holds true, even for such acts, which persist in thought and project until further notice, that a last impulsion is necessary to set the projected action in motion—i.e., in this case, the projecting. In cases where the action has to overcome an external resistance, it becomes all the more obvious that something like a volitive "fiat"—to use William James's term—is necessary to translate the project into deed. Unless something is added, no progress is made beyond the project. In common parlance, the missing link between the project and the action proper is called a decision.

It was already mentioned earlier that action does not of itself follow from the project.[36] Now it will have to be shown briefly that for all kinds of action a decision to take the first step is necessary, but that this decision is also different in character for the various kinds of action. Depending on whether it concerns habitual action, or simple decisions for a familiar project, or the result of a hard choice between carefully weighed projects, and depending on the importance of the action for the actor, the last impulse to act will be "strong" or "weak."

To this point we have concerned ourselves mainly with describing how an actor prepares to act, or, to put it more precisely, how a prospective actor gears himself for a possible action. Certainly, without a project there is no act. But whereas a project is a necessary ingredient of action, not all projects necessarily lead to action. However seriously a person may feel when he visualizes a particular future possibility (his death by lung cancer), however carefully he deliberates between different projects (to give up smoking immediately, merely to cut down on smoking at first, or to continue smoking as usual), and however unreservedly he may decide in favor of a project (to stop smoking), still nothing has happened. Whether or not he is serious about it, the actor has up to this point just been playing with the thought of action. He can still turn back—or, since he has not taken a step, he can still stay right where he is. This is true both of past deeds and of deeds left undone (as is shown by the example of smoking and the act of nonsmoking, which is quite difficult for many persons), and it holds good, as we have already seen, both for operation and work as well as for pure thinking (e.g., designing projects).

The choice between conflicting projects is basically an act of interpretation. Choosing is not an act of thought undertaken from the distance of the theoretical attitude, but an interpretative decision that stands under the pressure of action and time in an actually present situation. It is also clear that the actor thinks because he must: he has a more or less cogent, practical motive for choosing, and he is more or less urgently interested in the result of choice. Nevertheless, envisionings of the future are nothing but fantasies. However, they are fantasies that come into question seriously for the actor based on his biographically predetermined interests. But the weighing and deliberating with which he must occupy himself is an act of interpretation. The actor establishes themes in his consciousness and reflects upon them; but he still does not want to commit himself to "reality."

The decision itself is an altogether different kind of performance of consciousness. It is an act of will. The concepts, and even more the words with whose help a person tries to grasp and understand the essence of this act, differ at least in nuances from society to society and from epoch to epoch. But one thing they have in common is the actor's consciousness that the *ultimate* impulse to realize the project comes from himself. The actor notices that he is in the process of crossing a boundary, that he can now still go back . . . but now no longer so. He knows that he can later interrupt the action or bring it to a complete stop; he also knows that what has begun has begun. In most cases, this boundary is crossed without particular significance: in habitual action one hardly notices it. In the crisis situations of life, by contrast, when it is a matter of "life or death," one knows very well that by this first step one is in the process of burning down all the bridges behind oneself.

How clearly a decision stands out from the foregoing project and the subsequent action and enters consciousness as a sharply delineated act of the will depends thus on the combination of two circumstances (it is, moreover, clear that the two do not "vary" independently of one another). First, there is the importance of the act's consequences for the actor's life—of course, as the actor sees it at the time of making the decision. Second, it makes a difference whether the action is oriented habitually by an already-existent, ingrained project (so that no polythetic mental act of projecting takes place, and project, decision, and the first steps of action merge together), whether a project competes just with the weakly weighed alternative of preferably not steering toward the possibility envisioned in it and the decision comes easy, or whether the actor has to choose step by step between projects requiring ever more precise weighing and can break through to a decision only after long vacillation.

It is perhaps unnecessary to point out that all these considerations must always be related to the actor's subjective, biographically anchored relevance system, which characterizes his complex of attitudes, his character. Just as there are people who hesitate in the valuation of weights, in the decision between various possibilities, there also are "weak-willed" and "strong-willed" persons. Of course, it must not be forgotten that these categories belong in some form to the typification of the social world in the natural attitude and are stamped in their concrete empirical form by the respective relative-natural worldview.

However much a given situation seems to restrict the possibilities of choice, however immediate the decision for a particular alternative may be, and however much or little the decision stands out from project and action, in any case the actor remains conscious that the decision is not imposed on him. Everyone knows the difference between what he wanted or did and what happened against his will. Afterward he may, naturally, pretend to have done something that merely happened to him—and on the other hand, he can pretend that something he did merely happened. We have already discussed the difficulties of ascribing responsibility.[37] What matters here is only to point out the fundamental (and subjectively graspable) prominence of decision in the act as a whole, with all the empirical nuances that result from whether or not a language knows the word "decision" or its equivalent and what system for ascribing responsibility a relative-natural worldview contains (whether, for example, it already encompasses the imagining of the project so that one can already "sin in thought," or whether it is oriented strictly by the consequences of the deed, so that a vendetta is continued for generations; whether it defines the individual or a collectivity as the bearer of responsibility, etc.).

2. The Course of Action

a. *Beginning and End*

The action proceeds—how else could it proceed—between a beginning and an end. Every act, every project is, as we have seen, preceded by doubt. The beginning of the action proper, however, is set by the decision to act. The events of consciousness that led to the decision may have been long and complicated—from the initial doubt, via the choice between conflicting projects that had to be weighed, to the decision for one project. But the decision itself is, in the last analysis, a simple matter. And as soon as the decision has been made, the actor, as if in the same breath, begins to take the first step. This step has been established with sufficient clarity for the action, as the first of a series of steps that, in the project the actor had decided upon, lead to the goal. Naturally, depending on the kind of action, "sufficient clarity" can be a habitual initiation of steps that then unreel of themselves or a contrived move in an overarching strategy. In any case, nothing more intervenes between the decision to act and the action itself. For what could intervene, if it really was a decision to act and not a decision to postpone or a decision not to act? Doubt is eliminated, hesitation is over: the action begins.

Things are not quite so simple with the end of action as with the beginning. The multiplicity of concrete circumstances in which an action ceases is so great that it seems inexhaustible. What difference between a rider whose horse gallops across the finish line ahead of all the other horses running in a race, and another who broke his neck jumping over the first hurdle; between a man who has stopped eating because he is satiated, another who becomes ill from overeating, and a third who stops because he has nothing more to eat; between a reader who throws away a book because he is enraged at its style or content, another who late at night is tired and falls asleep over the book, a third who reads the book intently to the end, and a fourth who reads exactly fifteen pages every evening (except Saturday) before turning out the light. But if the reasons that lead to the end of the action are examined, one sees that they can, without too crude a simplification, be divided into three groups: realization of the project, interruptions, and cessations.

The simplest case seems at the same time to be of the greatest significance for the person acting in the everyday world. It is characterized by the fact that the actor has accomplished his original project in a manner that is satisfactory to him and adequate for all practical purposes. The future envisioned *modo futuri exacti* has come about in its essential features, of course (for the actor, too) with one exception, namely the mode. The *futurum exactum* has been changed into the *praesens* or, respectively, the *imperfectum* or *perfectum*. Now the act is in the process of being accomplished . . . now it is accomplished . . . just a moment ago, it was accomplished. The action has found its natural end by reaching the goal. It becomes an act.

However, the reservations that were just made—"satisfactory to him," "adequate for all practical purposes," "in its essential features"—are indispensable. For, no matter how well the actor may have estimated in advance the chances and practicability of any given project, and no matter how little what is unusual and unexpected has happened since the beginning of the act: the completed act can never coincide perfectly with the projected one. The reasons for this have already been enumerated often enough. But since perfection is rarely necessary in the everyday life-world, it suffices in most cases of everyday action if the average type of performance can be made to coincide with the average type of project. If that succeeds, then the act is unproblematically successful. In the natural attitude of everyday life there is not the slightest occasion for the hairsplitting reflection that in principle no act can be identical with its project or be made to coincide perfectly with it. What matters is that the act did not fail, that I galloped across the finish line, finished reading the book, that I am satiated.

Things are somewhat more complicated when the action is ended not because the project has been accomplished but because it must, for some reason or other, be interrupted or brought to a halt. Interruptions can be called a temporary halt and cessation a permanent halt in the course of the act. Interruptions must be divided into two kinds: those that are more or less clearly planned in the project itself as a kind of empty place in the action proper, and those that occur unexpectedly.

It is obvious that a halt in the course of the action proper may have been foreseen from the first in the original plan for executing an act of thought and, even more so, an act of effective operation. This holds good especially for acts that cannot in any case be accomplished in one sweep, i.e., those that are scheduled for longer spans of time. A school program that is designed for four years of regular matriculation cannot be finished any sooner by studying day and night, on school days and holidays. Many acts thus foresee a sequence of phases of action proper, which alternate with phases of inaction, followed in turn by new phases of action. This case, involving the sequence of phases of action and inaction, has close affinity with another, involving a sequence of phases of different acts. In this way, a phase of act B begins before act A is finished.

Both kinds of prearranged interruptions of the action proper (by determining rest-breaks and by intertwining acts) can become habitual, either separately or conjointly. They then find their systematic place in the more or less strongly routinized provinces of daily plans and lifetime plan. The latter, in turn, are co-determined by the social objectivations of acts as types of acts and by the institutionalization of courses of action. A good illustration of the systematic interlacing of act, non-act, and other act is provided by the most important type of everyday action, namely socially organized work. The degree of systematization, the rhythm, and the content are different, but in the basic principle of interlocking, all societies resemble one another: a wandering horde of hunters and gatherers in the Old Stone Age, an advanced culture planting and harvesting grain, and modern industrial societies with their work at an assembly line or in an office.

But not all interruptions prearranged in the project are characterized by the fact that action is brought to a stop on schedule and unconditionally at a given time or after certain phases have been passed through. Many actions follow plans that foresee in advance only the possibility of stopping the action after the first, second, third, or a later step, depending on the circumstances (until further developments or once and for all). Obviously we are dealing here with a narrower formulation of the general maxim of action: "One thing after the other." The empty formula, *a, b, c, d,* etc., is often applied with the addition of hypothetical relevancies (if . . . then . . .) as follows: first *a,* then *b,* then also *c;* but if not *b,* then also not *c,* . . . but perhaps *d* or nothing at all. And that fits our case: if my *a* is followed by *b,* I will do *c;* if not, I leave *c* undone. The principle holds good again, of course, for the (now hypothetically formulated) sequence of phases of action and inaction, as well as for the interlocking of phases of different acts. Most projects of acts provide more or less clearly for certain intersections with alternative possibilities for continuing, including some consisting of an interruption or cessation. They thus take the form of a more or less richly branched "decision-tree." Moreover, only possibilities that are relatively firmly calculated come in question here. The empty anticipation ("Something or other that is not anticipated can always happen") is of no significance for the course of the act.

The best illustrations of decision-trees with calculated inter-ruptions and cessations are again provided—not at all surprisingly—by various forms of social action: if he (or she) does this, then I will do this: if he (or she) does that, I will do something else—for example nothing. The latter applies to fistfights (but not to a sports match, where one must do *something* within fixed time-periods or else receive penalties for inactivity) and to courting the other sex (but presumably not to the sex act itself). Even mediate social action on high levels of anonymity can follow projects of interlocking action, inaction, and alternative or other action. This applies to war (a *cunctator,* a "dawdler" or "slowpoke," has even gone down in history), agriculture, and in-dustrial production. Naturally, the structure of such decision-trees is already more complicated because it is based on a long-term collective organization of acts. The staggering of phases of action with inter-ruptions, for instance, in rice farming, in steel production, and in advertising agency "output," is dependent not only on very different natural and technological conditions (e.g., the rainy season or blast furnace temperatures), but also on the extent to which the "addition" or "substitution" of work processes is possible.

This should be enough said on the interruptions and cessations prearranged in the plan of action. In addition, we have already dealt with a few important formal aspects of planned stopping in other contexts, e.g., in the descriptions of the temporal stratifications of the everyday life-world,[38] of hypothetical relevance[39] and of the time-structure of action.[40] We therefore now turn to those interruptions or cessations that the actor has not foreseen and that were not firmly calculated into the original project.

In the course of action, conditions can always occur that the actor in no way foresaw, not even with the help of a very general but action-relevant typification of occurrence. As was said before, we are completely disregarding premonitions because they are devoid of content. The original project has made no provision for conditions that occur unexpectedly. If the new conditions are favorable to the action, the case need trouble us no further. For the action is not held up but rather promoted—whether this takes the form of an accel-eration or of increased chances for a successful outcome with or with-out acceleration. What interests us here is when the new conditions are notably unfavorable and the chances have decisively worsened for the actor to realize the original project judiciously (of course, always in relation to the actor's subjective state of knowledge, his "objective" blindness or stupidity). Then the actor has two possibilities: either he tries despite everything "to ram his head through the wall," or he ceases (temporarily or permanently) to act. What a person then actually does in a given situation depends both on the nature of the act, especially of the risks accompanying failure, and on the actor's subjective relevance system (his "personality"). Thus the empirical thresholds will vary from person to person and from situation to situation. In any case, an actor will cease to act when in a given situation he thinks that further action does not seem advisable, at least for the moment.

b. The Sequence of Steps

Action often proceeds step by step from beginning to end. This does not mean that each actor must be clearly and distinctly conscious of every single step in every action. Whether one phase of an act stands out distinctly or only vaguely from the prior one depends on the interplay of two circumstances: on the kind of action (this goes from flowing movements to games in which one must wait after each play) and on the degree of habituation to the action in question. The pole-vaulter measures his approaching run in advance by the number of strides that he needs on the average until his leap. He still remains to some degree conscious of the individual steps even in the execution, more clearly so when things do not work out, and less clearly so the longer he trains on the same sports field with his own marked approach run. Someone walking home by a familiar route, in contrast, pays absolutely no attention to the individual steps that bring him closer to his destination. The chess player has the individual moves in his mind as separate components of a coordinated sequence planned in advance. It is, after all, integral to this game that it proceeds move after move and that what a move is, is precisely defined. An experienced master, however, in the initial moves of a standard opening that is answered with the moves of a standard defense, no longer thinks about the individual moves, and they seem almost to merge together in the first minutes. In arithmetic one learns to add one number to another, but once a high degree of routine is achieved, the distances between the individual events vanish almost completely. In a conversation the phases of facial expression merge together even when one tries to become aware of them and to control them consciously. Something similar is true of the gestures that accompany conversation, but not of separately planned, conventionalized gestures. And speech itself has from the beginning a more strongly articulated character, even when this articulation follows a rhythm that does not correspond completely to the written codification of word and sentence. And to cite one last example, in a court proceeding, the distribution of talk is to a considerable extent institutionally fixed. If a witness should ever forget not only that *he* is not supposed to ask any questions but also that he is supposed to give only sharply delimited answers, he will be reminded of it emphatically.

The steps of action are arranged in the project. This does not mean that while carrying out the steps of the act every actor consciously keeps each of the steps prearranged in the project with the same distinctness. Even less does it mean that he compares each step in the execution of the act in every detail with each corresponding step arranged in the project. We have just shown that how distinctly the steps stand in relief in consciousness during their execution depends on the kind of act and the degree of habituation. Furthermore, let us recall that already in the original project the individual steps—depending on the kind of action, the demands of the situation, and even the "personality" of the actor—were planned with a great variety of distinctness and may have been determined with different degrees of clarity in their details. If we take all these circumstances together, it cannot be surprising that the degree of agreement between the projected and the completed steps of the act is subject to considerable fluctuations. The actor can be hardly or very decidedly aware of the arrangement of his steps of action in terms of the project. The range extends from almost automatic coincidence between the projected and the completed steps in an action that unreels habitually, to active precise examination of $A1$ which is in process of being completed with the projected $A1$, then $A2$ in the process of being completed with the projected $A2$, etc.

This also holds true, of course, for the case of "successful" action, in which the actor comes step by step closer to the originally projected goal. Other possibilities have already been considered in the analysis of interruptions and cessations. In "successful" habitual action the agreement between the projected and the executed steps is, indeed, very high, but the actor no longer needs to orient himself very attentively vis-à-vis the project. Only when the automatic expectation that it will continue that way is crudely disappointed does *non*-agreement press to consciousness. On the contrary, when new and difficult life-problems are to be mastered and a person arranges his action strategically and plans it in advance in every detail, then in execution the steps are also carefully arranged according to the project. The project becomes a standard of execution arranged with meticulous precision. In everyday life, cases of such action are not very frequent. What comes closest are those forms of action in which the "moves" are subject to more or less binding social regulations and which at least in this respect show a certain similarity with play: football rather than soccer, the war games of the "mathematical nuclear strategists" rather than the Battle on the Berezina, the strictly regulated reciprocities of "primitive" bartering rather than the black market in a planned economy. We know, however, that even in such forms of action, in principle no perfect coincidence between the projected and the completed sequence of steps can result. But we also know that a perfect coincidence is not at all required for most practical purposes of everyday life.

c. Changes during Execution

We have till now considered the course of action mainly from the vantage pont of "success" or "failure"—if not final failure, then at least a temporary setback. In the first case, as we saw, the action proceeded step by step in (more or less clear) orientation with the series of steps arranged (more or less clearly) in the project—indeed in relatively satisfactory agreement with it. This applied to simple processes following a single, planned line. And it also applied to acts whose project had the basic features of a decision-tree, except that in "if-then" acts the concrete course follows each concrete "if" that has occurred between one intersection point and the next. In the second case, action came to a stop—for whatever reasons, the original project could not be realized. To be sure, the possible forms of the course of an act have still not been enumerated exhaustively. Let us consider still further possibilities in the following passages, though we can still be brief, because they can be regarded as variations of the already described basic forms of the process.

It has already been stated that a person can notice in the middle of the course of action that the chances for realizing the project have worsened so fundamentally since the beginning of the act (more precisely: since the original estimate of practicability) that the execution of the original plan seems seriously endangered or even impossible. Depending on the circumstances, the actor will then continue to act, interrupt the act, or cease completely. The basic traits of how things go in these cases have already been clarified. If the person continues to act "blindly," the projected series of steps does not change: if he is lucky, the original project is realized after all and the action is "successful"; if he is unlucky, he simply does not reach the goal, and the action "fails." Either way the case is closed. And the case is closed from the outset, if the person gives up the act once and for all. But what is the situation if the person neither continues "blindly" to act nor gives up completely?

The possibilities of the further course that come under consideration here are all characterized by the fact that the person still holds firmly to his original goal, but that the steps which he takes to achieve this goal are no longer governed by the originally planned series of steps. This results in an "accidental" change in the execution of the act that is controlled by the actor and does not affect merely superficial details. It need hardly be stressed that here we are speaking only of further developments in the course of the "same" act, not of repetitions of the same type of act, since in such a case nothing essential really changes in the process itself. At most, a re-estimation of practicability results for later actions of such a type. Here we are interested, rather, in continued action, insofar as it is not "blind," or in other words a continuation or resumption of the action.

If, despite unfavorable circumstances, the person does not continue to act "blindly," but also no longer wants to interrupt the action in question (or its concrete time-structure does not perhaps permit an interruption), he will briefly (under some circumstances, with lightning speed) "stop and reflect." If even then he sees no other possibility, he will after all interrupt, cease, or continue acting somewhat "blindly." He may, however, discover a series of steps other than the one arranged in the original project, and assume that it has better chances of reaching the same goal. Further action is then oriented by the newly projected sequence of steps. Thus, in the midst of the action, components of the project are changed—to be sure, components that are subordinate to the goal. The project of the act, accordingly, follows the original project up to a certain point, then it follows the changed project. In relation to the forms of process, this means that after the fact a simple, rectilinear course was changed into an "if-then" course or respectively that an additional juncture was inserted in the decision-tree after the fact. For the performance of the action, this "after the fact" is, however, of decisive significance: the "if" had not been foreseen in the original project and the action was not oriented by it.

Besides continued action, we spoke above of continuations and resumptions of interrupted action. By this, we meant to point out a difference in the concrete conditions for performing action that is important for everyday life. Many kinds of acts can be continued from where they had been interrupted. This applies to daydreams and mental calculations as well as to operations and work. A process of addition can be continued, starting from the partial sum that had been reached before the interruption; one can continue plowing a half-plowed field on the next day; a half-inserted screw can later be tightened firmly. Interrupted while playing a sonata, one can indeed continue to play from the point of the interruption, but the form of the process is no longer the same. Fresco painting is limited to narrow time-spans, whereas Cologne Cathedral could be worked on for centuries. Some kinds of action must be begun all over again after excessively long interruptions. And from them, a boundary marked only unclearly in reality runs to forms of action that cannot be rightly interrupted, otherwise one must begin all over again even if it is not a matter of repetitions in the sense mentioned above. Such acts always lead from the beginning to the end; the end can be successful or unsuccessful, but one cannot continue from the middle—for example, a dive from a five-meter high diving board.

D. Rational Action, Rational Acts

1. Rational Action

Unrestricted rationality of action presupposes so much that ordinary mortals can hardly hope to achieve it. In provinces of the life-world where the conditions of everyday life cannot be abrogated, a rational person cannot even seek it. The question of whether or not a philosophical concept of unrestricted reason is suitable as the model for human action can be disregarded. Nor do we want to consider how useful models of rational action are in the social sciences, e.g., as ideal-typical constructs for economic theory.

We are not concerned here with provinces of self-contained meaning-structure (which are based on theoretical considerations) but with everyday practice in the natural attitude. No one will be surprised by the statement that there can be no unrestrictedly rational action in this everyday reality. If the results of the foregoing analyses (especially concerning the stratifications of the life-world, the origin and the structure of subjective stocks of knowledge, and finally the way projects are formed and the choice between projects) are kept in mind, no further proof for the claim will need to be sought. But if we have no contribution to make, either to the background questions of ethics and philosophical anthropology, or to the foreground question of social-scientific methodology, and if we consider a proof that there can be no unrestrictedly rational everyday action to be super-fluous, why should we turn the discussion to this theme at all?

We are not applying the excessively narrow standard of un-restricted rationality to everyday action in order to bring out and criticize irrationality. Nor is it for the opposite intention of showing how rational this standard itself is. By asking what the preconditions of unrestrictedly rational action would be, we are at the same time asking about the boundaries that the rationality of action in the every-day life-world must of necessity encounter—and not just occasionally because of a person's passion, blindness, or self-incurred ignorance. Thus, we want merely to play with the idea of the unrestricted ra-tionality of action, in order to see how the *practical* rationality of action is constituted under the limiting conditions of everyday reality. Playful thought helps us to draw the conclusions from the foregoing analyses with special clarity.

First, the actor, in order to be able to act with unrestricted rationality, would have to know himself just as he is. We need pre-suppose no perfect self-knowledge, whatever "perfect" could mean here—if anything definite at all. In order to encounter the first boundary of rationality in everyday action, a less demanding but more clearly defined presupposition is quite sufficient: the actor would have to see his interests clearly and distinctly in an orderly arrangement according to their importance. For this purpose he would have to trace back the multiplicity of their developmental contexts and lift them to consciousness out of the blind efficacy that they have as be-cause-motives of present action. Since in the action proper only in-order-to motives are in view, this inventorying of interests would al-ready have been done long before any action, but it still would have to be brought up to date prior to each action. Only with the help of such a clearly defined and uncontradictory inventory of interests could the actor balance benefit against cost in his decisions. In other words, only in that way could he rationally take into account the inevitable consequences of the fundamental rule of all projecting and action (in Spinoza's formulation: *omnis determinatio est negatio*). The part of self-knowledge essential for the rationality of a man's action would consist in having found a standard of comparison he believes valid for things that are otherwise incomparable. With this standard he could first distinguish the projects that seriously come into question for him in the given life-situations from all the conceivable ones and then fit them into a systematic context of superimposed, parallel, and sub-ordinate plans. But a plan-hierarchy related to knowledge of his present self would still not be sufficient, even if it had a maximum of clarity, distinctness, and freedom from contradiction.

Second, the actor would not merely have to know himself as he is now, but also as he will be at some future time. To reach the next boundary of the rationality of everyday action, we need not demand that the actor be capable of predicting the future that will later really happen with certainty in all its details. It is quite sufficient to suppose that he be able to foresee the possibly significant typical changes of his own self. He would thus (of course, here too, as always, with the "other things being equal" stipulation) have to know now at least how probable it is that his state of interests will remain constant in certain realms and on certain points and will change in others. Before he decides now to do or not to do some particular thing, he would have to know now, at least according to the kind of acts and their typical consequences, the extent to which what seems good and precious to him today might also be important and urgent to him tomorrow, in a month, a year, twenty years. And he would have to know, above all, to what extent something that is indifferent to him now will be worth striving for tomorrow, later, or much later. In short, the person would have to orient his action not exclusively under the somewhat natural assumption of the "And so forth" or even just pre-dominantly by the now prevalent state of interests. Even considering the consequences of his present action must not be done based only on knowledge of his present self. The actor should also take carefully into account the foreseeable state of interests of his future self.

Everyone knows, of course, that he could, according to his present state of interests, regret certain acts tomorrow—and this has considerable influence on his present decision to do or not do some-thing. Everyone also knows, although mostly in a very indefinite man-ner, that some things that now seem to him highly worth striving for will presumably be indifferent to him in later years. However, this knowledge need have no particular significance for his present action, since he is now hastening toward a goal that seems worth striving for. But, beyond this, the actor would have to be able to calculate whether he will in the future, according to a later but now foreseeable state of interests, regret having done something now that seems to him highly worth striving for today and that he knows he will most prob-ably not regret having done tomorrow. Only in this way is he in a position to decide now on a completely rational basis whether the later (now foreseeable) regret would outweigh the present (more precisely speaking: the now immediately foreseen) satisfaction. The person would thus have to build up not merely a clear and well-ordered hierarchy of interests and plans relative to his present self, but already now to orient it by his (presumed) future self. He would deliberate both between his present different interests as if they were meaningfully comparable, and between his present and successive phases of his future interests, insofar as they are now foreseeable. Incidentally, we will disregard completely that the person of whom we are requiring all this knowledge would, before all this, have to make calculations on his chances for a "later" life. But these calculations of his life expectancy would be based less on his knowledge of himself than on knowledge of the world, especially of his fellowmen and their typical life-spans.

Third, in order to act rationally, the person would have to know not just himself but of course also the world around him. To a degree, that is certainly always the case. To reach a further boundary of rational action, we again need not demand that the actor know all there is and ever was to know. It is quite sufficient to suppose that he knows what knowledge he needs and will need for the various acts in his world, that he then also wants to acquire this knowledge, and that he actually can acquire it. Thus he would have the full scope of knowledge that is necessary for action in a concrete, historical, everyday reality.

For the actor to be able to estimate the practicability of the various projects that seriously come into question and to consider the consequences of his action just as rationally, we must, however, suppose one more thing: that all this knowledge should have for him the highest degree of clarity, distinctness, and freedom from contradiction. The actor's stock of knowledge would, accordingly, have to be fundamentally different from what it actually is, both in its subjective structure and in its dependence on the social distribution of knowledge.

Perhaps we need not expressly mention, certainly not list as a separate point, that the actor would have to know not only the world that surrounds him now, but also that in which he will have to live in the future. For it belongs to the knowledge of everyday reality that in some respects it remains as it is, whereas in others it changes in typical ways. It is, however, clear that estimates of practicability, especially for projects with long time-spans, can be rationally grounded only by carefully including this time-perspective. The same thing naturally holds good for deliberating about the sequences of acts.

The points addressed above do not yet apply to the rationality of the choice between projects, and even less to the action proper. They relate entirely to what would have to precede choice and action: the clarity and distinctness of projects or their location in well-ordered contexts of interest and plan-hierarchies, the reliability of the practicability estimates assigned to them, and the precise calculation of the consequences of the act. As could be seen, the limits that are set for the rationality of action are essentially time limits. *Tempora mutantur et nos mutamur in illis*: Everyone knows *that* this is the case but no one knows exactly *how* this will be the case for him. Was Tiresias, then, a common mortal? Could Saul, then, know that a Paul was in him?

The next point also has to do with time, not with the future as the basic transcendency of present knowledge but rather with the actor's inner time:

Fourth, in order to be able to act rationally, the person would have to be able to choose between competing projects as if the choice itself were not an event in his stream of consciousness. He would have to be able to examine the projects that present themselves for their suitability in the actually present situation, without the pressure of time and decision. Even if, as was demanded in the first three points of this play of thought, we envision the plan-hierarchy that was "brought along" into the situation, the estimates of practicability, and the pre-weighings on a plane of perfection that is unknown in reality, the projects still have to be weighed for their situational importance and urgency. The steps of judgment necessary for this would have to be made not only fully consciously on the highest level of clarity and definition, but also be unburdened from all the disturbances and pressures usual in everyday life.

The fifth and last point concerns the action itself. Let us assume that the previously discussed reservations did not apply. Let us assume that the actor had clarified his interests perfectly and also related them to his future self, calculating the chances that such a self would exist in the time in question. On this basis he would have built a plan-hierarchy in which the individual projects would be ranked on the highest level of clarity, distinctness, and freedom from contradiction. Let us also assume that he had with the help of his fully sufficient knowledge calculated exactly the possibilities of practicability for the projects and carefully weighed the consequences of the acts eventually performed. As a perfectly rational actor he would, furthermore, keep up to date all decisions and weighings already made. Thus equipped, he would enter the decisional situation and, relieved of the time pressure, make the logical choice fully consciously, step by step. Even then, in the course of the action proper, still unexpected circumstances immediately affecting the further course of the action could occur. (Otherwise, we would have had to demand that the person actually have the power to predict the future. If we had tried this, even for the purpose of the play of thought, it would presumably have exceeded the bounds of even the most fantastic idea of human action.) The supposition that would thus have to be made for every occurrence of unexpected circumstances in the course of action is that made for the situation of choice: relief from the pressure of time and decision.

The actor's nature, especially his temporality, as well as the nature of the reality around him, especially its temporality, set uncrossable limits to his knowledge. The idea of the unrestricted rationality of action thus remains what it is: an idea. But discussion of the rationality or irrationality of action does not therefore become meaningless. How close one comes to the boundaries drawn in every life-world depends, as we have seen, both on the actor and his life history, as well as on the kind of action and its natural and social conditionality. The possibilities of practical reason are determinable only if an act (whose universal structure was described) is measured against *what* a concrete actor, a living person, can do in a concrete historical life-world and *how* he can do it.

2. Rational Acts

Just like past experiences, acts, after they have been performed, can also be called to memory immediately afterward, somewhat later, or years and decades later. Common sense is not wrong: important and rare acts, but even more so, unique acts, tend to be remembered more than unimportant, often repeated, or even habitual ones. And moreover, as everyone knows, some things are remembered more preferably than others . . . And some things one would like to forget but cannot . . .

Still, acts are not called back to memory quite the way simple experiences are. For something that merely happened to oneself is not remembered, but rather events that one tried to direct. One remembers *acts,* but under normal circumstances of everyday life not the action. Acts that have run their course do not rerun it once again in memory even in a copylike fashion—not even abbreviated as to details. One perhaps remembers them approximately as one lived them: a house from childhood, the face of a deceased person, the taste of the wine one drank ten minutes ago. On the contrary, acts are generally not brought back into the memory in such a way that one could—with a highly unusual exertion of consciousness—believe that they really occurred exactly, or at any rate approximately, so. At least in the natural attitude of everyday life, acts are *not* re-enacted in the memory in their complex time- and meaning-structure, and therefore not as action.

Of course, memories are present events of consciousness. They unfold in inner time and are determined by the present relevance system of the one who remembers. Memories of simple experiences are not interpretative *performances* of consciousness, at any rate not in and of themselves. They can, naturally, always be transformed into complex interpretative performances of a remembering action—but that is not the topic of discussion here. In their occurrence in memory they are determined by the present relevance system, but primarily in passive events. What one remembers is automatically represented as determined by the relevance system at the time and it is preserved in its basic form as experience. The memories of acts refer to something that had a completely different time and meaning structure from that of simple experiences. The achievements of consciousness that become operative here are either already higher-level complete interpretative acts, or nearly so, or else they have sunk back down from that level to that of routine occurrences. Memories of acts are actively determined by the present system of the actor's interpretative relevances (of the one who has acted!). The interpretative act is a re-presentation (*Wiedergabe*): neither something itself given nor a simple memory, but also not fantasying imagination. That it is a reconstruction holds true already for the typifying presentiation of a completed act ("quarreled with the neighbor yesterday"), but even more for attempts to re-enact the former occurrence as faithfully as possible ("then I said . . . then she said . . .").

In daily life there is seldom a motive for a precise, gradual re-presentation of the former action exactly as it was performed step-by-step in its turn. Now one knows how the story ended—and generally that is what matters. Why, then, should one strive to go back only to wind up later where one had already arrived long ago? Certainly, typical interests, typical projects, typical results, even typical processes (arranged under categories such as "fast" or "slow," "easy" or "laborious," and the like) can readily be called to mind as characteristics of a past act. The memory of the action proper, however, runs into a great difficulty. How can one put oneself back in the state of not knowing the course of the action or its outcome? In the action at the time, the future was still uncertain and open; now it is absolutely certain and definitively over. It has become past. The knowledge of the person who now calls the past act to memory is not the knowledge of the person who acted at that time. Then he had to look forward, projecting, estimating chances of practicality, deliberating about consequences, weighing projects; now he looks back. Precisely what he did not know then, he now knows. The state of negative knowledge at that time is, of course, no longer restorable as a present state. But it is already difficult enough and requires a very unusual exertion to call forth in crude, typical features the former state of negative knowledge that was significant for the action at the time. That by itself requires an interpretative act. "I really could not know that at the time . . . ," "If only I had known then what I know today . . ." The problem is highlighted in expressions such as these.

In everyday life, the memory of past acts is evoked mainly by the practical requirements of the present or of the anticipated immediate future: the projecting of a similar act, narration among friends, a report in professional contexts, a confession, a witness's statement. Whether they involve foresight or boasting, duty or gossip, justification or accusation, the motivational contexts that enable subjective memories to become communicated memories are mostly also already motivational contexts that determined subjective memory (of *acts*) as self-communication. Certainly the impulsion may come from "within" or from "outside." And the original meaning of an act, the motive for its re-presentation in memory and the meaning that the communication of a remembered act has, can on the whole be regarded, in various mixtures and ways, from two opposite sides: the "objective" location of an act in social act-contexts (a location that is of course also relevant for the actor, but only mediately so), and the role of an act in the actor's life history. From both vantage points, however, the typically most important aspect of action is the completed act.

For the completed act, in turn, typically the most important aspect is success or failure. In case of success, a question will hardly be raised concerning the rationality of the act, at least not by the actor himself. (Under certain circumstances other persons, rather, feel compelled to do so, e.g., under the envious motto "beginner's luck.") For acts that have failed, on the contrary, the question arises as if by itself: "Did I attempt the impossible?" "Could I have done better?" "Could I have foreseen that it would end this way?" Such questions, touching more or less directly on the rationality of the act, are raised after the act has been completed and one knows what it led to. Hence, one could believe that the rationality of the act could then be judged better or in any case differently. On closer inspection, it turns out that this is not the case—or is so only to a very limited extent. One now knows more and is relieved of the pressure to act, but only the second circumstance is really of considerable significance. One can be annoyed now at not having known more then, but it does not follow from this that one now regards the action as unreasonable at that time. Only when it also becomes clear from present knowledge that one should already have known then, for example, that the plan was impracticable can one be said to have acted irrationally. The same is true of the foreseeing of the consequences. Now one knows what the consequences of that act are; but only if our own negligence is determined to have been the cause for our not pre-calculating these consequences will the act be called irrational. In regard to the clarification of one's own interests, one perhaps "becomes wiser with age," but if at that time the present state of interest was, with some foresight, included in the choice of projects, one must not today elevate the current state of interest to the exclusive standard of action at that time. If one establishes that the former act was reasonable according to soundest knowledge at that time, this fact cannot be shaken even from the standpoint of current knowledge.

But the judgment of what could have been the "soundest knowledge" at that time has shifted. Naturally, this shift is quite enough to require a change of judgment about the rationality of an act in retrospect. The basis for this change is, however, not a state of knowledge construed after the fact, a knowledge that was unattainable at the earlier times.

In short, both future action and past acts are judged as to their rationality not from the standpoint of omniscience (not even, to paraphrase Pareto, from the respectively highest level of science), but rather in regard to the knowledge that an actor *could* have had in a concrete, historical life-world.

E. Social Action

1. Action in Society

a. The Socialized Actor

Humans are the ones who can do or not do something. And humans are humans—and first become humans at all—only among their own kind. In other words: the person who acts is in society. But does it also follow without qualification and necessarily from the actor's sociability that the acts which a person undertakes are social? Let us consider somewhat more closely premises from which one should be inclined to draw such a conclusion.

There is no question about it: humans act. But it is questionable whether only humans act. For according to serious data from many persons at different times and in different places, plants, animals, spirits, devils, angels, and gods also have acted. In our modern Olympus, "systems" act, and even of the unconscious we have heard that "it" acts. But this need not concern us too much, since such acts are recorded in a different attitude from the natural one. In myth and epic, in fable and science, other rules apply than in the reality in which one acts because one must, in the primary and completely ordinary reality of everyday life. In this core province of the life-world, a person acts based on the assumptions of the natural attitude and notes the action of other people based on the same assumptions. The concept stems from the province in which the most important of the assumptions relative to the sociality of the life-world is valid first, foremost, and last: namely, the assumption of the reciprocity of perspectives (the interchangeability of standpoints and the congruence of the relevance systems). Unless one wants to level off the meaning of the concept of act completely, it is not even applicable to all human experiences and still less so to all occurrences of whatever kind in the world. If it is transferred to nonhumans, then it is always in an attitude that is relieved of the immediate everyday requirements. This is not meant to deny that non-everyday theories of the most various kinds have had a share in shaping the historical transformations of sound common sense. But prior to every theory, in the natural attitude of everyday life, only humans act.

Second, it need hardly be explained at length that the actor is "always already" within society. For everyone's unquestioned ground of life is that others existed before him, exist together with him, and will exist after he is gone. The normal adult can remember no state of prior solitude. He thinks of others, speaks with them and about them, acts for or against others, even when they are not present at all, indeed even when they have long been dead or still are not born. But everyone is also alone in society insofar as he alone remembers something, plans something for the future, speaks with himself. Socialized man is a pregivenness of the experience of the world and of oneself—not just a theoretical construction. Everyone can remember moments or even longer time-spans of solitude. But a mighty, indeed violent exertion of the fantasy is needed to envision a person who was alone from the first, but otherwise of the same nature as we. Robinson Crusoe entertains us because he is like everyone, except that he got into unusual circumstances. Kaspar Hauser repels us because he is nobody, a nobody who got into ordinary circumstances. We play with Robinson; Kaspar strikes us as unimaginably alien. [Kaspar Hauser (1812–33), a foundling in Nürnberg, Germany, who had spent his childhood locked in a dark room, became a famous psychological specimen of sensory deprivation.—*trans.*]

Well then, humans act, and the actor is socialized. From this it still does not follow that acts are socialized. So bracketing the actor's sociality, we were finally able to describe the basic structures of action as an event in the inner duration. But it need hardly be stressed that there are various events in the inner duration of a person, however socialized, that it would hardly be meaningful to claim are socialized. Thus people certainly do classify a stomachache into a pattern of body parts, pain thresholds, and suspected causes that have been already socially constructed and learned at some time or other; they learn self-control and pain description from and in the presence of other people; they adopt problem-oriented solutions for diminishing pain and treating sickness (herbs, medicines, operations, exorcism rituals, etc.) from the social stock of knowledge. But the lived experience of pains naturally comes "before" every social "reshaping" of the lived experience and interpretation of encounters, and also can be envisioned without it. We see how a child that still has not learned a single word has pains; we see that animals suffer.

But it is different with acts. Let us stay with our example and consider the acts that are motivated by pain. The diagnosis ("What on earth did I eat? . . . Aha, unripe plums"), self-control ("Get a hold of yourself"), the visit to the doctor, and the story later told to friends about the pains endured are all acts. From the "solitary" interpretative achievements to the acts of social operation, they were projected into the future, and their course was oriented by the project. The sociality of the actor simply cannot be mentally removed from all this. Of course, various extra-societal achievements of consciousness must be presupposed "before" action. Action itself, however, is based on the sociality of the actor. The project, the choice between projects, and the performance of the act—and not only later narratives about the act—presuppose various, mainly linguistic or languagelike social objectivations of subjective processes, objectivations in which the subjective processes take on form and stability. This has already been discussed in the example of the social conditions of choice.[41]

It is therefore not surprising that not only individual acts, but in a certain sense also action in general, must be learned and require social communication. Mothers (and sometimes also fathers) begin early with general instruction about action. This goes hand in hand with the progressive socialization of subjective relevances: interpretations are put into language, motives become graspable, and to a certain degree become available to the actor, with the help of a socially objectivated catalogue of motives (C. Wright Mills introduced the expression "vocabulary of motives" for this); the practicability of plans is estimated with the help of knowledge that is mostly derived from the social stock of knowledge. In summary, the actor is "always already" in society and the act is socialized from the beginning.

b. Socially Oriented Action

Actions are always socialized, but not always social. As we have just seen, essential components of all acts have a social origin. In all acts, the original context of motives is social, and only a socialized person has so memorable a past and so clearly envisionable a future that he can make plans, choose between competing projects, and act in view of a projected goal. But this still says nothing about the meaning an act has for the actor. There are many acts that the actor directs immediately or mediately to other people; but there are also many acts that have nothing to do with others. Someone who buries beets in order to store them for his own use, safe from the frost through the winter, is thinking of himself, not of other people. He could, of course, be easily convinced that he learned to bury beets from other persons; perhaps he would even agree with the statement that in everything he does or does not do he is, in a certain sense, "always in society." He could, however, rightly state that, as he now is, he is indeed socialized, but by himself would act no differently with the beets even if he were meanwhile the last person on earth. And he would point out that not only he but also his fellowmen see a considerable difference in whether he plants the beets for himself or for others, not to mention the possibility that pits are dug not just for beets, but sometimes also so that others may fall into them.

We thus remain in the vicinity of sound common sense when—with Max Weber—we speak of social action only when the *meaning* of the act is social. It was not hard to show that the meaning of all acts is social as soon as we take into consideration its context of genesis and the conditions for its possibility. "Others" enter into the meaning-horizon of all action. But for us to speak of social action, it is not enough that others are somehow and somewhere included in the meaning of the action. Social action is characterized by the fact that others appear in its thematic core or at least in the thematic field of the *project*. What "others" may mean here and especially how "others" enter into the project still needs a brief elucidation.

It was said above that the "others" in everyday action are other humans. The boundaries of the social world are also drawn very differently in different societies, and we must not conclude from what seems to us today to be a "sound" expression of common sense to human understanding as such, at least not on this point.[42] In non-everyday provinces of the life-world, quite different creatures than humans can—today as always—be the "others." Here, however, we are interested only in what is decisive for the structure of social action—and that is the way in which other humans appear in the projects of everyday acts. In the analysis of the stratifications of the social world, it was described precisely how other persons are experienced.[43] What applies to the mode of givenness and the meaning of other persons in the thou-orientation and the they-orientation holds good in principle as well for the mode of givenness and the meaning of other persons in the project of an act. We can thus here recall briefly the results of those analyses.

I can immediately encounter other persons within my reach, in flesh and blood, in the greatest possible abundance of appearance—and I know, naturally, that this is normally also the case for them. That I encounter them immediately does not mean, however, that I can "at the same time" also think of them. In contrast, I can *only* envision absent persons in presentiating memory or in mental constructions that are more or less full or devoid of content. Obviously, I can act immediately only on persons whom I immediately encounter, and who are in my reach. But of course I can form the project for such action even in the absence of the other person concerned, insofar as I can assume that he is in my restorable reach. The other person then enters my project based on my earlier encounters and my knowledge, depending on my interests, as a uniquely named or as a typical role-fitting person. To be sure, in this case the fundamental though graduated uncertainty of the outcome of all action at the time of the project is joined by the—also graduated—uncertainty concerning the existence of the addressee of my action. This uncertainty is removed, naturally, when the other person toward whom my act is directed appears already at the time of the project, not exclusively as envisioned, but already in person.

The mode of givenness of the other or others in my project, but especially in the course of the action, is, as will be shown, of great significance for the forms of social action. The meaning that others have for me in the project is, however, derivable not merely from its mode of givenness. It is influenced essentially by my interest in them in a given situation and, more generally, by my attitude toward them, which transcends the situations and is determined by over-arching relevance-structures. Thus, my interest may aim at the other as an individual person in his uniqueness; yet I obviously also apprehend him with the help of various typifications, from the beloved wife to the still-unborn oldest grandson who is remembered in my will. My interest may, however, also be directed to the other person only as a type, e.g., as the bearer of a particular, socially circumscribed role; of course, I always take into account that a concrete, living human being is "behind" or "in" the role. But my interest may also relate to completely anonymous types, under the almost-empty assumption that human beings are indeed "behind" them (e.g., behind the tax collector's office). And finally the others in my project may be no apprehensible, concretely envisioned humans, but just operative contexts that presuppose other people but only mediately and generally, e.g., an author.

The mode of givenness of others, my momentary interest in them, and my attitude toward them thus jointly determine the sense in which I have them in my projects. My interest and my attitude are, moreover, not completely independent of the mode of givenness. A mere "operative context" (an institution, a social formation, class, nation, and the like) is not entirely the same if it occurs as a piece of paper or as a flesh-and-blood person. An individual in all his uniqueness is not entirely the same if he has not been seen for twenty years or if one meets him daily. To express it once again with Max Weber: my attitude toward others is influenced, not exclusively but to a considerable extent, by the subjectively intended chance of the regular repetition of certain modes of givenness. As far as I am concerned, the bus-drivers of a line I use daily can change every day as long as they do their job. The same does not hold true of a wife, a child, or a friend—regardless of the fact that one can befriend a bus-driver with whom one has been riding for years, and that one's own child who never writes and whom one has not seen for ten years can become a stranger.

2. Forms of Social Action

a. Immediacy and Mediation; Unilateralness and Reciprocity

Social action, that is, action whose meaning relates to others by its very project, can in its performance be either immediate or mediate.

It is immediate, in principle, when the person toward whom the project is directed is in the actor's reach during the course of the act. As we have just seen, it is not absolutely necessary for the other person to be in the actor's reach already at the time of projecting; it suffices for him to be within achievable (or restorable) reach. On the other hand, action is in principle mediated when the other person is beyond the actor's reach during the course of the act. This is immediately clear in cases of reciprocal operational action; the mediation can occur only via the common world that is now in my reach, later in his. But even in cases of unilateral social action, we also speak of mediacy if the other person is not himself present during the course of the act: it is still social action when I undertake to reflect about a quarrel I had yesterday, until the opponent's motives become understandable to me—but it is neither reciprocal nor immediate. Mediate social action is directed not at fellowmen but at contemporaries (apparent contemporaries: the person I am thinking of could already be dead), at successors, and precisely speaking also at predecessors. If the action is not at all directed at a concrete other person, but tries to engage in an anonymous operational context, the action can in any case only be mediated—although the human "substratum" of the anonymous operational context under some circumstances encounters me through an immediately experienced representative. In an earlier passage, a precise description of the various strata of reach as well as their temporal dimensions was given, and we also touched upon the question of technically mediated possibilities for expanding the original reach, conditioned by the build of the human body.[44] We can therefore here simply refer to those analyses and use their results to describe the various forms of social action without any further comments.

For the construction of an act as a whole, but mainly of course for the actual course of action, it is decisively significant whether it is immediate or not. Just as important—perhaps more important for the significance that an act has for the actor—is the "sidedness" of the act, i.e., whether an act is unilateral or reciprocal. Social action can be either the one or the other, although in concrete cases the boundaries may not be clearly recognizable. At any rate, an action that the other person toward whom the project was directed does not "answer" is unilateral; only when it is answerable can one speak of reciprocity. And this still says nothing about the kind of "answer," except that it must be an action or inaction motivated by the "question." So it holds true: not to answer is also an answer. It must merely have been intended as such, as a non-answer. As to the kind of "answer," of course, and also as to the kind of "question," nothing else is known for certain except that it concerns an action or inaction directed to the other person, perhaps only as a suggestion of a first step of the act.

Therefore, there is not any fixed temporal boundary within which "answers" must be given—except perhaps the actor's lifetime (but even this restriction applies only to everyday action). How long an "answer" can still be considered an "answer" to the original "question" depends on the time-span with respect to which the act has been planned. But even if the "answer" is to be regarded as delayed within the time-spans applicable to the kind of act, it is still an "answer," but precisely a delayed one; the action is, in any case, reciprocal. In the natural attitude we know that in daily life there are actions that are designed for "answers" and normally also receive an "answer." We also know that the "answers" have to follow within a time-span typical for the kind of action, and generally also do follow. The answer to the question, "What time is it?" cannot first be given an hour later; one cannot wait ten years to avenge oneself for a slap. "Typically," however, does not mean "always." Exceptions are imaginable; exceptions do occur. Of importance in this context are socially objectivated typifications of acts that have been taken over into the subjective stock of knowledge. These include the typical temporal restrictions concerning the "answers."

Immediacy and reciprocity (or respectively, mediacy and unilateralness) comprise the independent, though not completely unrelated dimensions of social action. From their various possible combinations, four forms of social action result: (1) immediate and unilateral; (2) immediate and reciprocal; (3) mediate and unilateral; (4) mediate and reciprocal. These combinations are not just logically imaginable; they also actually occur. But as will be shown below, the four possibilities are of very unequal weight, or of unequal importance, as forms of social action. With certain reservations, immediate reciprocal action—and indeed operation—can be considered the basic form of all social action, whereas the other forms can be regarded as derivations of this basic form. "Unequally important" thus refers to the significance ascribable to the various forms of action in the construction of the social world. "Unequally important" could, moreover, also refer to the frequency of occurrence of the various forms of action in various societies, their role in the socialization of people, their function within a historical social structure, etc. But this concerns empirical theoretical questions that need not be considered here. Still, not much imagination is needed to envision on all these points the difference between a horde of hunter-gatherers of the Old

Stone Age, the inhabitants of a Greek polis in the Golden Age, and the people of an urban, industrialized, bureaucratically organized modern society equipped with electronic mass media.

In the following pages all four forms of social action will be described, either precisely and at some length or only briefly, depending on their fundamental significance.

b. Unilateral Immediate Action

i. *Operation* Immediate social action is characterized by the fact that the other person, at whom the project is directed, is within the actor's reach. Unilateral action is characterized by the fact that the other person himself acts as an "answer" to the original question. Unilateral immediate action must thus be characterized by both of these traits at once. This is, at least at first sight, by no means so self-evident a combination. If the other person is within the actor's reach, inversely the actor is generally also in reach of the addressee of his act. Consequently, apart from certain exceptions, only pure acts of thought can remain unilateral. Acts that somehow engage in the common surrounding world of the actor and the one to whom the act refers— i.e., socially operative acts, and social work even more so—become motives of "answering" acts or at least occasions for acts directed back at the original actor. If a wide-awake, normal person notices that someone does something in reference to himself, he is challenged to give an "answer." However inactive he then actually remains, by doing or not doing something in such a situation, he is acting. The normal case of immediate social operation is, consequently, reciprocal. Unilateralness is limited to special cases or characterizes only the initial phases of an act, which then eventually becomes reciprocal.

First we will consider the, so to speak, "counterfeit" cases of unilateral-immediate action. The actor has designed them for reciprocity, but for various reasons they remain temporarily—and sometimes also permanently—unilateral. It is quite possible even in a common surrounding world for B not to notice at all that A has acted upon him. This may be due to inattention. (All societies know linguistic and extra-lingual conventions for calling attention that vary in character and richness of content: means for synchronizing two streams of consciousness.) The reason may also consist of obstacles that run counter to B's perceiving A's act, but to which A did not give sufficient consideration in his project. In both cases, A will generally repeat his act with corresponding improvements, and B "answers." The temporarily unilateral act becomes reciprocal—as originally planned. As has been said: if B has indeed noticed A's act, but from indifference, arrogance, or other motives "does nothing"—e.g., pretends not to have noticed the act—he has of course nonetheless "answered." For an action to be reciprocal it is by no means absolutely required that B himself "answer" A's operational act by an *operational* act.

Let us consider the "genuine" cases of unilateral-immediate action. A acts on B with the intention that his action remain unilateral. Here two possibilities come in question. First, it is quite conceivable even in a common surrounding world for A to direct his operation at B and then to carry it out in such a way that B notices nothing or else does not notice that the act came from A. Many examples could be cited from war, love, and play; let us settle for the especially graphic one of pocket picking. The example requires no further clarification. It brings us, moreover, in the neighborhood of the above-mentioned exceptions to the rule that when B is in A's reach, A is also in B's reach.

As in the above-mentioned example, A directs his action at B from the beginning with the intention that B should not "answer." In a contrasting example, however, A is *not at all* within B's reach. That is the case when B is unconscious or asleep. In addition, modern technology has various ways to make reach unilateral. The psychological laboratory is a relatively innocuous example. Under such exceptional conditions, the chances are naturally the greatest that an operation which aims at being unilateral will actually remain unilateral. The anesthetized person is killed; the patient, operated on; the sleeping person, kissed; the experimental subject, manipulated. Of course, even here the part of the original project that is based on unilateralness can fail. The anesthetized person wakes up in time and defends himself; the patient screams; the one kissed opens his or her eyes; the experimental subject storms angrily out of the laboratory. The projects can be adjusted to the new situation: the murder, the operation, the kiss, the experiment, still manage to succeed—and that is what the actor is, after all, interested in. The form of social action has, however, been changed from unilateral to reciprocal.

Moreover, everyone is familiar with acts that actually are reciprocal, but are based on a (unilateral or reciprocal) feigning of unilateralness. Although the dreamer has already awakened, he pretends still to be sleeping so that the kiss will continue. The one kissing may however also have noticed that the dreamer meanwhile has awakened, but pretends not to have noticed the deception. Another example is a monologue that is designed to be overheard. Some of these examples are familiar to us from everyday life, others from artistic genres such as comedy. All are based on the contrast between unilateralness and reciprocity.

ii. *Thought* Thought is thought, and can be nothing but unilateral. It has the basic structure of solitary action and retains this in its essential traits, even when it is done in the presence of others. This applies in principle even when thinking is occupied with others. Since the manner in which other people are apprehended[45] was treated in very great detail in an earlier place where it was shown what structure acts of thought have,[46] we can remain very brief here.

A person can experience other persons immediately, of course, only in their presence. In their absence he can remember them, fantasy about them, include them in his plans of action. The mode of givenness is an envisioning. Beyond this, even memories, if they are not fragmentary and as if spontaneous, are similar to acts. Many memories have entirely the structure of acts of thinking, and the same thing holds good for daydreams. Projects, no matter whether or how they are realized, are in any case acts of thought. In acts of thought others are grasped by means of various typifications that, however, as we have seen, can aim either at the other person's typicality or at his uniqueness.

A person can encounter others immediately in their presence, but he need not do so. When he meets someone, he cannot avoid experiencing him directly, but he need not unconditionally advert to this lived experience, and even less does he need to think of the other person expressly, step by step. The synchronization of two streams of consciousness need not unconditionally occur; the two people do not enter into a we-relationship with one another. If A has nothing to do with B and wants to have nothing to do with him, he can even in his presence close his eyes internally—under some circumstances even externally—and think of nothing at all, or of his lunch, or also of C. And vice versa. Thus, no strictly unilateral immediate social action even takes place.

On the one hand, A, who encounters B immediately, (also) thinks of B. However, he does not act on him; he seems not to pay any attention to him. He (still) does not enter into any we-relation with him—or else for a time he steps out of one that had already come about. Still, internally he occupies himself with B. If he restricts himself to a pure act of thought, we are dealing with a unilateral immediate action in the form of thought. B can also think of A: then we have to do with two unilateral immediate actions in unnoticed parallel.

This construction involves a difficulty that cannot be overlooked. Pure acts of thought lose their purity in the presence of others. In their presence, not being occupied with others is more or less explicit. Preoccupation with others that remains just internal (not to mention non-preoccupation) looks like a turning-away-from, and therefore comes at least very close to a minimal form of social action. It is thus not surprising that various societies have developed quite complicated forms of etiquette precisely for this province, which stands, so to speak, between social relations and nonrelations. In them, distance, stance, facial expression, and the like are more or less bindingly regulated (by classification into valuations such as "courteous," "importunate," etc.).

Even if A and B are in a common surrounding world, they naturally do not at all have to act upon one another. A can think of everything possible and do or not do things that have nothing to do with B. But he is always more or less clearly conscious that B can observe him and that, although B will undertake nothing that has to do with A, he occupies himself mentally precisely with him, A. It is not necessary to add more complicated stages or interlockings of "being able to think that the other person could think," to see that in a common surrounding world a certain self-consciousness on the part of the actors is necessarily present—however little they may perhaps be interested in one another, and however much the self-consciousness may be bridged by social conventions and blunted by routine. In the concrete encounter of two persons it is always possible for "pure" thought to acquire unintended expression: thought becomes operation, and unilateralness flows over into reciprocity.

c. Reciprocal Immediate Action

Without further elucidation it was stated above that reciprocal immediate action must be regarded as the basic form of social action. This statement could be supported, from various vantage points, by a whole series of findings. Thus it could be pointed out that this form of action acquires decisive significance in the social formation of a personal identity, and that in all the more complex mediated forms of social action a socialized actor must be presupposed. The preliminary stage—or, depending on the mode of observation, the earliest form—of reciprocally immediate action is found in the exchange of ever more finely attuned looks between a mother and her baby, in whom there can not yet be a question of a socialized personal identity. In later prelingual and then also in language events of intersubjective mirroring in concrete we-relations, not only is personal identity developed further, supported, and modified, but at the same time the capacity for more complex action is expanded. It could also be stressed that prelingual, reciprocally communicative action in the immediacy of we-relations is an indispensable precondition for the acquisition of a language and of the relative-natural worldview transmitted by language. That such action must have played an essential role in the developmental history of language as such as well as in the separate history of particular languages is self-evident. How else should language have originated, how else could different, constantly changing languages have developed? And if not shy of using grandiose words, one could say that life and death are the consequence of just any reciprocally immediate act and that death can follow from reciprocally immediate acts. Less impressive, but perhaps just as important, is the circumstance that the social everyday consists for the most part of routinized, reciprocally immediate acts.

Functional considerations, however, belong just as little in the given framework of our study as to ontogenetic and evolutionary ones. Even without such views, the perspective from which we are here considering the everyday life-world also can show clearly that social action without any form of mediation is possible. One could also without difficulty envisage a society based exclusively on immediate acts. In contrast, mediated forms of acts cannot be envisioned without immediate action. And however much a society may depend on mediated forms of acts, they are simply unthinkable without a foundation of immediate action. This simple consideration is joined by a second one. Our everyday dealings with nature show that a unilateral action is very well possible without reference to foregoing or subsequent reciprocity. But where social action is concerned, things are different. Here, unilateralness presupposes at least a preceding reciprocity. Not only are the others at whom a mediated social act is directed transferred in the actor's envisioning into a kind of apparent immediacy, they are also always apprehended as actors (sooner or later), although at the moment as recipients of unilateral acts they are not so.

All in all, we thus have good reason to assume that all forms of social action are based on reciprocally immediate action, even when they have in their forms of appearance departed far from it. In social action, not only is mediacy derived from immediacy but also unilateralness from reciprocity.

Unilateral immediate action is, as we have already seen, possible both as thinking and as operation, though both only under particular, restrictive conditions: as thinking, when it takes place in complete concealment; and as operation, when the Other for determinate reasons cannot at all notice that someone is acting upon him. In contrast, reciprocally immediate action is possible under the most varied, entirely everyday conditions. It can, however, in contrast with unilaterally immediate action, in principle only be an operation. Let us remember that we have envisioned as a limiting case of unilaterally immediate action the possibility for two people, both corporeally present, to think of one another respectively. As long as the other person notices nothing, the action remains unilateral, though parallel. It is evident, however, that in a situation in which two people stand face to face, the preconditions for "pure" thought—which would have to be assumed in the envisioned case—rarely exist. Let us determine once more why that is so.

If A is in B's reach and B (normally) accordingly in A's reach, B can construe whatever A does or does not do in his presence (more exactly: in the assumed consciousness of his presence) as related to him, as concerning him directly or indirectly, and under some circumstances even as projected at him. And vice versa: whatever B does or does not do can be understood by A as having to do with him. According to the principle of the reciprocity of perspectives anchored in background knowledge, A is beyond this also always aware that B could apprehend his action or inaction in this way. And of course the converse holds good for B. This has an extremely important consequence. Even if A should initially not have thought of B (and B not of A), he will in view of B (or respectively of A) be unable, at least peripherally, in addition to what he is actually doing, to avoid thinking that the other person could think that he is perhaps thinking of him. More simply expressed: face to face, people are in reciprocal self-consciousness. Since they stand corporeally facing one another, this self-consciousness *must be expressed* in one way or another. We see also that unilaterally immediate thinking, parallel or only potentially parallel, merges into reciprocally immediate operation, insofar as no special conditions prevail.

Since reciprocally immediate thinking would be a contradiction in itself, reciprocally immediate action can only be an operation. It must be an operation, but it need not occur unconditionally in the form of reciprocally immediate work. Although work is the normal and certainly the most important case of social operation (more will be said about this below), other forms are conceivable at least without contradiction. That concretely they mostly merge into work is another matter.

All operation engages in the surrounding world. When B is present, A's operation naturally engages not simply in his own surrounding world, but at the same time in B's. A may or may not notice his engagement in the surrounding world; that entirely depends on what he happens to be doing at the time. A's operation is in any case a lived experience for B; generally, he will advert to it, and it will become an encounter for him. But we must go back one step, since "operation" and "engagement in the surrounding world" here appear simultaneously in the perspective of the actor and the observer. Certainly, the actor is at the same time himself an observer, and the observer an actor. Nevertheless, the concepts have a different nuance of meaning, depending on whether they relate to the perspective of the present actor or of the present observer.

In the common surrounding world, A's animate organism is a rich field of expression in all its possibilities of change and persistence. By means of this field of expression, B experiences and encounters A's "inner life," his moods, intentions, etc.—even if A does "nothing in particular." At the same time, B apprehends A's animate organism, his feet, hands, knees, elbows, head, face, sexual organs as that with which A does something whereby he realizes his projects. A, on the contrary, indeed also encounters his body as that with which he does something and to which something happens, but his own animate organism is for him not a field of expression by means of which he detects his own moods and intentions. On the other hand, A must, as we have explained, always count on it that in B's presence much that perhaps merely "happens" to him corporeally is ascribed as controlled by him. And he must always count on it that his animate organism serves as the field of expression for the other person. The boundary between the Other's animate organism as a field of expression for me and the Other's animate organism that realizes his projects (including those that relate to me) is, thus, flexible. But for that reason, the boundaries between reciprocally immediate operation, which is not (or not yet) work, and reciprocally immediate work, are blurred. In everyday life, the boundary is constantly crossed. It is often of little consequence, anyway, whether the "right" classification can be made—and so in the natural attitude of everyday life one will not strive at all to undertake it. Sometimes such a classification is, however, of great practical significance. Is what the Other is doing (or seems to be doing) a challenge or not? An insult or not?

A person must find answers to questions of this kind in order to master the not-fully-routine, problematic situations that constantly recur in everyday life—and he must do so even before he can turn to the further question as to what concrete meaning the operation or the work of a particular fellowman has in a given situation. Only the actor himself can have ultimate certainty about whether he acts at all or something merely happens to him, whether he operates or merely conducts himself, whether he works and in what meaning-context his work is imbedded, what range the project of the act originally had and what has changed during the performance of the act. But in most of these respects, acts are intersubjectively pre-interpreted, and the interpretations are socially solidified to a sufficient degree for most practical purposes of everyday life. The social stock of knowledge contains typifications of various social situations, various motives of acts, goals and courses of acts by different kinds of actors, and it contains typifications of various corporeal modes of behavior that as a rule are classified as acts. Thus everyone has at his disposal a stock of elements of knowledge not only acquired in his own experiences, but mainly adopted from the social stock of knowledge—elements of knowledge with whose help he can more or less reliably estimate the relation between the observed conduct and the intention of his fellowmen. Although only the actor can have ultimate certainty, his fellowmen still have a good and mostly sufficient chance to apprehend what another person is really doing and why he is doing it.

Typologies that assign external conduct and intention to one another approximately according to the pattern "mere conduct, operation, work," are indispensable for orientation in social everyday life. This of course does not mean that the classifications are always the same and the interpretations of acts identical. In different societies, they are modified by the theoretical (mythical, religious, philosophical, scientific) categories for ascribing responsibility, mostly based in special knowledge, refined in etiquette, and bound by law. This has already been discussed above. In any case, in a relative-natural worldview the ways in which these typologies mesh will be either rough or exact, depending on the prevalent social conditions, on whether they are supposed to apply to normal everyday cases or to difficult limiting cases, and on what forms of social intercourse they are intended for within and between various social groups and strata.

When B sees A cut down a tree, he will on the basis of his stock of knowledge without hesitation recognize that event as work, namely as a change of his surrounding world planned by A. If A is cutting down the tree now because of an assignment given to him earlier, B will apprehend the event, moreover, as work that immediately concerns him, since he will have to pay for it. Moreover, assuming that A and B together use the saw with which the tree is felled, B can hardly doubt that they are both working, in fact together. Something similar holds true not just for "obviously" directed changes in the natural surrounding world, but also for changes in the social world. When A answers a question asked by B, B will very well be able to judge what A is doing.

The matter is less clear for B when A changes his facial expression, moves his arms, sneezes, falls down. B will not be able to decide with certainty whether it is mere conduct, operation, or work. Depending on his state of knowledge and the prevailing circumstances, he will be able to say sometimes with subjective confidence, but mostly with only greater or lesser probability, whether the changes of facial expression, the arm movements, the sneezing, the falling down simply happened to his fellowman without his being able to do anything about it, whether it is a matter of accompanying corporeal phenomena of an act of A's that had not been projected by him as such but are associated with the performance of the act, or whether A himself controls the entire process. As was stated, depending on the state of knowledge and the prevailing circumstances, B will either believe with some confidence or only cautiously suspect that a passerby's sneezing on the winter street is the result of a cold and not a spy's sign of recognition, that his conversational partner's gesticulation was not planned by him but necessarily accompanies and underscores his speech, and that a clown's falling on his nose in the circus should not be ascribed to his awkwardness but represents laboriously practiced work.

In these examples, the interpretation of one person's conduct by another was the topic of discussion. But in reciprocal action, the observer is himself an actor. Here, the mere conduct of one party is still significant only as the occasion for the operation or the work, but of itself has nothing to do with reciprocity. In contrast, both operation and work must be considered in "corresponding" reciprocity: A and B operate reciprocally; A and B work reciprocally. Of course, mixed and transitional forms are conceivable: one "merely" operates, while the other works. But since they come close to or merge with the case of reciprocally immediate work—which interests us most—we will not attempt to study the various mixed and transitional forms in detail. Before we deal with this case, however, we will, in contrast with it, describe the case of reciprocally immediate "mere operating" and illustrate it by an example.

If reciprocally immediate operation is not also supposed to be work, then the operation, the respective engagement in the outside world, cannot from the very project itself be directed at one's fellow-man who is within reach. This holds true naturally both for the original action and for the fellowman's subsequent one. "Directed at" does not mean "related to": we have seen that it is absolutely inevitable that every action in the presence of a fellowman "somehow" and "also" relates to him. Thus when A's action in B's presence engages in the common surrounding world, the engagement must either not have been an essential component of the project at all or—in case that really was the case—at any rate not have been directed at B from the very project. As soon as this first condition is violated, we are no longer dealing with "pure" operation in reciprocal immediacy. So much for A. And now, for B's operation. B, who notices A's engagement in the surrounding world, cannot avoid assuming that it could somehow concern him, B; but he must not apprehend it as immediately directed by A at him, B. Otherwise the second condition of "pure" operation in reciprocity would have been violated. And finally, B's operation, which then follows and is influenced by knowledge of A's operation, must in turn not be directed immediately at A. Of course, it remains "somehow" related to him.

Let us take as an example A's facial expression on picking up a heavy burden and B's viewing of this expression while passing by. From A's standpoint, his facial expression is nothing but an accompanying phenomenon of the act he projected and has just performed: he wanted to lift the crate onto the table; nothing is further from his mind than his facial expression. And B's presence has for A nothing to do with his act. If now B understands A's facial expression in this way, i.e., interprets it "correctly," his passing by cannot be apprehended as a refusal to help—at least not in a society where in such a situation assistance is offered from the outset and needs no invitation, however covert, on A's part. A's facial expression is a necessary but not projected component of his action (which indeed is work, but not social work). B's passing by is likewise an act that is not projected with A in mind. Nevertheless, A and B relate to one another even in their operation. A's non-asking and B's non-answering are components of reciprocally immediate operation.

The same or almost the same external events could, however, also be understood as question and answer, as controlled, immediate work directed at the Other person. From this we see how laborious and painstaking is the casuistry of a "pure" reciprocally immediate operation that does not phase over into work. The difference is hard to determine between an operation that "somehow" and "also" relates to a fellowman, because he happens to be in reach, and an action that from the beginning—even in the form of an engagement in the common surrounding world—is directed immediately at one's fellowman. The non-asking on A's part presupposes that it could be an asking. Have we not all at some time twisted our face while engaged in a strenuous activity in the hope that someone would spring to our assistance? And the non-answer presupposes that the Other person actually did not ask, so that the non-answer could not be considered an answer. Have we not all at some time hesitated to spring to someone's assistance, because we did not know whether help was wanted or would be burdensome? In any case, in the immediacy of a we-relation every operation of whatever kind is always on the verge of turning into reciprocally immediate work.

It has become clear what must be understood by reciprocally immediate work: an operation that is not just somehow related reciprocally to one another, but—by its very project directed at one another—is performed in the common surrounding world with synchronization of the actors' inner time. Since we had to establish how difficult it is, regarding an operation in a common surrounding world, to distinguish between mere relatedness and direct alignment (*Ausrichtung*) we will now grasp the difference more precisely from another angle. Reciprocally immediate work is characterized by the fact that the operation of the one is from the beginning directed at an *operation* by the other person.

Strictly speaking, this means that A undertakes to bring about or to prevent a particular future operation of B's, depending on whether he wants or fears this operation. At any rate, he has imagined this possible operation of B's, pondered it seriously and projected steps that should lead to the goal (bringing about or prevention). In the performance of these steps, B, on the basis of his stock of knowledge, detects A's intentions, considers them in the framework of his own contexts of interest, and projects an operation that in its turn is directed at a future operation of A's. Of course, it holds good here, too, that the idea of the other's future action can be clear and distinct or very vague, consideration of the meaning of such action can be precise or slack because of one's own interests, the projecting of the steps can be accurate or superficial. And of course, it also holds good that the reciprocally immediate acts can be characterized by very different levels of routinization both of the project and of the performance. The degree of routinization can, moreover, be approximately the same for A and B: this holds true for many forms of social intercourse between normal (i.e., at least more or less "competent" and adequately "socialized") adults. But it can also be asymmetrical, high for one party, low for the other: this is usually attributable to differences in the actors' stocks of knowledge, or more precisely speaking, differences in the stock of knowledge required for a particular action in a given situation. The reasons for such differences are naturally themselves various. Among the most frequent are age differences (acts in which "experienced" and "inexperienced" persons are involved), specialization of knowledge (acts between layman and specialists), and many other social disparities (e.g., class-conditioned differences of opportunity to gain access to certain forms of knowledge or to apply certain forms of knowledge in action).

Let us bracket out the differences in "content" of the stock of knowledge, interest-situations, and motives—all of which mark concrete action—in order first to grasp reciprocally immediate action. The topic is still the basic form of this action, reciprocally immediate work, which is characterized by intended changes in the natural and social surrounding world, insofar as these changes are directed at a fellowman. The in-order-to motive for one person's operation is to create conditions for the because-motive of a particular operation by the other person; the resulting in-order-to motive of the addressee of this operation is in turn directed at a particular operation of the first actor. And so forth. With a certain simplification, we can thus say that this form of action is determined by an immediate chain of alternating sequential motives of the actors, unbroken until the act has been completed. A's in-order-to motive becomes B's because-motive, B's in-order-to motive becomes A's because-motive, and so forth.

On closer inspection, we see, however, that a somewhat more complex state of affairs is concealed behind these formulations. Namely, A enters into the framework of an overarching plan or, in reference to B, enters accidentally into B's reach. Based on the situation of his interests, within the framework of his overarching plans, and after estimation of the existing situation, he envisions a particular operation of B's. (He fantasies this operation of the Other person's *modo futuri exacti.*) He compares B's envisioned operation with other possibilities of operating or not-operating on B's part that would come into question in this situation and decides on one of the possibilities. Then he ponders the steps that he, A, would have to undertake in order to provoke that operation on B's part. Thereby, according to the principle of *reciprocity of motives,* he puts himself in B's position. This principle is a particular variation of the principle of the reciprocity of perspectives relative to action. For that general principle reads as follows: the other person experiences and understands the world approximately—other things being equal—as I would experience and understand it, if I were in his situation. The other person thus understands even what I do more or less as I would understand it if I were in his place. And the particular variation concerning the motives of action runs: the other person is moved by more or less the same motives for certain acts as would also motivate a corresponding action in me. Of course, this principle is also not applied blindly, but under consideration of everything one knows about the particularities of the situation and the other person's peculiarities.

Now back to the point: A thus puts himself in B's position—naturally only insofar as this is necessary for an estimation of B's reaction to steps that A is now considering. A ponders his own steps on the basis of an anticipation of the probable interpretation and estimation of these steps on B's part. For this interpretation and estimation on B's part should lead in B to the because-motive of a particular operation. Thus after A has decided for a particular future operation of B's, he must decide also for certain steps of his own, so to speak, from B's vantage point. Only then does he make the decision to act and begin with its performance.

It is clear that even in case of social action, each of the steps can be carried out carefully, step by step and with attention. But it is also clear that individual steps or whole series of steps can be so highly routinized, from the choice between projects to the pondering of the estimations that could motivate others to act, to the decision and the performance, that they no longer at all need be taken into the grasp of consciousness clearly and distinctly. Many phases of action, including social action in all its multistratified constitution, can sink back into secondary passivity. For instance, forms of appearance and subjective correlates of a common tree-sawing contest among experienced lumberjacks are at first sight hardly comparable to a duel, and even less so to the calculations of a master chess tournament. But the basic structure is the same. In everyday life, social action is in any case so highly routinized (and often institutionalized—a word about this later) that this intermeshing of anticipations of an intersubjective future, or of one's own subjective future and another's subjective future, hardly comes into view. The most important precondition for this is the social stabilization of typical motives and acts in a social stock of knowledge. Immediately reciprocal actors, whose stocks of knowledge are not based extensively on the same social stock of knowledge, can act together or against one another, but—at least initially—not routinely.

When A gives B a slap, he will of course assume (if B is a person and not a tree or a stone) that B will not just feel the slap as a slap but will also understand it as a slap. How precisely he can anticipate *how* B will understand it depends on whether they both belong to a dueling aristocracy or stand opposite one another as utter strangers and more or less drunk in a harbor tavern. When A asks an old friend what time it is, of course he need make no lengthy calculation as to whether he understands his language and will understand him correctly, or will first ponder his own interests, whether an answer could perhaps not harm him, etc. But, of course, all these things that are taken for granted hold true only until further notice.

These two examples also show, moreover, that in a formal description of this form of action, we may generally disregard the differences in "content" of interests and motives. The intermeshing of motives does not, of course, necessarily mean agreement of interests and goals. It takes place both in collaboration and in opposition. A question is generally asked in order to be answered—and it often is answered. One does not generally slap someone in order to be slapped back—but often one is slapped back. Working in immediate reciprocity is arranged for "answers" of one kind or another.

What holds true for acts in general must of course also hold true for social acts, whether they are unilateral or reciprocal, mediate or immediate: the act performed is not identical with the project and, precisely speaking, absolutely cannot be identical with it. This statement is especially convincing in the case of reciprocal immediate action, since from the very beginning this engages in, so to speak, a doubly uncertain future, quite apart from the uncertainties that must accompany an action whose steps intermesh even in their performance. Yet the reservation that in everyday reality one need not take everything so exactly holds true for social action as well as for all action. In all acts and all the more so in all social acts, socially stabilized, already typified combinations of motives, goals, and processes guarantee the possibility of agreement between project, action, and performed act, sufficient for the practical demands of everyday life—and, for normal (for the most part "competent" and "socialized") adults, the possibility of an intersubjective agreement that is necessary here.

Compared with other forms of social action, reciprocally immediate action is arranged by a particularity that affects not the project, the choice between projects, or the interpretation of performed acts, but the course of the action itself. In this form of action, acts that were not projected at a fellowman are performed in his presence.

A person, of course, does not act alone, but rather together with or against other persons.

In another context,[47] it was already pointed out that in the immediate encounter between people, the fulfillment or the failure of the other person's projects can be observed in the *course* of the action. I can never establish with absolute certainty the goal toward which a person is aiming, not even when I see a runner in the hundred-yard dash running toward the finish line. Even less can I detect from the course of the act its place in a fellowman's overall plans, unless he gives me additional, accurate information concerning his aims (we will here not even consider the difficulties concealed in this added stipulation). But here I can apply my knowledge of typical combinations of motives, goals, acts, and *courses* of acts with the help of the principle of the reciprocity of perspectives *and* motives. I attend the step-by-step construction of his act; additional, immediate evidence is at my disposal when I see how an act becomes embodied. Certainly, what is perceived must be interpreted: an act is not simply perceivable conduct. And it is always interpreted within the prevailing stock of knowledge, and not measured by an "objective" apparatus valid for all and applicable in the same manner by all. But in the living presence of the other person I do not have to rely only on the chance that a typification reaching into the future could be accurate, nor must I be satisfied after the fact with a reconstruction based exclusively on the results of the act.

Interpretation and action fuse together. In the We-relation I check typifications relevant to my act by the immediacy of my fellowman; at the same time, in the reciprocity of action I arrange my concrete operation step by step by his operation. In reciprocally immediate action the *present* irrupts into the *futurum exactum* and precedes the *perfectum*.

d. Reciprocal Mediate Action

Reciprocal immediate action is action in *living* intersubjectivity. The participants in it can in their actions be in doubt about everything conceivable but not about the corporeal presence of the other person. In contrast, like all mediate action, of course, reciprocally mediate action is also characterized by a, so to speak, hypothetical intersubjectivity. Certainly, for all normal people the intersubjectivity of the life-world is one of the basic assumptions concerning reality that absolutely cannot be cast into doubt in everyday life. No one thinks he is alone in the world. But how things are with that Other person at whom his present action is directed is a different, more uncertain matter. In mediate action each of the actors is an individual whose project is directed at an other, absent individual. Of him the actor does not even know with certainty whether he is alive. His action must therefore be based on the mere *assumption* that the other (still) exists. Whether this assumption is justified can, however, be decided only after the fact. After the fact means, i.e., after the act—or a part of the act that calls for an "answer"—has been performed and after the other has "answered" in one way or another.

Depending on the kind of mediation that characterizes the action, the actor will very soon determine whether the assumption was wrong and he has acted in a void. And only then will he know whether the steps of his act, which are arranged for reciprocity, are "answered" and a reciprocal action actually does take place or not. Precisely speaking, the uncertainty of the assumption exists for each of the actors in each phase of the act, and the assumption must be confirmed in alternating sequence until the entire act is performed. In reciprocally mediate action, the Other is always given *modo subjunctivi* until he becomes accessible via the interpretation of the results of his operation *modo perfecti*. The *praesens* is, on the contrary, exclusively the *praesens* of the respective actor.

In mediated social action, too, the motives are interlinked precisely insofar as they occur reciprocally. But in contrast with immediate action, the steps of performances do not intermesh in the common experience of the actors, so to speak, before their eyes and in their ears. The action is done not in simultaneity of the streams of consciousness, in the flowing synchronization of the two actors' encounter, but in a succession of encounters: first of the one, then of the other, then again of the first, etc. The Other's consciousness is not graspable in its living forms of appearance but only via the "rigidified" results of his operation, his work. The one acts, the other experiences the results of this action and interprets them in one way or another and then acts in his turn, whereupon the first must interpret the results of this action (the "answer"), etc. According to what has been said, the following would perhaps need no separate mention: reciprocally mediate action is necessarily an operation and will normally take the form of work.

The assumption that the other person (still) exists as addressee of the present act is naturally not the only assumption underlying reciprocally mediate action. This action is based, rather, on a series of further assumptions, which, however—with a further exception— underlie all social action. To be sure, they are, as we shall see presently, not equally effective in this combination and in this way in immediate social action.

Every encounter with reality presupposes the idealization "And so forth"; all action, the "I can always do it again" idealization. All social action presupposes the principle of the reciprocity of perspectives; all reciprocal social action, the principle of the reciprocity of motives. In reciprocally mediated action, the above-mentioned first assumption concerning the presence of an addressee of an act is already based on the "And so forth" idealization. It may be directed at the addressee as an individual ("there is no reason to fear that my friend Peter, with whom I was speaking just yesterday evening, has suddenly died"), or as a functional type ("Since I have not heard that the postmen wanted to go on strike, I will tape to the mailbox the letter the postman put there by mistake yesterday, for him to take back"). As the examples show, the assumption can refer either to the existence of the addressee of the action as such, or only to his role—that depends on the kind and the degree of anonymity of the act. In reciprocally mediate action, all further assumptions presuppose the validity of this first assumption.

The next assumption concerns the typifications with whose help the steps of the act are concretely projected at the other. It is in principle no different in mediate action than in immediate action. The actor assumes that the Other has not changed in the respects that are known to him, the actor, and are significant for the present action (interests, attitudes, motives, typical interpretations of an action similar to the present one, etc.)—or respectively that the changes are typical in kind and can be taken into consideration in the project. Even under this assumption, the "And so forth" idealization is in force. That is obvious. It is, however, combined with an idealization of the "I can always do it again" relative to the Other: *he* can always do it again. As in all social action, here, too, the principle of the reciprocity of perspectives and motives applies; here, too, it is restricted and modified by particular knowledge about the Other person. As distinguished from immediate social action, however, the assumption here is made not just in the project and then confirmed immediately in the performance or adapted to a deviating living reality. In mediate action, it must also be maintained without confirmation even in the performance. Accordingly, the restrictions of the principle of reciprocity must not just be imposed *in absentia*, but also carried out *in absentia*.

Moreover, in reciprocally mediate action, the above-mentioned assumption must find its own continuation to this action. The actor does not merely assume that the other person has not changed up to the time of his present action; he also assumes that by the time he responds to the present action, he will not have changed (or will have changed only typically) in the respects essential for the action. Of course, this additional assumption can be almost completely trivial or it can attain great significance—depending on which changes are typically predictable and which ones escape all prediction, on which respects are essential for the particular action and which not, and especially on what time-spans between act and "answer" are involved.

In accord with previously experienced and now rememberable simultaneity of the (or an) Other in reciprocally immediate acts, the actor in mediate social action also imagines the Other as if he were simultaneous with him. This as-if simultaneity of the streams of consciousness may turn out afterward to be an illusion: the Other is not only not present, but he presumably also is not thinking of the actor at this very moment. That is hardly ever of relevance for the act, unless it turns out, besides, that the idealizing "other things being equal" assumption on which the as-if simultaneity of the idea is based has been misapplied: namely, the assumption that somewhere and somehow the Other is located in the same world and in the same world-time as the actor. The further distant an act is from the Other's immediate presence, the more fictional in any case becomes the lived-experiential simultaneity that binds the actor with the Other. This state of affairs can be illustrated by the various transitional forms between immediacy and mediacy. Depending on the state of communications technology, the symptoms whereby the Other is apprehended can decrease while the synchronization of the streams of consciousness can still, to a certain extent, be maintained: a conversation face to face but in the dark, a telephone conversation, smoke signals, drum language, televideophone, letters.

The further the action departs from the maximum of symptom-fullness that characterizes a we-relation, the more important becomes—if a reciprocal act is to take place successfully—the correspondence between the anticipation (on the part of the actor) of the Other's interpretation of his present action and the actual interpretation of this action that the Other undertakes (via its results). In other words: the more important an objectivation of the interpretative schemata becomes for the typical results of an act. This objectivation can encompass very different kinds of results of acts: markings, sign-systems, exchange values, etc. More on this below.[48] Whatever the meaning of objective interpretative schemata may otherwise be for a person and for the society in which he lives, in mediate social action

they help to produce "successful" reciprocity. In contrast with immediate action, the typifications, assumptions, and principles that were
applied to the Other in the project cannot be overwhelmed by his
living presence. Mediate action can be adjusted to the circumstances
and the changes of circumstances only after the fact. Improvements
of the project cannot flow into the action itself; they must be added
to it by his own act, or at least by a partial act. It can hardly be avoided
that they thereby acquire a different weight, a different meaning.

On the other hand, in mediate action there is some chance
(more or less, depending on the circumstances) of eliminating results
of an act by further acts, before knowledge of them reaches the person to whom they had originally been directed. A letter is easier to
stop than a word; a mine can perhaps still be defused, but not a shot.
In contrast with immediate action, there is some chance (again more
or less, according to the circumstances) of denying the authorship of
certain results of the act (an unknown perpetrator fired the shot, the
letter is forged). This is normally, not always, of little importance for
mediate acts that are arranged for reciprocity. On the other hand, it
plays a more important role in unilateral mediate action.

e. Unilateral Mediate Action

Genuinely unilateral mediate action is characterized by two circumstances: it was arranged from the outset by the actor in his project to
remain unilateral, *and* it then actually remains unilateral in the performance. Only brief reflection is needed to discover two forms of
action that look similar to genuinely unilateral mediate action and are
related to it, but fulfill only one or the other of the above-mentioned
conditions.

Thus, an action designed as unilateral—whether mediate or
immediate—can, after all, under some circumstances quite opposed
to the actor's intention, include an answer from the one at whom the
original act was directed. It thus obviously becomes a reciprocal social
act, which need not occupy us here again. Inversely, an action designed for reciprocity can, of course, fail on this essential point and,
contrary to the actor's intentions, remain unanswered. Whereas in
immediate action such a development is hardly conceivable, in mediate action it is nothing unusual. In the description of reciprocal
mediate action, we have therefore already considered the possibility
that the assumptions underlying reciprocity can prove wrong. In reality, the person then, contrary to his intention, acts unilaterally. In any
case, action that actually remains unilateral but was not projected as

unilateral is, in its meaning, fundamentally different from genuinely unilateral mediate action. The same holds true for action that was designed to be unilateral but became reciprocal in performance.

Unilaterally mediate action is thus foreseen as such already in the project. The actor from the beginning expects no answer to his action directed at the Other. He may regret receiving no answer deeply or wish for an answer ardently, he may count on an answer with certainty or assume it as only somewhat probable. Depending on his motive for action and his goal, and on the weight of a perhaps still possible answer in the framework of his interests, on the kind of communication (and communication technology) on which his own action and, above all, a possible answering-act is based, the actor will sometimes assign but little significance to the matter and sometimes deliberate carefully; sometimes he will do absolutely nothing and another time do everything to avoid as much as possible the risks of a possible response. The precautions he takes for this purpose will also differ from case to case.

The person who designs his action as unilateral may, e.g., believe that absolutely no answer *can* result. He is convinced that the pregiven structure of everyday reality, with its spatial, temporal, and social stratifications, makes an answer impossible from the outset. The eighty-year-old testator who bequeaths to his still-unborn great-grandson a piece of land on which he has just planted a nut tree expects no thanks in his own lifetime from the great-grandson for the nuts he will enjoy in the distant future. The head of state who rejects a murderer's pleas for clemency hardly expects to become the next victim of this man who has received the death sentence. This case is clear. Either the actor is right: he need not bother about the possibilities of an answer, and the action in fact remains unilateral. Or he is mistaken: then the unexpected reciprocity will surprisingly bring him joy or suffering.

In the opposite instance, the actor believes that the possibility of an answer exists in principle. Then he will first try to estimate how great or slight this possibility is under the prevailing circumstances. Next, he will have to estimate how much or how little an answer would affect him. However, he will have to calculate what he must ask in the next step: how much trouble is he willing to take upon himself to prevent an answer? The answer to this question, however, presupposes that he has reflected as to which precautions on his part could at all prevent an answer, or else—if preventing one would be either impossible or perhaps not at all desirable—what could be done so that the answer does not reach *him*. Only then will he be able to make a more or less founded decision. There are thus many possibilities presented to the person who gears his action for unilateralness.

Thus the actor can try not to let the Other even notice that an act was directed at him. The conditions for this are generally more favorable in mediate action than in immediate action: that is the difference, for example, between a murder attempt with poison and one by strangling. A similar case is characterized by the fact that the actor cannot—or, under some circumstances, will not—prevent the Other from noticing that an action has been directed at him. But he has an interest in not letting the Other know that a *particular* act was directed at him. So if an answer does come, it should not be the answer to *this* act. Frauds, political propaganda, and commercial advertising have (at least) one thing in common: although sometimes the motive, sometimes the steps, sometimes the goal (sometimes probably all three together) of a certain act or partial act are concealed, it is essential for the intended effect that the addressee of the act not notice which act as a whole was directed at him. The act or the parts of the act are thus "packaged" into other acts so that the answer should not be adequate to the question. Frauds, propaganda, and advertising certainly are not in principle designed to be unilateral; indeed, they aim at an act-relevant effect. They are not, however, based on a reciprocal concatenation of corresponding motives (that these need not at all be in harmony for reciprocity was already stated), so that we are still dealing with an example, however complicated, of unilaterally mediate action.

In another, similar case, the actor tries neither to conceal the act nor in principle to prevent an answer; he tries only to delay the answer. In many kinds of everyday action, both immediate and mediate, from conversation to an answer by mail to meet a certain deadline, an answer must be given to certain acts within a narrower or wider time-span, otherwise the answer becomes meaningless or at least ineffective. If the unilateral actor thus believes that he cannot prevent the Other from noticing sooner or later that a particular act had been directed at him, or if for sound reasons he does not at all wish that the Other notice nothing, he will postpone the time of noticing or of a subsequent answer so long that any answer would go up in smoke.

One case of answer-prevention is stratified somewhat differently. In it the author tries to camouflage his authorship of a particular act. Although the Other person notices that an act has been directed at him, and he can determine adequately what kind of act it is, and although nothing stands in the way of answering on time, he does not know at whom he should direct his answer. In most cases he will then not answer at all. It is naturally conceivable that one "answers" an insult in an anonymous letter by an anonymous letter to an unknown party, but it is not very probable—and if one does so, the "answer" does not reach the right addressee. An undirected "answer" of this kind, in any case, does not lead to reciprocal action.

Yet a further possibility of answer-prevention, important under certain circumstances and in some societies, should be mentioned. Not the giving of the "answer," and not its appropriate direction, but its effect, e.g., its "arrival," becomes the object of precautions by the actor. The actor removes himself temporarily or definitively from the reach of the one at whom the original act has been directed, e.g., by flight, or in the extreme case by suicide.

Finally, the actor can undertake various steps that are suited to eliminate every motive for an answer on the part of the one at whom the acts are directed, or at least to weaken it so that the probability of an answer is decreased. He can try to have his own act seem so insignificant that it is not worth the Other's effort to do anything; he can try to portray the conceivable answers as unjustified; etc. Or he can try to counter the motive for answering by an even stronger motive for not giving an answer (e.g., threatening punishment for meeting during a state of emergency). Naturally, there are also cases in which the addressee of the act is not interested in giving an answer anyway (if the actor knew that, we would be dealing with the first of the above-discussed possibilities). However, the actor does not know this, and so he tries in vain to maintain unilateralness, and may, as is known, under some circumstances achieve just the opposite.

3. Social Action and Social Relations

Everyone can address another person in principle both in his uniqueness as a fellowman and as a mere reference point of highly anonymous typifications. This holds good for immediate and mediate, for unilateral and reciprocal action. Nothing stands against the intention, even in unilateral mediate acts, to want to direct one's operation at a particular irreplaceable flesh-and-blood person. And inversely, one can, no doubt, even in immediate action regard a corporeally present person as a type of function (embodied, so to speak, accidentally in him and not in someone else). Let us stress once again, moreover, that on the one hand anonymization can characterize not only mediate but also immediate reciprocal acts, whereas on the other hand highly anonymous and mediate social acts can be not only unilateral, but also reciprocal. All this is possible and occurs in everyday reality. To be sure, anonymization is unusual in societies based on immediacy and reciprocity; and reciprocity in anonymously mediate acts typically presupposes very complex technical and social arrangements and functions (such as, e.g., buying a newspaper by dropping a coin in a vending machine).

Yet it must not be forgotten[49] that people are grasped in mediate social acts only by remembering their former presence, by fantasying anticipation (of real opportunities) of future meetings, and with the help of more or less anonymous typifications (intersecting at the envisioned point of individuation). The uniqueness of a fellow-man is naturally not derived from these performances of consciousness themselves, but from performances of consciousness in original encounters of reciprocally immediate acts. By contrast, in immediate social acts, even people who were envisioned in the project only as the locus of functions (as "role-bearers") by their presence, fill the typifications applied there with life.

Social relations originate in social action. Their continued existence is based on reciprocal expectation of the regular recurrence[50] of reciprocal acts (frequent or rare, depending on the kind of relation)—indeed not just any, but of determinate reciprocal acts: determinate also in regard to their immediacy or mediacy, or respectively to a sequence of mediacy and immediacy. The form of the social acts at which such expectations point, therefore, comprises the core of social relations. The social order is built on social relations; the changeable share of various forms of social action in social relations is consequently an important feature of historical social orders, whatever the real causes for the change of the respective shares may be.

With these observations, however, we evidently come quite close to the boundary of a phenomenological description of universal structures of the life-world. Beyond this lies the province of sciences that proceed empirically and "inductively" in their study of the historical formations of human social orders. If we nevertheless venture to add a few remarks on the relation between the form of social action, social relations and the social order, we are aware of the danger that even with the most fleeting reflections of such a kind, the investigative framework already given could be exploded.

It is self-evident, and was moreover emphasized often enough, that all societies presuppose immediate action. Less evident is the significance of mediate action, which plays a very different role in various societies. Certainly, even in societies in which almost all action is immediate and almost all acts are reciprocal, unilateral mediate action is not unknown. The possibilities of mixing poison are, of course, not limited to modern industrial societies. Just as clear, on the other hand, is the fact that even in the modern world most of the subjectively significant—and an indissoluble part of the socially important—acts are immediate.

But *unilaterally* mediate acts first attain a greater general significance in such societies as are at the same time characterized by anonymization of many social relations essential for the existence of society, and by a highly developed communication technology—both of which apply entirely only to modern industrial societies. The technology for communicating acts has undergone an ever more rapid development since the invention of book-printing; moreover, in the present context the increasingly bureaucratic constitution of large public institutions with division of labor can be conceived as a social technology of act-mediation. The centralization of the state and the rationalization of the economy—and to a certain extent also the development of the mass media—have promoted a far-reaching anonymization of some (important) social relations. These developments— which are not uninvolved in the great "successes" of modern industrial societies—have assigned a new role to mediate action, by organizing it supra-personally and inserting it into complex systems of action.[51] The depersonalization of these systems of acts is a (presumably) unavoidable consequence of the supra-personal organization of acts. In these systems, the concepts of reciprocity and unilateralness have lost something of their concrete meaning.

In any case, these developments first created the conditions, in broad provinces of social life, for unilateral mediate acts to be addressable to large crowds of mere recipients. The anonymous bureaucratic intermediate agencies and the structurally conditioned unilateralness of "mass media" communication do not allow "answers" to many social acts even to arise in the province of meaningful possibilities of action. If the extent of the specialization of knowledge in the social stock of knowledge is added to this, it is not surprising that the reality of modern societies has become subjectively transparent only with difficulty.

Social relations that come about *only* via mediate social acts, and are maintained only in them, remain essentially anonymous. They refer to other persons at most on the basis of comparative judgments; the others in such relations are, so to speak, only analogous fellowmen. (We are here leaving out of consideration various symbolic repersonalization strategies that are applied to support the legitimacy of suprapersonal systems of action.) Essential anonymity all the more characterizes such social relations as come about exclusively in unilaterally mediate acts. Incidentally, whether one should here still speak of social relations is in any case questionable. Reciprocal expectation of reciprocal action is, of course, not given. Moreover, in such "relations" the *actual* point of reference of social orders of every kind, namely, the assignment of responsibility to an actor, remains mostly concealed. If one can still speak of social relations here, they probably would have to be located between the poles of charitable foundations and Adolf Eichmann (if we are also here allowed a symbolic repersonalization).

The Boundaries of Experience and the Boundary Crossings: Communication in the Life-World

A. The Boundaries of the Life-World

1. Boundaries of Life

Everyone knows that he lives in a world that must have existed before him, and no one doubts seriously that it will continue to exist after him. Even if no one has instructed us concerning this, in the natural attitude we take it for granted that the world does not depend on us, but rather that we depend on the world. If we sometimes bring about something or other in the world, we may for a moment, but only for a moment, forget that we are constantly and irrevocably changing in it. When we close our eyes, we have not removed from the world the reality of the objects that we had just seen and now no longer see. When we open our eyes again, the objects are still there, and when we walk on with our eyes closed we collide with them. Only seldom can we change the already-given course of things; generally, we do not even manage to speed them up or slow them down. Again and again we must wait—and often we wait in vain. Much that we had done vanishes away; other deeds, against our will, leave traces that we stumble upon long after the deed has been forgotten.

Every human being, every normal person notices sooner or later that he is not alone in the world. He encounters others who are "like him" and yet other. In the encounter with others he simultaneously comes upon the antithesis to not-being-alone, namely loneliness—and his own self. He sees other people grow older and die; he sees that other people are born and grow older. He knows that he himself had once been born, he sees himself aging. Everyone discovers that he outlives other men, and the conclusion imposes itself upon him that others will outlive him. Everyone knows that there was a world of *people* before him and he expects that there will be one after him.

We become accustomed to waking up again day after day, and to falling asleep again at night. We become accustomed to certain performances, to other people; we put order in everyday life, insofar as nature and other people permit it; we adopt orders created long ago, for precisely in the everyday realm we are not alone and not the first. But what if old habits abandon us and new ones do not make life more bearable? What if the orders of day are threatened at night; what if the possibility of not waking up dejects us? And what if the orders crumble apart by day? Is life a dream?

It is not necessary to go on further: everyone knows about the "transcendency" of the world in which he lives; everyone knows about the boundaries of his life in it. We live in a world concerning which we know that we will die in it.

This knowledge of the boundaries of life in the world does not stem from *one* experience of some "transcendency" or other, nor does it stem, really, from *experiences* of a "transcendent" world. (How could "world" as a whole be experienced? All we can know is that we experience in the world whatever we experience. And how should such a thing as "transcendence"—i.e., precisely what transcends experience—be experienced? Experience can, at most, point to what cannot be experienced. But a few things will have to be said on this topic presently.) It can, furthermore, be established that knowledge of the "transcendence" of the world is not acquired at a theoretical distance from the "world." Rather, this knowledge, originating from daily life and from its shocks, first provides the original occasion for theoretical reflections. On the basis of this knowledge, to be sure, the attempt is then made to reduce "transcendence" to a concept, to make it graspable and accessible to accustomed experience, to tame it. Here we would surely be dealing with a root of the various religious worldviews and also of philosophy.

Finally, it should be noted that this knowledge of the "transcendence" of the world does not at all have to guide concrete projects of a person who acts, like a kind of worldly wisdom or maxim, in order to be, nevertheless, the constantly underlying ground and pragmatic motive of all his action. It does not have to become the theme of experience, and yet it stands on the horizon, though not always in the thematic field, of all his experiences. For knowledge of the manifold limitation of one's situation in the world does not necessarily belong to the stock of explicitly formulated knowledge—which then is called upon and presentiated only in determinate, relevant experiences. But it does belong to the fundamental elements of every subjective stock of knowledge and it accordingly stands "behind" all concrete experiences.[1]

In the natural attitude the boundaries which a man comes upon during his life in the world seem to him to be fixed, irremovable givens. Irremovably fixed boundaries? But some are crossable for short periods; and although we cannot cross others, it is possible to look over them at the foreign land that lies beyond; and, finally, are there not also boundaries which are firmly locked and surrounded by impregnable walls?

Everyone repeatedly runs up against the spatial and temporal limits of his experience, but in memory and project of action he crosses them with the greatest, only seldom shaken, confidence. He uses various means to do this. The most important ones are indications and marks; they help him to interpret and to act in order to bridge the spatial and temporal boundaries of his experience.[2]

Every man encounters those of his own kind. Simply for practical reasons he must try to understand them. There, too, indications and marks can help him. In a common surrounding world with other people, and acting with, for, and against them, he will, however, more than anything else have to try to communicate with them. It is obvious that for this purpose a certain mutual understanding is a necessary but not sufficient condition. For communication, he must use determinate means which are not just already given to him by nature, but rather were created by his own kind before his lifetime and must be recreated by himself and others. These means of communication are summed up under the concept of the sign.[3] The constitution of the most important system of such signs, namely language, will be discussed below.[4]

And sooner or later everyone runs into the boundary of everyday life, in crises, after the collapse of familiar orders, in the ecstasy of a "different state." If he tries to look beyond the boundary of daily life or to bring back something out of the "other state" into daily life, he uses a means which we call a symbol.[5]

All the means that man uses in his various boundary-crossings will be investigated more exactly in the following pages. In preparation for this investigation, however, the real nature of boundaries in the life-world must first be discussed more carefully. Indeed, up to this point nothing more has been done than to establish that in the natural attitude such boundaries appear as givens of life-world experience. No more has been said than this: everyone knows that the world in which he lives "transcends" him. Now, it will have to be shown what performances of consciousness are involved in the *experience* of such givens. After these general reflections concerning "transcendence" and experience, we will then recall some of the findings from our description of stratifications in the life world[6] and our structural analysis of the subjective stock of knowledge.[7] This must be done in order to show and explain what the story is with the spatial and temporal limitations of experience, how everyday reality is located in the life-world with reference to other finite provinces of meaning, and how the individual relates to his fellowmen.

2. Boundaries of Experience, Experience of Boundaries

In the natural attitude no one would even get the idea that he himself is the whole world. Every child learns sooner or later to recognize the limits that are set for his action; everyone runs into the boundaries of his experience. No one believes that he could return to yesterday, no one leaps over a mountain, no one tries to bring down the moon from the sky. When a man tries to slip into another person's shoes, he fails. And on a given occasion, everyone eventually reaches the conclusion that he too cannot escape death. Such assumptions, which are eventually taken for granted concerning the conditions of experience, the limits of action, and the boundaries of life, together constitute the background knowledge that can be called knowledge of the "transcendence" of the world. At this juncture it is necessary to establish, as precisely as possible, from which experiences this knowledge stems or else, in case it does stem from particular experiences, in which strata of experience its origin is located.

We have just ruled out the possibility that knowledge of the world's "transcendence" stems from one's own immediate experience of transcendence. If "transcendence" is taken to mean something extra-worldly—that is, in principle not accessible to human experience as such—an experience of such "transcendence" would probably have hardly anything to do with knowledge of the "transcendence" of the world. Moreover, it is in any case clear that the possibility contains an intrinsic contradiction. As long as we remain on the ground of everyday reality, this contradiction is not resolvable. Only when we give up the natural attitude and withdraw to a religious worldview, does nothing stand in the way of the assumption that something transcendent in an extra-worldly sense could be directly revealed to man. Once one has taken this position, moreover, everyday reality itself is so unconditionally put in question that intellectual contradictions that are insurmountable in the natural attitude must seem insignificant.

Yet it cannot from the outset be ruled out that there might be experiences aimed at a transcendent, although "merely" an inner-worldly transcendent. The possibility that the transcendent is grasped not merely by an inference, but rather could somehow belong to the "content" of experiences must therefore be considered. We then run into an obvious but highly remarkable structure of experience. Some experiences present themselves to a person as self-related, others as other-directed. Everything that presents itself to a person as not from him, as not really his, he then experiences not as Self and as his own, but as an Other reality that transcends him. This reality need not remain alien to him; he can familiarize himself with it. But he does not have the choice as to what it is and what it is not. It is clear that even prior to any more sharply delineated boundary of experience, this "natural" distinction between Ego-related and Ego-transcendent experiences underlies knowledge concerning the "transcendence" of the world.

In everyday reality, this distinction is hardly shaken. It can, however, lose its validity for a time in other states than the natural attitude: e.g., in dreams, in ecstasy. And at a religious or philosophical distance from everyday reality, things may present themselves differently. In mysticism, the distinction between the Ego and the non-Ego of the natural attitude is abolished; and in materialism or in idealism, it undergoes completely different ontological interpretations. In phenomenological reduction, on the contrary, after socially objectivated worldviews, theories of reality, and conceptions of identity that co-shape the concrete experiences of Ego and non-Ego have been bracketed out, this distinction is shown, in the last analysis, to be traceable back to performances of consciousness in which what belongs to the Ego's own genuine sphere is constituted.

So much for the possibilities and the impossibilities of a "contentual" experience of transcendence! Now let us ask whether there is in the structure of experience itself something that flows into knowledge of the "transcendence" of the world—or perhaps even is its main source. For as important as the organization of experiences into Ego- and Other-related certainly is for orientation in everyday reality, is it not itself based on a fundamental distinction that characterizes all experiences, namely, the distinction between what is actually and directly given in experience and what is only somehow "co-given"?

First of all, in experience everything that is presented as itself present is distinct from everything that is given as remembered, expected, fantasied, representing or replacing something else. But everything that is presented as present and as itself, simultaneously refers in this presentation to something else that is not present. (This naturally also concerns experiences which are aimed at Otherness.) Expressed in a general form: no experience is self-contained. A present kernel of experience always points also to something not-present. The self-constituting noema brings along with it a thematic field. This thematic field contains references to something else that is relevant for the present experience: retentively and as evocable remembrance, to previous experience components, experiences, and courses of experience; protentively and as more or less determinate expectation but with a clearly defined province of relevancy, to future, possible experiences. In its thematic field each noema thus brings with it contentually determinate references which are, however, not presentiated as content. Moreover it also brings along horizons that (precisely as horizons) are components of the present experience but (precisely as horizons) remain devoid of content.

The noema is experienced so and not otherwise than it is given. That is how what is called noema is determined. But as we have just emphasized, it does not give itself as hermetically self-contained, but rather as pointing to something no longer experienced, not yet experienced, and, perhaps, also not at all experienceable. Compared with the present kernel of experience, what is presently not experienced, to which the kernel of experience points, is transcendent. In the broadest, but precise meaning of the word, experience of "transcendence" means that the actually present content of experience, whatever it may be (thus even if it does not make present or apprehend something Other), points beyond itself.

Let us summarize: by the fact that it constantly goes beyond itself in thematic field and horizon, every experience of every content whatsoever becomes, let us say, a "co-experience" of transcendence. In the natural attitude this "co-experience" is not itself taken into the grasp of consciousness as theme; however, it forms the lowest stratum of the foundation on which knowledge of the "transcendence" of the world rests. A particular case of incompleteness and imperfection of every single experience is the mediated experience of a "content" that is not given: the means is expressly presentiated as a reference to something else. We will have to consider this later.[8]

As we have seen, an experiential "content" of transcendence rests on the distinction that is made in experience between one's own and something Other. This distinction, combined with the general "co-experience" of transcendency, is the foundation of the concrete consciousness of the boundaries of experience in the life-world. Depending on whether the non-experienced reality that is indicated in the present experience is in principle just as experienceable as what is presently experienced; or, although itself present, experienceable only through indications; or is absolutely not experienceable in person (in the same reality), we want to speak of the "little," "medium," and "great" transcendencies (den "kleinen," den "mittleren," und den "grossen" Transzendenzen).

Even the "little" transcendencies are not matters of no account. Nevertheless, in the natural attitude we take it for granted that we can master them in principle and apart from any "technical" difficulties. The boundaries of experience that we run into here are crossable. To remember what happened yesterday; to note where one has hidden the key; to walk through the door behind which there is nothing more mysterious than the kitchen; to shout "Fire" after one begins to smell the smoke: everyone can do all this. We can do so until precisely those little "technical" difficulties arise: of memory, logic, or the project of the act. Only then do we notice that even the mastery of the "little" transcendencies of space and time is a considerable achievement, which is in part innate and in part learned, but certainly not simple and unforgettable. And of course we always stand at a new boundary; after having crossed one, we come to the next. Experience progresses as long as we live.

The same is true of the "medium" transcendencies of understanding and communication with fellowmen. To read the facial expressions and gestures of other men is no big thing in the natural attitude, once we have learned it (the kernel of normality consists in having learned this skill). We experience something, however, that is not itself immediately given but shows itself, although present, only in a transformation. For we know that our own facial expression is not the joy or the fear we feel, but only their expression. And we know that one can conceal or simulate joy and fear. All the more so are we aware of difficulties in communication; even in the natural attitude, where it seems self-evident to us that we ask and answer, plead, command, and scold, indeed, just like our fellowmen, we may sometimes become aware of uncrossable boundaries. We must begin again, correct, reinterpret, and even then we are not certain that the other person understands us.

And finally, the "great" transcendencies. What does the dream that had such a disturbing effect on me mean in the daytime? Is it a misguided weakness to fold one's hands by a deathbed? Is the mortal danger someone underwent for me as much an absurdity as my emotional reaction on seeing a chain of mountains in my homeland? And if all this may have a meaning, what do dream interpretations, parables, prayers, paintings have to say about it?

What we experience are indications; what we run into are boundaries. Insofar as it is experienceable, we can experience something not yet or no longer experienced; we can understand fellowmen only from what they do or what happens to them, in exaggerated or abridged form, from stories they tell; the non-experienceable presents itself in ciphers and secret languages that we do not know. Nevertheless, sometimes we believe we understand; mostly, however, others, wise men and scholars, tell us that they understand the strange language, and we believe—or do not believe—their translations.

3. The "Little" Transcendencies in Everyday Life

The "little" transcendencies, as was stated above, are characterized by a person's encountering spatial and temporal boundaries of his experience and his action that are in principle crossable in further experiences and later actions. A present experience, either in its kernel or in its thematic field, or merely on the horizon, points to something not experienced but which is presented as just as experienceable as what is at present experienced. Yesterday is indeed irretrievably lost, but not everything that was yesterday is relegated to mere memory. Much that one saw, sensed, tasted, felt, endured, and did yesterday, one can certainly do today as well, and perhaps tomorrow also see, sense, taste, feel, endure, and do.

In the case of the "little" transcendencies, what is not experienced but indicated in the present experience is either the same as had already been experienced, or it belongs to the same type of objects and events as were previously experienced, or it stems at least from the same province of reality, namely, everyday life. More carefully phrased: a person knows that what the present experience points to he has already experienced before in itself, or that it is known to him as a type (he has seen other examples of the type), or that it could at least be accessible to him without any drastic modification of his style of experiencing and tension of consciousness. "A man knows," means here simply that his consciousness could grasp one particular characteristic of the indications among those enumerated, if he adverted to these indications and followed them to the subsequent experiences. It does not mean, however, that he apprehends this knowledge at the time of the current experience itself. Nor does he become expressly aware of this in the normal course of familiar experiences, as long as the "And so forth" and "I can always do it again" idealizations at work in these experiences are not unexpectedly deactivated. Recognition or type-assignment takes place first of all in automatic, conscious processes, then in indications that are pursued no further.

As in all other things, a person can also be wrong concerning the experienceability of what is not experienced. If he has ever in the past experienced "in person" what the present experience refers to, he will, habitually applying the above-mentioned idealizations, have no doubt of its re-experienceability. If the non-experienced is known to him only according to type, but the type is very definite and examples of it are very familiar, he will be confident that he can re-experience it. The more indefinite the type or unfamiliar the examples, to be sure, the less the confidence. But as long as no express counterindication is present, he will at least suspect that the indication relates to something from the same province of reality. All this will depend on where the indication comes from: whether the experience in its kernel refers to the non-experienced, or whether the indications stem from the thematic field—and then whether from a highly determinate field made explicit in detail or only weakly defined from former experiences, or whether even the experiential horizon points only to something lying beyond. If we just spoke of "not having any doubt," "confidence," etc., of course what was said before about "knowledge" applies here too. They are not normally in the grasp of consciousness, but they can be apprehended in problematic cases.

The "little" transcendencies of everyday reality are typically experienced as objects of experience that were once in reach but are now out of reach. For this reason, and because we can cite the results of the detailed investigations of reach and the province of manipulation,[9] we will study being-out-of-reach as the fundamental lived experience of the "little" transcendencies. "Reach" need not, in any case, be understood only in the strictly spatial sense of the word.

Every moment in which a person moves, he changes the world in his reach, sometimes only slightly, sometimes decisively. Apart from the case of complete immobility, the province that is actually in a person's reach is subject to constant changes. These changes are mostly gradual, but under certain circumstances they can also be abrupt. Whatever was still in reach just a moment before may disappear from reach in the next. Now if the subsequent experiences contain an indication of what was still in reach before, we can say that it transcends the present experience.

Let us assume that I leave my room and set out for my friend's apartment. Halfway there, it suddenly dawns on me that I have forgotten a book that I wanted to bring to him. I remember leaving it on my desk in the room. The questions why I originally wanted to bring the book, why I then left it there despite that decision, why after having left it behind I remembered again that I wanted to bring it, and why I remembered it precisely halfway there are certainly not uninteresting questions, and they permit various more-or-less-coherent answers. But what matters for us in this context touches only upon the last of these questions. What in my flow of experience was the direct cause for remembering?

Let us play through a few possibilities. Halfway to my friend's apartment I pass by a bookstore. In the showcase I see the book I wanted to bring to my friend. The same book. One copy reminds me of the other one, which is now out of my reach. The remembrance concerns, of course, not just the object as such, but the project of the act in which the object played a principal role and which had not consciously been given up. Variants: not the same book, but a different book by the same author; a book with a similar title by a different author; just any book. Or, since leaving my room, I have been mentally occupied with the content of the book. In my thoughts, I have been playing through an argument against the book's author that I want to try out on my friend. Precisely halfway there, I trip slightly; my briefcase strikes my leg and feels strangely empty. It was supposed to contain the book. Here, it was not even a concrete experience that led me to think of a concrete object. Here a kind of lived experience of lack (too little "content" in the briefcase) pointed to an empty space, the gap in my plan of action.

The different variants have one thing in common: a present experience points back to an earlier one—and, since a plan of action is involved, forward to a future. The object of experience is out of reach, but it was in reach; according to the project it should have stayed in reach, and it can be brought back into reach. Of course, the everyday idealizations are applied automatically: "And so forth" (the book is still lying on the table); "Other things being equal" (no one has stolen it in the meantime); and "I can always do it again" (just as I came here, I can go back, and then come back again); or, another "Other things being equal" (if it is all right for me to arrive at my friend's house one hour late). And of course, on the basis of my store of knowledge I judge the chances of restorability: did I leave the book on my desk or did I leave it in the coffee shop where everyone knows me, in the subway, in a sinking ship?

In any case, I have run into a "little" transcendence. Much as I would wish it, the book is not in my briefcase. But it is a crossable boundary: I can put it back in the briefcase if I return home. If I left it in the coffee shop, it is in principle recoverable, but that is not certain. Here, "technical" difficulties on a larger scale begin: who knows whether it will be turned in to the subway's lost-and-found office! And finally I come up against the boundary not of my own life, but of the book's "life." Paper will not keep for long in water.

4. "Medium" Transcendencies: The Others

a. Fellowmen

The world in my reach overlaps to a considerable extent, as was explained above,[10] with the Other's world; however, it can never be completely identified with it. The same applies to our manipulatory sphere (*Handhabung*). However close we may be to one another, the Other's world necessarily transcends mine. But we generally disregard this. Based on the various idealizations of daily life and on the principle of interchangeability of standpoints, we take it for granted that objects in my reach (with few exceptions) are also objects in his reach and that his experience of these objects (with few exceptions) is like my experience of the same objects. But that is the rub: the few exceptions! He sees what is happening behind my back; and I know this because I see what is happening behind his back. In short, we are here dealing with a social dimension of "little" transcendencies that forms a transition to the "medium" ones. In my experience of Others I come upon a limit to my own experiences and at the same time I come to the limit of my experience of Others.

The "little" transcendencies of everyday life are characterized by the fact that people reach limits of experience and action over which they can under normal circumstances cross without further notice. Everyday reality also has a part in the "medium" transcendencies, and, like all transcendencies, these too are characterized by the fact that a person comes to a limit of his experience. But in contrast with the "little" transcendencies, he cannot cross this boundary. On the other hand, these "medium" boundaries are distinguished from the "great" transcendencies, because one can not only look over across them but also recognize the landscape on the other side in clear outlines. In its main features, this landscape resembles the one he is familiar with in his homeland.

In all transcendencies, the current experience points to something else located beyond the boundary of this experience. In the "little" transcendencies, this other thing is something that is not present at the moment, but could be present sooner or later and thus is directly accessible to experience. In the "medium" transcendencies, however, the present experience points to another thing, which in principle can never be directly experienced. In this regard it is thus irrelevant whether the other thing indicated in the present experience is itself present or not: it can never be experienced except mediately.

The reason for this is that the other thing is like myself: an Other person. If I see a stone within my reach, I simply see it, and that is the end of the matter. If I see an Other person in my reach, I necessarily discover that, inversely, I am also in his reach: he sees me. But obviously I can see only *that* he sees me, not *how* he sees me. To be sure, I can also try to find out how he sees me, reading this from various indications. If successful, I will not only learn that he sees me, but also know with more or less reliability how he sees me; naturally I can never experience this directly, otherwise I would indeed be the Other person.

Whatever else he may be, in my reach the Other person is a body that I can perceive like other objects in my surrounding world. I experience the Other immediately, in his corporeality. The experience of the Other rests on the perception of the typical shape of a body, but it is not exhausted by that. The body I perceive refers to something I cannot perceive, but which I "know" is co-present: an inwardness. In the perceptual kernel of experience, the other person is given to me from outside, but not simply as a mere outside; in complete experience his inwardness is co-given to me. The Other person, whose body I perceive in experience, is from the first "like me."

This remarkable "knowledge" is not added after the fact, by interpretative acts, to an event of perceiving a body; I am not free to superimpose this "knowledge" on perception or to settle for a mere perception of the body. Rather, the "knowledge" (of someone like me, an inwardness "behind" the exterior) is connected with the current experience's perceptual core in automatic syntheses. Judgments based on separately weighed evidence become necessary only when the experience of an object turns out to have been either inadequately defined as the experience of an Other's body already in the core of perception, or (then was) falsely determined in subsequent perceptions. That is always the case when, from the very beginning or later, various (equally relevant) thematic and interpretative elements come into conflict with one another. The unity of perception and typification breaks apart temporarily. Sometimes I may be in doubt as to whether a shape within my reach is another of my own kind or a scarecrow that has moved a little in the wind. Sometimes doubt sets in only afterward as to whether what I consider to be a mannequin in the showcase was not perhaps a decorator who did not move for a while. In its basic characteristics this event is, of course, no different from an event in which I at first cannot decide whether a knot of rope in a badly lit corner is not perhaps a snake. Since in the investigation of the relevance systems at work in storing up experience or knowledge, we have already described at some length the general nature of this event, we can now content ourselves with this reference.[11] The question at issue here is a different one, anyway. What is the source of this "knowledge" that a different body of an Other person is of my own kind?

The peculiarity of this "knowledge" consists in ascribing an inside to an outside. Obviously, a transference of meaning from myself to something else is at work here. The question of how fundamental this transference of meaning is—namely, whether it is not "originally" characteristic of all objects in my surrounding world— cannot be discussed here. Nor can we raise the other question: if the meaning-transference really is fundamental, why does the restriction of the meaning "like me" to people seem in some way self-evident?[12] In any case, the meaning "like me" or "almost like me" or "perhaps like me on just a few points" or "not at all like me" is ascribed to some objects with a typical shape and with typical courses of movement. Obviously, these distinctions in the typifications underlying transference of meaning to something else are established somewhat arbitrarily. The fundamental schemata that are developed from perceptual roots (*Anhaltspunkte*) in identifying and comparative performances of consciousness do indeed correspond approximately to those cited above. In the concretely expressed typifications in historical life-worlds, however, superimposed elements of knowledge derived from the socially objectivated interpretative systems play an important role. To what extent such interpretations of nature and society (synthesized differently from society to society) flow in the natural attitude into the experience of something Other, or else how general the "presocietal" fundamental patterns are—this question is one that belongs to the problematic field bracketed out above.

The common denominator of all these typifications is that the "knowledge" that an inwardness is revealed in this particular exterior is fused with the perception of the shape- and movement-characteristics of determinate, typical bodies. This "knowledge," which determines the experience of many another being, has its origin in the remarkable manner in which I experience myself. In other words, this "knowledge" consists in a transference of meaning from myself to something Other. All my experiences, whether of myself or another, carry the meaning "my experiences." I vividly experience myself in the unity of feeling, willing, remembering, fantasying, and projecting—events of consciousness that bear this subscript as inward. At the same time I experience myself as turned outward in the unity of perception, of action upon the surrounding world, and of the endurance of occurrences acting upon me from the surrounding world. I can envisage whatever I want; I can recall what is long forgotten independently of the present situation; or I can plan future events. But if I thereby pay no attention to my surrounding world, I am butting my head against a tree. Much that I do not want happens to my body; but my body also does much that I do want. By no means do I experience myself "only" as a body turned to the outside; but at least in everyday reality I always experience myself "also" as a body—from within. I livingly experience myself as a unity of inside and outside, but as a unity that can fall apart under certain circumstances.[13] In the natural attitude, I take it for granted that my inner life and my exterior are not separate "objects"; but I find it just as self-evident that there is a difference between what shows itself on the outside and what goes on within. My inner life is "always there"; my exterior only when I advert to it or when something happens to me from the outside, or when—if we presuppose that an Other is watching me—I am presented to Others.

It is this knowledge grounded in self-experience, therefore, that is transferred to Others. Others are those "behind" whose exterior an inwardness is found, as in me. A body that could show an inwardness as my body does, movements that could be acts, just as are similar movements of mine: all this triggers the meaning-transference. In further experiences the transference is confirmed for the most part as if spontaneously; occasionally, incongruent experiences convince me that I was wrong. If I grimace and he grimaces in reply, if I raise my hand and he falls back, that may already be enough. If I offer him my hand and he clasps it, there can be no doubt: he is "like me." He acts in tune with my exterior, as I act in tune with his exterior. I do not get the idea that God or nature has conspired against me and is merely deceiving me that other men like myself exist.

Now, I experience myself from within as turned to the outside. Naturally, I do not experience the other person from within, but from the outside, yet not as a mere exterior, but rather as an interior that is turned toward the outside, at the moment even toward me. In the natural attitude I take it for granted that his inner life is not immediately accessible to me. The principle of the reciprocity of perspectives and motives is, in case of doubt, applied first hypothetically: does it move as I would move if I were in its place? But the case of doubt is an exception. In the normal case, so many relevant traits agree and are so evidently confirmed in further experiences so self-evidently that the principle is applied without further ado. And the application entails an automatic "conclusion." At the moment, I "know" that the Other indicates his inner life in his exterior to me now. I also "know" that he "knows" that my inner life is embodied in the exterior that is turned toward him.

It is his body in living presence that "immediately" communicates to me his feeling, willing, and thinking. The fellowman is embodied in my presence. This circumstance, his presence for me and my presence for him, which I detect from him in my experience, gives us the justification to speak of immediate experiences of a fellowman in the we-relation. Although even in the simultaneity of our streams of consciousness, the fellowman's interior is not given to me as immediately as his body; it is embodied in my presence. This contrasts with the mediacy of remembrance of Others or of the direction of projects of action at Others, not to mention anonymous traces and signs that others have left. There, the Other person becomes apprehensible not just as a point of intersection, however unique, of typifications, but, so to speak, in dual mediacy.

Obviously, I grasp my fellowman as a unity in immediate experience of his exterior and in mediated experience of his interior. Nor do I experience myself as split into an interior and an exterior. But I know very well that his exterior does not indicate everything that is inward and that it could, under certain circumstances, indicate something that is not at all there. In other words, I always bear in mind the possibility that I could be wrong in an individual case, and I know that the Other can deliberately deceive me. This knowledge stems from my experience of the experiences that Others have of me—simultaneously with my own corresponding experience. There is certainly no doubt that for me in the natural attitude the existence of Others is not a problem. The everyday world is intersubjective from the outset.[14]

This means that the existence of Others as like me is not a theoretical problem that occurs in everyday reality. In the practical ontology of this province of reality, I am not alone (an idealist solipsism can be played out only at a distance from everyday life), and the Other is as far from being a thing as I am (in the natural attitude, no materialist metaphysics has a place). But the action of Others—and thus their willing, feeling, and thinking—is a constant problem for the practical hermeneutic of daily life. This, namely, the interpretation of all the indications of the Others' inner life, will be discussed below only after we move from the examination of the transcendences themselves to a description of their "overcomings."

b. Contemporaries and the Generations

In corporeal presence the Other person is experienced immediately-mediately. But as soon as he moves out of reach, the *kind* of experience changes fundamentally. He is now graspable only in a double mediacy. While the kind of experience changes, the *sense* of the experience does not change as regards what it is about. A friend to whom I have said farewell and who has vanished from my sight remains a friend; a stranger who passes by on the street generally remains a stranger. We have already described above at some length the transitions from the we-relation to the they-relation, as well as the various levels of anonymity in the experience of the social world.[15]

We need not take up the results of those investigations again at this point, but we will point out a circumstance that is important for the present context.

The Other person always transcends me as the other whose inwardness is not immediately accessible to me. If he moves out of my reach, he also transcends me now, moreover, as absent. Even when we meet, the world in his reach cannot be completely the same as mine; after he has departed, the two provinces no longer intersect at all. But the Others' world, whether within or outside my reach, transcends my world in yet another sense besides the merely spatial.[16] Let us illustrate this by taking up again the example of a departing friend.

The friend has just gone around the corner of a row of houses. A moment ago I could still see him; I could still have called him back, if I had remembered in time that I had a message to give him. But I have an appointment to meet him in a coffee house this evening; time enough to communicate the matter to him. Among the various idealizations that are automatically at work in daily life—until revoked or in case of a reservation—my friend remains the same person for me, although, as was mentioned, the mode of experience has changed decisively. We have a long span of common life behind us; we have shared many experiences; we cherish many common hopes. We played together as children and went to school together. After having lived in different countries for a few years, we now see each other regularly and are planning a hike together in the mountains this summer; and in any case we will be seeing each other again this evening in the coffee house. The world of the Other, who is now my contemporary but was my fellowman and whom I will in all likelihood meet again frequently, is a world of many common experiences. Much that was immediately accessible to me was also immediately accessible to him, often in common experiences, sometimes separately but almost simultaneously. His world extends in principle beyond mine, but it is very familiar to me—indeed, in the abundance of immediate experiences it is not known only in more or less anonymous typifications and imaginable only by means of analogies, deductions, newspaper reports, books, etc.

To a certain degree, this holds true also of the world of some contemporaries whom I do not know personally at all, but who can be assumed to have had in their life experiences that were the same as or similar to mine. They speak the same language, they grew up with parents whose attitudes have been stamped in a similar way by the same social stock of knowledge as my parents' attitudes, they went to the same sort of schools, they practice professions with which I am familiar, and in their lives the same historical events (economic crises, wars, epidemics, clothing fashions, and music, etc.) have played a role as in mine. But not all contemporaries speak the same language, nor are all of the same age.

It is clear that the world of contemporaries who speak a different language from mine, who went to completely different schools or to no schools at all, who heard different fairy tales or read different books, whose life was shaped by different local events (an epidemic brought under control, a "minor" limited war), whose parents belong to a different social stratum from mine, etc., is more and more remote from my world. Nevertheless, we are contemporaries; the same historical events have intruded upon our lives (for example, we experienced a world war on opposite sides). And although the past and the present of these contemporaries is accessible to me only mediately and by means of more or less anonymous typifications, I could share their future (e.g., by emigrating). They could become my fellowmen; I could immerse myself in their world, which is now essentially alien to me.

Things are somewhat different with the world of older and younger people. I share with both only a few provinces of complete familiarity in the fullness of immediate experiences. There are people whom I knew as a child, just as they knew my great-grandfather when they themselves were children. Our older contemporaries still remember well people in whose world there were no airplanes and no radio. Even though we are still alive together and though a great deal is, if not shared in common, at least accessible in similar and simultaneous (or almost simultaneous) immediate experiences, the world of older people contains provinces that are in principle excluded from my immediate experience. What is for me a horizon of more or less empty ideas, which can be filled only through the words of the elderly, photos, yellowed letters, old newspapers, etc.—i.e., through communicative documents of various kinds—is for them the immediately experienced past. As such it remains unreachable by me.

Older people and I do encounter the same situations, but they have already mastered such situations numerous times, whereas I am overtaken by many a situation "for the first time." The elderly know from their own experience how such situations tend to develop. I can incorporate a situation into my stock of knowledge only through another person's report, or by relying on general maxims of action. What for me are more or less anonymous elements of knowledge, are living experience for an older person. This living experience inevitably exceeds mine, just as inevitably I gather my own "life experiences." Incidentally, what role such "traditional" stocks of knowledge play in a society, with what emphasis they are handed down to the young, and the like, of course depends on the social structure on the one hand, and on the "tempo" of social change on the other—namely, on whether the life experiences of the generations are rooted in the same situations of life or not. My world extends beyond the world of younger people analogously to the way in which the older generation's world transcends mine. However, these limits of experience look different, depending on the direction from which one encounters them.

Older people are my connection with our predecessors; they even become predecessors if I do not die before them. Younger people are my connection with posterity, unless they die prematurely before me. But even people of the same age indicate another limit that cannot be crossed in everyday life.

Let us go back to the friend for a moment. He has gone around the corner. What if he suddenly collapses and dies? Our common experiences have come to an end. I can now only remember him. And who will remember him after I am dead? This is a final limit, which points beyond everyday reality.

5. The "Great" Transcendencies: Other Realities

a. Turning Away from the Everyday in Sleep and Dream

The flow of experience is, in everyday life, a constant sequence of adverting and turning away. This says no more than that the consciousness of an experience advances to the next experience instead of holding firmly to a single one. A man gets thirsty, leaves his work aside, and gets a glass of water. A loud noise behind him causes him to stop eating and turn around. He interrupts a conversation to observe a heron flying by. He turns his back to a disagreeable contemporary and goes away. Arriving at an intersection, he stops, closes his eyes, and tries to remember whether he had turned left or right the last time he went to that baker's shop. On the way to the chalet, his tooth begins to ache.

The performances of consciousness underlying the various kinds of adverting and turning away have already been studied above from the standpoint of thematic and interpretative relevance,[17] and of the interruption and progress in the acquisition of knowledge.[18]

Here we want simply to recall that although we are dealing with something that can rightly be called adverting and turning away, it still involves boundaries of experience that are set and exceeded in one and the same province of reality. The attitude prevalent in this is the natural one: the tension of consciousness moves from the carelessness of long-familiar experiences and the moderate attentiveness in habitual actions to the most urgent attention in unusual experiences and complete concentration on acts in problematic situations—and back again to carelessness. Crossings of such boundaries of experiences in new experiences are among the things taken for granted in the everyday life of normal people. Hardly anything changes in their taken-for-granted obviousness, even when they include changes of reach or relations to others.

The situation is different for the withdrawal from daily life that characterizes sleep and dream. Here experience encounters a different limit from that of its necessary own end, the respective parameters of reach or the barriers that separate the individual person from the other person. Nevertheless, it is a limit that is "crossed"—though only in a very restricted sense of the word. A few things concerning sleep and dream were already said above.[19] We cannot add a more detailed description here; but we will very briefly consider sleep and dream from the viewpoint of experiential limits and boundary-crossings.

Based on typical prior experiences that have been confirmed repeatedly (a single disappointment would indeed have sufficed to make everything further insubstantial), I know before falling asleep that I will indeed lose my accustomed wide-awake consciousness, but not forever. I know that the world in my reach, in which I feel to some extent at home, will fade away, but not for good. Thus I know that I will regain consciousness; I know that I will wake up again in the same environs, changed only typically (and of course in the same world), in which I fell asleep. In contrast with the experiential limitations and with the crossings of experiential boundaries in everyday life, I am this time not turning away from something in order to turn to something else. Rather, I turn away, so to speak, without a substitute. I therefore also do not experience myself growing older; I know only that I must have gotten older even while asleep. (I see that other men sleep while I am awake, and grow older with me without knowing it.)

For the world from which I turn away, the "And so forth" idealization continues to apply without interruption. The mountain I saw from the window will be there for me to see again tomorrow, if it is not covered with clouds. The weeds in the garden, which I did not get to hoe yesterday, will be pulled tomorrow. My neighbors, too, will not have aged more rapidly or slowly than myself (why the fascination with the Rip van Winkle story?). Moreover, the "And so forth" idealization applies to a certain degree also to me, since I know that after my turning away from the world I will somehow remain attached to it by means of my body. My feet will always still be where they are now, namely, under my ankles; I will not have grown a new tooth; and if I should fall out of bed, I will certainly wake up. Even the "I can always do it again" idealization will come back into force again without notice, as soon as I awaken. Should I actually fall out of bed, I will be able to get up again, as long as I did not break my neck— that is just the old "Other things being equal" stipulation—and as long as I first wake up.

For I cannot get back up while asleep (what is the source of fascination with sleepwalking?). The "I can always do it again" idealization holds good without exception and in contrast with "And so forth" for the time-span between falling asleep and waking up. In sleep, the abilities of the wide-awake state are suspended without question. After all, everyone "knows" that in sleep he can see nothing and taste nothing, neither eat nor carry on a conversation nor be with a woman; that he cannot even think (what is the probable source of fascination with shamans and witches, of whom it is said that in sleep they do not sleep at all but rather can do things that they are not capable of when awake?).

I know, of course, that while asleep I "can" dream. Memories of dreams have survived into my wide-awake consciousness. But this "ability" is an ability in the sense of "I can always do it again." When I am awake I can undertake to eat a slice of bread and carry out the project under most circumstances ("other things being equal"). I can also undertake mentally to picture eating a piece of bread in every detail, and this project, too, I can carry out. I can indeed undertake to dream of eating a piece of bread, but I know I cannot count on realizing this project. I cannot even undertake with any hope of success not to dream some particular thing. In short, while sleep lasts, I have lost my ability to act, but not my ability to dream. For dreaming is simply not action; dreaming happens to me. *In* the dream, however, I can "act." From my memories of dreams I know that in the dream I can walk, run, eat a piece of bread, carry on conversations, be with women, and think. But I cannot plan all this in advance and then carry it out in the dream; after the fact, I can remember having been "able" to do it.

The cessation of my conscious activities brings me to a limit beyond which there is something totally different from what is on this side. It is not a familiar country where I can move as I can in everyday life, but it is one where I later cannot remember what happens there in the same way as I remember past occurrences from my daily life. Nevertheless, it is not a completely unknown country. Indeed, I have often been there before. I can even remember many details from it: landscapes, people, events, as well as myself and my experiences. But the context in which they stood is not clearly graspable. I am completely uncertain how successful my efforts are to reconstruct the context after the fact. Memories of dreams generally fade away into darkness with such attempts. I can only try very cautiously to list them in succession, as they light up, and to tell what happened, and even there language (with its obligatory orders of identity, space, time, shape, number, and sex) threatens to fail. Memories are immediately distorted by the idealizations of the natural attitude: I notice that they offer resistance. They are immediately inserted into the categories of a relative-natural worldview: I notice that they do not quite fit. People I know look "different," or have a new name, or do things they would never do "in reality"; cities stand in the "wrong" place; I find myself in a "wrong" time. Someone has said something extraordinarily funny—but what on earth was it that was so funny in his words? I dreamed of a river landscape that I recognized in my dream. I had often been there before—but "only" in the dream; for now, combing through my waking memories, I know that this landscape does not exist at all "in reality"; not only have I dreamed of a landscape, but of a dream landscape—moreover one that was known to me.

The knowledge we call upon to say what was and was not "in reality," what exists "only" in the dream, and what is the "wrong" place and the "wrong" time—that knowledge has its home in the natural attitude of daily life. The reality accent of daily life certainly always has practical priority in clear daylight and under normal, secure circumstances. But only when this reality character is set as absolute by a *theory* of reality that blindly denies the claim to reality of other provinces of meaning, does the dream (and other, non-everyday provinces) appear unreal (as illusion and deception, except perhaps in a purely "psychological" sense). Theories of reality of this kind form, as is known, the core of the more or less rationalist worldviews predominant in modern societies. They reshape the natural attitude of members of these societies in a way that produces the "sound common sense" with which we are familiar. It must, however, not be forgotten that completely different theories have shaped the worldview of other societies—not to mention interpolations of such theories in the modern world. In the historical reshaping of the natural attitude in these societies, in the common sense that is "sound" there, dream-reality may be equal or superior to, or even "more real than," everyday reality.

The point that matters here is that another reality is concerned than that of daily life—whether "reality" is placed in quotation marks or not. The "logic" of a dream is in no way the "logic" of everyday action. And what is remarkable about this other reality is that everyone enters it daily (viz., nightly) by crossing an experiential boundary behind which there is no experience of the same kind and out of which he returns by again crossing a boundary. In contrast with the boundary-crossings within everyday reality, he can, however, take but little with him and bring back even less: memories of indications and indications of memories.

b. Turning Away from the Everyday While Awake

i. *Half-Awakeness and Daydreaming* The vast province in which the tension of consciousness moves is, as was said, bounded on the one side by the carelessness of accustomed and usual experiences and on the other by the clear attentiveness of action in problematic situations. When he goes outside this province, a person is transported into exceptional states that are, almost without exception, of brief duration and can take him to the edge of a sudden change into complete unconsciousness. A few words will be said on this topic right away. But first, we will examine briefly what lies beyond the other boundary of the everyday province. There the tension of consciousness has not yet reached, or it has sunk back below, the level of attentiveness that must be maintained in normal advertence to the business of daily life.

Between unrestrained turning away from daily life in sleep and the lower limit of the normal absorption in everyday reality, there lies a province of tensions of consciousness with unclear gradations. The person who moves through it in one direction or the other, toward sleep or toward alertness, is not aware of crossing any boundaries. Nevertheless, here too, and not just in the crossings of the everyday province, he finds himself in an unusual state. Everyone must repeatedly devote himself to the urgent demands of everyday life and everyone must sleep now and then. But just as not everyone must fall into ecstatic, exceptional states, especially not recurrently, so not everyone need sink into the state of half-awakeness, especially not recurrently. The half-awake, intermediate stages can be practically nonexistent. Moreover it is unusual for the relevance-structures prevalent in everyday life to be mostly abolished, and this is another similarity to the ecstatic, exceptional states: the pragmatic motive loses its efficacy. Whereas these states can indeed be fostered regularly—even in society—but are of short duration, half-awake twilight states can take the upper hand and be long-lasting compared with socially defined normalcy. However, they find (only subjective) inclination in single cases.

On the lowest levels of this province the wide-awake activities of consciousness come almost completely to a standstill. Consciousness still flows along almost only in passive syntheses, and encounters hardly stand out from the flow of lived experiences. Typifications become automatic and are not appresented in judgmentlike performances; thematic and interpretative relevances are "imposed" and, compared to motivional relevances, recede into a kind of "disinterested" "just getting along" (Nur-Erleben). The coordination of inner time with world-time ceases. As long as a man persists in this state, he remains incapable of action. With open eyes and ears he gives himself over to the surrounding world. Qualities of perception are presented without mediation and almost without any ordered placement into the categories of a relative-natural worldview and with very little active linguistic reshaping. If a person closes his eyes and ears, however, he sinks into a twilight state of inner, lived experiences without experiential delimitation, until sleep overcomes him.

On the topmost level of this intermediary realm, however, motive-awakening qualities of lived experience emerge and impose themselves on consciousness. Experiences begin to stand out, activities of consciousness begin, "voluntary" advertence to experiential themes takes place. The person stands at the boundary of action. At this point there are two possibilities. If the motive-awakening qualities of lived experience stem from the inner imagination, if memories or fantasies follow one another in sequence—and if the "outer" situation permits a continuation of the turning away from everyday life—the person can become active with his daydreams. He can thereby move in old paths or walk on new paths: assertions of a relative-natural worldview and the influence of cognitive sediments from a unique course in life will no doubt play a significant role in the concrete expression (content, duration) of a person's daydreams. But when the motive-awakening qualities of lived experience are presented as urgent demands of daily life, i.e., when they come from the surrounding world (indeed in a manner that no longer seems deniable even in a half-awake state), the pragmatic motive is reactivated. The person finds himself back in the natural attitude. As in the conscious reception of daydreams, the tension of consciousness has been heightened and the boundary to the wide-awake state has been crossed. In both cases, one brings back from the other state only memories that are not clearly delineated and seem strange to the natural attitude.

ii. *Ecstasies* The usual province of daily attentiveness can be crossed either in a slow, gradual increase or in sporadic increments. The occasion for the crossings can be either "imposed" and the tension of consciousness increased by itself, or the person acts with a goal in mind, whereby he willingly takes such crossings into account. He can even make the crossings themselves his goal. In this state, the person can either "just" string together experiences or he can act: thinking or even engaging in the surrounding world. The departure from the everyday can be blind; one does not know where one is going. It can also be well planned, even aimed at regular repetitions and subjected to a body-technique or a discipline of "pure" consciousness in order to attain a determinate other state. Techniques and disciplines of boundary-crossing are, moreover, mostly combined with a theory of reality: then one leaves the everyday for a different, extraordinary, but not unfamiliar and indeterminate province of reality.[20]

The common denominator for all these boundary-crossings is that the everyday is abandoned in a *wide-awake* state, though not necessarily intentionally and in some cases of heightened tension of consciousness almost "blindly," but always consciously. Daily life loses its reality accent in favor of the other state; what the experiences in this state point to, can, insofar as only a minimum of credible possibilities of interpretation ("theory offerings") are available, receive not only a fleeting reality-accent, but one that retains its *theoretical* pre-eminence after the return to everyday life. The natural attitude is shaken off, the pragmatic motive deactivated, the relevance-systems of everyday action and everyday experience are mostly eliminated.

Here, too, we have crossed a boundary over which only indications and memories can be taken along. To be sure, they are indications and memories of experiences in a wide-awake state (with the exception of the above-mentioned possibility of the sudden change into unconsciousness). After the return to the reality of everyday life, they can be evoked as memories and—"translated" into language—be interpreted as indications, formulated into symbols (more about this below), and processed into systems of special knowledge. These can serve as guides for inquiries in provinces of reality outside every-day life; they can be "taken into custody" by experts as both lock and key, and be exploited for the quite practical purposes of daily life. Moreover, they can decisively influence the relevance-systems of daily life with or without general social approval, and even in everyday life they can put in question the pragmatic motive, at least in part and at least rhetorically.

There are many occasions for boundary-crossings. Just as nu-merous are the attempts to repress these occasions or, if that appears to be absolutely impossible, to bring under control, as much as pos-sible, the extraordinary experiences that are triggered by these oc-casions—this, already subjectively. Everyone is aware of the dangers that can be connected with the extraordinary; but these dangers do not merely deter; they also attract. And all the more so socially, if the objectivating phraseology is permitted, that societies can "try" some-thing, "repress" something, and even become "aware" of something. Expressed more briefly: everyday action is essential for the survival of the members of a society and for its existence, as it is seen by some of its members (at least some of them). The relevance-systems of everyday action are put in question by the non-everyday, directly or in roundabout ways. The suppression or an innocuous socialization of the extraordinary (in many religions, in rationalistic worldviews, "psychologies," and other sciences), its immurement in enclaves (in religious and "psychiatric" institutions), its temporary permission (e.g., in carnivals) and translation into forms of play (e.g., "topsy-turvy world") can therefore be found in one form or another everywhere and always. It is, however, impossible—and would be presumptuous—to want to exhaust the abundance and variety of human (and also almost inhuman) possibilities of transcending the everyday without meticulous historical and ethnological analyses of a few examples. It is clear that the universal structures of the life-world, not just of every-day but also of the extraordinary provinces of reality, undergo a de-cisive, concrete shaping in historical-social processes. Therefore, examples cannot, without a meticulous analysis of the above-men-tioned kind, claim to be more than examples.

And there is no lack of examples. An urgent case of "imposed" heightening of the tension of consciousness typically performed in leaps, is extreme, helpless anxiety. Something extraordinary that brings mortal danger (for the individual person, everything that endangers life is extraordinary) assaults a person and compels his attention. If it actually or even supposedly cannot be mastered, in everyday per-formances, nothing else is important any more. In case one survives the danger and returns again to the normalcy of daily life, the old things that were once important and urgent resume their place. One can again forget the moments when one was in the other state, beside oneself so to speak, just as one can forget a toothache after it is gone. If one nevertheless does remember it, one can also explain it with everyday reason. Otherwise, however, it is clear that memories of this kind, in which the relevance-systems of everyday life have been deeply shaken, are taken, in various religions, as the point of departure for revision of these systems and the development of an "unnatural" attitude.

Examples of a more or less self-guided turning away from the everyday and toward a different state—and thus generally also to a different reality—extend from relatively brief subjective experiences to socially elaborated acts. Whereas the Malayans' running amok can still be taken as a transitional form from the "blind" and "imposed" ecstasies to the self-guided ones, the battle-frenzy of the Assassins (with or without hashish) was socially approved and institutionalized. It is also a long way from the occasional orgasm to the dogmatically supported cultivation of sexual orgies. Similarly, it is a leap from the taking of hallucinatory drugs out of addictive dependence to the achievement of a union with God after hard, ascetic discipline. Despite different theoretical ballast, both rock-and-roll and the dancing dervishes are social institutions. Other examples: "exhilaration" (with or without pantheistic interpretation) when mountain-climbing; the planned, final turning away from everyday life in suicide (from "acts of desperation" to Bushido).

c. Distance from the Everyday

i. *Crises and Death* Death has been regarded as the essential experience of transcendence proper. But if one reflects more carefully on this view, one becomes aware that some confusion threatens here. One's own death cannot really be a life-worldly *experience* corresponding to the experience of other transcendencies. The changes of his own sphere of reach remind a man peremptorily of the spatial and temporal limits of his experience and at the same time allow him to experience how some of these limits are crossed with the greatest ease. One turns around, one moves to another location, and one can even remember past events in one's—utterly irreversible—inner duration. Even one's own experience of the Other person is an experience both of boundary and of a boundary-crossing—although an uncertain and, so to speak, well-guarded one. One can understand the Other and his acts or misunderstand him; sometimes one can even communicate with him. Whereas dream and ecstasy lie beyond the familiar province of the everyday, its boundaries and the crossings of these boundaries are nevertheless lived and encountered as such. Beyond the boundary, the nature of the encounters and lived experiences then does indeed change—they remain encounters and lived experiences, but precisely not everyday ones. Even of the realities that lie beyond these boundaries, everyone brings back to his daily life certain memories and indications. However different they may otherwise be, all these experiences of boundary and boundary-crossing have one thing in common: they are not unique. Some are being repeated constantly, others frequently, and a few at great intervals.

That death is a boundary, certainly no one will doubt; and hardly anyone will deny that it is an ultimate boundary. Opinions diverge on whether it is also a final boundary beyond which nothing exists and—in case one assumes that beyond that boundary another reality after all awaits us—what its nature might be. But that is just the point on which death as limit or boundary of the life-world differs from all other boundaries that are drawn within the life-world (in the everyday itself and between the everyday and other life-worldly realities). From dream and ecstasy everyone has brought along indications of another reality, although he may upon returning to the natural attitude reinterpret it as misleading or not. Has everyone brought something from death into life? Certainly, one can even believe in the news that someone once returned from beyond this limit, but that is not everyone's experience. Should there be indications making it possible to intimate a reality beyond this boundary, such an experience certainly does not have the character of memories. These indications would from the outset have to be discovered either as indications in this-worldly experience itself or as two-sided indications in the experience of other transcendencies.

In any case, death is not a life-worldly experience of a boundary. One *knows* only that one will die. The "only" refers, naturally, not to the certainty of this knowledge, for one *knows* of one's own death with certainty. It refers rather to the fact that this is not an experience of one's own, but rather a knowledge derived from other kinds of experiences. Everyone has at some time experienced not his own death, but surely the death of others, even if one perhaps was not present at the time of death. And everyone has experienced his own aging in person. These are, as was mentioned above,[21] the two sources of knowledge of one's own death. It was also pointed out that knowledge of the finitude of all life is one of the fundamental elements of the subjective stock of knowledge.[22]

Knowledge that death is a final boundary is indubitable. But knowledge of what lies beyond is not indubitable. Since, in contrast with other transcendencies, this boundary is crossable in only one direction, what—if anything at all—could lie beyond it is certainly not immediately derivable from everyday experience. The other experiences of transcendence, however, offer some indications. Sleep has understandably time and time again been offered as a point of departure for the assumption that another reality awaits us beyond the boundary of death. It is a boundary at which the fundamental idealization of life, the "And so forth," apparently comes to a standstill—quite as one believes about death—and yet again and again reasserts: there is an awakening—as if there were an overarching "And so forth." And people have taken all the other experiences of transcendence that are connected with a return, simply and in manifold combinations, as a point of departure for ideas of what could lie beyond this last boundary. In fear and hope, people have drawn conclusions from the spatial and temporal transcendencies, from the experience of the Other person and of the generations, from ecstasies and dreams, concerning the nature of that completely different reality, which cannot be experienced in life.

Once knowledge of one's own death has been acquired, it enters into the horizon of all experiences. Moreover, it becomes a component of the thematic field of those experiences in which finitude is in some way interpretatively and motivationally relevant: hypothetically relevant. It accompanies the "And so forth" and "I can always do it again" idealization with the faint remembrance: "until further notice." It stands behind the pragmatic motive of the natural attitude, sets the framework for life-plans, and flows into the things of lesser importance and urgency in the course of the day. But this knowledge determines the kernel of experiences only in those situations that intrinsically warn of death. In the serious crises of daily life, knowledge of one's own death must be taken into the grip of consciousness. The thought of death is then imposed upon the thought of one's own future.

While a person can become frantic from fear of dying and either plunge into ecstasy or freeze into a stupor, in the crises of daily life he retains his self-composure. Certainly, when they press him hard in all their menacing gravity, his condition may draw him "downward" ("as if lamed") into a kind of semi-conscious numbness, or, under certain circumstances, upward ("in wild despair") to the edge

of ecstasy. Typically, however, he remains in the state of clear attentiveness and wide-awake reflection, which preserve his ability to act.
The everyday does not completely lose its reality-accent; one by no
means renounces it, though crisis threatens to destroy it. Even in
grave crises, a person does not turn away completely from the everyday; but, since now the possibility of a definitive turning away becomes
sharply visible, he distances himself from it.

The reality-accent is not withdrawn completely from the everyday, but at the thought of death its claim to validity, which had been
taken for granted, is now questioned. This means that a person raises
at least *one* foot from the ground of the natural attitude and could be
ready to set it on that of an "unnatural" one. The fundamental anxiety
associated with knowledge of one's own death does not lose its power;
on the contrary, it is what, in the serious crises of life, motivates putting the everyday into question. But everyday reality with all its relevancies is at least temporarily put in brackets. We are dealing here
with a peculiar suspension of the validity-claims with which everyday
reality occurs in the natural attitude (a suspension that, in many respects, is related to the theoretical *epochē*). While a person persists in
the reality of daily life, in serious crises he annuls the naturalness of
the natural attitude.

If his life (or what he considers to be the meaning of his life)
seems threatened, he must then ask himself whether what just seemed
so urgent and important is still so urgent and important. The relevancies that had previously operated so matter-of-factly are then subjected to an explicit interpretation in the light that the present crisis
casts on his previous life and on his future life (which has been put
into question). What results from this interpretation is another matter: the relevances can, as the case may be, turn out to be void, or
still remain valid. The person can hold on to the results of his reflections as a *memento mori* for his further course in life, or else forget
them again as quickly as possible (especially after the crisis has faded
away). That will depend on the most varied biographical and social
conditions. What traces have other experiences of transcendence left
in his memory? How does he interpret them now in view of the crisis,
and how does he interpret the crisis and its possible outcome in view
of these traces? What do the interpretations already within the social
stock of knowledge offer him for such crises? What degree of credibility did these interpretations have for him before, in the corresponding phases of his "socialization," and how much credibility do
they have for him now? How bindingly have they been transmitted
to him, and through what social relations? What inner connection did

they have as religious, philosophical, scientific systems? But with these questions we are, naturally, already touching upon the problem of "overcoming" the transcendencies in their concrete historical formations.[23]

In all societies and at all times, man stands "in the midst of death." But not only the visibility of death and the availability of this knowledge for mastering crises and for consolation in those that cannot be mastered (e.g., as general knowledge or special knowledge) differ from society to society. Even the occasions for crises, and especially their forms of appearance and their course, also differ. The reason for this is simple. Occasions and forms of appearance of crises are in part determined immediately by society (as in the case of war, enslavement, unemployment, and the like), co-determined by it (as in the case of famines, natural catastrophes partly caused by people, serious hardships caused by dishonor, love's sorrows, and the like), or else at least mediately dependent on social conditions (as in questions of health and "natural" death). Some of these occasions are of such a kind as to drive a person into a different state. Many, however, cause a person, even in the "normal" state, to transcend the everyday by distancing himself from it in thought.

ii. *Theoretical Orientation*   Knowledge taken into the grip of consciousness in the serious crises of daily life causes a transformation of the natural attitude: the finitude of one's own life appears by no means natural. By bracketing out everyday relevances, a person draws close to a fundamentally different attitude, namely, the theoretical orientation; under some circumstances he even places himself in it, at a stoic distance from his own fate. But even in pre- and semi-theoretical transformations of the natural attitude (in which the accent of reality is not completely removed from the province of daily life and its taken-for-grantedness is not unreservedly drawn into doubt), a person begins to ask himself and the world questions that he would never think of in the natural attitude. He is not outside himself; but since he is distanced, he is in a certain sense outside this reality, which had been so familiar to him and which now shows an alien, threatening face.

In the theoretical attitude, the accent of reality is withdrawn, so to speak, hypothetically—but only hypothetically—from the everyday province, and the relevances prevalent in it are put in question unreservedly, although only for the time being. Whereas the pre-theoretical transformations of the natural attitude are motivated by fundamental anxiety—this lived-experiential correlate of knowledge of one's own death—and fundamental anxiety is preserved in them, *after* the transition to the theoretical attitude this fundamental anxiety is bracketed out. Knowledge of one's own death remains as knowledge, but it is transferred to objective interpretational contexts. The further one is distanced in this way from the natural attitude, the more independent of the pragmatic motive does the interpretation (i.e., reinterpretation) of the reality of daily life become—above all, the indications and memories of other realities that are funneled into it. During the time that thinking is done in this attitude, even one's own Self, in its corporeality and finitude, is subjected to an *epochē*. Although originally it may have occasioned the transition to the theoretical attitude in one way or another, one's own state of interests is thereby suspended—temporarily and hypothetically, but decisively—for thinking and its results. Everything that is put in brackets—the entire everyday, the everyday province in its relations to other realities, limited sectors of everyday reality, one's own life in the world together with its crises and in its finitude—all this can, of course within brackets, be made the theme of thinking, interpretation, and reinterpretation.

The further reflections that could be based on these characteristics of the theoretical attitude concern no longer the foundation of the attitude itself, namely, the wide-awake distance from everyday reality and the unreserved putting-in-question of all that everyday reality takes for granted. Such reflections focus on the multiple possibilities of thinking in this attitude. Theoretical thinking cannot be unhistorical. Like all thinking, naturally, an individual's theoretical thinking also stands in relation to the results of previous acts of thought deposited in the subjective stock of knowledge. Above all, however, the individual's theoretical thinking is guided by the more or less systematic results of the theoretical acts of thought by other people who preceded him, which are deposited in the social stock of knowledge. Socially mediated theoretical traditions of thought have historical character. This becomes especially clear in the forms of specialized theoretical knowledge,[24] which become "independent" under certain social conditions. This stands within the span between the personalization of transcendencies in (some) religions and the anonymization of everyday reality in the modern sciences. Here we are thus again touching upon not only the question of "mastering" transcendencies, but also upon their historical prefabrication. As these themes are the proper concern of such disciplines as history of religion, philosophy of science, and the empirical sociology of knowledge—and not our specific concern here—we must stop this analysis at this point.

B. Boundary Crossings

1. Appresentation

We have been discussing the manifold limitation of human experience in the life-world. How boundaries are experienced and lived has been described in considerable detail. Something has also been said concerning the possibilities of encounters and lived experiences, which open up when one turns away or distances oneself from everyday reality. But the boundary-crossings themselves have not been studied sufficiently. Up to this point, little more has been said on this subject than that the barriers of space and time are crossed in memory and project; that in understanding and communication bridges are thrown across to the Other person's alienness, that the dissimilarity of realities outside everyday life is made more evident by the interpretation of the memories and indications that are brought back from there to the "normal" wide-awake state; and that death is "overcome," if at all, by the interpretation of indications of indications. In the introduction to these reflections, it was, moreover, suggested that in crossing the limits of his experience a person uses certain means that we call indications, marks, signs, and symbols.[25] Now it is time for these means to be subjected to a more precise examination. Do they really help in crossing the boundaries themselves? Or do they help, so to speak, in "overcoming" the boundaries, without these boundaries really being crossed, by sending back news from the beyond? Or do they do both?

The answer, summarized in two sentences and prefaced to an exact description of the relevant performances of consciousness that participate in the process, is this: First, indications, marks, signs, and symbols all convey news from beyond the boundaries of immediate experience by co-presentiating in the experience everything that is thematically, interpretatively, and motivationally relevant to the actually present experience but in some way or other transcends the kernel of the experience. Second, signs, even though essentially "news-bearers," also help us, in *reciprocal* communication with other people, to cross the boundaries to them; symbols, although essentially embodiments of a different reality in the everyday world, can, in combination with certain (namely, ritualized) acts, be of assistance in crossing the boundaries to other realities, including the last boundary.

An indication points to something other than itself, something disguised, hidden, or absent, and makes it accessible in the reference of experience. It brings a person the tangible news about what lies spatially and temporally beyond his reach. A particular form of indication, the corporeal expression, points to something that is not just "accidentally" outside one's spatial and temporal reach, but is in principle not apprehensible otherwise than through such a reference: the Other's consciousness. Marks help "overcome" the barrier to the future by projecting, now, memories for later; they transmit information to one's own future: like memories, but tangible and planned. Signs combine indicational and mark-like components in an intersubjectively compelling manner; in concrete and anonymous reciprocity they carry news of a like kind from one to the other—and back. Symbols give information concerning non-everyday realities, or news about the everyday realm from that non-everyday perspective, which is disclosed as completely different from it.

All these means are based on appresentation, a performance of consciousness that is essential to life-world experience. They are, at the same time, results of previous appresentational relations and occasions for present appresentations. In other words: they are vehicles for appresentative performances. Without these vehicles, a person would remain to a considerable extent caught within the limits of the flux of actually present experiences; without the appresentations themselves, completely caught. There would be life and lived experiences, perhaps even encounters, but no life-*world*.

Appresentation interests us here mainly as an active performance of consciousness.[26] But active appresentations are based on the more primitive syntheses of consciousness in which appresentative relations were built up. These syntheses, in turn, rest on the fundamental, original, passive syntheses of association, of "pairing." "In a pairing association, the characteristic is that in the most primitive case, two data are given intuitionally, and with prominence, in the unity of a consciousness."[27] It must, however, be observed that "the condition for the possibility of each unity of intuition" is the "unity of time-intuition."[28] Even in this form of pairing is found, as "essentially present here, an intentional overreaching, . . . a living, mutual awakening, and a self-overlaying of each with the objective sense of the other."[29] And further: "As a result of this overlaying (i.e., of the coincidence [T.L.]), there takes place in the paired data a mutual transfer of sense, that is to say: an apperception of each according to the sense of the other, so far as moments of sense actualized in what is experienced do not annul this transfer with the consciousness of 'different.' "[30]

The appresentative pairing and the analogous meaning-trans-ference that occurs in it differ from simple coupling. Through the primitive form of coupling, the unity of apprehension occurs in the simultaneous presence of two givens. On the level of "associative union," important for us here, in contrast, a synthesis of "present" and "non-present" occurs.[31] This is precisely the basic structure of consciousness that must be presupposed in all indicational perfor-mances—and finally in man's so-called capacity for signs: "Appresen-tation presupposes, as such, a core of presentation. . . . The two are so fused that they stand within the functional community of *one* per-ception, which simultaneously presents and appresents. . . ."[32]

Indications, marks, signs, and symbols refer, from a present given (more precisely stated: from an actually present datum of *per-ception*), to something at present not given. What is at present not given can be something that was once given (as a datum of perception) and could later be given again; but it can also be something that has a different mode of givenness than do objects of perception and events, e.g., an idea (a fiction, a phantasm), a dream, a beyond, a personalization or an abstraction of natural and social operational contexts. This means that it can belong to any area of everyday reality, including completely socialized reality, or even stem from a different province of reality.

This circumstance results in a great variety of possibilities not just of simple but also of stratified indicational relations. In life-worldly experience, however, an immediate given, a datum of perception, must always stand at the lowest level. This is therefore typically ex-perienced not as a mere datum of perception, such as it immediately presents itself, but as the vehicle of a reference. For, once the relation between the appresenting and the appresented poles of this refer-ential relation has been established, the vehicle is from the outset (let us say for the time being) experienced in its "meaning." For the ve-hicle still to be experienced as a mere object of perception after all, the person must transport himself out of the natural attitude into an "unnatural" one, for example, the scientific attitude. However it had originally been established in his life-history, later on the "meaning" grounded in appresentative syntheses comes into the grasp of con-sciousness as such and not just as a judgment after a series of cognitive acts. Although they could be taken apart again step by step—after the fact—the vehicle and its meaning comprise an experiential unity in "functional community" (as was said above).

Let us summarize: In the simple and fundamental ("associa-tive") forms of pairing, two data, *a* and *b*, are given simultaneously;

and both within one and the same perceptual modality as well as ("synaesthetically") between them, a displacement of meaning from a to b and from b to a takes place. On the next higher level of appresentative pairing, only a is given, and by analogical transference of meaning it evokes the idea of b. On the level of appresentative pairing at which indications, marks, signs, and symbols are constituted, a is again given, and again it evokes b; however, a is not apprehended as itself but rather as the "vehicle" of b, and b is thematized in experience. In this appresentative relation we are dealing with something we will, for the time being, call "meaning," and we notate B instead of b. ("For the time being," because this relation is probably the basis of all meaning, but we will speak of meaning in the strict sense only when this relation is intersubjectively ascertained as a sign.) In respect to B, there are two possibilities: either B is in principle experienceable in the same manner as a and is "absent" only at the time of the experience in which a is present, or B is fundamentally "absent" and can never be experienced in self-givenness like a.

Appresentative relations, of course, are but rarely separate, individual relations. They are inserted with other appresentative relations into larger experiential contexts, where they typically must be authenticated. This holds true especially of the relation between vehicle and meaning. As a rule, the meaning is inserted into overlapping contexts of meaning that are assigned (so to speak, all together) to determinate experiential contexts. Especially in the intersubjective use of the various forms of communication, relations of meaning are inserted into the currently existing contexts of meaning. Depending on how loosely or strictly systematic these contexts are, changes in an appresentative relation—of course, all the more so, new creations—condition more or less decisive changes in all other relations that stand in the same context. Accordingly, systems of appresentative relations, at any rate, have biographical character; and systems of socialized meaning-relations, moreover, also have a historical character. Meaning-relations are therefore above all subject to socially and historically variable regulations of their structure, their subjective application, and their intersubjective use. Even prior to all social regulations, however, meaning-relations rest on two simple general principles, the first of which essentially concerns the appresenting member of the relation and the second the appresented member.

The principle of the *(limited) arbitrariness of the vehicle of meaning* signifies that the presence of an appresentative relation, $a — B$, does not exclude that under certain (situational, biographical, or social) circumstances a new appresentative relation, $c — B$, can be founded.

Depending on the causes, viz. the motives, of the new foundation and the constraints of the context into which these two relations are inserted, the old $a - B$ can continue to coexist with the new $c - B$ (synonymy in a general, not just a linguistic, sense). But it can also be replaced by the new relation and be eliminated from the meaning-context (a modified traffic sign for right-of-way regulations, the particular case of phonetic change). This principle is limited by "prejudice," namely the already-established uses of the vehicle, which can be physical, namely, restrictions in the production and perception of vehicles, and social, e.g., "theories" of the meaning-relation itself, for some kinds of possible vehicles, and the like.

The principle of the *(limited) variability of meaning* means that the presence of an appresentative relation, $a - B$, does not exclude that a new appresentative relation, $a - C$, can be created under certain (situational, biographical, social) circumstances. Depending upon these, the old meaning can be preserved (homonymy, in the general sense) or vanish (change of meaning, in the general sense).

It must, therefore, be stated in general that appresentative relations are not established once and for all. Certainly, once they have been established in an experience or a series of experiences, some appresentative relations are confirmed again and again in later corroborating experiences and hardly change: $a - B$ is preserved as a typical patterned relation. This can occur in "natural" indications, self-posited marks, and socialized signs. Other appresentative relations are not confirmed in experiences subsequent to the original establishment; they turn out to be "false indications." These are dissolved and replaced by new, "correct" indications. And finally there are appresentative relations that have been established only in and for particular occasions. The person is fully aware of their arbitrariness, and if nothing further is added, these relations are dissolved again after the use planned in the original establishment.

2. Indications

Indications, marks, and signs (in an indicative sense) have already been discussed in another context. There, our interest focused on the communication of subjective knowledge.[33] We have seen that under certain conditions (agreement of the problematic situations, etc.) other people's observable problem-solving attempts and solutions can be interpreted as indications of subjective processes of knowledge acquisition. Already acquired knowledge, however, can be passed on, either intentionally or unintentionally, only by means of other appresentative relations—partly by marks, but principally by signs. In accord with our interests, we have focused on indications (as well as marks and signs) only from a very determinate vantage point: the appresentation of Other conscious life.

Now, certainly one of the most important functions of these appresentative relations is the "overcoming" of the transcendence of the alter ego. Corporeal expression and movements are taken for granted in the natural attitude as indications of conscious processes of the most varied kinds, i.e., not merely of knowledge acquisition but also of the intention to act, fear, anger, nausea, discontent, affection, doubt, pleasure.[34] In the continuing and repeated perception of Others, their expression and their acts, a context of congruent appresentations is constructed that opens up for me—with unavoidable limitation—the "inner life" of others. In this context, every single indication must be verified.

It is obvious, however, that our investigation of various objectivations of knowledge acquisition anticipated a general description of indications. There we already had to consider the case, particular and complicated though especially important, of an intersubjective use of indications (and marks). We must now step back and study indications in their appresentative basic structure. This is essentially independent of intersubjectivity, regardless of the empirical fact taken for granted in the natural attitude, that in the everyday world indications are inserted into the most varied communicative processes and thus begin to lead a proto-semantic existence. Not all indications are expression.

In everyday experiences, patterned combinations are established again and again between events and other events, objects and other objects, and objects and events. One thing follows the other; one thing emerges from behind the other or can be found behind, above, or under it; one thing passes over into the other, etc. When, for example, tall grass moves one way in a strong wind and another way when animals are creeping past, I will learn to "read" one kind of grass movement as an indication of strong wind and the other as an indication of animals creeping past. Whether I understand the relation between the appresenting member and the appresented one "rightly" or not is in principle irrelevant—although in the case of animals creeping past, it could end badly. In other words, the confirmation of appresentative relations in later experiences is not necessarily dependent on one's ability to explain the nature of this relation, which can be obscure just as well as transparent. So it is also without essential significance whether the appresentative relation was originally established step by step, like a logical argument, or as it were automatically, in a single attentive grasp.

Whatever the motive and occasion may originally have been, in a particular experience a present a appresents a non-present b. The latter can, however, with one exception—an extremely important one, to be sure—itself become present. Only in the case of expression can b, even later, not be experienced as itself but only in the embodiment in a. When the appresentative relation is verified and corroborated repeatedly in further experiences, a relation of meaning develops. Under usual circumstances, the a will no longer be experienced in its self-sufficiency but in its meaning, B.

3. Marks

Marks could, without oversimplification, be regarded as intentionally posited indications. Whereas the appresentative relation of an indication is grounded in perceptual experiences, the appresentative relation of a mark is indeed also associated with perception, but above all with the tangible result of an act. The motive for setting marks has already been discussed: a person seeks to ensure that he will still know later what he knows now. Or, to translate it into the terms that were used in the investigation of reach: the mark is supposed to point out within a later restored reach what was conceived to be relevant in the present reach.

If I want to mark where I have buried a rifle, I will try to mark the arrangement of the mountain chains, streams, stones, trees surrounding the burial place. If this arrangement is striking enough, we are dealing with a pure act of thought, and the arrangement will serve me later as an indication for the burial place. But, as the example shows, the boundary to the mark is flexible. I need only move a few stones, and already this operative act has marked certain components of the world in my reach. Moreover, the principle of the arbitrariness of the vehicle holds true almost without limit. Whether I move, notch, arrange, etc., stones, trees, or whatever else, has only practical, not fundamental significance. Whether I tie a knot in my handkerchief, or hang a ten-pound weight around my neck to remind myself that I am supposed to buy bread, depends on the availability of handkerchiefs, my neck, the degree of my forgetfulness, and the degree of urgency with which I need the bread. What matters is that all these vehicles are no longer experienced as trees, stones, knots, weights (although they are perceived as such) but as indications of something else. Further, it must be kept in mind that the indication in this instance was not experienced but posited. The motive for the positing is, as was mentioned, orientation in a future situation.

It was stressed that indications and marks are fundamentally subjective meaning relations independent of intersubjectivity. It was, however, also noted that they can be inserted in communicative processes, and there they begin to play a proto-semiotic role—proto-semiotic, but by no means fully as signs. To make clear the reason for this we will recall a few of the results of our investigation of the objectivation forms of subjective knowledge.[35]

The interpretation of indications as an expression of the other's processes of consciousness and the interpretation of marks as memories posited (earlier) by me (for now) are strongly situational. They can become effective as inter- and intra-subjective transmission of knowledge only if the structures of experience and relevance, from which a specific element of knowledge developed, coincide extensively with the experiential and relevancy structures of the person interpreting the objectivations, i.e., with the relevances of the Other—or, in case of intra-subjective "transmittal," with one's own, which then must remain extensively the same over a period of time. For the objectivation to be apprehended correctly, the problem whose solution was objectivated in certain indications or marks must be presented similarly for two people, or for one person over a period of time.

4. Signs

Among the various forms of appresentative relations with meaning-character it was not very difficult to bring out clearly the structural characteristics of indications and marks. In the framework of the general nature of appresentative relations (present $a \rightarrow$ absent b), unilateral and consolidated meaning relations (aB) develop. In their particularity, indications are constituted based on the observation of typical combinations of events and objects, viz. the apprehension of typical sequences of the occurrence of certain a's and b's. This produces $a \rightarrow b$, and finally aB. Marks, in contrast, are constituted not by mere observation of already-present combinations, but by intentionally positing a more or less arbitrary a for a subjectively given b. In the constitution of the indication, the b follows the a in the same sequence as in the later experience of this appresentative relation. In the constitution of the mark, however, a follows b. In the apprehension of this appresentative relation, once it has been established, naturally in marks too the b follows the a (i.e., $a \rightarrow b$, and finally aB). Despite the unmistakable difference in the constitution of the relation $a \rightarrow b$ (or aB), as we have seen, even in the concrete case, transitions between indications and marks are to be found. The boundary between experience and act, between observing and marking, is quite a bit sharper conceptually than in concrete everyday reality.

Transitional forms also exist between indications and marks on the one hand, and signs on the other. With a certain simplification, it could even be said that signs develop from the socialized combinations of indicational and marklike components. In order to clarify this, let us recall first a result of the investigation of those objectivations that serve for the transmission of knowledge.[36] We had asked ourselves why marks that are posited by one person can be apprehended by another not only as indications of any conscious processes whatever, but rather quite accurately as indications of a specific "marking problem" belonging to this person and of his attempt at a solution. We found that this succeeds all the better, the more simply a coordination can be established between *typical* marking problems and typical marks. A relatively accurate interpretation depends mainly on the kind of problem itself (Is it at all a problem that can in principle be "read" from events in the outside world? Is it typical in its particularity, or does it belong to a large class of similar problems?), and on the degree of agreement between the relevance structures of the participants. (We illustrated this by a few examples: the attached string in the cave passage, the knot tied in a handkerchief lying on the street, and the knot in the handkerchief that fell out of my friend's trouserpocket before my eyes—a friend whose forgetfulness of his wife's birthday is well known.)

The closer—both literally and figuratively—a mark is to the situation in which it was originally posited, the more the relevant components of the world then in reach are still on hand as relevant, the better known (in type or as a person) the person who placed the mark is to its present interpreter, the more likely can delimited, particular knowledge (and generally: determinable conscious processes, such as experiences, intentions to act, etc.) of one person be communicated to the other by marks. This is a remarkable pyramiding of appresentative relations: one person's marks are apprehended by the other as indications of marks. Naturally, like all other indications, they must be confirmed. Since they involve indications of an Other's conscious processes, they must, as we want to explain in advance, be confirmed in his further experience by congruency with other relevant indications, acts, consequences of acts.

When for the same kind of problems the same kind of marks is posited by one person and by the other, the interpretation of the respective marks acquires relatively high reliability. Positing and interpretation still remain subjective processes, but they are of the same kind for the participants. The last threshold prior to the complete intersubjectivity of the appresentative relation has been reached. It is crossed when the typical interpretation of a typical mark on the part of a (typical or particular) Other is included in the project of mark-positing by the person who posits the mark. This is so, assuming that the Other, who is experienced as someone to whom the principle of the interchangeability of perspectives is fully applicable, does or will do the same thing! In anticipation of his (presumed) interpretation, the mark is posited as an indication. Once this threshold too has been crossed, one person's marks become for the other person clear indications of his well-defined experiences, intentions to act, etc., and inversely. But then the indications are no longer indications, the marks are no longer marks. In positing and interpretation, act and experience, what we are dealing with is a reciprocal and, at least in this minimal sense, bindingly socialized meaning-relation. It does indeed contain the structural characteristics of indications and marks, but in *one* vehicle of meaning—moreover *conjointly* for the one who produces the vehicle of meaning and for the one who perceives it (X $\rightarrow aB$, Y $\leftarrow aB$). The level of the meaning-relation proper, for which we have reserved the concept of the sign, has thus been reached.

It might perhaps have seemed meaningful to distinguish signs from indications and marks not just by their intersubjective constitution, as we have done, but rather by the fact that in the appresentative relation the indication does not refer to other objects or events in the world but to the Other's consciousness. For in the description of indications, we had stated that some indications refer to something that just accidentally and momentarily is not experienced immediately, though it can in principle be experienced immediately. Other indications, however, in their exterior embody an interior that cannot be experienced otherwise than mediately. "At first" this is experienceable mainly through its expression (and "later" also through other objectivations, e.g., results of acts). The structure of the appresentative relation is here, too, basically the same as in other indications, but the character of the appresented member ("interior," "processes of consciousness") differs importantly from its character (objects and events in the world) in "natural" indications. We found it right to define expression and embodiment not as signs, but rather as a special form of indication, though a particularly remarkable and important one. It is an indication for the reason that it has the basic structure of an indication (the apprehension of typical connections); a special form, because embodiments do not have the same kind of verifications as "natural" signs. Embodiments are verified when an appresented B later becomes present and is experienced in self-givenness— as a is now. Embodiments cannot find a specific confirmation of this kind in an individual case. They must be verified in the continued congruency of a multiplicity of appresentations of the Other's conscious life (this particular person, this typical person, or human beings in general).

The extension of the sign-concept to all appresentative relations in which the Other's consciousness is apprehended would, furthermore, have brought us into great difficulties, even if taken by itself it had otherwise been convincing. It is more than doubtful whether in appresentative relations a generally valid life-world boundary could have been drawn along this line (indication of an interior, of an Other's consciousness). At best, "interior" and "conscious life" would have been almost empty of content, and "indication of an alter ego" would have had to be defined formally. As was pointed out in another passage, it cannot simply be presupposed that the distinction, "nature" versus "man" (ego and alter ego), is a universal category of life-world experience. It stems rather from a "regional ontology" that is grounded theoretically (mythically, religiously, scientifically) and that appears one way in some relative-natural worldviews, and differently in others. We cannot here go into the difficult question of the constitution of the alter ego as nature, animated nature, animal, man (e.g., *homo sapiens* in the modern conception), or fellow tribesman—depending on the socially solidified restrictions of the credibility of an originally universal transference of meaning: like myself.[37] It may be sufficient to point out that even today not everyone has yet forgotten to apprehend the expression of animals as the indication of an "interior." However, in contrast to many other societies and epochs, we would hardly ascribe "physiognomic" traits any more to trees, flowers, mountains, rivers, the moon, thunder. If we wanted to extend the concept of sign to that which in any way ascribes "subjectivity" to a subject, we would have to accept the fluctuations of what has been considered to be subjective and consequently was experienced as such in various historical life-worlds. This difficulty can be avoided if signs are conceived in terms of their intersubjective constitution and validity in everyday action. These are universally human.

We thus persist in considering only such appresentative relations to be semiotic as can be posited and interpreted reciprocally and similarly—indeed in such a way that the positing itself is geared fundamentally toward interpretation. Signs combine the essential traits of indications (apprehension of typical combinations) and marks (positing) in reciprocal social action. For the positor, the positing of signs stands immediately in the subjective "in-order-to" context of wanting-to-be-understood (whatever may be the background of because-motives of his action and whatever the overarching in-order-to motives in which his action stands). For the interpreter of the posited sign, the interpretation stands immediately in the subjective in-order-to context of wanting-to-understand (whatever the because-motives and the in-order-to motives may be in the context of *his* action). This process is one of intersubjective communication. This is not at all changed by the fact that signs can also be presentiated only subjectively, e.g., as inner language, or that signs can be used only subjectively, e.g., in a monologue. Signs are intersubjectively constituted, and an already-constituted system of signs such as a language is intersubjectively acquired. The essential function of signs in the everyday life-world is communication; it goes beyond the understanding function of indications and marks.

Like all other appresentative relations, signs also "overcome" life-world transcendencies for the individual person. In their basic indicational and marking components, they "overcome" the "little transcendencies," the spatial and temporal limitations of experience. An embodying indication in the sign already "overcomes" the boundary to the Other person; but only *as* a sign does it facilitate the crossing of the boundary between fellowmen in both directions.

While we have till now been able to speak of meaning-relations only with restrictions (for, in the case of indications and marks, "meaning" always had to be understood by one individual), meaning in the strict sense is essentially intersubjective (meaning is the means in the process of communication between men). Meaning is meant in the same way as it is supposed to be understood by the Other person. I thus presuppose that the Other has the same—or, in any case, almost the same—knowledge as I do in regard to the appresentative relations in question. In the natural attitude, this is not for us a fundamental but merely a practical problem. We take for granted that he and I have at our disposal a system of already-completed meanings independent of ourselves. My fellowmen and I have already learned or still need to learn how this system is made—and already we can communicate. In the natural attitude, the question of how such a system of socialized meanings could have developed cannot be asked. Nevertheless, the question must be raised in our investigation of the life-world. But the answer will have to be postponed briefly until after our description of the constitution of language in the everyday life-world.[38] For obvious reasons, language will serve as a good example for the constitution of signs in general. It will have to be shown how linguistic signs developed from particular forms of expression in reciprocally immediate social actions. To be sure, we will then also have to consider whether the grounding of linguistic signs in eventful forms of expression (hence, in "temporal objects")—and not in results of acts in the form of marked objects (written signs, as well as more primitive notations, can be taken as a complex example of this)—leads to noteworthy particularities in their basic structure as signs. But there can be no doubt that language is the most important sign-system in the reality-province of daily life.

Thus, in completely developed systems of signs, naturally above all in language, not just "solutions to problems" but also "posings of problems" are transmitted relatively detached from the limitations of experience in space and time and with *relative* independence from the boundary separating a person from his fellowman and from earlier and later generations.[39] At the same time, systems of signs—again language is the most important one—are the presupposition for the detachment of the individual from the limitations of experience (and the limitations of self-acquired knowledge) of his own course of life. In our description of the constitution of language, we will show that these possible applications of systems of signs, in which the manifold boundaries in the life-world are "overcome," mean a remarkable reversal of one's own constitutional conditions in the immediacy of the we-relation.

In the historical life-worlds, the individual in association with other individuals develops systems of signs by no means out of nothing, nor by independent socialization of indications and marks. Everyone finds fully developed systems of signs already present, particularly of course a language. These systems are "imposed" elements of his situation in the world. As systems of boundary-crossing they are, at least under relatively normal circumstances (the wild boy of Aveyron; Kaspar Hauser), "imposed" on everyone by society, just as the boundaries of his experience in the life-world itself are "imposed" naturally.

5. Symbols

Symbols have already been discussed in various passages of our investigations.[40] It must have become clear, at least in general outline, what symbols are and what they achieve for life-world experience; they throw a bridge from one province of reality to the other and play an important role in "overcoming" the "great" transcendencies. Now, after describing the other appresentative relations, we will capture somewhat more precisely the structure and function of symbolic relations.

In symbolic as in all other appresentative relations, to repeat it once again, something immediately given refers to something absent, which is however co-presentiated in experience by means of this reference. Disregarding their special form (the expression and embodiment of conscious processes), in indications and marks what is absent is only "accidentally" not present or, so to speak, cannot be apprehended immediately at the moment, as it were, for technical reasons. With the special form, things are different, since other consciousness can never be apprehended immediately in self-givenness, but is experienced at all only in expression and embodiment—or in signs. In their fundamental indicational and marklike constitution, signs can indicate all conceivable objects and events in the surrounding world. But as a result of their intersubjective constitution, signs indicate the objects and events by means of an intersubjective, consciousness-related "intermediary world" of meanings, a stabilized context of typical experiences (one's own or Others'). Moreover, like indications and embodiment, but likewise in intersubjective prior typification, signs of course also refer to one's conscious processes as such, e.g., to intentions to act, frames of mind, etc. Like the special form of indications, signs too are appresentative relations in which the appresented member is not just "accidentally" not present, but rather fundamentally cannot be apprehended immediately even later on.

Now, in this general form, this holds true also for symbols: in the symbolic relation too the vehicle of meaning points to something that in principle cannot be apprehended in the same manner as the vehicle—namely, immediately. What distinguishes symbols from embodiment and sign is something different.

Whereas objects now out of reach transcend my present experience only temporarily, since later on they can perhaps be brought back in reach, the Other person transcends his fellowman in principle. Nevertheless, it is a matter here of an entirely everyday transcendence. The everyday is populated with people; people become accustomed to one another, act routinely together, communicate. We have taken this circumstance into consideration even in the choice of linguistic designations: it is a matter here of a "medium" transcendence. In one respect, the "medium" transcendencies are like the "little" transcendencies. The boundaries of experience that are being crossed are everyday ones, and the crossings themselves are likewise everyday ones. In other words, what is co-presentiated in indications, marks, and signs belongs to the same province of reality as the vehicle of meaning itself, namely, everyday reality.

In symbolic relations, however, what is appresented is not merely absent (as in all appresented relations), not "merely" absent in principle (as in embodiments and signlike transmittal of conscious processes), but belongs to a totally different province of reality than the vehicle of meaning itself. Now, vehicles of meaning are components of everyday reality. They are events and objects that I experience in perception; under some circumstances I can stumble over them. Certainly, in such perceptions I can already be on the way to an "other" state, ecstasy, semi-awakeness; or the perceptions may accompany me back to the "normal state" of the natural attitude. But those are limiting cases. When the boundary is crossed, the symbolic appresentative relation is dissolved. The "other" reality is experienced immediately in intoxication, dream, mystical union, etc. That is, at any rate, the news that the memory of such experiences brings back to everyday reality for us. The memories themselves are now indications of other realities; they are almost symbols or are completely anchored in symbols. For, as "pure" conscious process, they would dissolve into indefiniteness during the shocking experience of crossing the border into the indeterminate; what is constituted in a relevance-system is not by itself preserved if it is transposed into a different relevance-system. For it to be preserved as a memory, a marklike solidification is needed. It can use any vehicle of meaning, even some from the surrounding world, and it can be determined formally as sign and mark—but precisely with a symbolic function. The solidification of memory, which is nearly or already symbolic, can of course also use signs—language, in particular. Both "inner language" and communicative retellings of experiences in "other" states are, literally, telling examples of this. They "overcome" the "great" transcendencies of another reality: on the one hand, as mnemonic devices for one's own memory, in order to assist it in indicating the experience of another reality; on the other hand, as an announcement to one's fellowmen of what has been seen beyond the boundary of everyday life.

The symbolic meanings attached to particular vehicles of meaning are thus memories of experiences outside the everyday sphere that have been brought back from other states to the normal everyday state. Now, in the description of the "great" transcendencies, we have seen that besides the turning from the everyday to other states, distance can also be gained from the everyday even when wide-awake. Full of fear and hope amid the grave crises of life and more or less routinized in the theoretical orientation, one seeks explanations for the forces at work in nature and society, which engage fatefully in daily life, and asks questions about the meaning of the whole and its parts. As long as the natural attitude is not given up through critical shocks or through a routine transition into the theoretical attitude, such a quest and such questions are bracketed out. At a distance from the natural attitude, such questions can be asked. The answers found are, however, not indications of *other* realities: rather, the everyday itself has become alien and extraordinary. For this reason we can also call "symbolic" the meanings that arise from such a distance (e.g., in the various developmental stages of the theoretical attitude: myth, religion, philosophy, and science). Of course, even these ideas (about everyday reality from a distance) are attached to vehicles of meaning. As in memories of other realities, it is *not* "pure" conscious processes that are at issue here; what was symbolic representation and embodiment there, is here symbolic representation and notation.

According to the principle of its (limited) arbitrariness, the vehicle of meaning can be (almost) anything conceivable. Vehicles of meaning range from objects of the surrounding world, e.g., from a distance: sun, moon, stars; or closer: e.g., mountains, rivers, ravines; or quite close: e.g., springs, trees, stones; or objects produced by men: e.g., tools, weapons, graves, houses, crowns, flags. They run the gamut from natural events, such as lightning, thunder, rain, high and low tide, drought, seasons, plague, epilepsy; to animals, such as owls, snakes, lions, turtles, bears, beavers, spiders, kingfishers, bulls, sheep, coyotes, foxes, ravens; to body parts, eye, head, fist, phallus, vagina, breast; to body movements, knee-bend, kiss, hand-kiss, slap, nose-rubbing, two outstretched fingers, outstretched index finger, dance, song, copulation, farting, hand-clapping; to historical events: crossing the Rubicon, the suicide of the Maccabeans, the Olympic games; to social occasions: coronation, execution, marriage, burial.

It is clear that many of these vehicles of meaning are no longer simple objects or plain events, but consist of meaningful components, e.g., acts of the most various kind. But furthermore, vehicles of meaning themselves can be pyramided on appresentative relations, indications, marks, signs. We have already discussed indications of indications. Breasts or the vagina can symbolize fertility, mountains the breasts, and ravines the vagina. Mountains and ravines can be modeled or drawn, etc., just like breasts and vaginas. An animal can symbolize courage, slyness, sexual desire, etc.; animals can be portrayed, their movements danced, their voices sung. For events: liturgical and dynastic calendar, anniversaries, etc. The list of examples and of pyramidings of example on example is almost inexhaustible. Everything follows what we will call the principle of the (unlimited) transferability (or pyramidability) of meaning. Everything that is an indication of something else can become an indication of another reality; everything that is an indication can become an indication of an indication.

With this, we have reached the point to note that the intersubjective establishment of symbolic meanings leads to an extraordinary multiplicity of socio-historical forms. We have been discussing nearly symbolic and symbollike appresentative relations, as well as the symbolic functions of indications and marks. All this means is that these relations indicate another reality, but still in purely subjective experiential contexts hardly shaped by society. Indications and marks with symbolic functions can be made and used without intersubjective fixation. But even that holds true only for individual memories from other cognitive states, not for the ideas and cognitive results applied to Others' everyday reality from a radical distance. Symbolic meanings in the full sense are, like signs, intersubjectively constituted, either by themselves or in a form pyramided on signs. They obey general principles: (1) the (limited) arbitrariness of the vehicle of meaning; (2) the variability of meaning and the transferability (i.e., pyramidability) of the symbolic function. But this list includes, so to speak, just the marginal conditions for the regularity of symbol production and symbol use, of the socialization of symbolic meanings and their internalization by the individual. Symbols are intersubjectively constituted and form historical contexts, often even hierarchically arranged systems institutionalized as special knowledge. Indeed, their constitution is in principle dependent on the general conditions of the universal structure of the life-world and on the above-mentioned principles for appresentative relations. But one of their essential features is their historicalness. The quest for the patterns and perhaps even the laws governing the historical constitution of symbols therefore leads to the empirical sciences of man, historiography, and the social sciences, from anthropology to political theory and the sociology of knowledge.[41]

c. Communication in the Life-World

1. The Constitution of Language in Everyday Reality

Signs were defined above as intersubjective meaning-relations that—under a reciprocal and complete application of the principle of exchangeability of standpoints—combine indicational and marklike components. Signs are intersubjective on the basis of their original constitution and in their validity or rules of use. The constitution of signs is intersubjective in the strict sense of the word. In contrast, the intersubjectivity of the rules of use in the communicative processes of a we-relation presupposes not only the process of intersubjective constitution of the signs, but moreover a socially more or less solidified ("institutionalized"), historically pregiven system of signs, a "natural" language.

During the description of signlike appresentative relations, we postponed a more precise investigation of the constitutive process and of the general framework of the social conditionedness of the rules of use. It was said that we would study these problems through the example of language, certainly the most important of the life-world systems of signs. Now that we are drawing to the conclusion of our investigation of the structures of the life-world, the time has come for us to turn to these problems.[42] Let us begin with a description of the intersubjective constitution of language; after that we will provide a few reflections on the social regulation of language use, in particular on the presupposition for such regulation, namely, the social "distribution" of language.

Let us, then, ask which performances of consciousness enter into the intersubjective constitution of language, and reflect on the nature of this process itself. The preconditions for answering these questions were already developed in the studies on the we-relationship, on reciprocally immediate social action, and on appresentation.[43] We can now refer to their results without unnecessary repetition. Indeed, the basic conditions for the constitution of language are the reciprocal mirroring of fellowmen in a we-relation, action in concrete intersubjectivity that is based on this relation, and the pyramiding of complex forms of appresentation upon simpler ones.

As long as the normally socialized man (therefore also in a pregiven language) persists in the natural attitude of daily life and as long as the habitual action that serves for communication in the we-relation is not disturbed and interrupted, he does not pay attention to the phonetic foundation of what his fellowman says. He does not thematize the vehicle of meaning as such, as an object of perception (*a*), but rather the meaning appresented in it (*B*). He now apprehends the meaning both in the meaning-context of the language system (as its "objective" sense) and in the context of the communicative situation, e.g., through the prior history of what has just been said and the motive-context in which the fellowman's action stands—insofar as he can apprehend it typifyingly (its "intersubjective" sense)—and also in the in-order-to context of his own action (its "subjective" sense). But what is said does not have for him its own significance as an object of perception. The subjective *lived experience* (*Erleben*) of sounds (not their *encounter* [*Erfahrung*], as was just explained) is, however, the underlying grounding stratum for the constitution of language. Without *a*, there is no *B*. In order to grasp the pregivenness of *a*, we must thus first try to bracket out *B*. In other words, in the experience of language forms we must bracket out what belongs to higher levels of constitution, i.e., what first makes sound patterns into language forms. But even then the lived experience of sound patterns, considered as a lived experience of "natural occurrences," exhibits a few remarkable characteristics. As distinguished from the lived experience of many other everyday objectivities, language forms present themselves in a single modality of meaning. They are apprehended as temporal objects. In contrast with many other events in the common surrounding world they pass away instantly, although at the moment of their production they are an undeniable component of the "objective" surrounding world. The lived experience of sound patterns is constituted in the continuous synchronization of inner time-syntheses and "external" processes, in various nuances of pitch, volume, rhythm, and melody. These nuances form the thematic field around the kernel of the sound formation.

These lived experiences are constituted as typical lived experiences. In the current situational context, it happens that, as a consequence of prior encounters deposited in the subjective stock of knowledge, the Ego turns toward a *typical* kernel of sound formation in a characteristic thematic field of such nuances. The lived experience of sound patterns is, through Ego-advertence, transformed into a well-circumscribed memorable pre-encounter. This pre-encounter serves as perceptual foundation, first for simple, but then also for higher-level apperceptions. In the we-relation, the lived experiences of sound patterns refer to events apprehended by people in the situation as events within common reach. I experience the series of sounds as something that my partner in the situation experiences approximately as I do. In the we-relation I also have the immediately transmitted lived experience of my fellowman. I thus have not only conscious evidence of the polythetic constitution of *my* lived experiences of the sequence of sounds, but, transmitted by his living organism, also immediate evidence of the polythetic constitution of *his* lived experiences of the same sequence of sounds. The series of sounds is experienced as "objective" and can at the same time be apprehended as an indication of the fellowman's subjective lived experiences.

If I experience the series of sounds as produced by my fellowman, it is apprehended as an indication of him, as an appresentation of his subjective experiences. Yet it does not at all lose its characteristic as an "objective" event in a common surrounding world.

The sounds produced intentionally or unintentionally by fellowmen are paired with *other* indications of their subjective events. They are apprehended by me together with the series of sounds as appresentative references to *his* lived experiences or encounters. Typical combinations of observed indication-syndromes and inner states (moods, attitudes, motives, plans, etc.) are deposited in the observer's stock of knowledge as interpretative schemata.

Interpretative schemata, which appresent the fellowman's "inner life," can in principle be grounded on any modality of perception, in any chosen combination of indications. (The privileging of sound over our most important sense for orientation in the surrounding world, the sense of sight, and over touch and taste, is presumably connected with the structural plan of the human body, the empirical nature of sound, and the early ecology of the species.) It is also important that sound patterns are temporal objects: their polythetic constitution, in combination with the perceptual nuances of pitch, volume, rhythm, etc., makes possible a nearly inexhaustible number of combinations of simple and complex patterns of sound.

Another circumstance is even more important. On the one hand, sound patterns are forms of expression, i.e., indications that are apprehended as produced by other beings. Forms of expression become elements in patterns of interpretation that appresent the consciousness of fellowmen. On the other hand, they are "objective" events in the common surrounding world of partners in the we-relation. This means that I experience them in the way I assume my partner approximately experiences them himself. They thus appresent a fellowman's subjective lived experience, but at the same time they serve as the foundation for the synchronized *intersubjective* lived experience of the partners. This does not apply to the most important (phylogenetic) competitor of sound, the sense of sight.

Although the forms of expression on which language is based are "objective" in this sense, "objectivated" forms of expression as such still do not constitute signs. The constitution of signs has yet a further essential presupposition: the mirroring of the self in the lived experience of fellowmen. This condition is fulfilled *only* in the we-relation. Only there do we vividly experience the fellowman as immediately mediated, and indeed not only on the basis of "objective" patterns of interpretation (just as we vividly experience "natural" events), but also in contexts of subjective ascriptions of meaning.

As soon as "objectivated" forms of expression are interwoven into the intersubjective mirroring process of reciprocally immediate social action, the preconditions for the constitution of prototypical signs are given. A form of expression in common reach of the partners in the given situation can be produced intentionally by the one or the other, experienced in the same way by both, and apprehended by both in the same kind of interpretation contexts. Fellowmen now no longer merely express an inner state; nor are they turned only toward an event in the common surrounding world; nor do they act simply in the reciprocal relation of social action. Rather, they act to express something, which they experience in their encounter with the Other in continual reciprocity. They anticipate the explication of their expressive act and interpret the partner's similar expressive acts with the same interpretative schemata.

The conditions for the constitution of language in the everyday life-world are thus: "objectivity" of the lived sound experiences, indicationality of the sound patterns, expressivity (i.e., appresentative reference to "inner life") of typical sound patterns in acts. The constitution of prototypical signs can be derived from these conditions. But before prototypical signs become signs in the full sense of the term, they must be detached from certain conditions of their origin in concrete intersubjectivity.

First, language forms are to a great extent detached from the respective momentary subjective experiences. *All* forms of expression are apprehended more or less as indications of typical, repeatable lived experiences. For *language* forms, however, the reciprocal social control of the partners in the mirroring process and the subjective control of the "objective" event promote agreement between the production and the interpretation of language forms.

Second, language forms are also to a great extent detached from the spatial perspectives of the concrete we-relation. The idealization that leads to the bracketing of the partners' different apprehensional perspectives is an application of the assumption of the interchangeability of standpoints. In combination with temporal idealization, which includes the actuality of the lived experiences within the appresentative reference, there occurs a further detachment of the meaning of the language form from the dependency of encounters on the surrounding world.

Third, language forms are to a great extent detached from the individuality of encounters. To a certain degree this holds good even for the mutual typification and interpretation of forms of expression. The resulting limited anonymization of language forms is now generalized in connection with the temporal and spatial detachments. The meaning becomes "objective." Further, language forms also become detached from other forms of expression with which they originally constituted an expressive syndrome. Those forms become fundamentally irrelevant for the objective meaning. In situations of concrete intersubjectivity, but also only then, other forms of expression can take the place of the language forms. Moreover, they can enter (so to speak, renewed) appresentative combinations with them.

And fourth, language forms become detached from the concrete imbeddedment in social action. The meaning of language forms becomes relatively independent of the immediate pragmatic situational context. The great advantage of the language forms is that they can enter determinatively and corroboratively into the planning and the coordination of social acts that reach out beyond the boundaries of the we-relation. The use of language forms, speech, is indeed an act; but language, as a quasi-ideal system, is the precondition of nearly all acts that display a certain complexity or are deployed over longer periods of time.

With this detachment from their original conditions, language forms as prototypical become signs, almost in the full sense of the word. "Almost" because something is still missing: the systematic nature of the signs. Every concrete social relation, every sequence of social actions, is deposited in subjective stocks of knowledge. Protosigns are obviously intersubjectively relevant, so that they are extraordinarily rich in memories. Every proto-sign receives an identifiable place in the intersubjective tradition. The first is the first, the second is the second, etc. Every proto-sign thus contains in its own thematic field a reference to the previous intersubjectively constituted proto-signs. With the constitution of proto-signs, the construction of a system of signs begins.

2. Language as a Social System of Meaning

Language without structure is thus inconceivable on account of its intersubjective constitution. For every person who has ancestors, at any rate, language is already present with a particular structure as a social pregivenness of his biographical situation. In other words, the human being is born into a historical life-world in which language has a concrete, predetermined structure. The child "repeats" the steps of sign-constitution to the very last step, the constitution of the *system* of signs. The events of intersubjective mirroring, into which sound patterns are interwoven as objectivated indications of subjective processes, are repeated in the "normal" child, but with a decisive difference. The subjective appropriation of language does not re-enact the historical development of the language structure. Rather, this structure from the outset enters into the processes of intersubjective mirroring between child and adults and is not first built up there "de novo."[44] The structure of every "natural" language is the result of a sequence of sedimented social acts in which communication took place. The language structure, and, more generally, the structure of "natural" sign systems, is determined immediately by past acts of communication—and thus mediately by the social structures that comprise the external framework of these acts. These structures can, in general, be considered as institutional consolidations of human action and human orientation in the world.

Systems of signs, among which language is by far the most important (phylogenetically, ontogenetically, and socially), are appresentative structures that are built up intersubjectively, stored historically, and transmitted socially. The basic function of systems of signs, which we have discussed above, can be "read" from this. Such systems act as "bridges" between a person's present experience and something else, or even something entirely otherwise.

"Something else" is the individual's past encounters and also his projects for future action. Already on the subjective level, all the more complex interpretations of meaning, but especially also solidifications of meaning, rest on the highly developed systematic mark-like nature of language and on the systems of signs derived from language, above all writing. It is obvious that *in principle* the subjective storage of experience does not presuppose a system of signs. But *empirically,* that is really an important subjective function of the social systems of signs. The semantic-taxonomic establishment of patterns of typification helps subjective orientation and action.

The life-world function of systems of signs can be summarized as follows. Appresentative references serve to "overcome" the life-world boundaries of a spatial, temporal, and intersubjective character. Beyond this, socially consolidated, socially transmitted, and intersubjectively used appresentative references of a concrete *system* of signs—and, empirically, language more than everything else—have a distinct advantage over the ambiguity and ephemerality of merely subjective, situation-bound, appresentative indications and typification patterns. The semiotic nature of communication promotes, first, the routinization of subjective action, particularly the higher-level and more complex action, but it serves mainly as precondition for the taken-for-granted reciprocity of social action.

This performance of language is based on the establishment of the presentative function of signs and their semantic-taxonomic rigidification in the system. The presupposition for this is the detachment of language from its conditions of origin in the everyday we-relation. This has obvious consequences for the structure of life-world communication. The origin of language is, however, shown again in the full everyday concreteness of the situation. Here language again combines with other, for the most part less univocally structured, more weakly institutionalized, nonlinguistic forms of expression rigidly bound up in the situation. The rules for language use, for social action, and for the use of nonlinguistic forms of expression are interwoven in reciprocally immediate action, so to speak secondarily, after they had in the primary interweaving been the point of departure (naturally also the phylogenetic one) for the construction of language. In any case, one thing ought to be clear with respect to human society: the multiply-grounded forms of communication in social action presuppose language as a quasi-ideal system, as the authority for clarification, appeal, and mediation. Language is the principal means for the social construction of every *human* reality; but it is also the chief medium for transmitting a particular, hence historically and socially already-constructed reality. From both vantage points, language is essential as a quasi-ideal system of signs; it is the presupposition for de-subjectivation, i.e., for the historico-social determination of the subjective orientation of the individual in his life-world. As a product of the we-relation, however, language is at the same time also always already presupposed in the intersubjective production of every historical social world.

3. Language and Social Structure

Languages, in their particularity, in their inner phonological-syntactic and lexical arrangement, as well as in their external stratification into levels and dialects, originate in principle under different social conditions. They are then also used under different social conditions; the manner of their use across the generations in turn affects the stability and change of language structure and language stratification. Consequently, social structure determines language in two ways. First, a particular historical social structure has governed a particular chain of typical communicative processes: by stabilizing and changing elements already on hand, these processes produced a particular language structure and stratification. But second, a given social structure governs more or less bindingly, and in a more or less functional manner, the typical uses of existing means of communication in typical situations, starting from the early phases of language acquisition (e.g., baby talk in mother and child relations) up to the institutional establishment of semantic, syntactic, and rhetorical elements of communication.

So even the access of socially pretypified members of society to the social component of the means of communication is determined within a certain range of variations of individual possibilities. The access barriers are not the same in caste-, estate-, and class-societies: they extend from sacral barriers all the way to mere economically and socio-psychologically conditioned "tendencies." Opportunities of access to language are socially distributed. This is an essential component of the historically changing forms of the social distribution of knowledge—and of social inequality.

Furthermore, the actual present use of the means of communication is, in concrete situations, socially regulated. The regulations can consist of strictly or loosely enforced negative and positive rules of selection. Among these rules are prohibitions and word taboos, the forbidding of certain stylistic variants in certain situations or toward certain types of persons, commands for the use of certain forms of language or of entire strata of language, as in the binding (symmetrical or asymmetrical) use of status-conditioned formulas of address, stylistic variants, etc.

By means of communication we understand, of course, both "purely" linguistic and para-linguistic means as well as strongly or weakly conventionalized nonphonetic forms of expression (facial expressions, gestures, distancing, body stance). The typical relation of the various communicative means to one another is neither accidental nor purely idiosyncratic. It is, rather, regulated differently within a society depending on the situation, and from society to society, and indeed more or less clearly and with differing (often socially distributed!) binding force.

The use of means of communication is thus determined both by the historically available structure of the means of communication and by the concrete social regulation of communicative processes. But now even in the long run, continual use stamps the historically available structure of the means of communication in a society. It would be idle here to pose the question as to what came first. The actual use of the means of communication is, in any case, composed of rule-following, routine, and action in the we-relation, however limited. Structural preservation and structural change result from this.

4. The Social Distribution of Language and Its Subjective Correlates

The social structure, both as an operational context of institutions and as a system of social inequality of chances in life and in the way of living, determines both the fundamental structure of communicative situations and the opportunities for access to the social stock of knowledge and means of communication. One of the consequences of this is that the capacity to master typical communicative situations adequately displays a social distribution. This distribution is arranged according to the knowledge of means of communication relevant to the typical courses of life of typical groups and strata of members of society and, combined with this, knowledge of the relevant rules of language use.

Subjective knowledge—leaving aside the question of how objective it is and what "objective" can at all mean here—of the social distribution of the means of communication plays a role in the typifying apprehension of fellowmen in social action. Often this knowledge is superfluous, since the fellowman is in any case known, or the institutional framework of conditions facilitates an unmistakable placement. Often a communicative, but not explicitly transmitted typification is however of considerable significance for the definition of a situation, particularly where this situation is negotiated between the participants and not rigidly predetermined.

In every society, there are communicative situations of various kinds pregiven by the situations in life and interests, which institutionally are more or less clearly determined. By combining the historically available communicative system with social rules for use—and on the basis of individuals' different, socially determined access to the means of communication—these situations are mastered in typical fashion. Yet the act of communication is not exhaustively determined by the language system, rules of use, and social structure. Apart from freedom of action in the concrete we-relation there exists in every society—in regard to every individual "normal" member—a certain surplus of forms of communication and patterns of procedure in communication (strategies). Societies differ in the extent of this surplus (or perhaps rather: these possibilities of choice).

Within the historically and socially established degrees of freedom under which, e.g., rhetorical and stylistic variation is at all possible, the actual choice of means of communication now itself fulfills particular communicative functions. These, namely the indicative (indicating the speaker's type, personality, and mood) and phatic (creating or disturbing a relation), are superimposed on the meaning function determined by the system of signs. The members of a society learn to recognize more or less adequately these components of communication—or of misunderstanding. They can then use them more or less consciously as building blocks of their communication "strategies."

APPENDIX

Arrangement of
the Appendix

Editor's Preliminary Remarks

This appendix contains the manuscripts foreseen by Schutz himself as the material basis for the book *Structures of the Life-World,* as well as the file cards prepared by him for the organization of the book. Presented before the notebooks are a "Survey of Contents" begun by Schutz and list of index words. The file cards contain a broad division into chapters (blue file cards), a subdivision of the chapters (yellow file cards), a more detailed outline (red file cards), as well as the corresponding page references to the notebooks (white file cards). This outline is presented in the appendix; the respective file-card color is abbreviated by a letter in parentheses to the right.

The notebooks were written in the year 1958 in Seelisberg, Minnewaska and New York City (as indicated in the table of contents) and are of varying content. They contain, first, rough outlines for the book, especially for Chapter I; secondly, German translations of a few essays published by Schutz in English, which were supposed to be worked into the text. But even these translations led Schutz to further questions, continuations, and commentaries. I already pointed out in the introduction to Volume I that the chapter division of *Structures of the Life-World* differs from Schutz's rough draft [cf. Project Outline below—*trans.*]. Chapter III ("The Knowledge of the Life-World") is followed by a new Chapter IV ("Knowledge and Society"). In Volume II, Chapter V corresponds to the Chapter IV planned by Schutz ("The Life-World as the Realm of Practice") and Chapter VI to the chapter entitled "Sign and Symbol." In the introduction to the first volume, it was already stated that Schutz's Chapter VI ["The Sciences of the Social World," cf. pp. 177–80 below—*trans.*] would not be included. Work on the analyses also resulted in changes of the subdivisions, which can be recognized by comparison with the Table of Contents.

This appendix is intended to give the reader not only some insight into the original plans for the book, but also some idea of Schutz's preliminary work. Interested scholars can make a more precise reconstruction of my procedure and of the insertion of Schutz's preparatory works into the present volume by examining Schutz's original manuscripts and my own manuscripts in the archives of the University of Constance.

The notebooks are preceded by an outline of them based on Schutz's survey of the contents of the first two notebooks, continued by the editor, in which parts not written by Schutz himself are contained in brackets. Page references refer to the original page numberings, which are retained in the present edition. The first number of the page reference indicates the number of the notebook, and the other numbers indicate the page in the respective notebook (e.g., p. 2035 indicates Second Notebook, p. 35; 4105 indicates Fourth Notebook, p. 105). The page references refer respectively to the immediately following text, although occasionally—for technical reasons—they are given at the end of the text of the preceding page.

Minor changes of the text were made and, except where they involved mere orthographic changes, are indicated by brackets. As far as possible quotations and references were also checked and added by the editor as footnotes. Otherwise an effort was made to render the original faithfully. Schutz's abbreviations are explained in the List of Abbreviations.

I will not neglect to thank the Center for Advanced Studies in the Behavioral Sciences, Stanford University, for making its facilities available to me; let me thank also the Volkswagen Foundation for the financial support that made work on this book possible. It would also hardly be forgivable not to thank Ska Wiltschek, Anne Honer, Ronald Hitzler, Matthias Michailow, and Hubert Knoblauch for their work on the manuscript, and Hildegard Eble-Warndorf for typing it. Merely to thank Mrs. Ilse Schutz would be to underestimate her importance. Her help was absolutely necessary for the book to be completed.

Thomas Luckmann

Schutz's Project Outline
for *Structures of the Life-World*
Based on His "File Cards"*

Chapter 1

The Life-World of the
Natural Attitude (b)

A. As Unexamined Ground of the Natural Attitude: (y)
Characteristics of life-world thinking (r)
Basic Assumptions of constancy
—of the world structure
—of the validity of previous experience
—of the power to act
Idealities of "And so forth"
"I can always do it again"
1001, 3021, 3022, 3023, 3034, 3035, 3036, 3069, 3070, 3073, 3090, (w)
3091, 3092, 3093, 3094, (3095), (3096), (3097), (3098), (3099),
(4006), 4027, 4028, 4029, 4030, 4031, 4060–4067, 4087

B. That Which is Taken for Granted and the Problematic (y)
(1) How what is taken for granted becomes problematic and the (r)
problem is transferred to new questionableness
(2) Explicable horizons of questionableness surrounded by the
unquestioned.—Interpretational horizons of the self-evident
(3) Opaqueness of the unexamined pre-interpretedness
(4) The tested recipe
1002, 1003, 1004, 1005, 1014, 3069, 3070 (w)

C. Structuredness of the Life-World for the Experiencing Subject (y)
It stands in contexts of meaning (r)
contexts of interest
contexts of plans
projects and practicabilities
1052, 1053, 2067, 4012, 4070 (w)

---

*The abbreviations (b), (y), (r), and (w) refer to blue, yellow, red and white file cards.
See on this the editor's preliminary remark. Missing file cards—always noted in the
following text—were replaced by resorting to an (unpublished) prior plan of Schutz's
for the arrangement of *The Structure of the Life-World*, which generally coincides with
the "file cards."

D. Plans and Practicabilities   (y)
   Plans, systems of plans, plan-hierarchies   (r)
   Laws of pragmatic consistency
   Spheres of incompatibility

                             [white card missing]

Chapter 2

The Stratifications of
The Life-World   (b)

A. The Spatial Stratification of the Life-World   (y)
   The Here and Now   [red card missing]*
   World within actual reach
      within potential reach (a) restorable
                  (b) attainable
   The problem of empowerment (a) imposed
                        (b) controllable
   The manipulatory sphere
     World within your actual and potential reach
     World within your actual and potential manipulatory sphere
   Your and my empowerment
   Third parties; everyone
1007, 1008, 1009, 3023, 3024, 3025, 3094, 3095, 3096, 3097,   (w)
3098, 4009, 4095–4099, 4103, 4104

B. The Temporal Structure of the Life-World   (y)
   (a) (1) The physical and social world existed before my birth   (r)
      (2) It will continue to exist after my death
      (3) Historicity of the inanimate and the human world
      (4) What does "First things first" mean?
   (b) Subjective correlates of the actuality of reach   (r)
      (1) Reference to interpretable horizons and stock of experience
      (2) Reference to restorableness: retention and recollection
      (3) Reference to attainableness, protention and anticipation
      (4) Problem of sedimentation and wakening (association and
          passive synthesis)
      (5) My death
   (c) The subjective experience of time   (r)
      (1) The "specious present"

---

*Outline items of this card reconstructed on the basis of Schutz's unpublished preliminary draft on the arrangement of the book.

(2) Flying stretches and resting places
(3) Articulation (breaking-off of the musical theme as example)
(4) Time-dimension of biography
(5) Objective time
(6) History
(7) What I have in retrospective (anticipatory) view, is
determined by relevance, situation, and problem
1001, (a) 1011, 3098, 4100, 4101, 4102, 4105, 5004, 5005   (w)

C. Social Structure of the Life-World   (y)
(a) Axioms of the existence of others   (r)
(1) Intelligent fellowmen exist
(2) I was born into an existing social structure
(3) The life-world is accessible to others
(4) My knowledge of it: socially derived
socially approved
socially distributed
(5) The so-called reciprocity of perspectives
(b) Articulation of the social world   (r)
(1) Surrounding world—fellowman
(2) Contemporary world—consociate
(3) Prior world—predecessors
(4) World of posterity—successors
(5) Transitions—aging, my-your death
generations
(6) Digression: The dead, the unborn, gods, demons as
members (of) society, totemism
(c) How the other person is experienced   (r)
(1) The pure Thou-relation (shared *durée*)
(2) We, You, They
(3) Typifications and anonymity   cross-reference
(4) Self-typifications   to *Type??*
(d) Subjectivity of the world beyond question   (r)
(1) My, Your, Our, Their world beyond question
(2) Differences of the biographical situation
(3) Subjective-objective meaning
(4) In-group—out-group (cross-reference to III D d 7)
(5) Self-interpretation of the out-group
(6) Objective interpretation of the out-group
1008, 1009, (b) 1012, 1013, 1035, 1036, 1052, 1053, 1054, 1055,   (w)
1056, 1057, 1058, 3035, 3036, 3043, 3046, 3048, 3049, 3050, 3098,
3099, 4001, 1009/10, 4013, 4042, 4043, 4103, 4104

D. Reality Spheres of Finite Meaning Structure   (y)
(1) The paramount reality; what distinguishes it   (r)
(2) The fantasy worlds (a) their time-character
(b) their social structure

(3) Attention à la vie; tension of consciousness
(4) The transcendental experience
(5) Transition to the theory of the role of the systems of signs
and symbols in the life-world
4022-4029, 4034-4036, 4076, 4077, 4078, 5001, 5006, 5001-5009,   (w)
5010, 5011-5014, 5015-5023, 5024-5030

E. Signs and Symbols in the Life-World   (y)
  (1) Appresentation (a) of objects of perception   (r)
               (b) on understanding the Other
               (c) on the structure of signs
  (2) Marks
  (3) Indications
             in solitude   in the social world
  (4) Signs
  (5) Symbols
    (2)–(5) only cross references to Chap. V
4048-4049   (w)
II: A–E: 1006, 3094-99, A: 1007, 1008, 1009, C: 1008, 1009

F.? Relevance Spheres   (y)
5002-5003   (w)

Chapter 3

Knowledge of the Life-World: Relevance and Typology   (b)

A. The Stock of Knowledge at Hand and its Structure   (y)
  (1) Knowledge about and knowledge of acquaintance   (r)
  (2) Mere belief, its levels, blindness
  (3) Degrees of clarity and distinctness—Cause of the inequality of
     the levels of clarity
  (4) The pragmatic motive and operationalism
  (5) Subjective correlates of the structuring
     of the stock of knowledge (a) situation   (r)
                   (b) biography
                   (c) interests
  (6) The incoherence of the stock of knowledge explained by its
     genesis, especially by the many forms of interruption of the
     stock of knowledge
1015, 3030, 3031   (w)

B. The Situation   (y)
  (a) The ontological world structure is imposed   (r)

(1) Ontological world-structure of the physical world
temporal (sugar-water, waiting)
spatial (N.Y.—London)
causal (experienced causality, in-order-to, because, means, ends)
(2) Ontological world-structure of the social world, historicity, superordination, subordination
  (b) Biographical: (r)
    Content of the stock of knowledge
    Its genesis: from experiences of various
        duration
        intensity
        sequence
  (c) "Definition of the situation": its subjective and objective meaning
1016, 1017, 1018, 1019, 1048   (w)

C. Plan-determined Interest   (y)
  (1) Again: the pragmatic system of motives   (r)
  (2) The definition of the situation as a function of selective interest
    (a) by selection of components of the objective world
    (b) by selection of elements of the stock of knowledge (biographically therefore)
    which are relevant for:
  (3) (a) Orientation in the situation
    (b) Mastery of the situation
1016, 1018, 1019, 1020, 1022, 1048   (w)

D. Relevance   (y)
  (a) The three kinds of relevance   (r)
    (1) Motivational relevance: its insightfulness
    Connection of the stock of knowledge and definition of situation in the sense of motive-relevance
    (2) Thematic relevance: that which is worth inquiring into; Connection with advertence, attention, passive synthesis, problem of "First things first"
    (3) Interpretational relevance: clarification of association, habitual acquisition, overlapping, concealment, wakening, pairing
  (b) Connection of the three kinds of relevance   (r)
    (1) The context of meaning in which each of them stands
    (2) The context of meaning between them; how this is established by the consciousness
    (3) Doubt and the genuine situation of doubt
    (4) Carneades' problem as an illustration

(c) Conclusions from the theory of relevance   (r)
    (1) Relevance and typification
    (2) Accessibility of the stock of knowledge
    (3) Opaqueness of the life-world
    (4) When is a problem transferred to questionableness?
    (5) Aporias and empty places
    (6) To live in the relevances and to look at them   (r)
(d) Social conditionedness of the structure of relevance
    (1) *General:* Dependence on the arrangement of the social
        world into surrounding world, contemporary world,
        world of predecessors, posterity; the paramount position
        of the surrounding world
    (2) The social distribution of knowledge
    (3) Socially derived knowledge
    (4) Socially approved knowledge
    (5) The well-informed citizen
    (6) Models
    (7) Self-interpretation of the in-group and the out-group   (r)
        (following up on II c d 4)
    (8) Language
    (9) Pragmatic techniques for mastering life
    (10) Standardization of ends and means
    (11) Problems of a genuine sociology of knowledge
(e) Digression on relevance and world   (r)
1016, 1020, 1021, 1022, 1023, 1024, 1025, 1027, 1029, 1030, 1031,   (w)
1032, 1033, 1034, 1035, 1056, 1057, 1058, 1059, 4044, 4045, 4046,
4050, 4051

E. Typification
    (1) Husserl's theory of pre-predicative typification   (r)
    (2) What is atypical?
    (3) Typifications in the sphere of predicative judgments
        S is p, but also q and r
        Cross-reference to the connection with relevance
    (4) Type and concept
    (5) Type and eidetic reduction:
        Where do the types which are to be run through in free
        variations in the fantasy and their typical styles come
        from?
    (6) Piaget—Goldstein on the formation of types
(b) Typology founds similarity   (r)
    (1) Husserl's view
    (2) "Typical, "same," "similar" experiences
    (3) The recurrent experience
    (4) "Suppression of the primes"
(c) Types as construction
    (1) Ideal type and constructive type

(2) Course-of-action and personal type
(3) Remark on the change of the concept of type in Max
Weber's thinking
1028, 1037, 1039, 1040, 1044, 1045, 1046, 1047, 1049, 1050,   (w)
1051, 2003, 3089

F. Typology, Stock of Experience, Knowledge of the Future   (y)
(1) The typified stock of knowledge as source of new
type-formations
(2) Clarity and distinction of the pre-established type
(3) Its consistency (harmony)
(4) Normalcy (Husserl)
(5) Essential and non-essential types
(6) Adequacy of the type
(7) Future knowledge: the problems of Tiresias
(a) The possible   difference between
(b) The probable   future imposed events
(c) The plausible   and such as are under
my control
1043, 1049, 5003   (w)

G. Typology as relevance-conditioned   (y)
(1) Problem-relation of types, hence situation and   (r)
relevance relation
(2) There is no absolute type, each type has a
problem-referring index
(3) Are all three kinds of reference involved in type-formation?
1025, 1026, 1063   (w)

H. Types from the Social World   (r)
(1) Typification of the Other in the co-worldly relation
(2) Apprehension of the partial contents of one's self
(3) Fullness and anonymity
(4) Self-typification: I and me
(5) Social role
(6) Alter ego and alter tu (Ortega)
1059, 1060, 4048–4049, 4052–4058   (w)

I. Socialization of the type-formation   (r)
(a) Pre-position of the typification of the Other and self-
typification in the social world
(1) —as store of socio-culturally derived knowledge, which is
mediated by tradition, and indeed as habitual property
(2) —as standardized form of the stock of knowledge with
predesignated relevance structure
(3) —as institutionalization (law, mores)
(4) —as social restraint
(5) —as etiquette (China)

(b) Some prominent writers on this problem   (r)
   (1) Heidegger: one, talk, authenticity
   (2) Berdyaev: solitude
   (3) Buber: I and thou
   (4) Ortega: custom, alter tu
   (5) Parsons: social rule
1061, 1062, 4041   (w)

Chapter 4

The Life-World as the
Realm of Practice   (b)

A. Behavior, Action, Motives   (y)
   (1) Definitions of behavior, conduct, action   (r)
   (2) Critique of behaviorism
   (3) In-order-to and because-motives
   (4) Time-structure of motivations and
   (5) of the project
   (6) Wm. James: flying stretches and resting places
1065, 4068, 4071–4075, 4079–4086   (w)

B. The Project: Its Fantasy Character   (y)
   (1) Its fantasy character   (r)
   (2) Limitations by the postulate of practicability
   (3) Conditions of practicability:
      potestivility (Husserl, "power to act")
      Ontological structure of the world
      I can—you can etc.
      World within reach and manipulatory area
   (4) What does "possibility" (praxological) mean?
      Open and problematic possibility
      (a) In connection with relevance structure
      (b) Choosing among projects of actions
      (c) Cross-reference to sciences of action in the social sciences   (r)
   (5) Projecting = thinking *modo potentiali*, not optatively
   (6) Projecting is typical action, not course-of-action
   (7) Project and sciences
   (8) The relevance of ends and means
   (9) The expected, the unexpected, the new
  (10) Objective and subjective chance; power to act
  (11) Revocability of the project, irrevocability of the act   (r)
  (12) No choice for the past, but probably reinterpretability of the
      past by the respective present

(13) Why the completed action is necessarily different from the
project
1041, 1042, 1043, 1064, 1065, 1066, 1067, 2001, 2002, 2003, 2004   (w)

C. Choice between Projects of Action   (y)
    (1) Origin in genuine (problematic) situation of doubt (even if   (r)
    only one project: whether to carry it out or not)
    (2) What is the meaning of "open to choice"?
    (3) Husserl's theory of choice (doubt, weight)
    (4) The world beyond question, the general framework of open
    possibilities
    (5) Choice between objects within identical reach
    (6) Choice between goals of action
    (7) Bergson's theory of the act of choice; critique of the same
    (8) Leibniz's theory   (r)
    (9) Comparison of the Husserl-Bergson-Leibniz theories
    (10) Positive and negative weight based on relevance structure
    (11) The systems of interests as correlates of the system of action
    Action systems
    Motivational systems
    End-means systems
    Project-purpose systems
    (12) Plan-hierarchies, life-plan
    (13) Connection with the stock of knowledge at the time of
    projecting
    (14) The horizon of indeterminancy of choice
2005, 2006, 2007, 2008, 2009, 2010, 2011, 2012, 2013, 2014,   (w)
2015, 2016, 2017, 2018, 2019, 2020, 2021, 2022, 2023, 2024, 2025,
2026, 2029

D. Reciprocal (Social) Action   (y)
    (1) Concatenation of motives: A's in-order-to motive becomes B's   (r)
    because-motive
    (2) Underlying general assumption:
    Idealization of the reciprocity of motives
2033, 2034, 2035, 3036, 3037   (w)

E. Interpretation of the Act   (y)
    (1) Understanding the course of the act, understanding motive,   (r)
    understanding the personal type
    (2) Understanding motives and chains of motives as a type
    (anonymity), as an individual event
    (3) Meaning of subjective and objective interpretation
    (4) Only the actor knows the scope of his project
        (a) What is given in the Other's course-of-action?
    (5) Limits of understanding
    (6) Standardization increases its chances

(7) Partner and observer: difference of the situations
  —motives—relevance systems
2030, 2031, 2035, 2036, 2037, 2038, 2039, 2040, 2041, 2042,   (w)
2043, 2047, 4070, 4088, 4089

F. Action in the Surrounding World and the Contemporary World   (y)
  (1) Possibility of subjective interpretation in the pure we-
    relationship: To live in the Other's duration by simultaneity
    with external event
  (2) Contemporary-world social action: its anonymity series
  (3) Typification of the Other and self-typification
  (4) G. H. Mead's theory of the "generalized other"
  (5) Cooley's "looking-glass effect"
  (6) Example 1: the letter
  (7) Example 2: the team
4090–4094   (w)

G. Rational Action in the Life-World Attitude   (y)
  (1) Purpose-rationality and value-rationality in reference to stock (r)
    of knowledge and relevance system
  (2) Rationality in life-world impracticable;
    What its prerequisites would be
  (3) Can only projects or also completed acts be rational?
  (4) Is rationality a subjective or an objective concept?
  (5) Reasonableness is not rationality
  (6) Rationality within a pregiven framework of typicality
2027, 2028, 2043, 2044, 2045, 2046, 2047   (w)

Chapter 5

The Transcendences of the Life-World and Their Overcoming by Signs and Symbols   (b)

A. Introduction: Signs and Symbols as Stores of the Life-world   (y)
  (1) Reference to arrangement of the life-world in manifold areas
    of reality
  (2) The Thomas theorem on the reality of the social world
  (3) "Reality" of the contemporary world, the world of
    predecessors, and the world of posterity
  (4) Communication possible only by means of signs (symbols)
  (5) Ernst Cassirer's view: The *animal symbolicum* in the life-world
3007, 3008   (w)

B. Survey of the State of the Problem in the Literature   (y)
  (1) Problem of the "natural" and "conventional" sign   (r)

(2) The "conventional" sign already presupposes the life-world social structure

(3) "Interchangeability" of the sign with the "signified"

(4) Husserl's theory of "indication," "sign," "meaningful sign," "sign as expression" in the *Logical Investigations* and *Ideas;* critique of this theory

3031, 3002, 3003, 3004, 3005, 3006, 3032, 3033   (w)

C. Husserl's Theory of Appresentation, Expanded and Applied   (y)

(1) Description of the theory   (r)

(2) Appresentation: Its style of verification and realization

(3) The orders involved in appresentation: The apperceptual; appresentational scheme, referential scheme; contextual or interpretational scheme

(4) Why each of these 4 schemes can serve as reference scheme

3009, 3010, 3011, 3012, 3013, 3014, 3015, 3038, 3039, 3040,   (w)
3041, 3042, 3092, 3093, 2094, 3095, 3096, 3097, 3098, 3099

D. Bergson's Theory of Multiple Orders   (y)

(a) Bergson:

(1) The concept of disorder; "The two orders and disorder"

(2) His theory applied to controversial views, e.g., sign and symbol

(b) *Principles of the structural change of appresentative relations:*

(α) Principle of the irrelevance of the vehicle

(β) Principle of the variability of appresentative being

(γ) Principle of figurative transference

3016, 3017, 3018, 2019   (w)

E. Signs and the Experience of Transcendence: (y)

(I) *Solitary persons*

(Motives for developing and using signs and symbolic relations)   (r)

(1) World within reach, the manipulative sphere transcended

(2) Actual reach and reach presumed to be restorable leads to *marks*

(3) Transcendence of contexts in the life-world as opposed to opaque pre-given and taken-for-granted relations leads to the *indication*. The indication helps the individual to transcend the life-worldly world within reach.

3007, 3008, 3020, 3021, 3022, 3023, 3024, 3025, 3026, 3027,   (w)
3028, 3029, 3030, 3031

F. Signs and the Experience of Transcendence;   (y)

(II) *Intersubjective*

(a) Husserl's theory of understanding the Other   (r)

(1) Appresentational knowledge of the Other's consciousness

  (2) Appresentational knowledge of cultural objects
 (b) The three transcendences of the Other's world by means
  of the sign:
   (1) The Other's world within reach (and the Other's
    manipulatory area) transcends mine
   (2) Transcendence of the Other's existence itself in the
    pure we-relationship because
     (α) only a small sector of biographical intermeshing is
      shared
     (β) only a part of the personality enters into
      relationship
     (γ) the relevance systems transcend
   (3) the we-relationship as such; sociality in general   (r)
    transcends my and your existence
 (c) The analysis undertaken under (b) refers only to the pure
  life-worldly we-relationship (face-to-face relationship).
  Transcendences of other social spheres and display of their peculiar
  styles.
   (1) the contemporaneous world
   (2) the world of predecessors
   (3) the world of posterity
3034, 3035, 3036, 3037, 3038, 3039, 3040, 3041, 3042, 3043,   (w)
3044, 3045, 3046, 3047, 3048, 3049, 3050

G. The World without Question Interpreted by Signs   (y)
 (a) Comprehension, manifestation, communication   (r)
   (1) Definition of the terms
   (2) Preconditions
 (b) Signs, definition and kinds
   (1) Provisional definition
   (2) Kinds of sign:
    purposive movement ⎫
    expressive movement ⎬ according to Snell
    imitative movement ⎭
 (c) Signs in communication proper   (r)
   (1) Vehicle in the outer world as bearer
   (2) Interpretational and expressive scheme (attitudinal
    relation [in reference to (1) and (2)])
   (3) Discursive (linguistic), pictorial, expressive, mimetic
    depiction (see V G b 2)
   (4) Polythetic and monothetic positing and interpretation
   (5) The communicative process as time-object
   (6) Examples: Making music together   (r)
      Mozart
      Knight, Death, and Devil (Husserl)
 (d) Connection of the systems of signs interpreting the world
  with the system of types and relevances

(1) interpreted according to apperceptual schemes
(2) interpreted according to appresentational schemes
(3) interpreted according to interpretational schemes
(4) Realization of the world with appresentational
    meaning factors
3051, 3052, 3053, 3054, 3055, 3056, 3057, 3058, 3059, 3060,   (w)
3061, 3062, 3063, 3064, 3065, 3066, 3073, 3074, 3075,
(4001–4005), (4007–4008), 4029, 4028, 4040

H. The Transcendence of Nature and of Society   (y)
   Its Overcoming by the Symbol
   (1) The experience of this transcendence   (r)
   (2) Provisional definition of the symbol
   (3) Origin of symbolic appresentation
   (4) Peculiarities of symbolic appresentation
   (5) Symbol as appresentation of multiple spheres of reality
   (6) Final definition of the symbol
   (7) The experience of the leap (shock) in the transition to other
       spheres of reality
   (8) Examples of systems of symbols
       (a) Poetry
       (b) Science
3067, 3068, 3071, 3072, 4009, 4010, 4011, 4013, 4014, 1015/16,   (w)
4017–4021, 4022–4028, 4029;
3076–3099, 4001, 4006, 4007–4008;
4030, 4031, 4032, 4033, 4034, 4035, 4036, 4037, 4038,
4039, 4048, 4049, 5010

I. Symbol and Society   (y)
   (a) "The symbol establishes community without communication"   (r)
       (Jaspers), his theory
   (b) The dependence of the appresentational symbolic relation on
       the social environment
   (c) Society itself symbolically appresented
       by the self-interpretation of the in-group,
       by interpretation of the out-group
Note: the above outline (a)–(c) has to be articulated even more closely
4017, 4018, 4019, 4020, 4021, 4040, 4041, 4042,   (w)
4043–4047, 4052–4058

Chapter 6

The Sciences of the Social World   (b)

A. Life-World as Unexamined Ground of All Sciences   (y)
   (1) All scientific inquiry begins with that which has become   (r)

questionable, but was previously unquestioned, and ends by transferring it to new unquestionedness

(2) Husserl's doctrine of the origin of natural science in the life-world

(3) Husserl's doctrine of the genealogy of logic in the life-world

2069, 5031–5049 (w)

B. On the Phenomenology of the Natural Attitude (y)
(1) Husserl's view in the "Postscript" (r)
(2) Husserl's views in the *Crisis*
(3) Husserl's views   B   I   15 & 16
(4) Is a real ontology of the social world possible as an eidetic science?
(5) Husserl's concept of the "human and social sciences" *(Geisteswissenschaften)* and their tasks
(6) Husserl's successors: E. Stein, G. Walter, Scheler

2073 (w)

C. Natural Science and Social Science (y)
(a) The alleged difference between natural-scientific and social-scientific methods (r)
(1) State and causes of the controversy
(2) Both [are] empirical sciences
(3) To what extent is logical positivism (behaviorism) justified?
(4) What the logical positivist posits as simply given—the social world—is the subject matter of the social sciences
(b) Understanding and clarifying (r)
(1) Understanding is not a category of the social sciences, but a method of life-world practice
(2) Three methodical meanings of the concept of understanding
(3) Understanding and subjective meaning
(4) Arguments against behaviorism
(c) Fundamental difference between objects of thought of the natural and the social sciences. The two-levels theory

2060, 2061, 2062, 2064, 2065, 2066, 2067, 2070, 2071 (w)

D. What is the Subject-Matter of Social Science? (y)
(1) Does social science refer to life-world reality? (r)
(2) What is social reality?
(3) Common sense and scientific interpretation
(4) Are social collectivities "real"? And if so, for whom?

2032, 2063 (w)

E. The Social Scientist and his Situation (y)
   (1) The difference between scientific activity and the theoretical (r)
   scientific attitude. To what extent theoretical science is carried
   on within the life-world, as Husserl believes.
   (2) What the decision to make the theoretical leap involves for
   the (social) scientist
   (a) he is an observer
   (b) he stands outside the life-world situation
   (c) he brackets out his biography and the relevance systems
   anchored therein
   (d) The scientific situation (r)
   The scientific problem-relevance
   The scientific decision
2050, 2051, 2052, 5031–5049 (w)

F. Life-Worldly and Scientific Interpretation of the Social World (y)
   (1) The scientific model of the social life-world according to the (r)
   two-level theory
   (2) Types of processes—types of motivation—homunculi
   (3) Nature ("consciousness") of the homunculi
   (4) Interaction of the homunculi
   (5) Postulates for the construction of social scientific
   thought-models
   (a) Postulate of subjective interpretation in the sense of
   tracing back all social phenomena to individual action
   (b) Problem of the objective grasping of subjective (r)
   meaning-contexts
   (c) Problem and "datum"; that which is posited as given
   without question (scientifically accepted)
   (d) The problem as "locus" of all types relevant to its solution
2048, 2049, 2053, 2054, 2055, 2056, 2057, 2058, 2059 (w)

G. Postulates of Social Scientific Construction (y)
   see card VI F 5 a–d (r)
   (1) Postulate of logical consistency
   (2) Postulate of subjective interpretation
   (3) Postulate of adequation
   (4) Postulate of rationality (in a few cases)
   (5) What does "rationality" mean in this case?
2058, 2059 (w)

H. The Unity of Science and the Problem of Continuity (y)
   (1) Critique of "monolithic science" on a logical-positivist (r)
   (natural-scientific) foundation
   (2) The true unity of science warranted by its origin in the
   life-world

(3) It is, therefore, oriented not natural-scientifically but human- and social-scientifically (in Husserl's sense)—

(4) whereby it remains doubtful whether eidetic and transcendental phenomenology can fulfill Husserl's hopes

(5) Such a science of the social world fulfills the positivists' justified postulate of "continuity."

2072 (w)

Survey of Contents
of the Notebooks

[The following survey was taken over from the survey of contents begun by Schutz. The survey of the additional notebooks was made by the editor of the manuscripts (Thomas Luckmann).]

First Notebook

1.

2.

3.

4.

Second Notebook

4.

184

APPENDIX

Fourth Notebook

7. continued

Fifth Notebook

7. *continued*

Contents of the
Notebooks and Dictionary

First Notebook

1. Bar Harbor Ms. 1957; (Theory of Relevance)

[I.] The Life World as Unexamined Ground of the Natural Worldview

That Which Is Taken for Granted. Its Dubiousness and Questionableness

The Relative-Natural Worldview

Spatial, Temporal, Social Strata of the Life-World

Structures of Reality

Subjective Correlate: The Stock of Knowledge and Its Structure

Interest

Situation: (a) Ontological Structure of the World
              (b) (Auto)biographical definition

The Interests (especially the Plan-Determined Ones)

Motivational Relevance

Familiarity: Its Role for the Unity of the Meaning Context

Thematic Relevance

Attention
First Things First

Interpretational Relevance

Typology as Problem-Oriented. Relation to Pre-Acquaintanceship

Pairing, passive synthesis

Carneades problem

Relevance and Typification
Accessibility of the Stock of Knowledge
Aporias of the Knowable, the Empty Place
Living within the Relevances
Social Conditionedness of Relevance

Social Conditionedness of the Relevance Systems

Communicative (?) Environment (Husserl)

Typification, Experience and Judgment

Typification according to the Structures of Relevance

What Is Atypical?

> Prepredicative Typification, Sartre, Merleau-Ponty
> The Sphere of Predicative Judgments

Type and Concept

II. *Choosing Among Projects of Action*

Open and Problematic Possibilities

Science of Rational Action: Transformation of the First into the Second

Stock of Experience—Typology—Relevance (continued in Notebook II)

III. Tiresias problem

IV. *Common Sense and Scientific Interpretation of Human Action*

Typology

Definition of the Situation

Repeated Action (Suppression of the "Primes")

The Intersubjective Character of the Life-World and of Our Knowledge of it

Axioms of Life-World Knowledge (Idealizations)

Social Origin of Knowledge: Genetic Socialization
> Social Distribution of Knowledge

Articulation of the Social World: We, You, Fellowman, Consociate, World of
> Predecessors and Posterity

Self-Typification

Socialization of the Type-Formation of Human Action

Typification and Relevance

Course-of-Action and Personal Types

Theory of Action

"I Can" and Its Declension

Project and Empowerment

Second Notebook, Seelisberg

IV. Common Sense, Theory of Action and of the Project continued

Choosing: Doubt

III. *Again Choosing:* Choosing between Projects of Action

Choosing: Husserl, Problematic and Open Possibilities; his Point of Departure
> from the Modalization of the Prepredicative Judgments

The Choice Itself
  Choice between Several Projects of Action
Bergson's Theory of the Act of Choice
Motives: Leibniz's Theory of Volition
Positive-Negative Weight
(Perfectly) Rational Order
Intersubjectivity and Mutual Understanding of the Actors in the Life-World
Interpretation of Action in the Social Life-World by the Social Sciences
IV. Common Sense continued
Social Action (Relations of Acts)
In-Order-To and Because Intermeshing
Idealization of the Reciprocity of Motives
Subjective Determination of the Project (Where is the Ink?)
Scope of the Project
Subjective Interpretation of the Action
The Observer
Rational Action Within the Life-World
The Construction of Objects of Thought by the Social Sciences
Difference between This and the Construction of Life-World Thinking
The Scientific Model of the Social Life-World
Postulates for the Scientific Construction of Such Models
V. Concept and Theory Formation
Social Science—Natural Science
Social Reality
Arguments against Behaviorism
Life-World *a priori* Intersubjectively Meaningful
Understanding
Fundamental Difference between Thought Objects of the Natural and the
  Social Science
The Unity of Science. Postulate of Continuity
VI. Thematic Areas from the Essay for Van Breda's Husserl
  Commemorative Volume

Third Notebook

VI. Sign & Symbol
For further elaboration:
Equality

Making Music Together
Well Informed Citizen
Stranger
Homecomer
Language and Language Disturbances
Tiresias
Gurwitsch Polemic against Multiple Realities

Dictionary

mark	merkmal
stratification	Schichtung
taken for granted	als gegeben hingenommen
beyond question	froglos gegeben
indication	Anzeichen
sign	Zeichen

First Notebook

from Seelisberg, Switzerland

August 12 – 16, 1958

Contains: pp. 1001 – 1067

Motto to the whole:
The greatest miracle of all
is that the true, the genuine
miracles can, and should come
to seem so commonplace to us.

Lessing, *Nathan the Wise*,
Act I, Scene 2

(Bar Harbor Ms. 1957)
[1001] The life-world as the unexamined ground of the relative natural conception of the world

Characteristics of life-world thinking
the idealities of "and-so-forth" and "I can do it again."—
Basic assumptions: constancy of the world-structure
                   constancy of the validity of previous experience
                   constancy of the power to act upon the world

Hence:
       Its familiarity;
          pre-interpretedness;
       our power to act upon it

Restriction of the investigation
       to *wide-awake* experience of the world by *adults* [1002]

Nature of what is given without question

       Its self-evidence
          as incomprehensibleness; opaqueness;
          which can nevertheless be brought to self-understanding

APPENDIX

Its unquestionedness
which can be put in question, if it becomes questionable—above
all in the sense of being worth questioning.

It becomes problematic,
a theoretical, practical-emotional problem

Everything problematic originates on the ground of unquestionedness—problem-solving consists in transferring what has become
questionable to a new unquestionedness.—
Antithesis to Dewey's theory of inquiry [1003]

The relative-natural world-view (Scheler)
(a) has stood the test so far
(b) is therefore assumed as given until further notice
(c) the experiences, beliefs, etc. are by no means necessarily consistent and
    compatible one with the other
(d) but their intrinsic inconsistency and incompatibility merely discovered if
    a novel experience not subsumable under the so far unquestioned
    frame of reference turns up.
(e) *Truth* not a goal of this type of knowledge, merely *plausibility*.

Digression on *epistēmē* and *doxa* [1004]
    Horizons of questionableness surrounded by the unquestioned. Ho-
rizon as determinable indeterminacy =
    unquestionedness assumed in principle to be questionable (though not
    worth questioning at the moment, but surely as open to question) (Must
    be checked closely)
Even what is taken for granted without question has its horizons of
    explication.
The unending task of explicating horizons.

Second main question: When does this process of explication stop?
                         When do we declare the problem we are con-
                         cerned with as solved "for all good and useful
                         purposes"?

First main question: How does the posing of a problem come about at all?
                        [1005]

Opaqueness of the unquestioned preinterpretedness.
The true recipe; incomprehension of its effect;
    Modifiability of the recipe; [1006]

A. Stratifications of the life-world [quasi-ontologically] in three ways:
    I.   Spatially
    II. Temporally
    III. Socially

B. Stratifications of the life-world into its reality structure

The *paramount* reality of everyday life

—in which actions that change the world are possible; other actions can undo a change, but mere cancellation does not suffice,

—in which communication with the other reality becomes possible, precisely because actions can gear into the outer world;

Fantasy worlds in various stratifications

The world of dreams

C. *In structures of signs and symbols* [1007]

AI. *Spatial structuring of the life-world*

My Here and Now as orientation (coordinate) center

World within actual reach

> Within (?) this—sometimes overlapping with it—the world within the actual manipulatory sphere

World within my potential reach

> (a) World that was formerly within actual reach no longer is so, but can be brought back within actual reach: world within my *restorable reach*.
>
>> Underlying idealization: I will, after reach is restored, again find the world within former reach to be "the same," or possibly, "the same, but changed," with the same gradations of feasibility.
>>
>> Meaning of this statement.
>
> (b) World that was never within my reach but can be brought into it; *attainable reach*
>
> Here several groups of subproblems result [1008]

A. Differences of possibility and power

> I can, I could ⎫ Husserl
> I could, but I cannot ⎭
>
> Technical, logical, physical impossibility;
>
> Variations of the spheres of possibility with the help of tool, implement, instrument

B. Social articulation:

> (c) World within your actual reach that can be brought into mine by changing locations.
>
>> With respect to power to act:
>>
>> (You can move from there, I from here;
>>
>> If I were there, I could do what you can.)
>>
>> Is this statement reversible?
>
> What are the conditions for the restoration of such an articulation? [1009]
>
> On the other hand: Although theoretically from your position I

could see what you see (could reach, perform, etc.) I cannot because I am myopic (too short, too weak) etc.

Degree of familiarity of this zone: based on the typology of the actual restorable world previously experienced by me.

The range of variation of my possible experience from your actual experience (is) attributed to the difference of our respective biographical situations.

 (d) world within your former and
  (α) restorable
  (β) nonrestorable reach
 (e) world within your attainable reach by reference to actuality, or to restorable potentiality
  (α) of a third party
  (β) of everyone
 (f) world within potential reachableness for everyone willing, able, and fit. [1010]

Basic differences of the world and thus of the situation
 (a) as imposed upon me
 (b) and as within my actual or potential control (mastery)
  (a) unmodifiable
  (b) transformable

Relativity of this division of respective knowledge; yet limitation by the metaphysical fact: e.g. my finitude; Fink's discussion-remark on my death and that of the Other, my answer thereto. [1011]

A II. Time structure in objective time has the following subjective correlates
 Actuality: refers to interpretable horizons and stock of experience.
 Restorability to retentions and recollection
 Reachableness: to protentions and anticipations
Special problems: the world existed before my birth—both the physical and the social world.
 Historicity:
 of the inanimate
 of the animate world
 Sedimentation of prior events—as signs or indications [1012]

A III. *Social world*

surrounding world	fellowman
contemporary world	consociate
prior world	predecessor
subsequent world	successor

surrounding world: face to face; commonness (of) time and space: the bodies of both within reciprocal reach; but nevertheless: merely overlapping of the manipulatory spheres

contemporary world: no reciprocal reach, but common time
$\qquad$ articulation according to the typification of $\lessgtr$
$\qquad$ fullness or emptiness
$\qquad$ intimacy $\qquad$ anonymity
$\qquad$ distance
$\quad$ contemporary world as restorable (or not) or attainable surrounding
world

prior world: it acts on us, we do not act on it;
$\qquad$ historicity; ever new interpretability

world of posterity: in principle, empty anonymity;
$\qquad$ we act upon it, it not upon us; [1013]
Special problems of the social world:
$\qquad$ (1) the dead $\qquad$ Husserl: on Thomas theorem
$\qquad\qquad\qquad\qquad\qquad$ witches
$\qquad$ (2) the unborn
$\qquad$ (3) totemism
$\qquad$ (4) the gods
$\qquad$ (5) social world on the same levels of reality,
$\qquad\qquad$ (a) in the paramount reality: basic supposition of all commu-
$\qquad\qquad\quad$ nicableness through events in it;
$\qquad\qquad$ (b) built up on (a) diverse fantasy-communication; children
$\qquad\qquad\quad$ playing, congregation praying, the schizophrenic's voices;
$\qquad\qquad\quad$ varieties of religious experience; playing together; but
$\qquad\qquad\quad$ not dreaming together.
$\qquad\qquad$ (c) built up on (b): highly complex communication by sym-
$\qquad\qquad\quad$ bols 1st, 2nd .., nth valency; e.g. the work of art. [1014]

$\quad$ The life-worldly social world as taken for granted:
$\qquad$ in its typifications
$\qquad$ symbolizations
$\qquad$ recipes of our action upon it
$\qquad$ its action upon us
$\qquad$ degrees of our—its power to act
$\qquad$ { our expressive schemes upon it
$\qquad$ { our interpretative scheme in it
culture → in group—our-group
$\qquad$ { Everyone "who is one of us" = shares our expressive and
$\qquad$ { interpretative scheme
codeterminative for:
$\qquad$ what has to be considered a type
$\qquad$ meaning of the concretely used symbols
$\qquad$ what is taken for granted as "self-evident"
$\qquad$ what is questionable and worth questioning
$\qquad$ statements of the problem and interlockings
$\qquad$ typical admissible solutions of problems; when is a problem
$\qquad\quad$ considered adequately solved?

APPENDIX

socialization of knowledge:

instruments	socially derived	which leads to new expressive
recipes	socially approved	and interpretative schemes taken
user's instructions	socially distributed	for granted and accepted [1015]
maxims		

structure of the stock of knowledge

knowledge about, how	knowledge of acquaintance
knowledge of acquaintance, what degrees	knowledge of familiarity
of clarity	certainty, uncontradictedness

mere belief

ideal-typical nature of this division	well-founded
	plausible
	presumable
	reliance on authority
	complete ignorance

Digression on *doxa* and *epistēmē*
Digression on William James and Bergson
Digression on Kallen interpretation
Change of these degrees: learning
                                         trial and error
Change within [the] individual
            from individual to individual
Change within a social group
Change from group to group
Inequality of this social distribution
            of knowledge as a main problem
            of the sociology of knowledge [1016]

Reason for the inequality of the levels of clarity: *relevance*
Motive for the transferral of what is taken for granted into the
            questionable: the problem of becoming-problematic;

Subjective correlates of the structurization of the stock of knowledge: (of the forms
of knowledge)

Interests of the perceiving, thinking individual, acting in the world
            —from his "standpoint" within
                        { the physical
                        { and social } world
                        the world of nature
                        the world of culture
                        historicity
(Leibniz: progress to ever-new apperceptions)

Interests and *situation*
    Concept of the situation
    Concept of the definition of the situation
    Objective and subjective definition of the situation
Mead and Sartre, Merleau-Ponty, *Dempf* [1017]

Two components of the situation
    (a) *ontological structure of the world*
        (i) *temporal* Bergson's sugar water: waiting
        (ii) *spatial* New York–London, Atlantic
        (iii) *experienced causality* in-order-to givenness, means and goal
        relation
    (b) *biographical after previous experience*
      refers not only to the content of experience
      but also to intensity   of the experiencing (lived experiences)
              duration   of the experiencing (lived experiences)
              sequence   of the experiencing (lived experience)
    One-eyed twins, first Plato, then Aristotle, and vice versa
    Bergson's canons, Peter and Paul

(a) in terms of (b):
Biographically, [the] ontologi[cal] structure is experienced as conditions of
spontaneity, latitudes of freedom, barrier and diving board, obstacle and
promotion, as *imposed* and *instrumentally manageable*. [1018]

Selection of elements of the ontologically pregiven world
World is always prestructured
    Its elements stand for the experiencing subject in meaning contexts
        of orientation
        of mastery
    Formation of theoretical
        axiomatic
        practical
        and how reference would have to be made symbolical
    structural contexts, subjectively experienced as
        contexts of interest
        problem areas
        systems of projects with inherent practicabilities.

All these, together with their intermeshings
    experienced by the individual as
        system of his plans
          for hour and day,
            work and leisure,
            life plan.
"Plan," as used here, involves neither transparency
                nor intentionality
                nor voluntariness.

Plan and plan-system can also be imposed. There is also an in-order-to and because-relation in the realization of a plan. Exclusions and incompatibilities: in short, laws of *pragmatic* [1019] consequence, just as there are laws of *axiological* consequence. Presumably the laws of pragmatic consequence are based on the components of the situation contributed by the ontological world structure, those of axiological consequence [on] components contributed by the biographical and *social* components. For, besides the ontological and biographical components of the situation, there is, as still has to be elaborated upon, the social determinant of the individual situation.

On the ontological structure of the world: here there are *spheres of incompatibility.* These [are] important for describing, e.g., the problematic and open possibilities, the end-means choice, the practicability of the planned project, the alternatives "open to choice," etc.

But are there also spheres of incompatibility in the biographical (perhaps the "feasibilities" = "I can and yet I cannot" are of such a kind) and social (here certainly) components of the situation? This [must] be investigated. [1020]

The plan-determined interest selects
> *on the one hand* the components of the objective world that the individual chooses in order to define his situation subjectively,
> *on the other hand* (Husserl would say "together" with it) those elements of the stock of knowledge at hand, with whose help the situation is defined.

In other words: in the last analysis it is interest that determines which
> elements of the ontological structure of the pregiven world and of the stock of knowledge at hand are relevant to define his situation
>> in thought, action, emotions,
>> to find one's bearings in it,
>> to master it

Since this relevance is experienced subjectively as motive for defining the situation it shall be called

Motivation-relevance [1021]

Degrees of insight into motivational relevance
> as imposed from the outside
> as a manifestation of inner spontaneity of every form
>> (*petites perceptions*—drive—depth-psychology up to rational action)

Degree of clarity of insight dependent upon the structure of the actual stock of knowledge, out of whose elements [the] situation is defined.

Connection between the stock of knowledge and definition of the situation in the sense of motivational relevance

Stock of knowledge as the sediment of our experiences of prior definitions of the situation of the world within one's own or another's reach in all its variations.

Situation to be defined at present may be the same, similar, modified, varied, or new from those standing ready in the stock of knowledge—
at least typically (see Type [cf. Index, Vol. I, p. 335; Vol. II below,
p. 339–*trans.*])
Here a study or digression on Husserl's synthesis of recognition [1022]

Important: that the subsumption of the situation now to be defined under
elements of the stock of knowledge can refer to such different levels of
knowledge and clarity.

Two cases: These elements are sufficient to define the new situation: Then this situation is experienced as "self-evident" and taken for
granted; *routine.*

The elements are either not "foreknown" with "adequate" familiarity, or the situation to be defined cannot—at least with respect to type—
be made to coincide with pre-experienced ones by synthesis of recognition:

Then I must try to "know more" about the pregiven elements,
either by acquiring new elements of knowledge or by transferring old ones
to other degrees of clarity.

Such elements are *relevant* to defining the situation, but this relevance is not motivational relevance, although it is based on it. The relevant
element is no longer taken for granted but is questionable and worth questioning [1023]

This element now becomes the theme of our cognitive consciousness and
should thus be called

Thematic relevance

Relation of thematic relevance to the problem of *attention* (Pradines and
Lalande should be consulted, as well as Bergson).

The hereby-accomplished "isolation" of the theme as a problem to
be mastered, from pregiven problem contexts of a motivational kind,
which are, however, preserved as outer horizons of the theme and are in
principle questionable in new advertences.

We do this in order to determine when we have to break off questioning the thematically relevant because the problem at hand is
"adequately" solved.

First things first—the most important thing first—
Let us cross the bridge when we get to it:
These are all definitions of thematic relevance.

Still to be investigated: What makes "first things" *first?* Here references to ontological structure presumably of the greatest importance.
[1024]

Solution of the thematically relevant problem

It must be made to coincide with [the] elements contained in the stock of
knowledge by penetration into the inner and other horizons—especially its
typical appurtenance to typically foreknown world-phenomena must be
discovered.

But not all elements of the actually present stock of knowledge arranged according to degrees of clarity and certainty are relevant, or equally relevant, for the "theme."

This relevance is of a third kind and shall be called

Interpretational relevance

Associational psychology has studied this, but simply taken for granted the complicated mechanism of interpretational relevance with motivational and thematic relevance, without clarifying how it comes to temporal, spatial contiguity of similarity. [1025]

Clarification of the association from the structure of the stock of experience. This is sedimentation of former thematically relevant material, which now was transferred to taken-for-granted unquestionedness, [and] therefore is no longer a theme but "habitual acquisition" (Cart. Med.).

Transferral to habitual acquisition occurred genetically, based on biographical and situational *motivational* relevances, which determine under what conditions the previously thematic problem has to be considered solved.

All these acquisitions, such as our entire "knowledge" of the life-world—prepredicatively given or arranged in predicative stocks of judgment—are, however, a knowledge of the *typology* of the object and events. This typology [is] in turn dependent on prior *thematic* situations, which had to be defined and which it had to "come to terms with." The degree of familiarity of the knowledge-elements is also determined by this typology (cf. the same) has [a] style of its own in [1026] every degree of familiarity.

Therefore (as must be indicated on closer analysis of the type) there is *no absolute type, but only problem-oriented types* (referential index).

What shall be made to coincide with these pre-existing types—the new thematically relevant problem—is, by a synthesis of recognition (Question: Is it indeed a matter of such?), referred to horizontally and habitually given elements of the stock of experience of the same level of familiarity:

We have already experienced "such a thing" before, or heard of it; the situation to be defined now has—probably, credibly, unfortunately, hopefully—typical similarity with former ones, etc.

Or is it "atypical" (see Type [cf. Index, Vol. I, p. 335; Vol. II below, p. 339—*trans.*]) [1027]

Now, however, even the elements of the prearranged stock of knowledge that are interpretationally relevant stand from the outset in a context of meaning, precisely because the prearranged knowledge originates in "the" transferral of formerly thematic (problematic) material into acquisitions that have become habitual.

The "unity" of the context of meaning is thus "established" by *motivational relevances* that were formerly effective and have been kept within the horizon (are they now neutralized? Is there any such thing as neutralization?) that can now be "questioned."

This constitutes—or at least is co-determinative [of]—autobiography. [1028]

Digression and the main question to be studied:

What is the meaning of "to make coincide"?

What is the meaning of "pairing"? as passive synthesis e.g. of recognition in Husserl's theory?

Is there a passive synthesis in general or is this a *sideroxylon* [iron wood, contradictio in adjective—*trans.*]?

How is all this related to the Kantian three-way synthesis (*Critique of Pure Reason*, 1st edition):

(1) of apprehension   in intuition
(2) of reproduction   in imagination
(3) of recognition   in the concept

Why did Kant, in the second edition, omit this threefold division, or summarize it in the "synthesis of apperception"?

What does all this mean for the clarification of the problem of association?

What does it mean with respect to the problem of learning? [1029]

(Estes Park Ms.)
The problem of Carneades

as illustration of the scheme of relevance [1030]

(BHM [Bar Harbor Ms.—*trans.*] 57)

Conclusions from the theory of relevance.

(1) Relevance and typification

The typifications arranged in the stock of knowledge that result from the solution of formerly thematic problems designate, so to speak, the line of demarcation between the explicated horizons of formerly thematic problems and problems that are left pending until further notice; this [is done] with consideration of the problem-contexts (*systems* of thematic relevances), originating in the subjective correlate of the systems of motivational relevances; i.e., the respective hierarchy of plans arranged under the superordinated life-plan.—For precisely this reason, not only relevances of motivation but also thematic and interpretational relevances, indeed even the typifications resulting from them in processes of sedimentation and habits, and the corresponding degrees of familiarity as our stock of knowledge, stand in a systemic context.

(2) The stock of knowledge is accessible in each case. As such it comprises an element (perhaps the most important one) [1031] of the individual biographical situation. It is the taken-for-granted substratum for the definition and mastery of the physical and social world.

(3) This world is, in principle, opaque, not-understood, and incomprehensible in its ultimate ground by the natural attitude. All this lies in the

nature of its "givenness"; in subjective terms: of my being born into it (Heidegger: thrownness). Only partial contents of the world can, as was just described, be brought into the context of everyday life to the required extent and thereby made transparent.

(4) Insofar as this is not possible, the zones of the world that come in question cannot be transferred to unquestionableness and they remain problematic.

Aporetic categories:
  (a) the unknown, but knowable
  (b) that which is known to be unknowable
ad   (a)   From this results the fact of the empty spot (jigsaw-puzzle problem).
ad   (b)   Multiple Realities, made accessible by Symbols [1032]

(5) *Within* the life-world, i.e. before any reduction is made, the important distinction of attitudes (characterized by Husserl in another context) of "living-in-the-relevances" (whereby the systems of relevances do not come into view at all but are "in grasp") and of reflecting (though not necessarily reflective) "looking-at-the-relevances."

Every vitally important decision places the actor before a set (or sets) of thematic relevances of a hypothetical nature, which are to be interpreted and questioned for motivational incorporation into the life-plan.

Here reference to "Choosing among Projects of Action."

The technique of these referential experiences and decisions would constitute the "art of becoming aware of what one knows," which Leibniz called for. [1033]

(6) Social conditionedness of the relevance systems and of the corresponding typifications (B) *Special* (A follows later).

They are socio-culturally co-determined; namely:

(a) By language (vocabulary and syntax) as typical comprehension of what can, should, and must be said; all this in contrast with what is presupposed as "self-evident" and "self-explanatory"; inner form of speech.

(b) Social (cultural) structuring of the distribution of knowledge (secret knowledge, shared knowledge, etc.) based on political (in domination, group, class, sex, age), economic, professional, professional organization. Here also belongs the technique of the mediation of knowledge and its forms of organization (Scheler); conservation of knowledge by tradition; learning and education.

(c) Pragmatic (praxeological) techniques of mastering life in forms of organization of sub- and super-ordination, of cooperation and conflict; here tools, procedures, social institutions; mores; ethos (Scheler); morality (Sumner);—
and again the Thomas theorem, *perhaps* also Merton's "self-fulfilling prophecy." [1034]

(d) (b) and (c) as means-goal, promotion-impeding for individual planning within the group;

Standardization both of the goals and of the available means; relevance of all these factors;

(e) all this socially derived and socially approved;

(f) self-interpretation of the in-group; interpretation by the out-group—indeed, out-groups; reference to subjective and objective meaning, as suggested in the *Equality* essay;

(g) "models" (Scheler); "types of knowledge" (Scheler);

(h) Systems of symbols, signs, indications—as preconditions for communication;

(i) What belongs to social reality? (see also earlier: the dead (ancestors), the unborn, gods, totem-animals?);

(j) "prelogical" and "postlogical" thinking;

(k) The well-informed citizen; experts; eyewitnesses, etc.

This grouping of the problem (a) to (h) is completely provisional and needs most precise elaboration. [1035]

(BHM 57) (Common Sense)

Social conditionedness of the systems of relevance

(6) (A) *General*

Dependence of the systems of relevance on the arrangement of the social world into surrounding world, world of contemporaries, world of predecessors, and world of successors;
their distance;
their anonymity or contentfulness;
partner, team;
outsider, observer; social scientist;
intermeshing of the problematic of objective-subjective meaning;

Surrounding world: paramount position *because* as a common sector of the spatial and temporal elements equally relevant thematically for both partners; above all, the existing mutual givenness of the Other's body as equally accessible interpretational field of expression and phenomenology (field of the interpretationally relevant).

Husserl's problem of communicative surrounding world; Ortega's problem e.g. of the greeting—and of the ego as "other thou."

Modification of the common or similar systems of relevance of the environmental situation [1036] in increasingly anonymous zones of the contemporary world,
of the world of predecessors and of the surrounding world;

on the other hand:
identicalness or similarity of "relevance-isohypses" |contour lines| as precondition and constitution of any possible communication and of the corresponding communicative environment.

Here particularly worth noting:
(a) Husserl's profound definition of the communicative environment
   (a) as constantly in a state of flux,
   (b) as including only those elements of which the individual defining
   his environment *knows* (cf. in this respect, what was said above about the
   definition of the situation from the acquisition of knowledge).
(b) Sumner (and others) on ingroup—outgroup theory (especially Park,
   Stonequirt)
(c) W. I. Thomas's concept of the definition of the situation
(d) Cooley's "looking-glass effect," William James's "social self," especially
   G. H. Mead's *"generalized other"* as expression of the defining of the situation and of the conformed social system of relevance posited as
   standardized. [1037]

Typification

(1) *Husserl: Experience and Judgment; prepredicative typification*
The world of everyday life is neither the sum of the data of experience nor
the mass of individual things isolated and without relation to one another,
but as types.

   (Similar problematic in W. James's radical empiricism, in Bergson,
in Whitehead, indeed in Dewey.)
   Typification according to structures of relevance:
My dog Fido in typical behavior as healthy and sick (of Theaetetus:
Whether the healthy or sick Socrates is the same person; work through the
entire Theatetetus again with respect to this question), as individual mam-
mal, living being, something in general.

   Which type I choose is determined by thematic relevance!

(2) Atypical objects (or processes):
Ambiguity of the atypical [1038]
Atypical can mean:
(a) Incompatibility of the "atypical" condition experienced in the present
   situation with the previously experienced typifications;
(b) compatibility of the two on a higher level of familiarity is indeed possible or attainable;
(c) what is now thematically relevant shows absolutely new traits that do
   not coincide with elements of the previously acquired stock of
   knowledge;
(d) the "untypified";
(e) what is "untypifiable" because in relation to types at hand precisely
   uniqueness and unrepeatableness is what is of interest.

(Interesting material on this can be found in Fink's chapter on
Parmenides.) Perhaps a terminological distinction between atypical and
type-transcendent could be indicated. [1039]

(3) Compare on this further development of the prepredicative problematic in Sartre and Merleau-Ponty.

(4) Predicative sphere of judgment:

S is p elliptically, for it is also q, r, t . . . , but at the time of making the judgment 'S is p' I am interested thematically only in the p-being of S. Only this is thematically relevant for me at this moment, because this thematic relevance is constituted as theme by the motivational relevances prevalent at the particular biographical point in time.

Here attention and perhaps further elaboration: dialogically dramatic (Kenneth Burke) motivation of the modalities of judgment;

Particularly of the negative judgment: The statement that the whale is not a fish presupposes that I or my partner would have believed, hoped, feared, etc., that it is one. [1040]

(5) Prepredicative or judgmental subdivision of the types: of experientially conditioned sediments and habitualities of the stock of experience is varied, modified, subdivided, which leads to the origin of new subtypes.

(6) The main question still to be analyzed:

How is the transition made from the type to the concept? Possibilities to be investigated:

(a) function of discursive, and indeed mainly linguistic thinking; for are there not also typically musical themes? Is not also every pictorial representation a type? Ideograms (China), emblems, etc. [are] important here.

(b) Dewey's origin of generic concepts

(c) Bergson's attempt at a solution [1041]

(Choosing)

Husserl's distinction between open and problematic possibilities.

Of multiple importance (where should it be inserted?)

(a) What is thematically relevant and has become a problem can become a task both within the framework of the ontologically predesignated spheres of incompatibility (perhaps also of Others) and in the form of the alternatives open to choice. Then "problematic possibility" in which only a finite and relatively slight number of possible solutions to a problem are open to choice, each of which has its "weight." The thematically relevant problem is solved when it can be determined under which of the alternatives available for choice it must be subsumed, a process that in its turn again is predesignated by the comprehensive system of motivational relevances.

(b) Choosing among projects of action

(c) Goal of the sciences of rational action, e.g. economics: the actually existing [1042] open possibilities determinable within the life-world [are] to be interpreted as *systems* of problematic possibilities (see Choosing among Projects of Action, unpublished second part, and correspondence with Adolph Lowe). Illustration: Morgenstern-Neumann's theory of games, especially the Sherlock Holmes example of strategically selectable alternatives. [1043]

(d) Stock of experience, typology, relevance had been studied above only with respect to past (genesis of habituations) and present (synthesis of recognition) experiences and knowledge. What is the situation with our life-world knowledge of future events? Here belong all statements on the

Tiresias-problem [1044]
(Common Sense)
>   *ad types*
>   *Husserl* Experience and Judgment: Section 18–21, 82–85
>   *Schutz* Language: Social Research Vol. 17, 384–90
>> Common Sense 14, 5–7

Husserl: What is experienced in the actual perception of an object is apperceptively transferred to any other similar object, which (?) is perceived merely as to its type. Actual experience will or will not confirm my anticipation of the typical conformity with other objects. If confirmed, the content of the anticipated type is enlarged; at the same time the type is split up into subtypes; on the other hand, the concrete real object shows its individual characteristics, which nevertheless have a form of typicality.

(This is a translation of the summary in Common Sense p. 5)
Now I *can* take the typically perceived object as an exemplar of the general type and [1045] thus be led to the concept of the type, but I *must* by no means take the concrete dog as an exemplar of the general concept (dog).
Questions:
>   What do *can* and *must* mean in this context?
>   What regulates the scope of this capacity?
>   Of what kind is the freedom of the "must not"?
>   And what meaning of "must" is negated here?
Further question:
>   Does eidetic reduction lead through a series of negated types?
>   What is the guideline
>>   for running through
>>>   variations in the fantasy?
The successive reduction of typicality?
>   From where do the—really present or merely fancied—changes or mutabilities stem?
>   From what store of experience?
>   From typical practicabilities of mutability?
>   From analogization of finished changes?
>   And in what direction, to discover what *eidos*, do I perform the fantasied variation in the red wooden |1046| cube? To prepare out the *eidos* "cube," "color," "wood," "material object of the outer world," "geometric object"? But is this direction not already predesignated by motivational and thematic relevance? Is the fact of relevance not already pre-experienced in the life-world? Does a pragmatic motive of perception— clarified by Scheler—here play a part (with cognition and work)? Did not Dewey or Whitehead see something essential in this regard?

Connection with ontological world-structure and spheres of incompatibility; real-ontological regions; "the sum of the angles of a triangle is the color green"; Whitehead's and Gurwitch's theories in this regard; Piaget would also have to be consulted.

All these questions must be clarified in the essay on types. [1047]

On the type:

Meaning of the question: What kind of *dog* is this? I have already grasped the object it refers to as an animal, and indeed as a dog. As dog it shows all the doglike traits and doglike behavior; it is certainly not a cat and most certainly neither a bird nor a fish. The dissimilarity of this particular dog, belonging to a breed of dogs unknown to me from all other dogs, I know arises and becomes questionable only against the background of similarity that this animal has with my unquestioned experiences of typical dogs.

On this also Piaget's studies on type-formation in children and Goldstein on type-formation in aphasic patients.

(Presumably in the formulation of types also the foundation for "symbol-transfer") [1048]

Definition of the Situation

W. I. Thomas

Subjective and objective meaning of such a definition

Biographical basis of determination: the historicalness of the situation is

(a) biographical;

(b) history in the objective sense of the objective thing-world.

William James's theory of the "history" of the object and its interpretation.

Connection of the objective side with ontological world-structure of the subjective co-involved 'purposes at hand' (Are these alone relevant? Are 'means,' especially 'availability of means' and their context in the situation also predesignated?) [1049]

Again on Type (Common Sense p. 15f.)

Experiences "are not repeated." There are no two "same" experiences in the strict sense (if for no other reason) not because my stock of knowledge at the time of the first experience must be a different one than at the time of the second one: For this second experience, indeed, differs from the first insofar as the experiencing of the first experience could be made to coincide with it or not, i.e. it has in any case enlarged and enriched the stock of experience. At the time of the second experience I thus have a stock of knowledge on hand, which through element E of the first experience must be different from the stock of knowledge that was on hand at the time of the latter, precisely by this element E (if by nothing else). In a word: I have grown *older* between E' and E''.

E.g. the experience of a repeated action: (It could also be shown with respect to the differently defined situations, the one in which it first

occurred, and the one in which it reoccurs.) [1050] The first action A'
began in a situation S' and led to the result R'. The repeated action A''
began in a situation S'' and will presumably produce a result R''. Now,
according to what was said above, S' and S'' are necessarily different, from
the very fact that my stock of knowledge K' at the time of the definition
of S' deviates from the stock of knowledge K'' at the time of defining S'' by
the fact that the experience of A' as having led to R' was not yet present
in K'—only the empty anticipation that this would possibly be the case was
there—but now a new element K'' has thereby been added to the definition of S''.

By the idealizations of the "and so forth" and "I can always do it
again" (itself very much in need of clarification) I turn my interest away
from the uniqueness of the experiences A', S', R', K' and A'', S'', R'', K'',
and am interested only in the A, S, R, K (without the 'primes') typified
by this term, i.e. in their typicality. [1051] The construction of the type
thus consists (figuratively speaking) in the suppression of the *'primes'* as
relevant characteristics of the experiences. [1052]

The intersubjective character of the life-world and our knowledge thereof

(1) Givenness of the Other as element of the life-world; mutual understanding, working on others and influenced by their work upon us;

(2) Social world as cultural world; meaningful world, given to our interpretation as established by men, ourselves and others, contemporaries and
predecessors: tools, symbols, language systems, works of art, social institutions, etc.—in their meaning and origin they all refer to human actions.

Therefore: constant awareness of the historicity of the cultural and
social world handed down in custom and tradition. This historicity can
be inquired into and interpreted. It can be traced back to the human activity from which it originated. This must happen if it is to be understood:

Tool = purpose for which it was made;

sign and symbol = what it stands for (in the mind of the person
who uses it);

social [1053] institution refers to its meaning for the person who
orients his behavior by it; here origin of the postulate of the subjective
interpretation of meaning.

Axioms (idealizations, constructs) of socialized life-world knowledge: (they
contain the reason why the life-world is not my private world, but the one
pregiven to all of us):

Basic axioms:

I. Intelligent fellowmen exist as elements of the life-world.

II. The objects of the life-world are, in principle, accessible also to the
experience of other persons, indeed of everyone; either known by them or
knowable to them.

A. *Reciprocity of perspectives* (structural socialization)
"The same" object must necessarily show differences for each of us, because: [1054]
(i) "Here and There," differences of reach and of the manipulatory realm; (in mine, but not in yours, etc.).
(ii) Difference in mine and the Other's biographically determined situation, our motivational, thematic, and interpretational system of relevances: i.e.,

however, of our interests, plans and hierarchies of plans; and finally also of our systems of types.

To overcome these differences and to constitute the common life-world as the world for everyone, it is necessary to accept the following basic constructs (idealization, axioms, postulates):
(i) Change of place (see also Fink's description in the book on space-time-movement), i.e. the idealization of the exchangeable time of the standpoints: If I were there and he here, I would see things in the same perspectives, reach, distance, typicality, as he does now.
(ii) Idealization of the congruency of the systems of relevance. I and he take for granted that differences in perspectives that originate in my biographical situation and his [1055] are irrelevant for the present purpose of [each of] us, and that he and I, *we* both would have selected and interpreted in an identical manner the objects standing actually or potentially within our common reach and their qualities—"identical" of course meaning "empirically identical," namely adequately for the objective purpose.

The idealizations of the interchangeability of standpoints and the congruency of systems of relevance comprise, taken together, the general thesis of reciprocal perspectives. These idealizations lead to constructs of objects of thought (Whitehead's term), which supersede the objects of thought of my private world. The mobilization of these idealizations in natural thought leads to the general assumption that the sector of the life-world that I accept as given is also accepted by you as given, moreover by *us*, by the We that is thereby established, finally by [1056] "everyone," in the sense: everyone who is one of us, who shares our relevance system to a sufficient extent. In this way the general thesis of the reciprocity of standpoints leads to the assumption that the objects perceived by me and their aspects known actually to me and potentially to you are or could be "everyone's" objects of knowledge (understood in the above sense).

The terms "objects" and "aspects of objects" must here be understood in the broadest sense as the objects of our knowledge of the life-world in the natural attitude accepted as "obviously given."

Meaning of this view for social scientific problems: what is uniformly known by everyone who shares our scheme of relevance is:

(a) the "way of life" recognized as good and right by the in-group (Sumner),

(b) the origin of recipe knowledge and thus of traditional action (Weber), [1056a]

(c) (origin) of what is "taken-for-granted"—"of course" statements in Middletown (R. S. Lynd) (and)

(d) the relatively natural worldview (Scheler).

In all these cases, it is a question of typical knowledge of highly socialized structure that supersedes objects of thought of the private knowledge of myself and my fellowmen. This knowledge is a part of my socio-cultural heritage, it has its history. This leads to the problem of genetic socialization. [1057]

B. *Social origin of knowledge* (genetic socialization)

(a) Socially derived knowledge; friends, parents, teachers of teachers.

(α) How my surrounding world (environment) is to be defined, and indeed the typical contents and aspects of the world, as it is grasped in the relative natural attitude as the unquestioned but ever questionable quintessence of things taken for granted until further notice;

(β) How types and typical constructs have to be formed in accordance with the systems of relevance from the anonymous, unified point of view of the in-group; this includes

(aa) the general way of life

(bb) how to come to terms [with] the environment

(cc) tested recipes for the use of typical means for bringing about typical purposes in typical situations.

Significance of the vernacular in this context.

(b) Socially approved knowledge. [1057a]

(Common Sense 12)

On the articulation of the social world

Only in reference to me do my relations with others obtain the specific meaning that I designate by *We*.

Only in reference to *Us*, whose center I am, are others "you" *(Ihr);* only in reference to "you" *(Euch)* [familiar form.—*trans.*], who refer back to me, yet others are "you" *(Sie)* [polite form.—*trans.*].

This complements the division of consociates, predecessors, successors.

Characteristics of the surrounding-world relationship.

(Face-to-face) physical presence: The Other and I within mutual reach;

Participation in a mutual inner time: an internally onrolling course of mutual life; growing old together (analyzed by Ortega); polythetic structure mediated by events of a physical kind in the outer world and the outer time-form; the surrounding-world "you"

graspable in true simultaneity, my own experiences only as past
(at least in the beginning phases); participation in the hopes and
fears, their anticipations of future planned actions; in brief, consociates are mutually involved in one another's biographies; *they grow
old together;* they live in pure we-relationship. [1058]

C. *Social distribution of knowledge* see above

The expert and the layman.
The knowledge and the social distribution of the degrees of clarity
and contents of the other's persons and my own stock of knowledge
is itself an element of my stock of knowledge. I know whom I must
consult as a specialist, and under what typical circumstances. I know
who is a "competent" specialist. The civilization of reference books
and sources of information. In other words:
    In daily life I construct types of the scope and texture of the
stock of knowledge that the other has on hand. In doing so I
assume that he does the same,
    that he is guided by a certain type of relevance structures by
the fact that a set of constant motives codetermines his typical
actions and even his "personality." [1058b]
In the pure we-relationship, the other person is grasped in the
uniqueness and unrepeatableness of his existence; here begins the
process of typification that leads to ever increasing anonymization.
    But the uniqueness of the other person grasped in the we-
relationship is necessarily always merely fragmentary insofar as
his personality becomes apprehensible; just as the other person's
finite biographical situation is only fragmentarily revealed by participation and involvement. In this sense I know more, in another
less about the other person than about myself.
    In other forms of social relationship: typification; Problem
of quasi-simultaneity; flowing transition from surrounding-world
relationship to the world of contemporaries; construct of "hypothetical meaning presentiation by the contribution of imagination"
(Whitehead);
    Kind of types: typical kind and way of behavior,
        typical concatenation of underlying typical motives,
        typical attitudes of typical personalities,
of which the Other's concrete behavior within and outside my reach
is only a typical example. [1059]
Social-scientific meaning of the doctrine of the social distribution of
knowledge:
In economic theory
as *true* problem of the sociology of science and grounding
of the most varied doctrines summed up
under this name,

as grounding of the concepts: Social role
social stratification
institutional behavior
organizational behavior
sociology of professions
prestige and social status etc. [1059b]

By typifications of such a kind (wherever this is to be treated in more detail) the other person is always grasped only in partial contents and partial functions of his self, never in his uniqueness in a unique concrete situation. He seems to be given to the observer or partner only with a part of his self; he enters into the we-relationship merely with one part of his self; with one part he always remains outside the social relationship (Simmel); herewith the concept of "role" becomes explainable; Cooley's "looking-glass" effect;

G. H. Mead's idea of the generalized other; all this implies the emptying of the meaning contents; social function and rationality.
Here perhaps a digression on:
Durkheim: collective consciousness
Levy-Bruhl: pre-logical thinking
Husserl's letter to Levy-Bruhl quoted in Merleau-Ponty, and
Merleau-Ponty's own theory [1060]

Correct: *Self-typification*

I too enter into the social relationship with only part of my personality: in defining the role of the other (as a component of my situation?), I define my own role as it corresponds to the expectations anticipated by me (even typical constructs of my production) of the other person; I transform myself into customer, consumer, passerby, friend, etc.
W. James: I and Me.
G. H. Mead: I and Me.
"Changes" of roles: Husserl's professional times and professional pauses.
Ortega y Gasset: The I as *other thou* [1061]

On socialization of the type-formation of human action

Both typification of the Other and self-typification, and indeed types of courses-of-action, motive, and personality (In James-Mead terminology "I," "Me," "Generalized Other") are in the relative natural worldview, located ahead of the social group;
(a) as a component of socially approved type-formation
(b) as a store of socio-culturally derived knowledge that is usually communicated traditionally
(c) as in part even standardized forms of the stock of knowledge with pre-designated relevance structures whose conformity is warranted by genetic socialization
(d) type-formations even lead to institutionalization, e.g. in law;

(e) Chinese etiquette—(Granet), greeting (Ortega); custom (Ortega)
(f) the problem of social coercion (constraint in Durkheim, Ortega theory).

On this subject, what Vögelin writes in Volume III on "Characters" from Aristotle's Rhetoric to La Bruyère; also commedia dell' arte, Molière, Mozart essay,

Situations!

also Kierkegaard's studies and Dostoevsky's types. [1062]
The "someone" of "talk," of authenticity;
    on [Nikolai] Berdyaev's loneliness,
     on Buber's I and thou.
On the "role": Parsons (also critique of his "expectation"). [1063]

Typification and relevance

There are no types in general, but only types that are formed for the solution of a particular theoretical or practical problem. Typification thus depends on the problem at hand, for the sake of whose definition and whose solution the type is formed. The problem is, so to speak, the geometric locus of all possible types leading to the solution. The problem, on the other hand, depends on my situation, its foundedness on the ontology of the world, my biographical situation, hence the system of relevances that grow out of it *or* enter into it. (In this "or" lies my greatest difficulty! What is prior? Or are relevances and definition of the situation "equally original," as Fink would say, or constituted "together," as Husserl loves to say? But what does that mean? What is said by this: "equally original" or "together"?) [1064]

Meaning of the typification especially of the course of one's own and the other's actions
    (a) for the mechanism of projects of my own action.
    (b) for understanding the Other's action,
    (c) for choosing between different projects of action.
Therefore, analysis of action is required. [1065]

Theory of action

Brief description: definition of action
        action and act
        the project, its temporal structure
        fantasy-nature of the project
The project is based on the stock of knowledge at the time of projecting.
    Therefore, the idealization of "And so forth" and "I can always do it again" is involved.
    Why the finished act can never match the project of future action—repression of the "prime" connection with typification. Again Tiresias.
    In-order-to and because-motives briefly explained from the time-structure of the project. (In-order-to and because-motives as constituents of

theories of interest, e.g. Bergson and Leibniz: Note 2 page 168, Choosing essay.) Project and fantasy (daydream). Problem of practicability,

Double meaning of practicability; both refer back to "situation" and involved horizons of comparison.

But the "I could" [1066] refers to ontological world-structure components of the situation as framework of open possibilities of an objective kind,

the "I can" to biographical (characterological, Husserl believes) components of the same, the subjective powers.

Differentiation of the "I could"—I can—you can; reference to this problem's connection with the principle of the reciprocity of perspectives, which undergoes modifications in such a way; further reference to concatenation with the typical situation, which is defined by the consociate in the social action so that a number of elements of the situation are common— for that is what consociate means—while for the outside observer in the social world—let alone in the social sciences—this is not the case.

Meaning of the "world within reach" for the practica- [1067] bility of the project: The means must either be within reach or be able to be brought within reach; this [is] the real meaning of the "principle of scarcity" in economics. (Here belongs also the problem of technology and technical progress; it is a matter of extending the boundaries of reach more and more. And namely in every dimension: spatially, temporally, socially (one world).

Projecting is thus fantasying within the framework of open possibilities of practicability, as they can be known to be given based on the stock of knowledge at the time of projecting. It is a thinking *modo potentiali*, whereas for instance the mere fantasying of the daydream is not bound by practicability but is a thinking *modo optativo*.

Second Notebook

from Seelisberg

August 17 – 18, 1958

Contains: pp. 2001 – 2073

[2001] *Theory of action and project continued:*

Projecting within the framework of open possibilities of practicability demarcated by the stock of knowledge means:

That for my projected action I can in fantasy draw upon only means and ends within my actual or potential reach and forgo, in my envisioning of future action, drawing upon elements that lie outside my actual or potential control;

that I estimate all chances and risks based upon my available knowledge of "similar" occurrences in the real world;

that, in a word, according to my present knowledge, the act would have been possible *as a type* and that its means and ends would have been in reach *as a type*, if the now-projected act had been carried out in the past in the "same" (*typically* the same) situation as the present one.

(This casts an interesting spotlight on the logic of "counterfactual statements") [2002]

The restriction *"as a type"* is important because, of course, strictly speaking, as was shown above, the *same* action, the *same* means and ends are never repeatable (the same thing when repeated is not "the same" for the very reason that it is being repeated). Every finished act in itself (as well as any finished action with means-end relationship) is necessarily unique, if it is not typified (like my "dog Fido") under the ideality of the "I can always do it again." (More will have to be said below about the "socialization" of this ideality).

If the restriction to typicality were not included in the characterization, then a "new act" could never come about. It suffices for practicability that the projected act, its ends and means, remain compatible and consistent with those elements of the situation that according to our knowledge at hand at the time of projecting have warranted the practicability, if not the success, of typically similar acts in the past. [2003]

(Again the "atypical":

What is the "unexpected"?
What is the absolutely new?)

Subjective chance, objective chance versus mathematical or objective
possibility.
Borel: the chance of my death and the mortality chart—life expectancy
90 to 10 chance [of] my surviving [from an] operation, 50 to 50
[depending on] the group to which I belong.
The "calculated risk."
The above consideration in regard to projecting on the basis of prior experiences and the problem of statistics, extrapolation, trend, stochastics
[random statistical probability—*trans.*].
(The "possible,"
the "probable,"
the "plausible"—to be noted, to what extent the categories of objective and
subjective chance are contained in the concepts of possible and probable,
while the plausible, moreover, also refers to the categories of objective and
subjective meaning.—All this must still be reflected upon very precisely.)
[2004]
Again: open and problematic possibilities
[Choosing p. 167f.]
"S is p," "S is q" [are] possibilities that are open until the counterproof; for the statement "S is p" is necessarily elliptical (S is, among many
other things such as q, t, v . . . , also p). "S is q," "S is p" do not contradict
one another until proven otherwise; any statement has its equal right and
its equal weight; "S is p" means that for the time of this statement I am
interested exclusively or predominantly in the p-being of S, while its
q-being, r-being, t-being are irrelevant for me.
"Every determination is a negation," [2005]
. . . probably belongs at the beginning as prelude to the Carneades
problem. (Choosing 169)

Doubt

Insofar as systems of interest arise: all interests in a biographically determined and biographically defined situation are bound together into a
system, but are not thereby fully integrated. Interests can overlap and even
enter into conflict with one another ("roles" can therefore also do this).
This results in doubt as to which elements of the world accepted as given
are in fact *relevant* for my concrete purpose, the problem to be mastered.
Is it the p-being of S or its q-being?
What was previously undoubted and unquestioned has now become
questionable (indeed it is essentially always questionable).
A *genuine* situation of doubt arises. [2006]
All choosing between projects of action originates from such a gen-
uine situation of doubt.
Dewey's description in Choosing p. 169, quoting *Human Nature and
Conduct* III. Modern Library ed. p. 190
But what makes "habits" and "impulses" conflict? What creates
opposing impulses?

I can choose only between projects that *stand open to choice*. What is the origin of such alternatives?

But action and project are always in the genuine situation of doubt of the problematic possibility, even if several projects are not open to choice and only *one* project is involved: I always have the possibility to carry out the project versus the counterpossibility of dropping it. [2007]

Husserl, *Experience and Judgment:* problematic and open possibilities

His point of departure: modalization of prepredicative? judgments?
(certitude, possibility, probability)

The object of experience (is) originally pregiven to passive reception; it imposes itself on our self, it affects us. The self turns toward the object, and this turning-toward is the lowest form of spontaneity. (This was frequently described as the receptivity of the self or under the title of attention)

Attention, as advertence to the intentional object, is only the beginning of an activity of cogitations in the broadest sense; the beginning phase of these activities, namely attention, carries with it an intentional horizon of later phases of activity that are either fulfilled or not, and this was anticipated in an empty fashion, indeed in an ongoing synthetic process, until the activity comes to an end or is broken off, perhaps in the form: "And so forth . . ."

Example: perception of an outer object wakens the subject's interest in comparing it with other images of the same object to make [the] unseen back side accessible, etc., which one, I do not know. [2008]

Any of these phases carries with it its explicable horizons of protentional expectations, [for there are] three possibilities:

(1) The process is held up for some reason or other, e.g. the field of perception blocked off, the originary interest eliminated by another, stronger one.

(2) Interest in the object continues, but our expectations are not fulfilled but disappointed by [the] advance of perception in later phases.

> (a) completely; explosion; destruction of the anticipation, dented (?), speckled red sphere. "Not that way, but . . ." creates a new meaning of the object, which supersedes [the] first anticipated one;

> (b) first anticipation not completely obsolete, but has been made doubtful by the ongoing process: man or model? Carneades: solution of this conflict between now *genuinely problematic possibilities* and counterpossibilities, each of which has a specific weight and "desires" to be heard "by me." ("Weighing out" *(Ab-wägen)* of the weights = "pondering" *(erwägen)*.

> Something speaks for the one possibility and something for the counterpossibility.

(On the other hand, open possibilities that nothing speaks for are all of equal weight: the unseen back side must have *a* color, which one, I do not know.) [2009]

Every anticipation has an indeterminate character, and this general indeterminacy extends a frame of free variability: Precisely this constitutes [the] essence of *open* possibility.

Problematic [possibilities] are motivated by situation; they are possibilities in a unified field, disjunctively; only one of these conflicting possibilities may be conscious, the others [may be] unconscious.

Open possibilities: Nothing speaks for one more than for the other. An indeterminate general intention shows the modality of empirical certainty until revoked.

The world taken for granted without question is the general frame of open possibilities, none [of] them having a specific weight and none [of] them, as long as believed beyond question, contesting the others. All are considered empirically certain until further notice, i.e. until a counterproof. From these things and facts that are taken for granted the individual chooses according to his biographically determined situation elements [2010] by which the same [are] transformed into problematic possibilities, which from now on stand open to choice. Each of these possibilities now has its particular weight, raises the claim to be examined, and shows the conflicting tendencies of which Dewey speaks.

(That is how it stands in Choosing 173, but is it also correct? Are there not such conflicting possibilities already in the ontological structure?) [2011]

The choice itself:

A. Choosing among objects within reach
True alternatives between A and B. I incline first to A, then to B, then back to A, finally I decide to take A. The basic assumption is this: that A and B are within equal reach and attainable with the same effort (costs). The alternative of the objects open to choice is created by my biographical situation, by the quintessence of my previous experiences. For these previous experiences have created my system of interests and this has created the problematic possibilities that stand in conflict.

The modern social sciences assume such alternatives to be the normal ones underlying human choice, that is, that man finds himself at any time placed among a number of well-defined problematic possibilities, and that he is determined to choose one of them by acts of preference. (What preference is remains unclarified; in Scheler's view, preference is an act *sui generis*.) It is practically a methodological postulate of modern social science [that] [2012] the conduct of man has to be explained as if occurring in the form of choosing among problematic possibilities.

Examples: The concept of "defining the situation" in sociology, by which the social environment is transformed into a unified field of problematic (possibilities) within which choice and decision—especially rational choice and decision—become possible; secondly, the marginal-use principle can be defined as the scientific postulate for interpreting the actions of observed subjects as if they had to choose between pregiven problematic possibilities. [2013]

B. Choosing among several projects of action

Perhaps the distinction between (A) and (B) was meant by the classical distinction between *technē poiētikē* and *technē*, the art of producing and the art of acquiring.

The distinction is as follows:

(A)

The problematic possibilities within equal reach are ready-made and well-defined.

Their constitution is beyond my control.

I have to choose one or leave them both as they are. [2014] The alternatives coexist in simultaneity in the outer world. The two objects A and B are within my reach; I may turn away from A and toward B, then back to A; here it is, still unchanged.

(B)

The project is produced by me and in this sense it stands under my control. But before I have tentatively rehearsed this projected action in fantasying my project it is not brought into my reach and, strictly speaking, at the moment of my projection no alternatives are open to choice. All that will later be open to choice will have been produced by me in fantasying projection, and I can modify it however I wish within [2014] the bounds of practicability.

The two projects do not coexist in outer time. By its fantasying acts, my consciousness (?) has produced them within the sequence of inner time, dropping one, turning to another, then returning to the first, or more exactly: re-creating it. But meanwhile I have grown older, have enlarged my stock of knowledge, and upon returning to the first I am no longer "the same" within the Heraclitean flow as I was when originally drafting it and when I dropped it; nor is the drafted project the same—or more exactly (?): it is the same, but modified—[*nicht* omitted based on Choosing p. 175—*trans.*]. In case B it is not a matter of problematic possibilities coexistent in outer time, but of possibilities produced by me successively within the *durée*. [2015]

Bergson's theory of the act of choice

Essai sur les durées

Associationistic psychology as the common false basis for determinists and indeterminists; for both substitute for the inner *durée* spatialized time, the juxtaposition of succession. According to the viewpoint of both (?) the ego finds itself placed between two alternatives, hesitating from one to the other and finally deciding for one of them. The ego and its tendencies, by which it is moved, are thus apprehended as well-defined things that remain unchanged through the whole course of operation. However the ego, by the very fact that it has had the first experience, has changed before it came to the second one. Hence it modifies, while running through the alternatives, not only itself but also the sentiments by which it is moved: Thus, a dynamic series of interpenetrating states of consciousness is created that influence one another and lead to a free act by a natural evolution. If I am choosing between two possible actions X and Y, this means that I am living through two series of states of mind depending on my inclination to X or to its opposite Y. [2016]

But even these opposite inclinations have merely one single real existence. X and Y are merely symbols for different tendencies of my personality at successive moments of my *durée*. As the ego runs through them, the ego grows and expands as it passes through the imaginary tendencies, which change during the process of deliberation as the ego changes. It is therefore purely a metaphor to speak of two directions or two tendencies. In reality there are neither two tendencies [nor] two directions but just an ego that develops as it lives through its hesitations until the free action detaches itself from it like a too-ripe fruit. Associationistic psychology, which is accepted equally by determinists and [also by] indeterminists, deals, however, with both possibilities as if they coexisted in space, as if the road run through by the consciousness bifurcated at a certain point and as if the ego, placed at the crossroad, had to take its decision which way to follow. He who makes such an assumption commits the fallacy of placing himself at a moment when the action had already been accomplished but of looking nevertheless at the process of the subject's activity as if the bifurcation of the road had existed before the deliberation took place [2017] and a decision [*Entwicklung*, a misreading for *Entscheidung—trans.*] was reached. Onrolling time and time past, *durée* and spatialized time, are thus confused and the irreversibility and irretrievability of time are disregarded. There was no bifurcation and no traced way before the action was accomplished, there was even no direction and no question of a way; only the accomplished action has traced the way. Deliberation cannot be conceived as an oscillation in space. It consists rather in a dynamic process in which the ego as well as its motives are engaged in continuous becoming. The ego [is] infallible in its immediate findings, feels itself free, and declares this; but in any attempt to explain its freedom it succumbs of necessity to a spatial symbolism with all its fallacies.

Translated into the terminology of the present paper: Bergson's criticism is directed against the assumption that problematic possibilities existed with respect to projects at a point in time when all possibilities were still open ones. The ego living in its acts knows merely open possibilities; genuine alternatives become visible only in interpretative retrospection, that is, when the act has already been accomplished and thus the becoming has been translated into existence. In our terminology one could say that, according to Bergson, all actions occur within open possibilities and that problematic possibilities are restricted to acts. [2018]

Critique of Bergson's theory:

(1) It relates only to actions that gear into the outer world. (Is this criticism accurate?)

(2) It tells only half the story. It is true that the ego in self-interpretation of its past acts has the illusion of having chosen between problematic possibilities. Bergson fails to add, however, that it is the accomplished act and not the action which is anticipated *modo futuri exacti*. According to our theory, projecting is a retrospection anticipated in the fantasy, in which the projected act is fantasied as accomplished. Therefore, the ways—to keep to Bergson's metaphor—were already traced, although merely as pencil strokes on a map and not as trails in a landscape. The ego does in fact, during the process of reflection that precedes decision, behave as Bergson describes. But what has been projected in such a projecting—or better: in such a series of successive fantasying activities—is the accomplished act anticipated *modo futuri exacti*, the outcome therefore of the action to be performed, not the action itself as it will go on. These various anticipated acts are now problematic possibilities [2019] within a unified field *modo potentiali*; they have their quasi-coexistence and *stand now to choice*. But their coexistence is merely a quasi-coexistence, that is, the projected acts are merely imagined as coexistent; they are not ready made and equally within my reach. Still they are all within my control and remain in their quasi-existence until my decision to carry one of them out has been reached. This decision consists in the supervening intention to turn one of these projects into my purpose. This transition requires a voluntative "fiat" that is motivated by the in-order-to motive of the chosen project. [2020]

Motives, says Leibniz, induce a man to act but do not necessitate him. He is free to follow or not to follow his inclinations or even to suspend his choice. (Scheler: Man as the no-sayer.) Man has the freedom of reasonable deliberation; reason guides (?) him in weighing the pros and cons of each possibility.

In our terminology: As soon as the possibilities of my future action have been constituted as problematic possibilities within a unified field, that is, as soon as two or more projects stand open to choice, the "weight" of each of them can be ascertained by operations of judgment. The "art of deliberation," the procedure by which conflicting motives after having passed the scrutiny of reason lead finally to an act of volition, has been carefully analyzed by Leibniz. [2021]

Leibniz's theory of volition (schematically)

Theodicy: "Good" and "evil" replaced by + and −
Leibniz's polemic with Bayle; Bayle's comparison of the soul to a scale where inclinations and reasons stand in the balance.
An emerging argument, a new idea, fear of displeasure may make one side heavier and thus upset the balance, etc. Decision [is] all the more difficult the more the opposite arguments approach an equal weight.
Leibniz's objections:

      (1) Mostly not two, but more eventualities are open to choice;
      (2) Voluntative intentions are at work from the outset;
      (3) There is no equilibrium from the outset.

Leibniz's own theory:

      Starting from Scholastic concepts of "antecedent" volition *(volonté antécédante)*, consisting in the opinion of producing an act in relationship to its inner weight, and "subsequent" volition *(volonté subséquente)*, he adds his own concept of an "intermediate" volition, *(volonté moyenne)*, which originates in counterarguments. With respect to the final, decisive volition *(volonté finale et décrétoir)*, the intermediate one is antecedent. [2022]
Decision results from the conflict of all antecedent wills and their combinations, those which correspond to the + as well as those which correspond to the −.

      Comparison of the final act of volition with the diagonal in the (parallelo-)gram of forces. The function of reason [is] to determine our choice and transform the *volontés antécédantes* into the *volonté finale*.

Limitation of this function of reason:

(a) Preferring always takes place within the framework of our knowledge, which originates in pre-experiences. But this knowledge is not homogeneous, [it is] either distinct or confused. Only distinct knowledge falls under the realm of reason. Our senses and passions furnish merely confused knowledge (thinking?) and we remain in their bondage as long as we do not succeed in basing our actions on distinct knowledge.

    The situation is complicated by the fact that we often feel our confused thoughts clearly, whereas our distinct thoughts are only potentially clear: They could be clear if we were willing to make the necessary efforts to explicate their implications, for instance by penetrating into the meaning of the words and symbols.

(b) (Agreeing with Locke) misjudgments in [2023] comparing present pleasure and displeasure with future disregard for the "time perspective"— or false anticipation of future things—or doubt that our decision will have the anticipated consequences.

(c) The accountant's balance sheet:
    —no item may be omitted.
    —all must be arranged correctly

—all must be added correctly

—error is possible in each of these steps

(d) To correctly estimate the consequences of our choice (modern social scientists: to arrive at a perfectly rational decision), we would need several techniques that we do not have:

(α) *l'art de s'aviser au besoin ce qu'on sait*

(β) a technique for estimating the likelihood of future events, namely the consequences of our decisions

(γ) a technique for ascertaining the positive and negative weights of the problematic possibilities (Leibniz: good and evil) Only then would we master *l'art des conséquences* [2024]

Comparison of the theories of Bergson, Husserl, Leibniz, see Choosing 180f.

Bergson: precondition for sciences, for Peter to predict Paul's future actions. (Then how come this is to a certain extent possible in the life-world?) [2025]

Positive and negative weight

Standards for this are not created by the projecting itself. On the contrary, the project is evaluated according to the pre-existent frame of reference. Positiveness and negativeness of the weights thus transcend the actual situation of a concrete choice and decision.

Keys: interest systems, their correlate

systems of action

systems of motivation

end and system of means

project and system of purposes.

Any end is a means for another end; any project is projected within a system of a higher order. Therefore, any choosing between projects refers to a previously chosen system of interconnected projects of a higher order.

The hierarchy of plans [is subordinated to the] life-plan. [2026]

Any choice relates to pre-experienced decisions of a higher order, upon which the concrete alternative standing to choice is based, just as any doubt refers to a pre-experienced empirical certainty that becomes questionable in the process of doubt.

Our pre-experience of the plan-hierarchy as the higher organization of our projects is the foundation of the problematic possibilities standing to choice: It also determines the weight of each of these possibilities: It is positive or negative merely with reference to this system of higher order. [2027]

The phenomenon of choice does not require a particular degree of clarity of knowledge. On the contrary, it takes place on any level of clarity, explicitness, vagueness.

In everyday life, full clarity and explicitness are unattainable.

Therefore

perfectly rational action

is impossible.

Reasons (according to the Choosing article)

(1) The system of plans upon which the constitution of alternatives is founded belongs to the because-motives of the individual in question. Because-motives can be disclosed merely in retrospective observation, but remain hidden to the actor who lives in his acts oriented merely by his in-order-to motives, which only he has in view.

(2) The actor's knowledge is founded upon his biographically determined situation, which selects the elements relevant to his purpose at hand from the world simply taken for granted; and this biographically [2028] determined situation, as prevailing at the time of the projecting, changes in the course of oscillation between the alternatives, if for no other reason than because of the experience of this oscillating itself. [2029]

Summary of the Choosing essay pp. 182/183

World taken for granted

       from it[s] biographically determined situation selects certain elements of this field as *relevant* for our purpose at hand.

(a) If this selection meets with no obstacle the project is simply transformed into a purpose and the action carried out as a matter of course.

(b) If by the very vagueness of our knowledge at hand at the time of projecting a situation of doubt arises, then some of the formerly open possibilities become questionable, problematic.

       Some part of the world formerly taken for granted beyond question and therefore unquestioned has now been put in question.

       The decision re-transforms what has been made questionable into a certainty, but an empirical certainty, so that it is again an unquestioned element of our knowledge taken for granted until further notice. [2030]

(Choosing, p. 183)

Intersubjectivity and mutual understanding of the actors in the life-world

(As application of the analysis of the problem of choice)
How does the observer in the social world understand ongoing or accomplished action?

       [There is] no warranty whatsoever that the world as taken for granted subjectively by the actor is in the same way beyond question for the observer. //Important. This is nonsense! That has nothing to do with it. [Marginal comment by Schutz—*trans.*]// The actor may suppose that what he takes for granted is beyond question also for "everyone belonging to us," but whether this assumption holds good for the particular fellowman depends upon whether a genuine we-relation has been pre-established between both. Yet even if this is the case, the biographically determined situation, and therewith the selection of the relevant elements among the open possibilities of the actor and the observer, must needs be a different one. In addition, the observer does not participate in immediacy in the process of the actor's choice and decision even if some of its [2031] phases were communicated to him. He has to reconstruct from the accomplished overt act the underlying in-order-to or because-motives of the actor. Nevertheless, to a certain extent at least, man is capable of understanding his fellowman.

How is this possible?

(This idea, dealt with in greater detail elsewhere, must be analyzed precisely. It is connected with the conformity of the relevance system of the two parties and is a key to the objective and subjective interpretation of meaning.

Important distinction: role of the partner in the social relationship versus that of mere observers; the "common situation" and its elements, determined (selected) by separate but corresponding objectives (plans, hence relevance).

All this must be elaborated, through the surrounding world and the world of contemporaries, predecessors, and posterity in various forms.) [2032]

(Choosing p. 183)

Interpretation of action in the social life-world by the social sciences

Nature of the idealizations and generalizations made by the social scientists. On the one hand, the social scientist is not permitted to take the social world for granted as "given." His "general plan" consists in putting this world into question and inquiring into its structure.

On the other hand, *qua* scientist (not as a man among fellowmen, which he certainly also is) it is not his biographically determined situation that ascertains what is relevant for his scientific work //important [Schutz's marginal comment—*trans.*]// as is the case for the actor in the social life-world with regard to his actions.

The question therefore is: Can the social scientist refer to the same reality of the social world that appears to the actor? If so, does he do this within his scientific practice? And if that is the case, how is this possible? [2033]

(Common Sense)

Social action (relations of acts)

Any form of social action is founded upon constructs relating to the understanding of the other person and the action pattern in general.

Example: Question and answer within the surrounding world relationship (with fellowman):

In projecting my question, I anticipate that the Other will understand my action (for instance, my uttering an interrogative sentence) as a question and that this understanding will induce him to act in such a way that I may understand his behavior as an adequate response. ("Where is the ink?" The Other points at a table.)

The in-order-to motive of my action is to obtain adequate information, which in this particular situation presupposes:

that the understanding of my in-order-to motive becomes the other's because-motive to perform an action whose in-order-to motive is to furnish me this information.

provided he is willing and able to do so, which I presume he is. Implied assumption: That he understands the language in which I formulate my question; that he knows where the ink is; that he is ready to tell me this if he knows it, etc. [2034]

(Common Sense, 17f.)

General assumption: He, the Other, would (?) be guided by the same typical motives by which in the past, according to my stock of knowledge at hand, I myself and many others were guided in a typically similar situation.

Thus, any social action in the life-world presupposes a series of common-sense constructs—in this case constructs of the Other's anticipated behavior—all of them based on the

idealization

that the actor's in-order-to motives become because-motives of his partner, and vice versa.

We call this idealization the

Idealization of the reciprocity of motives

It depends on the basic idealization (general thesis) of the reciprocity of perspectives, since it implies that the motives imputed to the Other are typically the same as my own and of many others under typically similar circumstances—all this within the framework of my originarily acquired or socially derived stock of knowledge at hand. [2035] This again involves the typical equation or corresponding intermeshing of the reciprocal motivational, thematic, and interpretational relevances.

Here the problem of social standardization must be considered. Closely connected therewith also standardized (socially derived and accepted) systems of symbols, systems of signs, etc.

Not discussed so far: The attitudinal relationship that must precede the establishment of all social relationships, including language.—This applies even (?) to the world of contemporaries. The letter needs an addressee.) [2036]

(Common Sense 18)

The chain of motives: The in-order-to motive [is] within the actor's view only subjectively; the partners or observers know only the revealed part, or they infer a chain of motives from the overt flow of action in the outer world.

Example: "Where is the ink?"
Omission or replaceability of intermediary sectors (subphases of the action); in regard to the state of affairs that constitutes the in-order-to

motive and is supposed to be produced by the action, they appear as
means, etc., which can be replaced or exchanged (typewriter instead of
fountain pen) (from the partner's or the observer's standpoint, the element
accessible to him seems to be autarchic). (This alone is reason enough for
the discrepancy between subjective and objective meaning.)

In other words: Only the actor knows when his action begins and
ends. The scope of his project determines the unit of his action.

Interpretation of this unit: again different for partner and observer;
the first necessarily has certain relevances in common with the actor; common or reciprocal goals. The observer does not have this, he stands outside
the actors' situation. [2037]

Consequences: In the commonsense thinking of everyday life there is only
a chance to understand the Other's action sufficiently for our purposes at
hand.

To increase this chance we have to search for the meaning a particular act has for the actor (Weber's postulate of the subjective interpretation
of meaning is, thus, not a methodological postulate of "understanding"
sociology, but a principle of constructing course-of-action types within the
life-world). [2038]

Digression on the scope of the project:
It constitutes the "specious present."
Arrangement of the course of action according to "flying stretches" and
"resting places."
For example: the interruption of a musical theme as recognizable again.
[2039]

(Common Sense 19)
Subjective interpretation of the action

by revealing the motives of a given course of action.
Course-of-action type—typical motives of the actor—personal type. The
latter may be more or less anonymous and, therewith, more [or] less empty
of content. In the pure we-relationship, the Other's course of action, his
motives (insofar as they become manifest), and his personality (insofar as it
is involved in the manifested action) can be grasped in immediacy; then
the constructed type will show a very low degree of anonymity and a high
degree of fullness. In constructing course-of-action types of contemporaries
([not] consociates), a set of supposedly invariant motives that govern their
actions are imputed to the more or less anonymous actor. This set is itself a
construct of typical expectations of the Other's behavior and is generally
studied by sociologists (especially American ones) under the title "social
role" or "functional behavior." In commonsense thinking such a construct
has a [2040] particular significance for projecting actions that are oriented
upon my contemporaries' (not my consociates') behavior. Its functions can
be described as follows:

(1) I take for granted that my action (say putting a stamped and

duly addressed envelope in a mailbox) will induce anonymous fellowmen (postmen) to perform typical actions (to deal appropriately with the content of the mailbox) so that in accordance with typical in-order-to motives (to live up to their occupational duties) the state of affairs projected by me (delivery of the letter to the addressee within reasonable time) will be achieved.

(2) I also take it for granted (by what right, really?) that my construct of the Other's course-of-action type corresponds substantially to his own self-typification and that to the latter belongs a typified construct of my, his anonymous partner's, typical way of behavior based on typical and invariant motives (whoever puts this duly addressed and stamped envelope in the mailbox is assumed to intend to have it delivered to the addressee in due time). [2041]

(3) Even more, in my own self-typification, i.e. by assuming the role of a customer of the mail service, I have to project my action in such a typical way as I suppose the typical post office employee expects a typical customer to behave. Such a construct of mutually interlocked behavior patterns reveals itself as a construct of mutually interlocked in-order-to and because-motives that are supposedly invariant. The more these types of behavior are institutionalized (?) or standardized, i.e. the more typified they are in the form of socially accepted laws, rules, regulations, customs, habits, etc., the greater is the chance that my own self-typified behavior will bring about the desired state of affairs.

(Here, reference must be made once more to Cooley's "looking-glass effect" and G. H. Mead's "generalized Other.") [2042]

The observer

is not a partner in social relations. His motives are not interlocked with those of the observed actors. He is "tuned in" upon them, but they not necessarily upon him. Thus, he stands outside the complicated mechanism of the mirror-effect by which in the social relationship among contemporaries the actor's in-order-to motives become understandable to the partner as his own because-motives (and vice versa). Precisely this fact constitutes the "disinterestedness" of the observer. He is not involved in the actor's hopes and fears of being understood by the partner or not, and of achieving the desired result by the interlocking of motives.

Thus, his system of relevances differs from that of the parties involved in the social relationship and permits him to see at the same time more or less than what is seen by the partners.

Under all circumstances it is merely the manifested fragments of the actions of *both* partners that are accessible to his observation. In order to understand them the observer has to avail himself of his knowledge of typically similar patterns of interaction in typically similar situational settings, and thus to construct the motives of the actors from that sector of the actions that is accessible to his observation. The constructs of the observer are, therefore, necessarily different from those of the partners, for the very reason that the purpose of the observer and his systems of relevances must be different from theirs. [2042a] There is thus a mere chance, although a chance sufficient for many practical purposes, that the observer in daily life can grasp the subjective meaning that Weber associates with the actor's acts. This chance increases with the degree of anonymity and standardization of the observed behavior.

The scientific observer has to develop specific methods for the building of his constructs in order to assure their applicability for the interpretation of the subjective meaning of the observed acts. More on this topic later. [2043]

Rational action within the life-world

Common Sense 21–26, must be condensed a great deal, if not added just as a note or appendix.

Of particular interest is the main theme:

(1) "purpose-rational"   "value-rational"
        this distinction is between two kinds of
                        because-motives

Within the system of the hierarchy of plans are different solutions of the problem, different ways of acting for the decision, and this decision is supposed to be rational	cannot choose between several projects equally open to the actor's choice within his systems of plans. The project is taken for granted; only several alternatives stand open for its realization, and these have to be determined by rational selection.

(2) Rationality (according to Weber and Pareto) refers, in the everyday thinking of the life-world, not only to the available stock of knowledge taken for granted by the in-group to which the observer belongs but also to the subjective meaning that the actor attaches to his action, i.e. to his stock of knowledge at the time of carrying out the action.

Several difficulties follow from this:

(a) Since our biographical situation determines the problem at hand and thus also the different systems of relevances under which the various aspects [2044] of the world are typified, the actor's stock of knowledge must, of necessity, differ from that of the observer. Even this principle of the reciprocity of perspectives is not sufficient to eliminate this difficulty because it presupposes that both the observer and the observed share a system of relevances that is sufficiently homogeneous in content and structure for the practical purpose. If this is not the case, then a course of action that is perfectly rational from the point of view of the actor may appear as non-rational to the partner or observer, and vice versa. Example: the rain-dance of the Hopi Indians and silver iodide twenty years ago.

(b) "Rational" seems to have a different meaning as applied to my future and my past acts. What I did has been done and cannot be undone, although an earlier state of affairs could be restored by countermoves. With respect to past actions, there is no possibility of choice (although there is the possibility of reinterpretation). Everything that was contained in an empty mode of interpretation [2045] in the project that preceded my past action has been fulfilled or refuted in the performance of the act. On the other hand, all future action stands under the ideality of the "I can do it again," which may or may not stand the test of experience in the performance of the act.

Closer analysis shows, however, that even in judging the reasonableness or rationality of a past action we refer to the stock of knowledge at hand at the time of projecting such action. Therefore in case the act once projected as rational should fail we may be accused of an error in judgment or a lack of foresight but not of irrationality or unreasonableness.

In both cases—of past or future actions—our judgment of reasonableness or rationality refers to the project determining the course of action and, still more precisely, to the choice among the several projects involved in the decision (including the alternative of carrying out the projected action or refraining from doing so.) [2046]

(Common Sense 25)

(3) Rational action on the level of everyday thinking within the life-world is always action within an unquestioned and undetermined frame of constructs of the typicalities of the situation (circumstances, setting, motives, means and ends, courses of action, and personalities involved), which is simply taken for granted.

All this is, however, not merely taken for granted by the actor; rather, he also assumes it is taken for granted by his fellowman. From this frame of constructs, forming their undetermined horizon, merely particular configurations of elements stand out that are clearly and distinctly determinable.

The commonsense concept of rationality refers to these elements.

On this level, therefore, there is only partial rationality, which has many degrees and levels.

E.g., the assumption that our fellowman in a business relationship knows its rational elements will never reach "empirical certainty" but will always bear the character of plausibility, i.e., of subjective (in contradistinction to mathematical probability). [2047]

We always have to "take chances" and to "run risks" and this situation is expressed by our hopes and fears, which are nothing else but the subjective corollaries of our uncertainty as to the outcome of our projected social interaction.

To be sure, the more standardized the prevailing pattern of action is, the greater the subjective chance of conformity and, therewith, of the success of intersubjective behavior. Yet—and this is the paradox of rationality—the more standardized the pattern is, the less the underlying elements are analyzable for commonsense thought in terms of rational insight. [2048]

(Common Sense 26ff.)
The construction of objects of thought by the social sciences

(1) The postulate of subjective interpretation for the purpose of grasping social reality.

(2) Objective phenomena (e.g., price movements) *can* always be ascribed to subjective action and they *must* be so for certain purposes.

(3) Constructs of the social sciences never refer to unique individual actions that [take place] in a unique, unrepeatable situation, but to models of sectors of the social world within which merely those typical events occur that are relevant to the scientific problem under scrutiny. In constructing these models the scientist uses special methodological techniques, one of whose results is that all irrelevant elements of the social world—irrelevant, namely, from the point of view of the problem formulated—are apprehended [2049] as mere "data," which are taken for granted as given—likewise by the particular methodological techniques such as the "clausula rebus sic stantibus" or "all other things being equal."—This does not contradict the possibility of constructing a model of the social world consisting of typical human interactions and analyzing within it typical courses of action as to the meaning they have for the typical personalities of actors who presumably originated them. [No (4) in original.—*trans.*]

(5) The social scientist as disinterested observer. He is not involved in the observed situation, which is to him not of practical but merely of cognitive interest. He does not act within it but is free of hope and fear as to the outcome of the observed act. He is "detached" like a biologist observing the occurrences in his laboratory. [2050]

(6) Difference between the scientific attitude and scientific activity within the social world.

(7) The biographical situation of the scientist and the systems of relevances that originate from it are replaced by the scientific situation with its relevances. In daily life the individual considers himself as the center of the social world that he groups around himself in layers of greater or lesser degrees of anonymity and intimacy. By the basic decision of adopting a scientific attitude—making science into his life-plan—[the] scientist detaches himself from his biographical situation. What is taken for granted in daily life may now become questionable for the scientist, and vice versa what is of highest relevance on one level is irrelevant on the other, etc. The center of orientation has been radically shifted and so has the hierarchy of plans and projects. The [2051] scientist, with the decision to carry out a plan for scientific work (governed by the disinterested quest for truth and in accordance with rules of scientific procedure, called the scientific method), has entered a field of preorganized knowledge called the corpus of his science.

He has to accept what his fellow scientists have achieved as solid knowledge or "show cause" why he cannot do so. Only within this frame of established knowledge may he pose his scientific problems and make his scientific decisions. This frame constitutes

the scientific situation

in which he is and which supersedes the biographical situation in which he experiences himself as a human being within the life-world.

It is henceforth
the scientific problem

that, once formulated, determines alone what is [2052] or is not thematically and motivationally relevant to its solution, and thus what has to be investigated (is worth inquiring into) and what can be taken for granted as a "datum"; furthermore, it determines the level of scientific research in the broadest sense, that is, the abstractions, generalizations, formalizations, idealizations, in short, the constructs required and admissible for solving the problem (indeed even the conditions under which it can be considered solved).

In other words, the problem is the "locus" of all possible constructs relevant to its solution. Each construct carries along its (mathematical) reference index referring to the problem for whose solution the construct was undertaken.

Danger of shifting the problem without revising the relevant construct. [2053]

Differences between constructs of the life-world by common sense and by scientific thinking

Commonsense thinking

Constructs, formulated from a "Here" within the life-world that determines the presupposed reciprocity of perspectives, take a stock of socially derived and socially approved knowledge for granted.

The social distribution of knowledge determines the particular structure of the typifying construct, for instance, the assumed degree of anonymity of personal roles, the standardization of course-of-action patterns, and the supposed constancy of motives. Yet this social distribution of knowledge itself depends upon the heterogeneous composition of the stock of knowledge at hand, a fact that as such is an element of commonsense experience. [2053–54]

Scientific thinking

The social scientist has no "Here" within the social world, or, more precisely, he considers his position within it and the system of relevances attached thereto as irrelevant for his scientific undertaking. His stock of knowledge at hand is the corpus of knowledge of his science, which he takes for granted—i.e., in this context, as scientifically ascertained—unless he makes explicit why he cannot do so.

To this corpus of scientific knowledge belong also the rules of procedure that have stood the test, namely, the methods of his science, including the methods for the right construction of types. [2053–54]

This stock of knowledge is of quite another structure than that

The concepts of "We," "You," "They," of "in-group," of out-group, of fellowmen, consociates, contemporaries, predecessors, and successors, all of them with their particular structurization of familiarity and anonymity, are at least implied, if not co-constituted, for the constructs of types in everyday thinking.

All this holds good not only for the participants in a pattern of social interaction but also for the observer of the life-world who still makes his observations from his biographical situation within the social world. The difference between him and the partners is merely that the latter, under the principle of reciprocity of motives, assume that their own motives are interlocked with those of the partners, whereas to the observer merely the manifest fragments of the actors' flow of action are accessible. Nevertheless, both, the participants and the life-world [2054-55] observer, form their commonsense constructs relative to their biographical situation. In either case, the constructs have their place within the chain of motives originating in the biographically determined hierarchy of the constructor's plans.

which is at hand in everyday life. To be sure, the scientific stock of knowledge also shows manifold degrees of clarity and distinctness. But this structurization depends on knowledge of problems still unsolved, of their still-hidden implications and the open horizons of other still not formulated problems.

The scientist takes for granted what he defines to be a datum, and this is independent of any belief and any opinion shared or accepted by any in-group in the world of everyday life. The scientific problem, once established, alone determines the structure of relevance.

Since the scientist has no "Here" within the social world, he does not organize the world in layers around himself as the center. He can never enter as a fellowman in a relationship of action with one of the actors within the social [2054–2055] life-world without abandoning, at least temporarily, his scientific attitude. The "participant observer or fieldworker" establishes contact with the group he is studying as a man among fellowmen. Only the system of relevances, which serves as the scheme for his selection and interpretation of the scientifically relevant elements, is preserved by the scientific attitude, otherwise temporarily dropped in order to be taken up again.

Thus, adopting the scientific attitude, the social scientist observes human, life-world, reciprocal courses of action or their results, insofar as they are accessible to his observation and open to his interpretation. These interaction patterns, however, he has to interpret in terms of their subjective meaning structure lest he abandon any hope of grasping "social reality," the life-world.

In order to comply with this postulate, the scientific observer proceeds in a way similar to that of the observer of the life-world, although guided by an entirely different system of relevances. [2056]

The scientific model of the social life-world

First step: Construction of typical course-of-action patterns, correspond-
                ing to the observed events.

Second step: Co-ordination of these patterns with a personal type, namely
                the model of an actor whom he imagines as being gifted
                with consciousness.
                Nature of this consciousness (Common Sense p. 32)

Third step: To this consciousness are ascribed constant typical in-order-to
                and because-motives.
                Nature of these motives.

Fourth step: Yet these models of actors or *homunculi* do not have any biog-
                raphy or any history; they are not in a situation defined by
                them, but in one that the social scientist has defined. He has
                also equipped them with a particular stock of knowledge, etc.
                In particular, he determines their system of relevances—and
                this is the system of scientific relevance originating in the
                scientific problem of its constructor and not in the biographi-
                cally determined situation of an actor within the world. The
                scientist defines the Here and Now of the model, what is
                within its reach, what is for him a We and a You or a They;
                he supplies it with a stock of knowledge that is not socially
                derived and, unless especially designed to do so, without
                reference to social approval. Only the scientific problem
                [2057] determines the limits of the model's knowledge of
                acquaintance as well as the zones of knowledge taken for
                granted, etc., and also what is familiar to him, what remains
                anonymous and on what level the typification of his experi-
                ence of the world imputed to him takes place.

Fifth step: The model is brought into a fictional reciprocal interaction
                relationship with other similarly constructed models. Hereby
                the intermeshing motives, the types of action and persons, the
                distribution of knowledge (?) are determined by the con-
                structing social scientist according to his problematic—along
                with the scope of reciprocal projects, etc.
                The homunculus is free from empty anticipations of the
                Other's reaction to his self-typification, etc.

Possible sixth step: Rational action and personal types possible. [2058]

Postulates for scientific model constructs of the social life-world
(1) *Postulate of logical consistency*
The system of types must be constructed by the social scientists with the
highest degree of clarity and distinctness of the implied conceptual framework so that it is fully compatible with the principles of formal logic. The
objective validity of the thought objects constructed by the social scientist is

thereby assured. The strictly logical character of the scientific construction of the thought objects distinguishes them from the constructs of common-sense thinking in everyday life that they have to supersede.

(2) *Postulate of subjective interpretation*
In order to explain human actions the social scientist has to construct the model of an individual consciousness and to ask what typical contents must be assigned to it to explain the observed facts as the result of the activity of such a mind. Compliance with this postulate warrants the possibility of referring all kinds of human action or their result to the subjective meaning such action or its result had for the actor. [2059]

(3) *Postulate of adequacy*
Each term in a scientific model of human action must be constructed in such a way that a human act performed within the life-world by an individual actor in the way indicated by the typical construct would be understandable for the actor himself as well as for his fellowmen in terms of commonsense interpretation of everyday life. Compliance with this postulate warrants the consistency of the constructs made by the social scientist with the constructs of commonsense experience in the social reality of the life-world.

(4) For certain purposes: *Postulate of rationality*
Rational interaction patterns and personality types have to be constructed in such a way that an actor in the life-world would perform the typified action if he had a perfectly clear and distinct knowledge of all the elements and only of the elements assumed by the social scientist as being relevant to this action, and if, furthermore, he had the constant tendency to use the most appropriate means at his disposal for achieving the purpose defined by the construct itself. [2060]

(Concept & Theory Formation)
On the alleged and actual difference between the methods of the social sciences and the natural sciences

Allegedly Social Sciences	*Natural Sciences*
ideographic	nomothetic
individualized (?) conceptualization	generalization
seeks individual assertory propositions	seeks general apodictic propositions
measurements and experiments impossible	has to deal with constant, measurable magnitudes
Its object: to understand psychological and intellectual processes	Its object: to explain material objects and processes

Untenability of these statements:

(1) [They have an] erroneous concept of the methods of the natural sciences.

(2) They identify special methods of one particular social science with the method of the social sciences in general. (History has to deal with singular assertory propositions, but not other social sciences; experiments are hardly possible in cultural anthropology, but they can be used in social psychology.)

(3) A set of rules for scientific procedure is equally valid for *all* empirical sciences, as for instance the principles of controlled inference and verification by fellow-scientists and the theoretical ideals of unity, simplicity, universality, and precision. [2061]

Reason for this unsatisfactory controversy:

The development of the modern social sciences occurred during a period in which the science of logic was mostly concerned with the logic of the natural sciences. [The latter enjoyed] a kind of monopolistic imperialism.

Without help and in revolt against this, the social scientists forged their own tools—without philosophical foundations and breaking off at the level that seemed necessary for mastering their problems. Therefore, inadequate formulations, without correct grounding, and many obfuscating misunderstandings. It is important to distinguish between what social scientists say and what they mean.

Agreement with Nagel and Hempel on the following points:

(a) All empirical knowledge involves discoveries through processes of controlled inference.
(b) Must be stateable in propositional form.
(c) Must be verifiable by anyone who is prepared to make the effort to do so through observation—though not necessarily sensory observation.
(d) "Theory" means in all empirical sciences the explicit formulation of determinate relations between a set of variables in terms of which a fairly extensive class of empirically ascertainable regularities can be explained.
(e) Neither the fact that these regularities [2062] have in the social sciences a rather narrowly restricted universality, nor that they permit prediction only to a rather limited extent, constitutes a basic difference between the social and the natural sciences, since certain branches of the natural sciences show the same features.

Instead of an analysis, the following simple propositions shall be defined as my standpoint. [2063]

Social reality

(1) The primary goal of the social sciences is to obtain organized knowledge of social reality.

Social reality (def.) = the sum total of objects and occurrences within the socio-cultural (life-)world as experienced by the commonsense thinking of men living their daily lives among their fellowmen, connected with them in manifold relations of interaction.

We are born into this world of cultural objects and social institutions,

we have to find our bearings in it,

we have to come to terms with it.

From the outset, we who act in it experience the world we live in as a world of both nature and culture.

not as private, but

intersubjective, i.e. common to all of us,

either actually or potentially

accessible to everyone.

This involves intercommunication and language. [2064]

The social reality simply taken for granted by the logical empiricists.

(2) Naturalism and logical positivism simply take for granted the social reality that is the proper object of the social sciences. Intersubjectivity, interaction, intercommunication are simply presupposed as the unclarified foundation of these theories. They assume, as it were, that the social scientist has already solved his fundamental problem, before scientific inquiry starts.

To be sure, Dewey: all inquiry starts and ends within the social cultural matrix.

To be sure, Nagel: Science and its self-correcting process is a social enterprise. [2065]

The postulate to describe and explain human behavior in terms of controllable sensory observations stops short before the description and explanation of the process by which scientist B controls and verifies the observed findings of scientist A and the conclusions drawn by him.

B must know: what A has observed

what the goal of his inquiry is,

why he thought the observed fact worthy of being observed, i.e. relevant to the problem, etc.

This knowledge is commonly called "understanding."

The explanation of how such an understanding can occur is generally left to the social scientist. But whatever the explanation may be, one thing is sure, namely that such an intersubjective understanding between scientist B and scientist A occurs neither by scientist B's observations of scientist A's overt behavior, nor by introspection performed by B, nor by identification of B with A.

Reference to Felix Kaufmann's proof that protocol propositions about the physical world are of an entirely different kind than protocol propositions about the psycho-physical world.

(= *Methodologie der Sozialwissensschaften* p. 126)[1] [2066]

Arguments against behaviorism

(3) Restriction to sensory observation and experience of overt actions excludes entire dimensions of social reality from scientific inquiry.

(a) G. H. Mead: Behaviorism can explain only observed behavior, not that of observing.

(b) The same overt behavior (a tribal ceremony) may have an entirely different meaning for the performers.

(c) "Negative actions," i.e., intentional refraining from acting. Not to operate, not to sell.

(d) The Thomas theorem: Social reality contains elements of beliefs and convictions that are real because they are defined as real by the participants, but escape sensory observation: Witches were a reality, not a delusion, to the inhabitants of Salem.

(e) Sensory observation possible only in face-to-face relationship. But other dimensions: Letter, France fears the rearmament of Germany [2067]

The life-world is from the outset experienced not only as intersubjective, but as meaningful.

The other's body is [experienced] not only as an organism but as a fellowman; its overt behavior not only as an occurrence in space-time, but as our fellowman's action. We normally "know" what the other does and why he is doing it now and under these particular circumstances, i.e. we experience our fellowman's actions in terms of his motives and goals. And in the same way we experience cultural objects in terms of the human actions of which they are the results. A tool, for example, is experienced not only as a thing in the outer world (which of course it is also) but in terms of the purpose for which it was designed by more or less anonymous fellowmen and its possible use by others.

The fact that in commonsense thinking we take for granted our actual or potential knowledge of the meaning of human actions and their products is precisely what social scientists want to express if they speak of understanding [*Verstehen*] as a technique of dealing with human affairs. [2068]

Understanding

is not a method used by the social scientist, but the particular experiential form in which everyday thinking takes cognizance of the social (life-)world.

It is also not a private affair, but controllable:
Jury, whether there was "premeditated intent" or "malice," etc.
Moreover, (highly reliable) predictions based on "understanding" are possible.
Nevertheless, the statement is justified that "understanding" is "subjective." Explanation of this unfortunate term.

To be distinguished:
(1) "Understanding" as the experiential form of everyday knowledge.
(2) as an epistemological problem.
(3) as a method peculiar to the social sciences.

ad (1): above

ad (2): the "scandal of philosophy," but the possibility of understanding the practice of everyday life in the world is taken for granted and constantly solved in everyday actions by everyone.—Born of mothers, the experience of the existence of other human beings and of the meaning of their acts is certainly the first and most original empirical observation. [2069]

The life-world as unquestioned but questionable background of the beginning and end of scientific inquiry.

On this topic, such different philosophers as
W. James
Bergson
Dewey
Husserl
Whitehead

agree.

Dewey: in the social matrix, unclarified situations [emerge] that have to be transformed by the process of inquiry into warranted assertability.

Whitehead: The aim of science [is] to produce a theory that agrees with experience by explaining the thought-objects constructed by common sense through the mental constructs or thought-objects of science. [2070]

Fundamental difference between the thought objects (constructs) of natural science and of social science

The natural scientist alone defines his observational field and (in accordance with the procedural rules of his science) determines the facts, data, and events within this field that are relevant for his problem or scientific purpose at hand. Neither are those facts and events preselected, nor is the observational field preinterpreted. The world of nature, as explored by the natural scientist, has no "meaning" to the molecules, atoms, and electrons therein.

The observational field of the social scientist, i.e. the social reality of everyday life, however, has a specific meaning and relevance structure for the human beings living, acting, and thinking therein. By a series of commonsense constructs they have preselected and preinterpreted this world which they experience as the reality of their daily lives. It is these thought-objects of theirs that determine their behavior by motivating it.

The thought-objects constructed by the social scientist [2071] in order to grasp this social reality have to be founded upon the thought-objects constructed by the commonsense thinking of the men living in it. Thus, the constructs of the social scientists are, so to speak, constructs of the second degree, namely constructs of the constructs made by the actors on the social scene, whose behavior the social scientist has to observe and to explain in accordance with the procedural rules of his science. [2072]

The unity of science
(Concept and Theory 272)

Dempf:

[There is] no different logic for natural science and social science.

But this does not mean that the social sciences have to abandon their particular procedures and slavishly follow those of natural science, especially physics.

[It is an] unjustified assumption that only the methods of the natural sciences, especially of physics, are scientific.

Perhaps the methodological problems of the natural sciences are special problems of the same and the general problem of knowledge and its basic presuppositions is more easily accessible to the social sciences.

The postulate of continuity
whether it means continuity of existence,
of analysis,
or of an intellectual criterion of
continuous checking upon the methods employed, is fulfilled by the two-level theory of social scientific constructs. [2073]

Thematic areas from the essay for Van Breda's Commemorative Volume, insofar as they were not discussed above:

(1) Act, motive, project, neutrality-modification of the positing presentation;

(2) Time-factor of the project, feasibility, choosing among projects of action;

(3) Monothetic, polythetic structure and sociality (synchronicity of the "Thou");

(4) Sign and symbol, appresentation, multiple realities originating in and referring back to the life-world.

Third Notebook

from Seelisberg

August 19 – 27, 1958

from (43) [below]: New York,

October 25 – 26, 1958

Contains: pp. 3001 – 3099

(Symbol 137)

[3001] *Whitehead*[2] in *Symbolism* and *Process and Reality* sees the origin of symbolic reference in perception, namely in the integration of percept in the mode of causal efficacy in our commonsense perception. *Cassirer* distinguishes signs (or signals), which are operators and part of the physical world of being, from symbols, which are designators and part of the human world of meaning. The former, even when understood and used as signals, have nevertheless a sort of physical and substantial being, whereas symbols have only functional value. Signs or signals are related to the thing to which they refer in a fixed and unique way, whereas the human symbol is not rigid and inflexible but mobile.

The So-called Natural Sign [3002]

(139)

Interchangeability of sign and signified

S. K. Langer: Sign and object would be interchangeable, if the latter were not different from the standpoint of the interpreting subject who uses the sign. Thunder may just as well be a sign that there has been lightning as lightning that there will be thunder. In themselves the sign and the thing signified are correlated. It is only where one of the two is perceptible and the other (harder or impossible to perceive) is *interesting* that we actually have a case of sign-function (signification) for one of the two terms.

(It is important to see, how in the Cassirer/Langer Theory the sign-function depends on interest, i.e. on relevance.)

Similarly John *Wild:* We take that member of a pair as a sign for the other which is better known to us than its signatum and, therefore, as a sign, dissimilar to it. The footprint of the animal is better known to us than the animal. But when neither the one nor the other is known, the sign may really signify the signatum. Signs are discovered, not made. [3003]

(140)
Yet in spite of these authors, everyday experience refuses to admit that fire is a sign for smoke, pain a sign for moaning, the physical object a sign for the concept.

Aristotle, De Interpretatione 16a 3ff.
"Spoken words are the symbols *(symbola)* of mental experience, and written words are the symbols of spoken words. Just as all men do not have the same writings so

all men do not have the same speech sounds, but the mental experiences *(pathemata tēs psychēs)* which these directly symbolize *(semeion)* are the same for all as also are those things of which our experiences are the images *(homoiomata)*."[3]
We have the rather complicated relationship:
Physical event (sound or penstroke) denoting the thing named, connoting the conception referred to. Therefore most certainly irreversible relations. The same holds good for all symbolic references of a higher order. [3004]

(140f.)
"Convention" and social structure of signs

Aristotle, De Interpretatione 16a 19f.:
A name is a sound that is significant by convention.[4] *(kata synthekēn)* This limitation is necessary, according to Aristotle, because nothing is by nature a name; it becomes a name only when it becomes a symbol. Inarticulate sounds, such as those a brute produces, are indeed significant, but nevertheless not a name *(onoma)*. For Aristotle, therefore, language and artificial signs in general are matters of conventions.
But the concept of convention presupposes the existence of society and also the possibility of some form of communication with the help of which the "convention" can be established. This leads to a series of important questions. [3005]

Questions associated with this:
(1) Does the statement of convention hold good also for all kinds of signs, including nonlinguistic ones?

(2) Or for all nonnatural signs?

(3) Or even for natural ones?

(4) Or still more generally: If it is true, as it is widely believed, that every sign and symbol-relation involves at least three terms, of which one is the subject or the interpreter of the sign, is this interpreter tacitly assumed to have already established communication with his fellowmen so that the sign or symbol-relation is from the outset a public one?

(5) Or are there sign- and symbol-relations even within the private psychological or spiritual life of the lonely individual?

(6) If so, how can these signs be shared with others, be com-municated to
them? And to what extent?

(7) Are my fantasies, my dreams, and the systems of symbols that emerge
in them also capable of socialization? [3006]

(8) Do artistic creation, religious experience, philosophizing presuppose
intersubjectivity?

(9) If, on the other hand, there are public and private symbols, does a
particular socio-cultural environment influence the structure of either or
both of them, and to what extent?

(10) Is it not possible that what is a sign or a symbol for one individual or
one group has no significative or symbolic meaning for another individual
or group?

(11) Moreover, can intersubjectivity as such, society and community as such,
be experienced otherwise than by mediation of symbols?

(12) Then, is it the symbol that creates society and community, or is the
symbol a creation of society imposed upon the individual?

(13) Or is this interrelationship between society and the system of symbols
a process of such kind that symbols, or at least some of them, originate
in society and, once established, influence in turn the structure of society
itself? [3007]

(142)
Symbol and the experience of transcendence

The place of man in a cosmos that transcends his existence, but within
which he has to find his way, his bearings. Sign and symbol are among the
means by which man tries to come to terms with his manifold experiences
of transcendency. We will have to show how the perceptible world actually
given to the individual at any moment of his biographical existence
(a) brings along its open horizons of space and time that transcend his
    actual Here and Now.
(b) How a common communicative environment originates in the compre-
    hension of the fellowmen and how the Other's existence and that of
    society transcends in still another sense the individual's actual
    experiences.
    It will have to be shown that a specific form of what Husserl called
appresentations—called marks, i.e. marking signs, indications, signs—
corresponds to each of these particular transcendences. [3008]
    All [these transcendences] have in common the fact that they are
experienced within the reality of everyday life. But this is not the only
reality in which man lives.
    There are other transcendences, beyond those mentioned so far.

W. James's theory of the multiple realities or "subuniverses," such as the world of religion, of art, of science, that can only be experienced in the unique form of appresentation for which we wish to reserve the term "symbol."

The world of everyday life, of everyday experience, has a paramount position above other provinces of reality, *since only within it does communication with our fellowmen become possible.* But the world of everyday life is from the outset a socio-cultural world, and the many questions concerning the intersubjectivity of the symbol-reactions originate within it, are determined by it, and find their solution within it. [3009]

Cart. Med. V §§ 49-54
Ideen II. §§ 44-47, § 50, Suppl. p. 410, §51, esp. p. 198
Symb. p. 143ff.

Husserl's Concept of Appresentation

The concept of pairing (here between sign and signified). A form of passive synthesis that is called association.

Particular forms of pairing: "appresentation" or analogical "apperception." Primitive form: two or more data are intuitively given in the unity of consciousness. The consciousness, by this very reason, constitutes two distinct phenomena as a unity, regardless of whether or not they are attended to. Illustration: Object in the outer world: a perceived front view involves analogous apperception of the unseen backside, an apperception that, to be sure, is more or less empty. But it can be verified by turning the object around. (Fink) *Anticipation is based on our past experiences of normal objects of this kind.*

      (N.B.: reference to the stock of knowledge on hand, its structuring, its typology.)

The red wooden cube; possible disappointment of anticipation; but *some* color, *some* material, *some* form.

      Appresentation is *not* an inference. [3010]

In Log. Unt. VI §§ 14f. and 26 (Farber pp. 410–15 and 430f.) and Ideen I, § 43, Husserl had already shown that significative relations are special cases of analogical appresentation, although there he used a somewhat different terminology. But he states clearly that if we perceive an object of the outer world as itself, no apprehension on a higher level, that is, no appresentational references are built up on the basis of this apprehending act of intuition. On the other hand, in the case of significative relations, we have the appresenting object as perceived in the intuitive field, but we are not aimed directly toward it, but through the medium of a secondary apprehension or an act of "founded grasping" toward something else which is 'indicated' or, in Husserl's later terminology 'appresented' by the first object. Thus, by appresentation, we experience intuitively something as indicating or depicting significantly something else. [3011]

Experience by Appresentation has its Particular Style
of Confirmation:

//Is that really so? Verifiability! [Schutz's marginal comment—*trans.*]//
Each appresentation carries along its particular appresentational horizons,
which leads to further fulfilling or confirming experiences, to systems of
well-ordered indications, including new potentially confirmable syntheses
and new nonintuitive anticipations.

But that is not all. So far we have tacitly presupposed that appresentation requires co-presence of the appresenting with the appresented
member of the pair. This, however, is just a special case of a general state
of affairs. In *Experience and Judgment* §§ 34-43, Husserl has shown that a
passive synthesis of pairing is also possible between an actual perception
and a recollection, a perception and a phantasm *(fictum)* and thus [3012]
between actual and potential experiences, between the apprehension of
facts and possibilities. The passive synthesis of association here involved
brings it about that the apprehension of the present element of a previously constituted pair "wakens" the appresented element, it being
immaterial whether one or the other is a perception, a recollection, a
phantasm, or a fictum. All this happens in pure passivity without interference of the mind. E.g. the present percept wakens submerged recollections
that then emerge whether or not we want them to. And, even further,
according to Husserl, any active remembering takes place on the basis of
an associative wakening that had occurred previously. In general, it is true
that by the functioning of a passive synthesis a unity of intuition is constituted not only between perception and recollection, but also between
perceptions and phantasms. [3013]

(Pp. 146f.)
The Various Orders Involved in the Appresentational Situation.
(1) Neither the appresenting nor the appresented object is involved (as was
previously assumed). Each stands within a field, carries along its horizon,
belongs to an order with its own particular style: The physical object is
interconnected with the whole of nature by spatial, temporal, and causal
relations; a mathematical object, e.g. an equilateral triangle refers to all
axioms and theorems that define it. The same holds good of all kinds of
objects. There is even an order of phantasms and an intrinsic order of our
dreams that distinguishes them from all other kinds of objects and constitutes them as finite provinces of meaning.

(2) Consequently, in any appresentative relation, several orders are
involved. This is the case whether the appresenting and the appresented
object belong to one or several realms of meaning. (Example for the latter:
a flag; for the former, smoke as a "sign" of fire). [3014]

In any appresentational situation we distinguish four orders:
(1) The order of objects to which the immediately apperceived object

belongs if it is experienced as itself, disregarding all appresentational references. (*apperceptual* scheme)

(2) The order of objects to which the immediately apperceived object belongs if it is taken not as itself but as a member of an appresentational pair, thus referring to something other than itself. (*appresentational* scheme)

(3) The order of objects to which the appresented member of the pair belongs which is apperceived in a merely analogical manner. (*referential* scheme)

(4) The order to which this particular appresentational reference itself belongs, that is, the particular type of pairing or context by which the appresenting member is connected with the appresented one—or, more generally, the relationship that prevails between the appresentational and the referential scheme. (*contextual* or *interpretational* scheme) [3015]

In describing an appresentational relationship we may take any of these orders as our starting point, our 'home base,' our system of reference, or, to use the term of Husserl, we may 'live in' any of these orders. Of course, we may at any time substitute any of these systems for any other as system of reference, and in the natural attitude of our everyday life we indeed continuously do so. But as long as we retain one of these schemes as the fundamental initial order, the other schemes seem to be characterized by arbitrariness and contingency, or as lacking any order whatsoever. [3016]

Bergson's Theory of Concurring Orders. *Evolution créatrice* ch. III[5]
        pp. 238-244
           252-258
The two orders and disorder.
The disorderly room
Chaos
The automatic order and the willed order.
      Application of Bergson's theory to a few of the controversial opinions concerning sign and symbol
        Symbol pp. 149-151 [3017]

(151)
The principles governing the structural changes of appresentational relations.

A. *The principle of the relative irrelevance of the vehicle*
      An appresented object X, which was originally paired with the appresenting object A, can enter a new pairing with object B, which henceforth appresents X. The new vehicle B, if apprehended (remembered, fantasied) in co-presence will waken in the mind of the experiencing subject the same appresented object X that formerly was paired with the vehicle A.

(a) longhand, typescript, print does not change the meaning of scientific paper.

(b) possibility of vehicle substitution is one (of the many) prerequisites for translating a term into other languages (two, deux, duo, zwei, etc.)

(c) In the pairing of X with a new vehicle, two cases are possible:
(α) *either* the original vehicle A is preserved and retains its appresentational functions along with the new B. Then A & B become synonyms in the broadest (not merely linguistic) sense. Example: vessel-ship, 10-ten, MDCCCCLIX-1959
(β) *or* the appresented object becomes completely detached from the originally appresenting A, [3018] in which case the original appresenting relation (A) − (X) is obfuscated or entirely forgotten. If this happens the originally appresenting A loses its wakening power.

B. *The principle of variability of the appresentational Meaning*
    Same situation as in (A) (c) (α), but the appresentative meaning changes with the substitution of B for A:
    Napoleon: [victor of] Jena—[vanquished of] Waterloo; equilateral equiangular triangle; A>B, B<A; Paris—Chartres [/Chartres—Paris]

C. *The principle of figurative transference*
    The opposite of irrelevancy of the vehicle: an appresenting object A was originally paired with the appresented object X, and now enters a new pairing with an appresented object Y, eventually also with a third object Z. Two cases are possible:
(a) *either* the original appresentational relation (A-X) is preserved and coexists with the new one (A-Y). Then a single appresenting object A may appresent two or several objects (X,Y, . . .). This is possibly the origin of the trope and of the figurative use of expression; it may lead to equivocal use of A; on the other hand, it makes higher-level constructions of appresentational relations possible. [3019]
(b) *or* the appresentational reference (A-X) is obfuscated or forgotten and merely the new one (A-Y) is preserved: change of meaning [3020]

Motive for the development and use of symbolic relations.
    The world within my reach and its dimensions.
Marks [i.e. marking signs] and indications. [3021]

(Symbol 154f.)
The world within my actual and potential reach and the manipulatory sphere
regarded from the standpoint of the isolated individual.
(1) In my natural attitude I take the world for granted as my reality.
(2) I have to understand it to the extent necessary to come to terms with it, to act within it and upon it, and to carry out my projects at hand.
(3) In this sense the world is given to my interpretation (for me to interpret).
(4) This interpretation is based upon the stock of my previous experiences, which in the form of my "knowledge at hand" functions as a scheme of reference.

(5) To this knowledge at hand belongs also my knowledge that the world I live in is not a mere aggregate of colored spots, incoherent noises, centers of warm and cold, but a world of well-circumscribed objects with definite qualities, objects among which I move and which I move, [3022] which resist me and upon which I may act.

(6) From the outset these objects are experienced in their typicality, as mountains and stones, trees and animals, and, more specifically, as birds, fishes, and snakes.

quoted: *Experience and Judgment*, Paragr. 18-22

> Common Sense, pp. 5 f.
> Language, Language Disturbances 340-390

(7) This world as experienced through my natural attitude is the scene and also the object of my actions. I have to dominate it and change it in order to carry out my purposes. Movements—kinaesthetic, locomotive, operative—gear, so to speak, into the world, modifying or changing its objects and their mutual interrelationships; on the other hand, these objects offer resistance to my acts, which I can either overcome or to which I have to yield. In this sense it can be said that a pragmatic motive governs my natural attitude in daily life.

(8) In this attitude I experience the world as organized in time and space around myself as the center. The place my body occupies at a certain moment within this world, my actual "Here" is the starting point from which I take my bearing in space. [3023] It is, so to speak, the center 0 of the system of coordinates that determines certain dimensions of orientation in the surrounding field and the distances and perspectives of the objects therein: they are above or underneath, before or behind, right or left, nearer or farther.

And, in a similar way, my actual "Now" is the origin of all time-perspectives under which I organize the events within the world, such as the categories of before and after, past and future, simultaneity and succession, sooner or later.

(9) The sector of the world of perceived and *perceptible* objects at whose center I am shall be called the world within my actual reach. It includes, thus, objects within the scope of my view and the range of my hearing. Inside the field within my reach there is a region of things that I can manipulate.

(10) (Already in the essay itself, it was pointed out that this depiction is highly sketchy and very imprecise but sufficient for the essay's purposes. The problem involved is much more complicated. Just think that we are living in a time when ICBMs [intercontinental ballistic missiles] extend the range of the manipulative sphere far across the world. [3024] It is said there that the expansion of the manipulatory sphere is perhaps one of the main characteristics of the state of our world situation today.)

Now, all this is insufficient as long as no precise analysis is under-

taken of the function of instruments, i.e. of the technical or terminological factor through which the world within actual reach is extended and of those other tools through which it can be manipulated. Much reflection is still needed on this subject but the overlapping of the world within reach and of the manipulatory sphere is a fundamental problem in both directions: I can perhaps manipulate the moon with rockets but not yet the fixed stars; I can cause atomic fallout, but I do not know how it influences future genetic developments.
(The essay continues)

(11) The manipulatory sphere (G. H. Mead, *Phil. of the Present*,[6] pp. 124ff., *Philosophy of the Act*,[7] pp. 103-106, 121ff., 151f., 190-192, 196-197, 282-284) is the region open to my immediate interference that I can modify either directly [3025] by movements of my body or with the help of artificial extensions of my bodily territory. The manipulatory zone is that portion of the outer world upon which I can operate by my current actions.

(12) In a certain sense, it can be said that the part of the world within my reach that does not belong to the manipulatory zone transcends it: it constitutes the zone of my potential manipulations or, as we prefer to say, of my potential working acts. Of course, these realms have no rigid frontiers: each one has a specific realm of "halos" and open horizons, and there are even enclaves within "foreign territory."

(13) It is also clear that the world within my actual reach including (the manipulatory zone) undergoes changes by any of my locomotions. By displacing my body I move the center 0 of my system of coordinates to 0', and this circumstance alone changes all coordinates pertaining to this system. [3026]

Marks [i.e. marking signs]

(14) I experience the world within my actual reach as an element or a phase of my unique biographical situation, and this involves a transcending of the Here and Now to which it belongs. To my unique biographical situation pertain, among many other things, my recollections of the world within my reach in the past but no longer within it since I moved from "There" to "Here," and my anticipations of a world which can be brought within my future reach, if I move from 'Here' to 'There' for this purpose.

(15) I know or I assume that, disregarding technical obstacles and other limitations, such as the fundamental irretrievability of the past, I can bring my recollected world in my former reach back into my actual reach (world in restorable reach).

I expect also to find it substantially the same (always perhaps: the same, but changed) as I had experienced it while it was within my actual reach; and I know or [3027] assume also that what is now within my actual reach will go out of my reach when I move away but will be, in principle, restorable to my reach if I return.

(Although this certainly cannot be treated at any length here, allusion would have to be made to Royaumont's discussion with Fink:[8] Finiteness of existence, my death as the definitive end (?), the restorability of all reaches).

(16) The latter case is to me of an eminently practical interest. I expect that what is now within my actual reach will go out of my reach but will come back into my actual reach. In particular, I anticipate that what is now in my manipulatory sphere will re-enter it later and either require my interference or will interfere in my life. Therefore I have to be sure that I shall then find my bearings within it and come to terms with it as I can now while it is under my control.

(17) This presupposes that I shall be able to recognize those elements that I *now* find *relevant* within [3029] the world within my actual reach, especially within the *manipulatory* zone, and which—as I assume on the basis of the idealization called "I can do it again" by Husserl—will prove relevant also when I return later on.

(18) This motivates me to single out certain elements of this zone and to *mark* certain objects. When I return I expect to find these marks useful as "subjective reminders" or as "mnemonic devices" (Wild's terms). Of what kind they are is immaterial.

Examples: a broken twig, selection of a particular landmark to mark the trail to the waterhole, bookmarks, underlined passages in a book.

(19) What counts is merely that all these marks, themselves objects of the outer world, will from now on be intuited no longer as "they themselves" in the pure apperceptual scheme. They have entered, for me the interpreter, into an appresentational reference. The broken twig is more than just that. It has become a mark for the location of the waterhole, or, if you prefer, a signal for me to turn left. In its appresentational function, which originates in the interpretational scheme into which I place it, [3029] the broken twig is henceforth paired with its referential meaning: "Way to the waterhole." [Two (19)s in original.—*Trans.*]

(19) The arbitrary character of my selecting certain objects as marks must be emphasized. The broken twig has "in itself" nothing to do with the waterhole. The two things are in one interpretational context merely because such a context was established by me. According to the principle of the relative irrelevance of the vehicle, I could replace the broken twig by a pile of stones and, according to the principle of figurative transference, dedicate this pile to a naiad, etc. [3030]

Indications and the stock of knowledge at hand

(20) The stock of knowledge at hand is, as W. James already saw, by no means homogeneous. Its structure is determined by the fact that I am not equally interested in all the strata of the world within reach. *The selective function of interest organizes the world into strata of major and minor relevance.*

From the world within my actual or potential reach are selected as primarily important those facts, objects, and events that actually are or will become possible ends and means, possible obstacles or conditions for the realization of my projects, or which are or can become dangerous or enjoyable or otherwise relevant to me.

(It must be examined precisely whether, as it seems, the relevance mentioned in the text refers to motivational relevance or also to other categories of relevance.)

(21) Certain objects and events are known to me as being interrelated in a more or less typical way, but my [3031] knowledge of their particular kind of interrelatedness is rather vague and lacks transparency. If I know that event B usually appears simultaneously with event A or precedes or follows it, then I take this as a manifestation of a typical and plausible relationship existing between A and B, although I know nothing of the nature of this relationship. Until further notice I simply expect or take it for granted that any future recurrence of A will be connected in typically the same way with a preceding, concomitant, or subsequent recurrence of B. I then apprehend A not as an object, fact, or event standing for itself, but standing for something else, namely the past, present, or future appearance of B. This form of appresentation is frequently called a sign. We prefer to reserve the term 'sign' for another form of appresentation and to call the present one an 'indication.' [3032]

"Indication" in Husserl I Log. Untersg. §§1–4, esp. p. 27, Farber p. 222

(22) Husserl's definition of indication: An object, fact, or event (A), actually perceptible to me, may be experienced as related to another past, present, or future fact or event (B) actually not perceptible to me, in such a way that my conviction of the existence of the former (A) is experienced by me as an *opaque* motive for my conviction for, assumption of, or belief in the past, present, or future existence of the latter (B). This motivation constitutes for me a pairing between the indicating element (A) and the indicated one (B). The indicating member of the pair is not only a "witness" for the indicated one, it does not only point to it, but it suggests the assumption that the other member exists, has existed, or will exist. Again the existing member is not experienced as "itself," i.e. merely in the apperceptual scheme, [3033] but as "wakening" appresentationally the indicated one.

(23) It is especially important that the particular nature of the motivational [connection] remain opaque. If there is clear and sufficient insight into the nature of the connection between the two elements, we have to deal not with the referential relation of indication but with the inferential one of proof.

(Therefore (known) footprints of the tiger are not an indication of his existence, but the halo around the moon, smoke for fire, the geological formation for oil, discoloration of the skin for Addison's [disease], the position of the needle on the dial of the car for an empty tank, etc.)

Most so-called natural signs fall under this category.

(24) The knowledge of indications helps the individual to transcend the world within his actual reach,[9]

by relating [an] element within it to elements outside it. The relation of indication again does not yet presuppose intersubjectivity. [3034]

(159)

The Intersubjective World and its Appresentational Relations: Signs

The world of everyday life is from the outset an intersubjective one.

(25) Marks [marking signs] and indications are appresentational forms that do not necessarily presuppose the existence of fellowmen and communication, but can be explained by the pragmatic motive governing the individual in his endeavor to come to terms with the world within his reach. To be sure, marks [marking signs] and indications can occur in the intersubjective context and indeed frequently do.

(26) So far the life-world within my reach and its dimensions have been analyzed without any reference to intersubjectivity, i.e. simply as I find them in the natural intuition of my everyday life.

Yet the life-world is by no means my private world. Intersubjective from the outset, I share it with my fellowmen; it is also experienced and interpreted by others, [it is] a world that is common to all of us.

(27) The unique biographical situation in which I find myself within the world at all times is only to [3035] a very small extent of my own making. I find myself always within an historically given world which as the natural world and the social world (cultural world) has existed before my birth and will continue to exist after my death.

(Death: see note 8, p. 331 below)

(28) This means that this world is not only mine but also my fellowmen's environment. Moreover, these fellowmen are elements of my situation, as I am of theirs: acting upon others and acted upon by them, I know of this mutual relationship, and this knowledge also implies that they, the others, experience this common [world] in a way substantially similar to mine. They, too, find themselves in a unique biographical situation within the world that is, like mine, structured in zones of actual and potential reach and [-] grouped around their actual Here and Now at the center [-] in the same dimensions and directions of space and time: an historically given world of nature, society, culture, etc. [3036]

(29) Without going into the phenomenological problem of the constitution of intersubjectivity, it is sufficient for this purpose of analyzing the everyday experience of the life-world to state:

—that man takes for granted the bodily existence of fellowmen; —likewise, that they have consciousness;

—that the possibility of communicating with them exists;
—that social organization and culture are historically given, indeed just as
the natural world into which we are born is taken for granted.

(30) If we abstract first from the fact that the social world into which I was
born already displayed a highly diversified social and political organization
and that I as well as the other members of such organizations have a particular role, a particular status, and particular functions within them. We
therefore restrict ourselves to considering first the appresentational references by which we have knowledge of others' mind; then, the structur-
[3037] ation of the everyday life-world that we share with our fellowmen,
and its inherent transcendencies, are to be investigated; and finally, the
phenomena of comprehension, manifestation, and communication and of
the appresentational relation, upon which they are founded, [namely] that
of the sign. [3038]

(161)
Our knowledge of the other mind is itself based on appresentational references

(31) Despite the difficult problematic of our knowledge of other minds and
the highly controversial theories that are offered for its solution by the
various philosophical schools, it can be stated that behaviorists and existen-
tialists, logical positivists and phenomenologists agree, if we disregard the
phenomenon of telepathy, that knowledge of the content of another's mind
occurs only through the intermediary of events occurring in the other's
body or produced by the other's body.

(32) According to Husserl (Med. Cart. V. § 50ff, Ideen II § 43-50 Schutz
Diskussion Ideas II. pp. 404ff.) this is a remarkable case of appresentation.
According to him, the other is from the outset given to me as both a material object with its position in space and time and a subject with its
psychological life. His body, like all material objects, is given to my original
perception or, as Husserl says, in originary presence. His psychological
life, however, is not given to me [3039] in originary presence but only in
co-presence. (*Nota bene* what Ortega says about co-presence.) It is not presented, but appresented. By the continuous visual perception of the other's
body and its movements, a system of appresentations, of well-ordered indications of his psychological life and his experiences is constituted, and
here, says Husserl, is the origin of the various forms of systems of signs or
expressions, and finally of language. The physical object, "the other's
body," events occurring on this body, and his bodily movements are apprehended as expressing the other's "spiritual I," toward whose *motivational
meaning-context* I am directed. So-called "empathy" in the other person is
nothing but that form of appresentational apprehension which grasps this
meaning.

All sorts of things can be said about this:

(a) Fink's remark on the unverifiability of this form of appresentation must

[be] regarded critically. For can it not be verified through the continuation of "consistent [3040] conduct"?

(b) The double (triple?) meaning [of] "expression" must be analyzed. What is expressed for me, the interpreter, is far from being expressed on the other's part, or rather: He had no intention whatever of expressing it. (The graphologist turns the page.)

(c) Here Husserl's transcendental approach still makes itself felt: Why, with the natural attitude, should not speech, and hence the other person who speaks, revealing and communicating himself, not belong from the outset to the social life-world?

(d) Sex, and perhaps also age, are aspects, as Merleau-Ponty and Ortega have remarked, of the other person's living organism.

(All this must [be] reflected on precisely; it is questionable whether this is the place to discuss these problems.) [3041]

(33) The same situation, according to Husserl, holds true of *cultural objects*. A book [is] an object of the outer world, a material thing. Here it lies before me, to my right, on my desk in a red binding. But when reading it I am not directed toward the book as an object of the outer world, but toward the meaning of what is written therein: I "live in this meaning," by comprehending it.

The same holds good of a tool, a house, a theater, a church, a machine, etc. The spiritual meaning of all these objects is appresentationally apperceived as being founded upon the actually appearing object, which is not apprehended as such but as the vehicle and expression of a meaning.

(34) Furthermore, if we listen to somebody speak, we do not experience the meaning of what he says as something connected with the words in an external way. We take his words as expressing their meaning-content: we live in their meaning by comprehending what the Other means and the thought he expresses. (Husserl: *Vom Ursprung der Geometrie*, Husserliana vol. 1[10]) [3042]

(35) To be sure, each person has only his own experiences given in originary presence. But by the intermediary of events in the outer world, occurring on or brought about by the other's body, especially by linguistic expressions in the broadest sense, I may comprehend the other by appresentation; by mutual understanding and consent, a communicative common environment is thus established, within which the subjects reciprocally motivate one another in their mental activities.

(36) These analyses of Husserl's are modeled after one specific form of intersubjectivity, namely the "face-to-face relationship." He further presupposes as self-evident that the appresentational comprehension of events in the other's mind leads immediately to communication. All these assumptions, however, require further elaboration.

First of all, what are the tacitly presupposed idealizations upon which the establishment of a communicative common environment in the "face-to-face relationship" is founded? [3043]

The general thesis of the reciprocity of perspectives

      (a) The idealization of the interchangeability of standpoints

      (b) The idealization of the congruence of the systems of relevancy

(37) Citing the "Common Sense Essay" there follows a summary of the theses developed there (cf. Notebook II)

      (Continuation of the general thesis of the reciprocity of perspectives in (56) and 58f.)) [3044]

The Transcendence of the Other's World

First Transcendence:

(38) So far only the "face-to-face relationship" has been treated, in which a sector of the world lies within both mine and my fellowman's actual reach.

      More precisely speaking, the world within my reach overlaps that within his. But there are necessarily zones within my reach that do not lie within his, and vice versa. As we sit facing one another I see things unseen by him, and vice versa. The same holds good for the manipulatory sphere. This object placed between us is indeed within my manipulatory zone, but not within his.

      In this sense, the Other's world transcends mine. But a corollary of the idealization of the interchangeability of standpoints is that the world within the Other's actual reach lies within my reachability (my potential reach), and vice versa.

      Within certain limits (to point them out would lead too far afield) (apparently I had in mind here the aporias of the "I can" and "I could": I can, introvert[ed] as I am, not do what you, extrovert[ed], can do), [it holds true] that even the world within the other person's restorable reach and [3045] within his anticipated reach lie within my potential reach (which then is a potentiality of the second degree, so to speak), and vice versa.

      (It must here be examined precisely how far the last paragraph applies only to the social environment. How is the problem of mutual reach modified in the various stages of anonymization of the contemporary world? Is there an—at least one-sided—problem of reach as regards the world of predecessors? or even the world of posterity? If not, how can the transcendencies of this other world be overcome?) [3046]

(164)

(39) *Second Transcendence:*

There follows a (good) description of the particularities of the face-to-face relationship for the constitution of the social world.

Only in it are the bodies within reciprocal reach, only in it do we experience one another in our individual uniqueness. In it we are mutually involved in one another's biography.

We are growing old together (Ortega!)
In it we have, indeed, a common environment and common experiences of
events that take place in it.
  "I and You," *We* see the flying bird. And this occurrence of the
bird's flight as an event in outer (public) time is simultaneous with our
perceiving it, which is an event in our inner time. The two fluxes of inner
time, yours and mine, thus become synchronous with the event "bird's
flight" in outer time and thereby with one another. This takes on particular
importance for the investigation of events in the outer world, which serve
as vehicles for communication, namely

(40) *Significant gestures and language.*
Nevertheless, here too another's existence transcends mine, and vice versa.
(a) We have in common only [3047] a small section of our biographies. (b)
Moreover, each of us, as Simmel has shown, enters the social relationship
with only a part of his personality, or, as modern sociologists express it, by
assuming a particular social role. (c) Finally, the other's system of relevance
is founded in his unique biographical situation and thus cannot be congruent with mine: it cannot be brought within my reach, although it can be
understood by me.

(This last statement is "dubious" in every regard. What does it mean for a
system of relevancies to be able to be brought into reach?
  Or does the concept of reach in general perhaps have to be
expanded? Is it justified to restrict it to things of the outer world and such
as are accessible to sensory apperception?
  Is not, in a certain sense, the deciphering of the Etruscan language
or the mathematics of quantum mechanics outside my reach? Or climbing
the North Wall of the Eiger? Is there a connection here with the problem
of "power to act" *(Vermöglichkeit)* and the idealization of the "I can"?) [3048]

(41) *Third Transcendence:*

This surpasses not only the world, but also the other's world: *this is the we-
relation as such;*
although originating in the mutual biographical involvement, it transcends
the existence of either of the consociates within the reality of daily life. It
belongs to a finite province of meaning other than that of the everyday
world and can be grasped only with the help of symbols. But these statements anticipate a set of problems that we are not yet prepared to
approach.
  (Here I probably went too far, although some authorities—Buber,
Berdjaev, Scheler, Jaspers, indeed also Peirce, Royce, Mead—could be
called upon as allies. The question still needs to be thought through very
precisely.) [3049]

The Other Dimensions of the Social World

(42) The face-to-face relationship studied so far is only one, although the
most central, dimension of the social world. If we compare it with the

world within my actual reach, then we also find dimensions in the social world comparable to the world within my potential reach.

This is [probably an attempt] to answer, perhaps partially, the question raised in the note to (38).

(a) The world of my contemporaries, with whom I am not biographically involved (badly formulated) in a face-to-face relation but with whom I have in common a sector of time that makes it possible for me to act upon them as they may act upon me, within a common environment of mutual motivations.

(In a primitive society in which the souls of the deceased are supposed to participate in the social life of the group, the dead are deemed to be contemporaries.)

(b) The world of my predecessors, upon whom I cannot act but whose past actions and their outcomes are open to my interpretation and may influence my own actions.

(c) The world of my successors, of whom no experience is possible, but toward whom I may orient my actions in more or less empty anticipations. [3050]

(43) It is characteristic of all social dimensions other than the face-to-face relation that I cannot grasp my fellowmen as unique individuals but only their typical behavior, their typical motives and attitudes in increasing anonymity.

(The theme of the transcendence of the others' experience and its overcoming by signs is continued (55) ff.) [3051]

Comprehension, Manifestation, Signs, Communication

(44) Always disregarding telepathy, every understanding of another's thought (another's soul) requires an object, fact, or event in the outer world, which, however, is not apprehended as such, but as a so-called "expression" of the cogitations of a fellowman. (Compare analysis of the equivocation contained in the concept "expression" in (32) (b).)

Cogitations discussed: they include in the Cartesian sense feelings, volitions, emotions.

Signs: Those objects, facts, or events in the outer world whose apprehension appresents to an interpreter another's cogitations shall be called "signs." [3052]

(166(a))
(45) *More Details on the Comprehension (Understanding) of Signs of Another's Mind*

The objects, facts, events mentioned in (44), which are interpreted as signs of another's mind, must be referred directly or indirectly to the existence of the Other's body.

(A) In the simplest case, that of a face-to-face relationship, events occurring on another's body (such as blushing, smiling), including bodily movements (wincing, beckoning), activities performed by it (speaking, walking, manipulating things), are made capable of apprehension by the interpreter as signs.

Here should probably be treated in more detail:

(a) Scheler['s] theory of the direct perception of the other's psyche, namely through "inner perception" (whose double meaning must be clarified);
(b) Scheler's view on the "idols of self-perception";
(c) Cassirer's three-stages theory [of] meaning (world as expression, as depiction, as concept);
(d) Snell's parallel theory (on this, see (47).) [3053]

(B) *Case of a tempero-spatial distance: modification of the "face-to-face relationship"*

To be remembered:

> "Presentation": attention to equivocations, particular study of the "neutralization modification" of "positing" and "passive presentation," etc. [Schutz's marginal note—*trans.*]

(i) Apprehension does not necessarily require actual perception of the appresenting member; this can also be a "presentation," i.e. a recollection or a phantasm. I can remember my friend's facial expression when he received some sad news; but I can also imagine what expression his face will have when he will receive this news; (furthermore, I can recall what expression I expected when I went to bring him the news, and how his actual facial expression (his reaction) differed from the one expected when I brought it). I can also fantasy a sad-looking centaur.

(ii) The result or product of another's act refers to his action from which it results and, thus, can function as a sign for events in his consciousness, [3054] his (the other's) *cogitations*.

(iii) The principle of the relative irrelevance of the vehicle (p. 151, A) is applicable here too. The printed lecture refers to the talk of the lecturer. [3055]

(167) (b))

(46) *Comprehension and manifestation*

That an object, fact, or event in the outer world is interpreted as a sign for another person's conscious processes *(cogitations)* does not necessarily presuppose:

(i) that the Other meant to manifest his cogitation by this sign, and even less that he did this with a communicative intent. An "involuntary" facial expression, a furtive glance, blushing, trembling, the other's gait, in brief, any physiognomical event can be interpreted as a sign. A certain hesitation in the Other's voice can convince me that he is lying although he tries precisely to hide the fact that he is doing so. Letter-writer and graphologist.

(ii) If the sign was planned with a communicative intent by the sign-setter the interpreter was not necessarily intended to be the addressee of the communication.

(iii) It is by no means a necessary presupposition of communication that the sign-setter and the interpreter of the sign are known to one another (example: whoever erected this signpost wanted to show any future passerby the direction). [3056]

On this section: Marty's theory of the function of giving and receiving information would have to be worked in. [Schutz's marginal note— *trans.*]

(47) *Types of Signs*

Here Bruno Snell's theory (in the *Structure of Language*[11]) to be described (anticipated in (45) (A) (d)).
Purposive movements, expressive movements, mimetic movements—as bodily movements.

      Differentiation of sounds
      Differentiation of words (singly or in context)
      Differentiation of morphological language elements
      Differentiation of syntactic structure
      Differentiation of literary forms
      Differentiation of types of philosophy
      What the communicator wants (purpose)
                    feels (expression)
                    is or pretends to be (mimesis)

(p. 167/168, (d))
Purposive signs are especially important for communication in the strict sense (48), namely because the communicator has mainly the intention of making the message understandable to the addressee, if not to induce him to react appropriately.

Expressive and mimetic signs (movements) as foundations of the symbolic function.
On the following: the terminology must be worked out precisely.
Especially: sign-setter—sign-interpreter
               information-giver—information-receiver
               communicator—addressee etc. [3057]

(p. 168)
(48) *Communication in the strict sense:*
    its particular presuppositions

(i) Signs used in communication are always signs addressed to an individual or anonymous interpreter by the sign-setter. They originate within the *manipulatory sphere* of the communicator, and the interpreter apprehends them as objects, facts, or events within his reach.

The conditions for understanding (comprehending) of the other's mind by signs (45) (B) (i–iii) apply to this situation. Consequently, it is necessary neither that the world within the interpreter's reach overlap spatially with the manipulatory sphere of the communicator (telephone, television), nor that the production of the sign occur simultaneously with its interpretation (Egyptian papyrus, monuments), nor finally that the same object, fact, or event chosen by the communicator as carrier and vehicle of communication be perceived (apprehended) by the interpreter (principle of the relative irrelevance of the vehicle.) [3058]

In more complicated cases of communication, any number of human individuals or mechanical devices can be inserted into the communicatory process between the original communicator and the interpreter.

(Example: I read in a German newspaper statements made by the President of the U.S.A. at a press conference; I attend a performance of Hamlet, read Cervantes's *Don Quixote*, etc.)

The decisive point is the insight into the facts that under all conditions communication requires, on the one hand, events or objects in the outer world produced by the communicator, and, on the other, events or objects in the outer world perceptible (apprehensible) by the interpreter.

In other words, *communication can occur only within the reality of the outer world*. And this is one of the main reasons why this world has the character of privileged or "paramount" reality—even the voices that the schizophrenic believes he hears are hallucinated by him as *voices*, and hence as events within the outside world. [3059]

(49) (ii) The *signs* used in the communication process are always pre-interpreted *by the communicator* in terms of their expected interpretation by the addressee. To be understood the communicator has, before producing the sign, to anticipate the apperceptual, appresentational, and referential scheme under which the interpreter will presumably subsume it.

The communicator has, therefore, as it were, to perform a rehearsal of the expected interpretation and to establish such a context between his cogitations and the communicative sign that the interpreter, guided by the appresentational scheme he will apply to the sign, will find the sign-producer's cogitations as elements of the related referential scheme. This context is, however, as was shown above (p. 146, (4)) nothing else but the contextual or interpretational scheme itself.

In other words: communication presupposes that the interpretational scheme which the communicator relates and that which the addressee will relate to the communicative sign in question *substantially coincide*. [3060]

(50) (iii) The restriction made at the end of (49): *"substantially"* is of particular importance. Strictly speaking, a full identity of the interpretational scheme that the communicator applies and adopts in anticipation, and the interpretation scheme that the interpreter in fact uses is impossible, at least in the commonsense world of everyday life, for the following reason: The interpretational scheme is determined by the biographical situation and the systems of relevance originating therein. If there were no other differences between the biographical situation of the communicator and that of the

interpreter, then at least this one: that one person's "Here" is the other's "There." This circumstance alone presupposes an insurmountable limit for a fully successful communication in the ideal sense. But, of course, communication can be, and is, highly useful for a whole series of important purposes. It can achieve an optimum of success through the use of highly formalized and standardized languages, such as, e.g. in scientific terminology.

These considerations, seemingly of a highly theoretical nature, also have important practical consequences. Success- [3061] ful communication is possible only between persons, social groups, nations, etc. who share a substantially similar system of relevances. The greater the differences between their systems of relevance, the less chance there is for successful communication, and complete disparity of the systems of relevance makes the establishment of a "universe of discourse" entirely impossible.

(51) (iv) The communicative process, therefore, requires a set of common abstractions or standardizations. The idealization of the congruency of the systems of relevance (see 36 (b)) leads to the superseding of the thought-objects that arise in the private experience of the individual by typified constructs of public objects of thought.

Typification is indeed that form of abstraction which leads to the more or less standardized, yet also more or less vague, conceptualization and therefore to the necessary ambiguity of terms in the ordinary vernacular. [3062]

This is because our experience itself, even in what Husserl called the prepredicative sphere, is organized from the outset under certain types. Therefore, the child learning how to speak is at a very early age capable of recognizing animals as dogs, fishes, birds, or objects of his surroundings as stones, rooms, mountains, tables, chairs, although the dictionary definitions of all these types are extremely difficult.

The vernacular (vocabulary and syntax) as a treasure trove of socially accepted typifications of the language group in question. [3063]

(p. 170)

(52) *Linguistic, pictorial, expressive, and mimetic presentation*

Language as system of signs combinable under syntactical rules; its function as vehicle of discursive (propositional) thinking; its power not only to name things but also to express relations among them; not only to formulate propositions, but also relations among propositions.

Essential for language that the language process and language communication necessarily is a process occurring in time; the *polythetic structure* of language communication; language as a temporal object; the *meaning* of communication, however, is monothetic.

Hence the capacity of language [to] synchronize the stream of consciousness [of the] speaker in inner duration and the stream of consciousness [of the] listener in inner duration both with the flux of the speech event in outer time and also between themselves in the truest sense. (?)

This holds true also for the quasi-simultaneity of writer and reader. [3064]

(53) *Pictorial presentation*

Susanne Langer:[12] [Visual presentations are:]

> not discursive
>
> not composed of elements having independent meaning;
>
> [have] no vocabulary;
>
> no sign not definable by other signs;
>
> their main function: conceptualization of the flux of sensory perceptions;

the appresentational relationship of a pictorial presentation is founded on the proportion of its parts, whose position and relative dimension corresponds to our idea of the depicted object.

That is the reason we recognize "the same" house in a photograph, painting, pencil-sketch, architectural drawing, builder's diagram.

Husserl (Log. Unt. VI sec. 14, Ideas I, sec. III, Farber 410-14) sees characteristics of pictorial figurative representation—in contradistinction to all other signs—in the *similarity relation* between picture and depicted object; whereas all other signs (except perhaps onomatopoeic ones) have nothing in common with what they designate—therefore the assertion of the arbitrariness of the language sign. Nonethe- [3065] less, even in pictorial presentation there exists an appresentational relation, although sometimes in a complicated way of interconnected levels. //Husserl's view hardly tenable! [Schutz's marginal note—*trans.*]//

Dürer's "Knight, Death, and Devil":

(1) (in an apperceptual way) the print as such, the page in the portfolio:

(2) (still apperceptual) black lines on white paper, small colorless figures.

(3) These figures *(appresented)* as depicted "realities" as they appear in the image—the knight [of] "flesh and blood," of whose quasi-being we are aware—and are the neutrality modification of being. (Ideas I, sec. III)

(Schutz, not Husserl)

(4) Appresentations under (3), founded appresentations of a higher order; the symbolic appresentation of man's position in the world between death and devil. [3066]

(54) Communication through *expressive and mimetic presentation*

Expressive: gestures of greeting (see now Ortega y Gasset's excellent description) (cf. E. Benz: Ostkirche (?))[13]

Gesture of prayer

movement of respect

expression of approval or disapproval

display of honor

(on this section, study precisely:

(a) Marcel Mauss: sociology of bodily movement;

(b) Buytendijk: expression and movement;
(c) Plessner: laughter and weeping;
(d) Granet: his book on China;
(e) G. H. Mead: significant gesture)
Mimesis (related with pictorial presentation)
    Kabuki dancers
to be studied: dance symbolism, perhaps based on
    Curt Sachs: World History of Dance[14] [3067]

(p. 172)
(55) *Overcoming Transcendence by the Sign*

The Main Thesis: Overcoming the experience of transcendence through the appresentational relation.

>(cf. "The Transcendence of the Other," above under (38) (39) (41) (42) (43).)

It has now been shown (in the analysis of the various forms of sign and communication) that the appresentational relations have the function of overcoming transcendent experience, namely the experiences of the Other and his world.

Through the use of signs, the communicative process permits me to be aware at least to a certain degree of another's cogitations and, under particular conditions, even to experience his inner duration (stream of consciousness) in perfect simultaneity with mine—this despite the fact that, as we have seen, fully successful communication is impossible. There still remains a zone of the Other's private life that is inaccessible to me and transcends my possible experiences. [3068]

(p. 173)
(56) *How Everyday Practice Solves This Difficulty*

Communication is possible for nearly all useful purposes, because the communicative process is based on a set of typifications, abstractions, standardizations, such as are stored up, e.g. in the ordinary vernacular.

The task here, however, is to clarify some basic features simply "taken for granted" by the commonsense thinking of everyday life, upon which the possibility of communication is founded. They are, in a certain sense, an amplification of the general thesis of the reciprocity of perspectives, analyzed in (36) (37). [3069]

(57) *What does it mean to accept something as simply given? "taken for granted"?*

= to accept until further notice our knowledge of certain states of affairs as unquestionably plausible.

Of course, at any time what hitherto seemed to be unquestionable can always be put in question.

(58) *What does commonsense thinking take for granted until a contrary proof?*

Things simply taken for granted seem to be:

(a) The world of physical and social (cultural) objects, into which we were born. This world is, in fact, the unquestioned but always questionable matrix within which all our inquiries start and end. (Dewey, *Logic* I, esp. pp. 19-20 and Part III *passim.*)[15]

 The process of inquiry consists in the regulated and controlled transformation of indeterminate situations encountered or emerging within this matrix into reliable assertability.

 //the process of inquiry: the task of transforming in a controlled or direct manner indeterminate situations encountered or emerging within this matrix into "warranted assertibility." [Schutz's marginal comment—*trans.*]// [3070]

(b) In my everyday thinking I take for granted not merely that my fellow-man exists, and indeed not just as a bodily existence, but as gifted with a consciousness that displays essentially the same basic structures as my own.

(c) Moreover, I take for granted that to a certain extent I can by appresentational relations analogically attain knowledge of my fellowman's conscious experiences (cogitations), for example, the motives of his action, as he can of mine.

(d) I take for granted that certain objects, facts, and events within our common social environment have for him the same appresentational significances as for me, which significances transform mere things in the outer world into so-called cultural objects.

(e) Until counterevidence is offered, I take for granted that the various apperceptual, appresentational schemes of reference and interpretation accepted and proved as typically relevant by my social environment are equally relevant for my unique biographical situation as they [also] are for my fellowman within [3071] everyday thinking in the life-world.

This means:

(1) With respect to the *apperceptual scheme*, that normally our apperception of objects, facts, or events of the outer world is guided by the system of typical relevances prevailing within our social environment and that a particular motive has to originate in the personal biographical situation of each of us in order to evoke our interest in the uniqueness, in the atypicality, of a particular object, fact, or event, or in its particular aspect.

(2) With respect to the *appresentational scheme* that we both, my fellowman and I, take for granted the typical way in our socio-cultural environment, by which objects, facts, and events in the outer world are apprehended not as "these themselves" but appresentationally as indications of "something else," that is, in the manner of "wakening" or "evoking" appresentational references. [3072]

(3) With respect to the *interpretational scheme* that in case of the existence of communication the other (whether he be the communicator or the interpreter) will apply the same appresentational (?) scheme to the appresentational references involved in the communication as I myself. I take it for granted, e.g. that in case of a communication through the medium of the ordinary colloquial language others who use this idiom mean by the linguistic expressions substantially the same thing that I understand these expressions to mean, and vice versa.

(Here a great deal must be added:

(1) Study on Heidegger's "co-being" and "co-existence"
(2) Sartre's "situation";
(3) Husserl's "communicational environment";
(4) Ortega's concept of habit;
(5) Durkheim's "collective conscience.") [3073]

(p. 174)

(59) *The world within reach and the everyday life-world*

If the terms "world of everyday life" or "everyday reality" do not merely designate the world of nature as experienced by me but also the socio-cultural world in which I live, then it becomes clear that this world does not coincide with the world of the outer objects, facts, and events.

(1) To be sure, the former includes the latter, namely insofar as these objects, facts, and events are either within the zone of my actual reach or within the several zones of my potential reach (among them also that within the actual and potential reach of my fellowman).

(2) In addition, however, the world of daily life includes all appresentational functional functions of such objects, facts, and events which transform natural things into cultural objects, human bodies into fellow-men, their bodily movements into actions or significant gestures, waves of sound into speech, etc. [3074]

(p. 175)

The world of daily life is therefore permeated with appresentational references that are simply taken for granted and among which I carry on my practical activities—my working activities, we have referred to them before—in terms of everyday commonsense thinking.

All these appresentational references belong, according to origin, goal, and direction, to the finite province of meaning called the "reality of everyday life." // Is this understated? // Nevertheless, our thesis stands that all appresentational references are means of coming to terms with the experience of transcendency.

This has been shown with respect to the appresentational indications studied so far, namely marks, indications, and signs. They all help to come to terms with transcendencies, but all these transcendencies themselves belong to that sphere which we have now characterized as the reality of everyday life. As transcendencies

—of my actual Here and Now

—of the Other

—of the Other's life-world, etc.

—they still belonged to the reality of my everyday life-world, as it is grasped by my commonsense thinking, and were co-constitutive for [3075] the situation in which I find myself placed in this life-world.

(60) But there are experiences that transcend the finite province of meaning of the world of everyday life and refer to other provinces of meaning, to other realities, or, to use William James's term, to other subuniverses, such as the world of scientific theory, of art, religion, myth, politics, but also of phantasms and dreams. And there is again a specific kind of appresentational references, called symbols, with whose help man tries to apprehend these transcendent phenomena in a way analogous to the apprehension of the perceptible world. The study of the essence of these symbols, however, requires an analysis of the problem of multiple realities. [3076]

(p. 202)

(61) *Professor Charles Morris's critique*[16] of my concept of the tendency of experience, the transcendence of experience.

(a) For the most part, the term "transcendency" is linked with experience (transcendent experience), but at times this is not so (when e.g., there is mention of the "inaccessible zone of the Other's private life, which transcends my possible experience"). It seems to me that an unnoticed passage back and forth between the *experience of transcendency* and the *transcendence of experience* obscures the argument at a number of crucial points.

(b) Connected with this is the question of the relation of transcendence to marks, indications, signs, and symbols (i.e. to appresentational relations). Does the experience of transcendence come first and exist independently of appresentational relations, or is the experience of transcendence simply the experience of these appresentative relations? I cannot see that this latter possibility is excluded by the analysis offered in the pre- [3077] sent paper. But unless it is, [then] the main thesis of the paper (namely that appresentational references are means of coming to terms with transcendent experiences of various kinds) [stands] on insecure ground. And if in the thesis "transcendent experiences" are taken to mean "transcendence of experiences," then it is difficult to see the sense in which the approach is a phenomenological one. [3078]

(pp. 202f.)

(62) *My answer to Prof. Morris*

The imperfection of the depiction of the relationship criticized by Prof. Morris between transcendence and experience must be admitted; likewise that this problem is fundamental for the entire argumentation. But more is involved than linguistic imprecision or an equivocal use of the term "transcendent experience."

(It is worth investigating whether the term "transcendent experience" used in the English version might not best be translated into German as "Transzendenzerlebnis," which consciously sums up the two states of fact separated by Morris. Indeed, Morris's problem comes up in the first place precisely because he understands "experience" in the empirist sense of the term and not as lived experience. In that case, of course it is possible to transfer the experience of the transcendent to the experience of appresentational references—for which no particular phenomenological apparatus would be needed. But if one speaks [3079] of the transcendence of experience and conceives experience in the empirical sense, then the entire term is absurd.)

(a) To answer the question posed by Prof. Morris, a long analysis of the problem of constitution would be needed. This would show that there are various levels of experience (lived experiences). Each of them may be selected as the basic system of reference, whereupon the other systems then seem transcendent in respect to it. Thus, for example, the world within my potential (restorable and attainable) reach transcends the world within my actual reach, once I have selected the latter as the basic system of reference; likewise, the intersubjective socio-cultural world transcends that of physical things; and the various "subuniverses" of science, art, religion, etc. transcend the paramount reality of the world of everyday life. In brief, transcendencies of this kind are experienced (lived) on each level, and man has to come to terms with them with the help of appresentational references. [3080]

// Certainly badly formulated [Schutz's marginal comment— *trans.*] // What was said above applies, however, only to the lived experience *of* transcendence. But this is only half the story. It is one of the basic findings of phenomenological analysis that there are no isolated and "ready-made" experiences (lived experiences). Each actual experience carries with it its inner and outer horizons, which are more or less empty; each experience is from the outset "thematic" within a marginal field. For instance, the actual perception of an object of the outer world in its particular perspective and adumbration refers, first, to a horizon of potential aspects of the "same" object in possible, different perspectives and adumbrations and, secondly, to other objects constituting the environment of the perceived thing. Some of these experiences are not actualized, but merely anticipated as possible actualizations. In this sense it could be said that any experience (e.g., a sensory one) [3081] transcends itself, if not otherwise, then by its reference to open horizons.

In this respect, phenomenological analysis meets with certain (although unclarified) basic tenets of *Gestalt* psychology, with William James's concept of "fringes," with Whitehead's theory of the principle of aggregation (that is, the transformation of the various sense-presentations into thought-objects of perception), and with certain points of the analysis of "common-sense experience" undertaken by G. E. Moore.

I submit, therefore, that the "passage back and forth" between the "experience of transcendence" and "transcendence of experience" is deeply rooted in the structure of the activities of the mind, the outcome of which is generally called "experience."

(b) What was said above probably also answers the second query posed by Prof. Morris, whether the experience of transcendence comes first [3082] and exists independently of the appresentation or whether the experience of transcendence is simply the experience of appresentational relations.

I can answer the second part of the question emphatically with "no." To be sure, man can come to terms with the experiences of the transcendences (transcendental lived experiences) only with the help of appresentational references. But this implies neither that the experiences of transcendence are simply the experiences of appresentational references, nor that there are not appresentational references of a very different kind.

(What I could have meant by this addition which begins with "nor" is completely incomprehensible to me.)

As to the first part of the question, it seems to me that the problem of whether the experience of transcendence comes first loses its meaning in light of the already given outline [3083] of the concatenation of experience and transcendence, let alone the highly equivocal meaning of the term "comes first."

(63) *The controversy with Prof. Morris, thought through once again* (October 25, 1958, Minnewaska)

Prof. Morris's questions, no doubt, concern an unclarified crucial point of my theory and are obfuscated rather than answered by my reply, which was written much too hastily. In part, the answer is completely off the track and beside the point.

What does Morris ask?

(1) Is there an experience or a lived experience of transcendence, or are we speaking of the transcendence of experience or the transcendence of lived experience?

What else could the lived experience of transcendence or experience of the transcendent mean but that the content of lived experience, the content of experience, the noema if you wish, always points beyond itself? [3084]

This is the sense that the experienced noema carries along its (inner and outer) horizons, which are experienced as horizons, but precisely as empty, not meaning-filling ones, always referring forward and backward to pre-experienced, retentive and protentive anticipated additional noemic contents, which in turn carry along further horizons of the same typical style of experience? The noematic content is experienced, so and not otherwise, in the way it gives itself to me as I find it, but I find it precisely with its references to what has not yet been or is no longer experienced, whereby it remains fully undecided whether this is experienceable or not.

If this is right, then the not-yet or no-longer experienced, whether it be in principle experienceable or not, is transcendent in respect to the actual [3085] content of experience, insofar as it goes beyond it, but the latter, on the other hand, pertains in a typically pre-experienced way to the actual content of experience: namely that I always experience the content of experience as transcending itself, when I experience it so and not otherwise than it gives itself. And that I can speak of this empty transcendence as self-transcending in the same sense as I say that the empty experience of horizon belongs to the intentional content of the noema as it gives itself to me in a way of typical pre-experiencedness, making precisely any experience of any content whatsoever into an experience of transcendence—and that means here not just into an experience of the transcendence of the content insofar as this must exceed every actually given content by its more [3086] [or] less empty horizon, but experience of the necessarily transcendent character of every experience in general, namely of the necessary incompleteness and imperfection of every isolated empirical act of experience. In this sense the transcendence of experiencing, as well as the experiencing of transcendence, corresponds to the Leibnizian definition of mind as the capacity to progress to ever-new experiences. Spontaneity is, in general, possible only because not just the content of experience is experienced as a self-transcending one by the fact that it is experienced just as it is, with all its inherent references beyond its actual givenness, but also by the fact that the act of experiencing, conceived as isolated, [3087] itself refers forward and backward to other, perhaps performable, perhaps not performable experiential acts, grounding them all in the unity of consciousness whether in Kantian transcendental apperception, or in James's "through-and-through-connectedness of the stream of consciousness."

This thus means: *experience of the transcendence of the experiential content is horizon-intentionality; transcendence of experience, namely transcendence of the act of experience, is spontaneity.* All this must still be studied in detail.

(2) Assuming that the present reflections are right. How, then, is Prof. Morris's second question to be answered?

What is the situation with the transcendental references of marks [marking signs]; indications, signs, and signals?

In general, how, if at all, is the phenomenon of apperception a phenomenon of transcendence? [3088]

What did I mean when, in the symbol essay, I constantly spoke of the main function of appresentation as being "to come to terms with transcendent experiences of various kinds"?

Prof. Morris formulates an alternative (in a second question); (a) *Either*, so he says, the experience of transcendence comes first and exists independently of the appresentative relations. As far as I can see he does not discuss this alternative further. It is probably also not worth discussing as long as "what comes first" is not more closely defined. If it is supposed to mean a life-world *"pros hēchas,"* then the thesis would have to be affirmed. The question is more difficult if "first" is supposed to mean an essential connection of the structural foundation. For it is by no means settled that [3089] sensory perception founds all appresentation. Husserl seems sometimes to have sensed this, particularly in the Cartesian direction of his thinking, just as in general he is inclined to regard perception, especially visual perception, as the basic model of all experience, and one sometimes has the feeling as if his entire theory of experiencing is just a single grandiose synecdoche. The assumption that all appresentation is indeed founded on sensory perception is favored by the remarkable thesis of the "passive synthesis," which establishes all pairing by way of analogy, with all its inherent appearances, concealment and overlapping. // non sequitur, obviously a breach of logic [Schutz's marginal comment—*trans.*] // The "wakening" or "evocation" of the appresented member of the pair by the appresenting one is, on the other hand, sometimes grasped by Husserl as a "primary fact of conscious life"—but what is that supposed to mean? [3090] I am at present inclined toward the view that this question, just as that of the actual experience of transcendence, can in fact be clarified only ontologically, but not phenomenologically. The original lived experience of transcendency is that of my knowledge of my aging (as constant enrichment or filling up of my intentionalities of horizon) and of my death (as the final stop to this enrichment of horizons, as the boundary state, in which, as it were, the horizons close, or rather: beyond which no intentionality of horizon can reach as long as I remain bound to subjectivity and do not include intersubjective posterity "as a horizon")—in other words the consciousness (a true primary fact), that the "world" will [3091] continue to exist after my death, just as it existed before my birth. But this amounts to saying that the finiteness of my being, or rather: my knowledge of it (can one still speak of experience or lived experience in this respect?), grounds all intentionality and above all its horizons. This may be accurate, but the idea [smacks] far more [of] Jaspers or Heidegger than [of] Husserl. As long as one clings to the latter transcendental ego, one must accept its immortality, as Husserl indeed did. But my own death is *life-worldly*—this "certain that, uncertain when"—certainly the first and original lived experience of the world's transcendency beyond my own existence. This requires no "pairing," no "passive synthesis" [3092] and no appresentational references. On the contrary, it could be asserted that all intentionality of horizon must come to a stop with my death, as it is, in all its emptiness and unfulfillment.

There are for this primary experience life-world correlates which would need a precise phenomenological analysis and which Husserl probably had in mind, when, in his very last period, he spoke of "genetic phenomenology." // This was written before I read Linschoten's excellent essay "Über das Einschlafen," in which he in part comes to similar results. (*Psych. Beiträge* II/1, II/2 (1955/56).[17] [Schutz's marginal comment—*trans.*] //

Such a life-world correlate would be sleep, the sentiment of "I will wake up again tomorrow," and that means, my horizons, which now come to a stop when I fall asleep—of course only to a temporary one, as I well know—will recommence their work [3093] and indeed precisely on the empty intentionalities which have just now come to a stop and which I will tomorrow sum up in a passive synthesis *appresentatively* by pairing the then actually presented but now appresentationally intuited member with today's lived experience of horizon now functioning as *appresenting*, but which tomorrow will be just an *appresented* reference, and thereby awaken what was concealed during sleep. This is an awakening in the truest sense of the word, and it could be said that awakening or being awakened from sleep means nothing else but to awaken appresentationally the intentionalities of horizon that existed before falling asleep (themselves then functioning as appresenting). That the intentionalities of horizon [3094] continue to perform their "dream-work" during sleep latently and in true passive synthesis would clarify some discoveries of depth psychology, especially dream symbolism, which is now seen both by Freud and by Jung but "explained" completely inadequately by both.

This phenomenological elucidation of the interruption of the activities of conscious life, which constitutes the intentionalities of horizon, by the process of falling asleep and their resumption ("wakening") by awakening is just *one* life-world correlate of the fundamental lived experience of transcendence, which my death is.

Another shall be called "turning away." Let us take this term first in its spatial meaning. Then [3095] the life-world correlate of the primary experience of transcendence (my death) consists in the same gliding transition of world within actual reach to world within former reach. I leave my room, I move away, I turn away from my world in actual reach. On the street I remember a book that I left lying on my table. The book was once within my reach; now it is no longer within it; it transcends my actual reach; but in this case it belongs to my experience of this transcendence that it lies within my restorable reach. I need only return to my room, and then I have a great chance—for many practical purposes the certainty—that I will again find this room with table and book, which I had turned away from, and indeed will find it just the way [3096] I left it. The house I live in will stand (unless a fire has burned it down), the table will be standing by the window (unless someone has moved it), the book will be lying on it (unless someone has taken it). (Here it can clearly be seen—which is a quite independent problem, which however cannot yet be thought through—what connection exists between typification, systems of relevance, and explication of horizon.) // namely what is posited as "constant" in a taken-for-granted way in all this? [Schutz's marginal comment—*trans.*] //

Now I am "turned away" from all that, and as long as I am, my possible "turning to," the restorable reach, is an achievement of the horizon-intentionality of my actual lived experiences; room, table, and book, as I now remember them, transcend the world within my actual reach. But the memory of the book left on the table—a memory that was wakened by appresentational pairing (the awareness of a lack is appresentational: "now I do not have with me the book I wanted to bring to my friends")—as well as the anticipation [3097] that I could—or I can—bring into restorable reach all that now transcends my world within actual reach, which was, after all, within my former reach—

(an anticipation which was likewise awakened by pairing, whereby the appresenting member is the problematic motivated by the awareness of a lack: "how could I remedy this lack?"—Thus both transcending elements, the memory of former reach and the anticipation of restorable reach, belong to the now actual lived-experience content of my "Now." They "belong" to it, but in the peculiar way that they transcend it and that the transcending elements are obviously achievements of the intentionalities of horizon of the actual content of consciousness, whose actual elements as appresenting members of the pairing "waken" the transcendent ones.

That the world I have turned away from [3098] continues to exist, and on the whole continues to exist just as I had experienced it when I was turned toward it, is, for instance, one of G. E. Moore's great problems in his *Defense of common sense*.[18] Kant too saw this problem, and for that reason Scheler scoffs at him when he speaks of Kant's transcendental anxiety that things could behave otherwise and arbitrarily if they withdraw from supervision by our consciousness that prescribes the rules of behavior to them.

That the described phenomenon of turning away has to do essentially with the transcendence of sleep (which is itself a phenomenon of turning away, the turning away from *attention à la vie*) is evident. Cf. on the other hand: *Partir, c'est mourir un peu.*

There remains yet to be investigated as a third life-world correlate of the primary experience of transcendence the Other and the Other's world. (This should by no means imply that these three correlates exhaust the problem and that there is not yet a series [3099] of others: probably aging itself is such a correlate.)—As far as the Other's transcendence is concerned, certainly the problematic of the "Here" and "There"—world within his current reach, hence of my first-degree potential reach, world within his potential reach, *hence* world within my second-degree potential reach, etc., as was discussed in more detail above (Notebook I) is of eminent significance.

But do we not have to introduce a new thought that stands in immediate relation with the primary lived experience of transcendence— my death? Is not the Other experienced in advance as the one who will *either* survive me *or* whom I will survive? Does this (essentially appresentative (?)) reference not contain a reference of the intentionality of horizon of my consciousness to the intentionality of horizon of the Other's consciousness? And is a new transcendence of turning away contained in the above "either-or"?

Continuation in Notebook IV

Fourth Notebook

from Minnewaska and New York City

October 26 – November 9, 1958

Contains: Pp. 4001 – 4105

[4001] Classification number (63) continued.

Continuation of Notebook III: Prof. Morris's objections reconsidered; the problem of the experience of transcendence; turning away; the Other as survivor or survived; all this still on Morris's second question; first alternative.

Turning away from my own actual situation with its unexplicated but explicable horizons. The phenomenological clarification of the problem of generations would have to be sought in the problematic of outliving (or dying before) the Other. What is for me in my situation an empty horizon, is already fulfilled for older persons in the same situation shared with me; what is anticipated by me—namely what is anticipated presumably as empty—is typically appresented to the older person by passive "wakening" of his typically analogous prior experience. He was already in a similar situation once and appeals to his "life's experience," which can, however, never become mine. But despite all autobiographical differences he disposes over the socially [4002] accepted typical recipes and solutions for typical problematics—at least he is able to *diagnose* the typicality of the present situation (which is for him a recurrent one, while it may be for me radically new). He knows "what it is typically a matter of in such a situation" and how one "typically" deals with it. He has himself lived through such situations or "heard of them," i.e. he knows of them through socially derived knowledge. And now he is ready to place this knowledge at my disposal, to pass it on in the form of recipes, maxims, rules, proverbs, and possibly *mores* and laws. Here it must be noted that a broad range of variation of traditional behavior, as it was called by Weber (reference is made again and again to its importance in his work), originates from this transcendence of the typified by its anonymity and its degree of fulfillment. It is instructive to think through the difference between [4003] traditional behavior (i.e. autobiographically limited as regards its typicality). On the other hand, a "genuine" knowledge-sociological problem is here added, which is most closely linked with the principle of the social distribution of knowledge. For, what status, and hence what prestige the individual generations have in the social order, will depend on the structure of the historico-cultural actuality of the respective social order (from ancestral worship, in which the ancestors perhaps are still members of the social group, via *gerousia* [veneration for old age], to the American system of idolizing youth, and the "Century of the Child").

Similar considerations, which need not be developed further here, can, of course, be made in respect to the generation that is younger than I am. Here, the fact of the transcendency of the Other's (the younger person's) life-world, which arises from the discrepancy between his unexplicated intentionalities of horizon and mine, as to appresentations relative to the [4004] same typical situation, but more or less typically filled, which are now "wakened," would give occasion to an explanation of the basic paradox of all education: We can present recipes and other solutions always just to the extent that typical prior experiences have been stored in advance in our stock of knowledge and are appresentationally evocable, i.e., are more or less filled, whereas the pupil must still anticipate in an empty fashion precisely these problems and developments (solutions) which we have already experienced. In a word, we can provide him only with knowledge of what has typically been confirmed or not confirmed in our life—whereas he has to live not our life but *his*. The "same" or "typically analogous" situation is, however, still radically understood, depending on whether (in the older person) previous experiences are "wakened" appresentationally or only (in the younger one) empty intentionalities of horizon implied or perhaps explicable. One of the younger person's problems will always be: (1) Which of these intentionalities of horizon are questionable? But mainly, (2) which are worth questioning? This would result in [4005] a philosophy of educability and education, which as far as I know has not yet been undertaken in this sense. The main goal of the education of the younger person is to learn to typify "correctly," to learn techniques of appresentational "wakening," methods of diagnosing the questionable, but especially to determine supervening motivational, thematic, and interpretational systems of relevance for the purpose of:

(a) Determining the value of questioning and the conditions under which the concrete problem is to be regarded as sufficiently solved for the present purpose;—in "adult education," an important distinction is that not just definition of the situation, but its empty and explicated horizons, are shared by the teachers and pupils, who belong to the same generation, in terms of the socially approved and derived schemes of relevance, including the derived typifications and methodological rules governing the posing and solving of problems. [No (b) follows—*trans.*]

But all this is a digression that is perhaps worth expanding [4006]

In summary, with respect to the first alternative to the second question raised by Morris—whether the experience of transcendence comes "first" and exists independently of the appresentational relations—it must be said:

(1) The question is meaningfully answerable only insofar as the lived experience of transcendence grounds all appresentations.

(2) The original lived experience of transcendence—can be cleared up only ontologically, [no] longer phenomenologically.

(3) This original lived experience of transcendence is my aging in its finitude, i.e. the constant enrichment of intentionalities of horizon with the frontier of their complete break-off—death.

(4) This primary experience (transcendence of the world beyond my life's end—transcendence of the world, which, while as such transcending my life, still belongs to my life-world) has immanent correlates in the life-world. The most important of the same are:

(a) falling asleep, awakening;

(b) "turning away";

(c) the Other (as outliving me and outlived by me) and his world, including the problem of the generations.

In all these correlates, the phenomena of appresentative awakening are detectable in their typical style. [4007]

On the Second Alternative to Prof. Morris's Second Question:

Relation of transcendence to marks, indications, sign, and symbol. Is the experience of transcendence simply the experience of these appresentational relations?

In my answer to Prof. Morris, I answered this question emphatically with "no"—perhaps too emphatically, in any case not clearly enough. I did, however, admit that experiences of the transcendental can be "mastered" (one can come to terms with them) only with the help of appresentational references. But what is this supposed to mean?

'To come to terms with' could mean, first, articulation into the stock of experience, therefore (at least analogical) understanding; achievement of knowledge, *what* transcends, how it essentially transcends, *where* the empty place is.

Further: how the unknowable can be analogously—appresentationally interpreted through the knowable and thus, although withdrawn from our power, be understood as an ontological determination of all powers and as an open framework of the same constitutive intentionalities; in this sense: determination of its validity-for-me.

Appresentation, however, here goes its particular ways in that every transcendence has its particular typical style of "coming-to-terms" by analogous appresentation. [4008] But the point of departure for analogous appresentation is always the life-world correlate emerging by passive "wakening," by the lived experience of transcendence. See above examples (a) to (c) for such correlates (e.g. Sleep—analogy with death, "wakened" by experiencing the transcendence of death; vice versa: sleep [as] starting member—appresenting member—of the pairing once established is grasped through death—as appresented member—taken as the limit of sleep, namely as sleep without reference to the horizon of awakening, as itself belonging to the world, as a "pause" after which nothing follows, as an everlasting "pause," so to speak, and through this character of the ever-lastingness transcending the life-world itself). (Something similar could perhaps also be shown for the phenomenon of "turning away"—turning-aways without implying a turning-toward that would again become possible—and for the Other and his surrounding world.)

All this is just tentatively recorded and requires very precise further reflection. [4009]

Symbol pp. 175f.
Continuation of the analysis of the symbol essay;
(64) continuation of (60) from Notebook III.

The Transcendence of Nature and Society

The lived experience of this transcendence: Within the life-world I experience the world as not of my own making within my potentialities, and this knowledge itself belongs to my biographical situation as an element of my stock of experience. *Nature* transcends my life-world: *in time*, as having existed before my birth and continuing to exist after my death, indeed as having existed before man appeared on earth, before any animals at all appeared; and as [—] possibly [—] surviving mankind as such;

In space: not only because the world within my potential reach transcends the world within actual reach, but because it belongs to my experience of the infinite horizons of my world within potential reach that every potential reach which is transformed into an actual one will show the same infinity of new horizons. Within the world in my actual reach are, moreover, certain objects (heavenly bodies, e.g.) that I cannot bring within my manipulatory sphere, on the other hand events within my manipulatory sphere (seasons, high and low tide), which I cannot bring under control.

The *social* world in a similar way transcends the reality of my everyday life I was born into a pre-organized social form [4010]; the social world will also survive me. This world is from the outset shared with fellowmen who are organized in groups, which have their particular open horizons in time, in space, and also in what sociologists call their social distance.

In time: a sequence of overlapping generations; *social distance:* my clan refers to other clans, my tribe to other tribes, and these are enemies or friends, speaking the same or another language, but they are always organized in their particular social form and display a particular life-style. My actual social environment refers always to a horizon of potential social environments, and we may speak of an infinity of transcendent social worlds and of posterities. [4011]

(S. p. 176)
(65) *The imposition of the transcendent natural and social worlds*
Both are imposed on me in a double sense:
(a) I find myself at any moment of my existence in the midst of a natural

and social environment; both are co-constitutive elements of my biographical situation and [are] therefore experienced as inescapably
belonging to it.

(b) Both, however, also constitute the framework within which I have the
freedom of my potentialities, and these include the possibilities for
defining my situation. In this sense, they are not elements of my situation, but determinations of it. In the first sense—as elements—I have to
take them for granted; in the second sense—as determinations—I must
come to terms with them; *they assign me my problems and hence determine*
[every] interest and the relevance systems of all sorts—motivational,
thematic, interpretative. In each of the two senses, I must *understand* the
natural and the social world *regardless of their transcendencies and precisely
in their transcendencies*, and indeed in terms of an order of things and
events. [4012]

(S. p. 177)

(66) *Intersubjective character of the lived experience of these transcendences as belonging to the "condition humaine"*

From the outset I know that every human being experiences the same
transcendencies imposed by nature and society, although in various
perspectives and adumbrations: The order of nature and of society as
such is, however, given to all men within lived experience as the same:
Each one experiences

his individual life-cycle of birth, aging, death,
health—sickness
hope—fear
participates in the rhythm of nature

movement, sun, moon, stars ⎫
day-night alternation   ⎬   are elements of each man's situation
cycle of the seasons   ⎭

Each man is a member of a social group into which he was born or which
he has joined and which continues to exist even if some of its members die
and are replaced by new ones.

    In every group there are systems of kinship, age groups, sex
groups, differentiations according to occupations (professions),
organizations of power and command, leaders and followers, and thus
coherent articulations (gradations) of status and prestige. [4013]

(67) *The "givenness" of the natural and social order for everyday thinking.*

In this [everyday thinking] we know that there is order in nature and the
social world; yet the essence of this order is unknown to us. It reveals itself
merely in images to our analogical apprehending. But these images, once
constituted, are taken for granted and so are the transcendences to which
they refer.

(68) This is so because we find in our cultural environment itself socially approved systems offering answers for our quest for the unknowable transcendences. Means and ways were developed socially to apprehend the disquieting phenomena transcending the world of everyday life in a way analogous to the experience of familiar phenomena within it. This is done by the creation of appresentational references of a higher order, which shall be called *symbols* in contradistinction to the marks, indications, and signs discussed so far. [4014]

(69) *Symbol: provisional definition.*

A symbol is an appresentational reference of a higher order in which the appresenting member of the pair is an object, fact, or event within the reality of the everyday life-world, whereas the appresented member of the pair is an idea that transcends our experience of everyday life. This definition will be reformulated later. (See [4033]) [4015]

(70) Reference to Jaspers's conception of symbol
(*Philosophie* III Metaphysik Chap. I, p. 15, First Edition)
"We talk of meaning in the sense of signs and images, of parables, comparisons, allegories, metaphors. The basic difference between mundane and metaphysical meaning is whether, in the relationship of the image to that which it represents, the represented thing itself could also be grasped as an object or whether the image is simply an image for something not accessible in any other way. In other words, whether that for which the image stands might be said or shown directly, or whether it exists for us only insofar as it is in the image. In the latter case alone do we speak of symbols in the exact sense of a metaphysical meaning that must be existentially grasped in the image and cannot be conceived as just an object. The parable that stays within the world is a translation or image of something which in itself is equally objective, of something thinkable or visual; but the metaphysical symbol is the objectification of something nonobjective in itself. The nonobjectivity as such is not given; the objectivity of the symbol [4016] is not meant as the object it is. We cannot interpret the symbol except by other symbols. To understand a symbol does therefore not mean to know its meaning rationally, to be able to translate the symbol; but what it means is that an Existenz experiences in the symbolic intention this incomparable reference to something transcendent, and that it has this experience at the boundary where the object disappears." pp. 15–16

The quotation continues (not used in the essay on the symbol):

"The object which is a symbol cannot be held fast as an existing reality of transcendence; it can only be heard as its language. Existence and symbolic being are like two aspects in the one world that shows itself either to consciousness at large or to possible Existenz. If I see the world as cognizable with general validity, as empirically given without signifying anything as yet it is existence. If . . . it is a symbol . . ."[19] Etc. [4017]

(S. p. 178)
(71) *On the Genesis of symbolic appresentation*

How does appresentational pairing between an element that belongs to the world of everyday life and an idea that transcends it come about?

This question can be answered on two levels:

(1) There is a series of appresentational references which are universal and can be used for symbolization because they are rooted in the human condition (in the general situation of man). To study this is task of philosophical anthropology.

(2) Particular forms of symbolic systems as developed by the various cultures in various periods of their history. To study these is the task of cultural anthropology and the history of ideas.

(72) *Examples of the first group:*

They should not be taken from our culture and historical epoch, which knows only systems of symbols existing loosely side by side and whose special feature consists in the attempt to interpret the cosmos in terms of the positive methods of the natural sciences. We, in our time and culture, take the world as it is defined by the mathematical natural sciences as the archetype of an ideal order of symbolic references and are inclined to explain all other symbolic systems as deviations from the archetype or at least as subordinated to it. Whitehead, however, has already proven that the [4018] founders of modern science, Galileo and Newton, defined the universe as an *ideally isolated* system and that the concept of an ideally isolated system is essential to scientific theory; so that without this concept science would be impossible.

As shown by investigations by Durkheim, Levy-Bruhl, Mauss, Granet, Malinowski, Cassirer, Snell, Dempf, Toynbee, and Voegelin, however, other cultures and historical epochs have grasped man's position in nature and society as equally participating in and determined by the order of the cosmos. The relationship between man, society, and nature in mythical experience, for instance, is of such a kind that any element in any of these orders may become a symbol, appresentationally referring to corresponding elements in any of the other orders.

The Cassirer quotation from the *Essay on Man* follows. Granet on the structural unity between the microcosm "man" and the macrocosm "universe"; produced by the structure of society and based on the fundamental principle: male (positive, yang), female (negative, yin) on the one hand; and master-servant in society, on the other. [4019]

(73) Continuation:
Universal systems of symbols genetically explained

(a) Man as the center 0 of the system of coordinates;—hence: up-down, before-behind, right-left; down-earth, up-sky; earth: producer of plant life, food; sky: not just the place where celestial bodies appear and disappear, but the place from which the rain comes, without which the earth would not be fertile.

On the other hand, the head [is] the carrier of the main sense organs; the organ of breathing and speech [is] on the upper part of the human body; the digestive and sexual organs [are on the] lower part.

Therefore symbolic dimensions of up and down:

China: head-*sky*- roof; fertilization by rain; male, positive, yang

foot-*earth*-floor; fertilized by rain, female, negative, yin.

Correlates of higher and lower in Chinese [exist in] medicine, music, dance, social hierarchy, etiquette—and can all be brought into symbolic interrelation.

Similarly: *before* (things that are visible and seen, and which one can face up to) and *behind* (invisible, therefore potentially dangerous things).

Right-left symbolism

(b) Movements of sun-moon-stars, rising and setting fix the direction for orientation; first 2, then 4 world regions; these have symbolic meaning as a result of their relation to day/night, light/dark, waking/sleep, visible/invisible, coming-to-be/passing-away.

Man's life-cycle—childhood, age, etc. [has its] analogy in the seasons and the cycle of plant and animal life and its meaning for hunting, fishing, [4020] cattle-raising and again independently of the movement [of] heavenly bodies.

Sub- and super-ordination in the social world. Consequently: cosmos, individual, social community form a unity, equally subject to universal forces that govern all events.

(c) Man has to understand these forces and, because he cannot dominate them, he must conjure and appease them. He cannot do this alone, but only in community with others; it is a matter for the group and its organization.

Symbolic forms, in which the forces of both nature and society are symbolized, e.g. *mana, orenda, manitu, yin-yang*, gods and their hierarchies; even the following can be symbols:

Expressive, purposive, mimetic movements (Snell); linguistic or pictorial presentations; amulets, magic articles, magical or religious rites, ceremonies, etc. Mythical symbols have, according to Malinowski, the particular function of justifying and vouching for the truth and validity of the order established by the other symbolic systems. [4021]

(Symb 182)

(74) (d) Snell *(Origin of Language)* cites as proof that on this level the sacred and the profane are closely interwoven: p. 150f. "Everything that is active is originally conceived as a deity. Many things carry the name of a deity which will later on be designated by an abstract term. Not only what is active in nature, such as the sun, the cloud, the lightning, the earth, the

tree, the river, is to the primeval mind a divine being, but also everything that acts within man, within the individual (such as love, fighting spirit, prudence), or within the community (such as peace, law, fortune or war, injustice and all forms of disaster). . . . but the question whether the sun was experienced first as a "thing" and thereafter interpreted in the mythical way, or whether first the noun denoting the thing or the name of the deity existed, is as wrongly put as the question whether the river or the river god existed first. The acting phenomena of nature are just divine. . . . It is meaningless to ask whether Eros was first a god or the emotion of love, since the emotion of love is apprehended as an intervention of the deity."[20]

Voegelin quote from *The New Science of Politics* p. 27[21] [4022]

(S. 186/MR 533).

(76) *Multiple Realities;*
    William James's subuniverses; finite provinces of meaning

In *Principles*, Vol. II, Ch. 21, William James analyzes our sense of reality. Reality, he states, means simply relation to our emotional and active life. The origin of all reality is subjective: Everything that arouses our interest is real. To call an object real means that this object stands in a certain relation to us. "In short, the word real is a fringe." Our first impulse is to affirm the immediate reality of everything thought, as long as it remains uncontradicted. But there are several, probably an infinite number of various orders of reality, each with its own particular style of existence. James calls them subuniverses and names as examples the sensory world or the world of physical things (as the paramount reality); the world of science; the world of ideal relations; the world of idols; the various supernatural worlds of mythology and religion; the various worlds of individual opinions: the world of the insane. [4023]

William James's subuniverses, continued
"Each world whilst it is attended to is real after its own fashion; only the reality lapses with the attention."[22] "All propositions, whether attributive or existential, are believed through the very fact of being conceived, unless they clash with other propositions believed at the same time, by affirming that their terms are the same as the terms of these other propositions."[23] [4024]

(77) *W. James, Finite Provinces of Meaning, continued*

Many other examples could be cited.
The play-world of the little girl, as long as it is undisturbed, is her reality. She is "really" the mother and her doll her child.

Only from the point of view of the outer world is the knight in Dürer's print a pictorial presentation in the neutrality modification. In the world of the work of art, i.e. in this case, of pictorial imagination, knight, death, and devil have "real" existence as entities within the meaning province of artistic fantasy.

While the play lasts, Hamlet is to us *really* Hamlet and not Lawrence Olivier, "playing" or "portraying" Hamlet. [4025]

(p. 187)
(78) *Interpretation of James's concept of subuniverses as finite provinces of meaning*
Need to detach W. James's ingenious theory from its psychological setting.
    Instead of speaking of subuniverses we speak of finite provinces of meaning, upon which we bestow the accent of reality. This change in terminology is supposed to emphasize that reality is constituted by the meaning of our experiences and not by the ontological structure of the objects. Each finite province of meaning has its own particular style of cognition (of lived experience?): The paramount world of the real outer objects and events into which we can gear operatively by our actions (and which we thus change), the world of imagination and fantasies, such as the play-world of the child, the world of the insane, but also the world of the work of art, the world of dreams, the world of theoretical-scientific contemplation—each of them has its own inherent cognitive style. It is this particular cognitive style, peculiar to a set of our experiences, which constitutes them into a finite province of meaning. All experiences within each of these worlds are, with respect to their cognitive style, compatible with one another (although not [4026] compatible with the meaning of everyday life). Moreover, each of these finite provinces of meaning is, among other things, characterized by a specific tension of consciousness (from full awakeness in the reality of the everyday life-world to sleep in the world of dreams) by a specific time-perspective, by a specific mode of experiencing one's own self, and, finally, by a specific form of experiencing the Other (sociability, sociality).
(Here add A. Gurwitsch.)
According to his presentation of my theory, every finite province of meaning is characterized by
    1. a specific tension of consciousness, including the *attention à la vie* founded on it
    2. a specific epoché
    3. a dominant form of spontaneity
    4. a specific form of self-experience
    5. a specific form of sociality
    6. a specific time-perspective [4027]

(79) *The Paramount (or Privileged) Reality*

This section must be compared precisely with the one in Multiple Realities; obviously it results in an important change that there—with W. James—the outer world of sensory objects was taken as paramount

W. James is completely right to call the subuniverse of the sensorily perceptible physical world the "paramount reality." But we prefer to take as paramount reality the finite province of meaning that we have

reality, while here it is the totality of the life-world. It must be precisely thought through, how—if at all—this change could influence Gurwitsch's critique.

called the reality of our everyday life. (Here reference is made to the analyses undertaken in (59)). We have seen (in 59) that the reality of our everyday world, which our commonsense thinking simply takes for granted, includes not only physical objects, facts, and events perceived as such within our actual or potential reach in the merely apperceptual scheme, but also appresentational references of a lower order by which the physical objects of nature are transformed into socio-cultural objects. [4028]

But since these appresentations of a lower order also contain objects, facts, and events of the outer world as their appresenting members, we believe that our definition is compatible with that of James.

We also agree with Santayana "that the spirit can never possess, much less communicate, ideas without a material means and a material occasion. The tongue must move; the audible conventional word must come to the lips and reach a ready ear; the hands, with tools or plans in them must intervene to carry the project out." [4029]

(Symbol 188)
(80) *What makes the world of everyday life the paramount reality*

(a) We constantly participate (live) in it, even during our dreams, by means of our bodies, which are themselves things in the outer world; (reference: Gurwitsch pp. 331ff. Merleau-Ponty: Phen. Perc. Part I, I-IV

(b) The objects of the outer world delimit our free possibilities of action and [do so] by offering resistances which must be overcome, if they can be overcome (Reference: Scheler: *Erkenntnis und Arbeit*, Maine de Biron)

(c) The world of everyday life is the realm into which we gear by our bodily activities and (which we) can change thereby;

(d) (this is just one corollary to the preceding points)

Within this realm, and only within this realm, we can communicate with our fellowmen and thus establish a common comprehensive [communicative] environment in the sense of Husserl (*Ideas* II. Paragraph 50, 51). [4030]

(81) *Socialization of other finite provinces of meaning*

The statement that communication with others can take place only within the paramount reality of everyday life does not mean that other finite provinces of meaning are incapable of socialization. To be sure, some finite provinces of meaning, such as that of dreams and (to a certain degree) of daydreams, cannot be shared with others. But there are others, such as the play-world of children, which permit intersubjective participation and even shared fantasies. In the world of religious experiences there is, on the one hand, the lonely vision of the mystic or prophet, but on the other hand the community worship service—there is solitary prayer and congregational prayer.

Without developing a typology of the individual forms, it is important to remember that in all cases in which intersubjective participation in one of these finite provinces of meaning takes place, the existence of "material occasion or endowment" is presupposed (on occasions, see the Santayana quotation [4031] in (79)). In other words, communication occurs only with the help of objects, facts, or events pertaining to the paramount reality of the sensory world, of the outer world, which are, however, appresentationally apperceived.

This holds good also for symbolic appresentations, insofar as they are communicated or designed to be communicable. Nevertheless, symbolic appresentations are distinguished from all other appresentational relations by a specific feature which must now be discussed and which leads to a deepened definition of the symbol. [4032]

(p. 189)

(82) *Specific features of the symbolic appresentational relation*

All appresentational references are, as was said, characterized by a specific transcendence of the appresented object in relation to the actual Here and Now of the interpreter. But with the exception of symbolic appresentation, the three terms of the appresentational relation—the appresenting and the appresented members of the pair and the interpreter—are located on the same level of reality: For, all three pertain to the paramount reality of everyday life. The symbolic reference, however, is characterized by the fact that it transcends the finite province of meaning of everyday life so that only the appresenting member of the pair pertains to it, whereas the appresented member has reality in another finite province of meaning, or, in William James's terminology, in another subuniverse. [4033]

(83) *Modified definition of the symbol*

We can, therefore, redefine the symbolic relationship precisely as follows: a symbolic relationship is an appresentational relationship between entities belonging to at least two finite provinces of meaning so that the appresenting symbol is an element of the paramount reality of everyday life.

(We said "at least two" because there are many possible combinations, such as religious art, etc., which cannot be further investigated here. [4034]

(84) *The transition from the paramount reality to other finite provinces of meaning follows through a leap, whose subjective correlate is a shock experience*

The world of everyday life is taken for granted by our commonsense thinking and thus receives the accent of reality as long as our practical experiences prove the unity and congruity of this world as valid. Indeed even more, this reality seems to us to be the natural one, and we are [not] ready to abandon our attitude toward it, unless a specific shock experience compels us to break through the limits of this finite province of meaning and to shift the accent of reality to another one.

Such shock experiences, however, befall us frequently in the midst of our daily life; they themselves pertain to its reality.

Examples: The curtain in the theater;
>
> Contemplation of a framed image; .
>
> Falling asleep;
>
> The Kierkegaardian leap into the religious sphere;
>
> [the assumption] of a theoretical attitude.
>
> [4035]

On the other hand it must be emphasized that the consistency and compatibility of experiences with respect to their peculiar cognitive style subsists merely within the borders of the particular finite province of meaning to which these experiences belong and upon which the accent of reality was bestowed. By no means must that which is compatible within the finite province of meaning P be also compatible within the finite province of meaning. On the contrary, seen from P, which is supposed to be real, Q and all the experiences belonging to it appear merely fictitious, inconsistent, and incompatible, and vice versa.

Here is a further realm of application for Bergson's theory of the multiple orders. [4036]

(Symbol 190/191)

(85) *Examples of the fictitious character of the everyday life-world, regarded with the help of systems of symbols pertaining to other finite provinces of meaning, supposed to be real.*

Example (1): Science

Reference to Whitehead's statement on ideally isolated systems (see § 72)
>
> Ph. Frank quotation from "Foundations of Physics."
>
> Herman Weyl quotations.

These statements show clearly that scientific theory represents a finite province of meaning that uses symbols which appresent realities within this field and—quite rightly, of course—works with them according to the principle that their validity and utility is completely independent of any reference to the commonsense thinking of everyday life and its realities. [4037]

(Symbol 192)

(86) *Example 2: Poetry*

T. S. Eliot on Dante: Selected Essays (1917-32, N.Y. 1932 pp. 199–241, 200, 201, 204.[24]

"Genuine poetry can communicate before it is understood. . . . Words have associations, and the group of words *in* association have associations, which is a kind of local self-consciousness, because they are the growth of a *particular* civilization. . . . I do not recommend, in first reading the first canto of the *Inferno*, worrying about the identity of the Leopard, the Lion, or the She-Wolf. It is really better, at the start, not to know or care what they do mean. What we should consider is not so much the meaning of the images, but the reversed process, that which led a man having an idea to express it in images. . . . Dante's is a *visual* imagination. . . . He lived in an age in which men still saw visions—a practice now relegated to the aberrant and uneducated—was once a more significant, interesting, and disciplined kind of dreaming." [4038]

Further, Goethe to W. Humboldt on the *Märchen* May 27, 1796: "It was rather difficult to be at the same time significant *(bedeutend)* but without interpretation *(deutungslos)*"[25]

The two terms show the poet's insight into the fact that within the finite province of meaning of the work of art the interrelationship of the symbols as such is the essence of the poetic content and that it is unnecessary and even harmful to look for the referential scheme that the appresenting elements would symbolize, if they were indeed objects of the world of daily life. But their connection with these objects has been cut off; the use of the appresenting elements is just a means of communication; whereas poetry communicates by using ordinary colloquial language, the ideas symbolized by this language are real entities within the finite province of poetical meaning. They have [turned], to use an expression of Jaspers's, [4039] into "ciphers" for transcendent experiences to be understood by those who have the existential key to them. And in this sense—and only in this sense—says Jaspers (III/p. 25) "The symbol establishes communion without communication."[26]

(Jaspers should be worked through precisely, particularly Vol. III, Chap. 4) [4040]

(Symbol 193)

(87) *Dependence of appresentational references on the social environment*

This is a main problem of any genuine sociology of knowledge that does not misunderstand its task.

(25) ff. We must start again from the experience of the reality of everyday life, which is itself permeated with appresentational references. In our discussion of the concepts of "marks" ["markings"] and "indications," we assumed for the sake of clearer presentation that a supposedly isolated individual has to map out the world within his reach. In truth, man finds himself from the outset in surroundings already mapped out for him by others, i.e. premarked, preindicated, presignified, and even presymbolized. Thus, his biographical situation in everyday life is always a historical one because it was co-constituted by the socio-cultural process that had contributed to the actual configuration of its environment. [4041]

(88) *Social structure of the stock of knowledge*

Hence, only a small fraction of the stock of knowledge at hand originated from the individual's own experience. The greater portion is socially derived and has been handed down to him by parents and teachers as so-called social heritage. It consists of a set of systems of relevant typifications, of typical solutions for typical practical and theoretical problems, of typical precepts for typical behavior, including the pertinent systems of appresentational references. All this knowledge is taken for granted beyond question by the respective social group and thus accepted as socially approved. This concept comes very near to Max Scheler's relatively natural worldview prevailing in a social group and also to Sumner's classical theory of the "folkways," that is, the quintessence of the life-form of an in-group, which is accepted by its members as the only right, good, and efficient way of life [4042]

(Symbol 194)
(89) *Definition of the situation, Thomas theorem*
Socially approved knowledge
consists, thus, in a set of recipes designed to help each member of the group to define and determine his situation in the reality of everyday life in a typical way. It is entirely irrelevant for the description of a world taken for granted by a particular society whether the socially derived and approved knowledge is indeed true knowledge. All elements of such knowledge, including appresentational references of any kind, if believed to be true, are real components of the "definition of the situation" by the members of the group. The "definition of the situation" must be understood in the sense of the well-known Thomas theorem by the famous American sociologist: "If men determine situations as real, they are real in their consequences." Applied to our problem and translated into our terminology, this means: If [4043] an appresentational relationship is socially approved, then the appresented object, fact, or event is believed beyond question to be in its typicality an element of the world taken for granted. [4044]

(90) *Role of learning the mother tongue in the process of transmitting socially approved knowledge*

The native language can be taken as a set of references that, in accordance with the relative natural conception of the world as approved by the linguistic community, have predetermined what features [of the world] are worthy of being expressed, and therewith what qualities of these features and what relations among them deserve attention, and what typifications, conceptualizations, abstractions, generalizations, and idealizations are relevant for achieving typical results by typical means. Not only the vocabulary but also the morphology and the syntax of any vernacular reflect the socially approved relevancy system of the linguistic group.

Example: Camel in Arabic
North American Indian languages; "I see a man";
Dual, Optative, Aorist, Medium in Greek;
Conscience in French
Experience in English

All these facts reveal the relative natural conception of the world approved by the respective language group. [4045]

(Symbol 195)

(91) *What is worthwhile and what is necessary to communicate*

depends, on the other hand, on the typical problems of a practical and theoretical nature that have to be solved. These will be different depending on whether they involve men or women,

young or old persons,

hunters or fishermen,

in general they will be different for the various social roles assumed by the members of the language community.

Each kind of activity has its particular relevance aspects for the performer and requires a set of particular technical terms. This is based on the *social distribution of knowledge*. Each of us has precise and distinct knowledge only about that particular field in which he is an expert. Among experts, a certain technical knowledge is taken for granted, but exactly this technical knowledge is inaccessible to the layman. Certain things can be supposed as well-known and self-explanatory, whereas others need an explanation, depending upon whether I talk to a person of my own [4046] sex, age, or occupation, or to somebody [not] sharing a common social situation with me, or whether I talk to a member of my family, a neighbor, or to a stranger, a partner or a nonparticipant in a particular venture, etc. W. James already observed that a language does not merely consist in the content of an ideal dictionary and an ideally complete and arranged grammar. The dictionary gives only the "kernels" of the meanings of words, which are surrounded by "fringes" of every kind: some originating in the speaker's personal use of this word; others originating in the context of the speech in which the term is used; still others depending upon the addressee of my speech or the situation in which the speech occurs, or the purpose of the communication, and, finally, upon the problem to be solved. [4047]

(Symbol 196)

(92) *General application of these statements to appresentational references of every kind*

What has been stated about language holds good in general for appresentational references. In communication or in social intercourse each appresentational reference, if socially approved, constitutes merely a kernel surrounded by fringes of the kind described. [4048]

(93) *Typifications of social relations*, etc.

All this presupposes an existing typification of social relations, of social forms of intercommunication, of social stratification taken for granted by the group, and therefore socially approved by it. This whole system of types under which any social group experiences itself has to be learned by a process of acculturation. The same holds true for the various [markings] and indications for the position, status, role, and prestige each individual occupies or has within the stratification of the group. In order to find my bearings in it, I have to know the different ways of dressing and behaving, the manifold badges, insignias, and emblems which are approved by the group as indicating social status and therefore as socially relevant. They show, among other things, what typical behavior, what typical actions and motives [4049] I may expect from a chief, a medicine man, a priest, a hunter, a married woman, a young girl, etc. In a word, I have to learn the typical social roles and the typical expectations of behavior of the incumbents of such roles, in order myself to assume an appropriate corresponding role and display appropriate corresponding behavior expected to be approved by the social group. At the same time, I have to learn the typical distribution of knowledge prevailing in this group, and this involves knowledge of the appresentational, interpretative and [other] referential schemes that each of the subgroups takes for granted and applies to the respective appresentational indications. All this knowledge is, in turn, of course, socially derived. [4050]

(94) *Summary: to what extent are the relevance systems socially determined?*

(1) The unquestioned matrix within which any inquiry starts is socially determined.

(2) The elements of knowledge which have to be considered as socially approved and which therefore might be taken for granted, but also those elements which might become problematic, are traced out by the social situation.

(3) What procedures of a practical, political, religious, poetic, scientific kind, i.e. what signs and symbols, are appropriate for dealing with the problems involved?

(4) The typical conditions under which a problem can be considered adequately solved, and the conditions under which further inquiry is broken off and the results can be incorporated in the stock of knowledge at hand. This point is of [4051] particular importance for the symbolic references to myths and to rituals. If the successful connecting of a problem at hand with a socially approved symbol is considered as its typical solution, then the appresentational reference thus established continues to function as an appresenting element of other and higher symbolizations which might be founded on the problem are deemed typically solved. [4052]

(Symbol 197)

(95) *The Symbolic appresentation of the social world*

Point of departure: what has been said under (42), (43):

The social environment of the face-to-face relationship is the center of the social world. Only in the we-relationship of the surrounding world do the partners, by their mutual biographical involvement, experience one another as unique individuals. In all the other dimensions of the social world—that of contemporaries, predecessors, and successors—a fellowman is not experienced in his individual uniqueness but in a series of typifications—typical behavior-patterns, typical motives, and typical attitudes, and in various degrees of anonymity. In social situations of everyday life all these dimensions are frequently intertwined.

Examples of typifications of the contemporary world that occur in a historical situation, i.e. one co-determined by the world of predecessors, namely under certain circumstances with respect to the still unfilled empty horizon of posterity. Nonetheless, in commonsense thinking [4053] we are familiar with most typifications which (all these) [occur] in the social life-world, indeed [they are even] taken for granted. How is that possible?

(96) *In commonsense thinking we experience the social world on two levels of appresentational references:*

(I) We experience *individual fellowmen* and their cogitations as realities within the world of everyday life. They are within our actual or potential reach, and through communication we share with them a common comprehensive environment, or at least we could potentially share such a world with them. Although we can apprehend these individual fellowmen and their mental experiences only analogously through the above-described (38ff.) system of appresentational references, and in this sense the world of the other transcends mine; but this is an "immanent transcendence" [4054] still within the reality plane of the life-world. Consequently, both members belong to the pair of the corresponding appresentational relation through which we apprehend this transcendence, and belong to the same finite province of meaning, the paramount reality.

(II) *Social collectivities* and institutionalized social relations are, on the contrary, not real entities within the province of meaning of the everyday life-world but constructs of commonsense thinking that belong to a different subuniverse, perhaps that which W. James called the subuniverse of ideal relations. For this reason, we can apprehend them only symbolically; but the symbols appresenting these entities themselves pertain to the paramount reality of the life-world and motivate our actions within it. [4055]

(Symbol 198)

(97) *Symbolic experience of social collectivities*

We are all in the same situation as Anatole France's Crainquebille: the state is a grouchy old man behind a counter. The government [is] represented by individuals: congressmen, judges, tax collectors, soldiers, policemen, public servants, perhaps the President, or the Queen, or the Führer. The political cartoon: Uncle Sam, John Bull, Marianne, the German Michel, the Globe. Meaning of this crude symbolism.

(98) *Symbolic experience of the we-relation*

The we-experience itself transcends, as was said above (39) (40), the existence of either of the two partners within the paramount reality and can be appresented only through symbols. My friend is to me and I am to him an element of the reality of everyday life. Our friendship as such, however, surpasses our individual province of meaning of the paramount reality. Since our notion of the we-relation is a purely formal one that includes all degrees of intimacy and remoteness [4056], the symbols by which the we-experience is appresented are of a great variety. Their appresenting member is always the common situation as defined by the participants, namely, that which they experience and use together, enjoy or endure together. A joint interest makes them partners, and *the idea of partnership* is perhaps the general term for the appresented we-relation: We are lovers, fellow sufferers, colleagues, comrades, etc.

The symbols became more discernible the more the social relation is stabilized and institutionalized. The dwelling place of the family gets the appresentational meaning "home," which is protected by deities such as *lares* and *penates*. The hearth is more than the fireplace, the fatherland more than a geographical term, etc.

All the examples refer, however, to social relations that can be brought within actual reach. [4057] These belong to the type of groups which Cooley wanted to designate by the highly equivocal concept of "primary groups" and which justify the interest of modern sociologists in so-called "small groups," which Homans, e.g., defines "as a number of persons who are few enough so that every person may communicate with all the others not at second hand through other people but face-to-face."[27]

When the group is larger, then Max Weber's definition holds true. (Chance that action is done in a certain specific manner.) But this is a construct by the social scientist and does not as such belong to the common-sense thinking of man within everyday life. A man experiences the social and political organizations by specific appresentations that Voegelin has described in the "New Science." (Every political society is a *cosmion* illuminated from within): "Society itself becomes the representative of something beyond itself, of a transcending reality."[28] [4058] Here it must be stated that the symbolic appresentations by which the in-group interprets itself have their counterpart in the interpretations of the same symbols by the out-group or out-groups. The latter will, however, necessarily be different from those of the in-group, because the systems of relevance of both groups and the systems of the apperceptual, appresentational, and referential systems based thereon cannot coincide in their function as schemes for interpreting "order" so created.

This problem is of great practical significance, for each manipulation of the system of symbols, for instance for propaganda purposes (cf. Pareto), requires at least a clarification of their intrinsic structure. [4059]

(99) *Goethe on the symbol*

"True symbolism is where the particular represents the general not as a dream and a shadow, but as vivid instantaneous revelation of that which cannot be explored." From *Kunst und Altertum* 1827 [4060]

(Multiple Realities p. 533)
(100) *The natural attitude of daily life and its pragmatic motive*

Purpose: Analysis of the world of everyday life that the wide-awake adult, who operates within it and upon it among his fellowmen, experiences as reality with the natural attitude: "Life-world" shall mean the intersubjective world that existed long before my birth and was experienced and interpreted by others, our predecessors, as an organized world. Now it is given to our experience and requires our interpretation.

All interpretation of the world is based upon a stock of previous experiences of it, [both] of our own experiences and [also] of such as were handed down to us by our parents and teachers. All these function in the form of a "stock of experience at hand" as a scheme of reference for our interpretation of the world. [4061]

(Multiple Realities p. 534)
(101) *A few of the elements of the stock of knowledge on hand taken for granted:*

(1) The life-world is a world of well-circumscribed objects with definite qualities, objects among which we move, which resist us, and upon which we may act.

The world is, for man in the natural attitude, never an aggregate of color spots, incoherent noises, centers of warmth and cold. These are philosophical and psychological problems, but not problems of the experience of the life-world in the natural attitude.

(2) The world is from the very outset not a private world of the single individual, but an intersubjective world, common to all of us, in which we have not just a theoretical but an eminently practical interest.

(3) The world of everyday life is both the scene and [also] the object of our actions and interactions. We have to dominate and change it in order to realize our goals, which we pursue in the life-world amid our fellowmen. Thus, we work and operate not only within but upon the life-world. [4067 follows 4061] our bodily movements of a kinaesthetic, locomotive, operative (manipulative) kind engage in the world, modifying or changing its objects and their mutual relations. On the other hand, these objects offer resistance to our acts, which we either overcome or to which we have to yield.

In this sense, it may be correctly said that the *pragmatic* motive governs our natural attitude toward the world of daily life.

World, in this sense, is something that we have to modify by our actions or that modifies our actions. [4068]

(102) *The manifestations of human spontaneity in the outer world and some of its modifications*

What does the term "action" mean, and how does man with the natural attitude experience his own actions within and upon the world and toward it? Obviously, actions are manifestations of spontaneous life. But neither are all manifestations of spontaneous life actions, nor does the actor experience all his actions as bringing about changes in the outside world. [4069]

(103) *Critique of Behaviorism*

The theory of modern behaviorism, with its distinction between overt and covert, or even "subovert," behavior, can contribute nothing toward solving the question of how the different forms of spontaneity are experienced by the mind in which they originate. Behaviorism can, at best, be an interpretation scheme for the observer of other people's behavior. Only the observer may be interested in observing the activities of man and animal from the vantage point of a stimulus-response or organism-environment relational system, and only from the observer's point of view are these categories accessible at all. Our problem, however, is not what occurs to man as a psychological unit and his response to it, but the attitude he adopts toward these occurrences and the steering of his response to them; briefly, the subjective meaning man attaches to certain experiences of his own spontaneous life. What appears to the observer to be objectively the same behavior may for the behaving subject have very different meanings or no meaning at all. [4070]

(Multiple Realities p. 535)

(104) *Meaning*, as shown in *The Structure of the Life-World* [I], is not a quality inherent to certain experiences emerging within the stream of consciousness but the result of an interpretation of past experiences looked at from the present Now with a reflective attitude. As long as I live in my acts and am directed toward the objects of these acts, these acts have no meaning for me. They become meaningful if I grasp them as well-circumscribed lived experiences of the past and, therefore, in retrospect. Only lived experiences that can be remembered beyond their actuality and questioned about their constitution are, therefore, subjectively meaningful. [4071–72]

(105) *Are there, in the sense of this definition, any subjective experiences of my spontaneous life that are not meaningful?*

The answer is yes. There are physiological reflexes, such as the knee-jerk, the contraction of the pupils, blinking, blushing; moreover, certain positive reactions provoked by what Leibniz called accumulations of [in]discernible and confused small perceptions; furthermore, my body stance, my gait, my facial expression, my moods, those manifestations of my spontaneous life that result in certain characteristic traits of my handwriting open to graphological interpretation, etc. All these forms of involuntary spontaneity are experienced while they occur, but without leaving any trace in memory; as lived experiences they are, to again borrow a very suitable term from Leibniz, indeed perceived but not apperceived. Unstable and undetachable from the surrounding lived experiences as they are, they can be neither well delineated nor well recollected. They belong to the category of *essentially actual lived experiences*, that is, they exist merely in the actuality of their being experienced and cannot be grasped by a reflective attitude.

(cf. footnote 4 on p. 536) on Husserl's view. [4073]

(Multiple Realities p. 536)
(105) *Conduct and Act*

Subjectively meaningful experiences emanating from our spontaneous life shall be called conduct. Conduct may be internal, or it may be external, gearing into the world. The first shall be called mere thinking, the second mere doing. Conduct by no means involves intentionality. All kinds of automatic activities of inner or outer life—habitual, traditional or affectual— fall under this class, called by Leibniz the "class of empirical behavior." Conduct which is devised in advance, that is, which is based on a preconceived project, shall be called action, quite regardless of whether it is internal or external. As to the latter, it has to be distinguished whether the project is followed by the intention to realize it, i.e. to bring about the projected state. Such an intention of realization [4074] transforms the mere forethought into an aim and the project into a purpose. If an intention to realization is lacking, the projected inner act remains a mere phantasm, such as a daydream; if it is present, then we speak of a purposive inner action or a *performance*. An example of such an inner act that is a performance would be the process of planned thinking such as the attempt to solve a scientific problem mentally.

As regards the external action that gears into the outer world by bodily movements, the distinction between actions with and those without intention to realization is not necessary. Every such act is a performance within the meaning of the above definition. But in order to be able to draw a convenient terminological distinction between performances in the sense of mere thinking and those [4075] requiring bodily movements, we shall call the latter working. Working, thus, is an action in the outer world, based upon a project and characterized by the intention to bring about the projected state of affairs by bodily movements. Among all the described forms of spontaneity, that of working is the most important one for the constitution of the life-world. As will be shown very soon, the wide-awakened self in its acts of working integrates its present, past and future; it realizes itself as a totality in its working acts; it communicates with others through working acts; it organizes the different spatial perspectives of the life-world through working acts. But what does the term "wide-awake self" mean? [4076]

(Multiple Realities p. 537)
(106) *The tensions of consciousness and the attention to life*

The planes of consciousness according to Bergson; from action to dream; each characterized by specific tension of consciousness (the highest— action, the lowest—dream; this important question, ambiguously treated by Bergson, must be reexamined precisely; Ingarden's interpretation, e.g., deviates from mine; Kallen's obviously likewise does);[29]

Tensions of consciousness are functions of our interest in life; action, the highest interest in meeting reality, dream, the complete lack of such interest; *attention à la vie*, therefore, the basic regulative principle of our conscious life; it defines the realm of our world that is relevant for us; it makes us either live within our present experiences, directed toward their objects, or turn back in a reflective attitude to our past experiences and ask for their meaning. [4077]

(107) *Wide-Awakeness*

denotes a plane of consciousness of highest tension originating in an attitude of full attention to life and its requirements. Only in performances and working acts is the self fully interested in life and, hence, wide-awake. It lives within its acts and its attention is exclusively directed to implementing the project. This attention is an active, not a passive one. In passive attention, I experience, e.g., the "surf" of [in]discernible small perceptions that are essentially actual experiences and not meaningful manifestations of spontaneity. Meaningful spontaneity may—to vary Leibniz—be defined as the effort to arrive at ever-new perceptions. In its lowest form it leads to the delimitation of certain perceptions transforming them into apperceptions; in its highest form it leads to performances or to a working that gears into the outer world and modifies it.

The concept of wide-awakeness is the starting point for a legitimate pragmatic interpretation [4078] of our cognitive life.
(Reread:
Scheler Cognition-work,
G. E. Moore, Critique of pragmatism
W. James in Phil. Studien)

The state of full awakeness of the working self traces out that segment of the world which is pragmatically relevant, and these relevances[30] in turn determine the form and content of our stream of consciousness; the form, because they regulate the tension of our memory and therewith the scope of our past experiences recollected and of our future experiences anticipated; the content, because all these experiences undergo modifications by the preconceived project and its being carried into effect.

This leads to analysis of the time dimension in which the working self experiences its own acts. [4079]

(M R 538)

(108) *Time perspectives of the acting self*

Distinction between action and act: life in the action-in-progress, directed toward the state to be brought about versus reflection on the experience of action—to stop and think—in which however I can grasp not acting (*modo praesenti*), but only act on past initial phases of action that is still going on (*modo praeterito*). (Here add an answer to Schaff's critique of my theory. (p. 539,—IInd paragraph.) "That does not mean that only completed acts are meaningful, but not ongoing action. We have to remember that on the basis of our definition, action is always based on a preconceived project and that it is this preconceived project that makes meaningful both our action and the act.") [4080]

(M R 539)

(109) *Time-structure of the projected action in general*

Dewey: Projecting (conceiving) is a rehearsal of my future action, that is, the future act *modo futuri exacti* [in the Future Perfect Tense]. This anticipation is empty; it may or may not be fulfilled by the act once it is performed. The act once performed is free of empty anticipations. Nothing is undecided or unsettled. To be sure, I may remember the open anticipations involved in projecting the act and even the protentions accompanying my living in the ongoing phases of the process of my acting. But now, in retrospection, I remember them as *past* anticipations, which have or have not come true. Only the performed act, therefore, and never the action in progress can be a success or a failure. [4081]

(110) *Time-structure of working*

What was stated in (109) holds good for all kinds of action. Working has a particular time-structure since it refers to bodily performances in the outer world. Bergson and Husserl have proven the importance of bodily movement for the constitution of the outer world and its time-structure. (Here insert Merleau-Ponty.) We experience our bodily movements on two different planes: as movements in the outer world they are events in space and spatialized time, measurable in terms of space run through; experienced from within, they are manifestations of our spontaneity pertaining to our stream of consciousness and to our inner time or duration. What occurs in the outer world belongs to the same time dimension as the objects and events of inanimate nature. It can be registered by appropriate devices and measured with our chronometers. This is the spatialized, homogeneous time which is the universal form of objective or cosmic time. On the other hand it is the inner time or duration [4082] within which and through which our actual experiences are connected with the past by recollections and retentions and with the future by protentions and anticipations. In and by our bodily movements we perform the transitions from our duration to the spatial or cosmic time and our working actions partake of both time-dimensions. In other words, we experience (live) our working action in simultaneity as a series of events in outer and inner time, whereby the two dimensions are united in a single flux which shall be called the "vivid present." The vivid present originates, therefore, at the intersection of inner duration and cosmic time. [4083]

(M R 540)
(111) *The self-experience of the self in the vivid present*

The I, living in the vivid present in its ongoing working acts, directed toward the objects and objectives to be brought about by its working, the self experiences itself as the originator of this ongoing action and, thus, as an undivided total self. It experiences its bodily movements from within and *lives in the correlated essentially actual lived experiences, which are inaccessible to all recollections and reflections:* its world is a world of open anticipations. The working self, *and it alone*, experiences all this *modo praesenti*, and experiencing itself as the author of these working acts, it realizes itself as a unity. // Is this also right? Is the "and it alone" not an overstatement? [Schutz's marginal comment—*trans.*] //

But if the self in a reflexive attitude turns back to its past working acts and looks at them *modo praeterito*, this unity goes to pieces. The self [4084] that performed the past acts is no longer the undivided total self, but rather a partial self, the performer of this particular act, that refers to a system of correlated acts to which it belongs. This partial self is merely the taker of a role, or, to use a rather equivocal term that W. James and G. H. Mead introduced into the literature: it is not an "I" but a "Me."
(Perhaps a digression on G. H. Mead in the sense of an expanded footnote 10, p. 541.)
For our purposes it is enough to refer to the fact that the inner experience of our bodily movements, the essentially actual experiences, and the open anticipations escape from reflective advertence, to clarify adequately that the past self can never be more than a partial aspect of the total self that experiences itself in its ongoing working. [4085]

(M R 541)
(112) *Performance and working*

Main structural distinction: In the case of a mere performance, such as the attempt to solve a mathematical problem "in one's head," I can, if my anticipations are not fulfilled and I am not dissatisfied with the result, simply cancel the whole process of mental operations and start again from the beginning. Nothing has changed in the outside world, and no vestige of the annulled process remains. Mere mental acts are, in this sense, revocable. Working, on the contrary, is irrevocable. Its result has changed the outside world. At best, I may restore the initial situation by a countermove, but I cannot make undone what I have done. This is why from the moral and legal point of view I am responsible for my deeds but not for my thoughts. But that is also the reason [4086] why I have the freedom of choice between several possibilities merely with respect to the mentally projected work, but not with respect to the past, i.e. only before the work has been carried through in the outer world or, at least, while it is being carried through in vivid present and therefore can still be modified. For the past, there is no choice. If I have realized my work completely or at least in part, then I have chosen what I did once and for all, and now I have to bear the consequences. I cannot choose what I wish I had done. [4087]

(M R 542)

(113) *The social structure of the life-world*
   Implications of the intersubjective structure of the life-world

(a) not my private [world], but common "to all of us";
(b) there exist fellowmen with whom I can enter into manifold social relationships: I act upon them, as they act upon me;
(c) especially important: intermeshing of the in-order-to and because-motivations;
(d) all communication is founded upon working relation.

I have to set in motion events or produce objects in the outer world that the Other is supposed to interpret as signs of what I mean to convey.

Gestures, speech, writing point back to bodily movements.

The behavioristic interpretation goes wrong by identifying the vehicle with the meaning. [4088]

(114) *The pure tuning-in relationship and synchronization of duration*

Two types of relation between communicator and the interpreter:

(1) The finished result of the Other's communicative action is given to me for interpretation. Example: road sign or tool.

(2) I participate interpretatively in the ongoing process of the Other's communicative action. Example: speech, letter; ad (2) polythetic performance of the meaning-positing acts; simultaneous with the polythetic performance of working—perception of the phases of the latter in full simultaneity, synchronously with polythetic performance of interpreting.

Two durations synchronized through mediation of the simultaneous process of working in the outside world.

In other words: communication takes place in the vivid present (speech) (see 110) or quasi-present (I read a letter).

(To be noted and analyzed, how—from the speaker's point of view—the meaning of the communication is monothetically preconceived while the monothetically interpreted meaning is revealed to the interpreter only after performance of the polythetic acts of interpretation and only as their result.) [4089]

Whereas the setting of meaning presupposes working, interpretation of meaning is a mere performance (105).

Based on the speech act that unreels in outer time, the listener does his interpretative performances as a series of retentions, protentions, and anticipations within his inner duration; these are linked together by the goal of understanding the Others (in regard to their relevance?).

The vivid present of the speaker, thus synchronized with the vivid present of the hearer, constitutes *our* vivid present, thus the we-relation. "We" experience this occurrence "in common," we each live in the Other's vivid present, are an element of his biography. *We grow older together* (cf. Ortega's assent to this formulation). [4090]

(M R 543)
(115) *Dimensions of the social world and their time perspectives*

(a) common time—common space;

The Other's body as an expressional field given to me for interpretation—although what I interpret as expression must by no means have been meant as an expressive announcement.

> // It can therefore be mere conduct (versus action), perhaps even just a reflex devoid of meaning. [Schutz's marginal comment—*trans.*] //

>> *Cassirer* on expression, reproduction, concept
>> *Snell* on purpose, expression, imitation
>> *Marty* on giving and receiving information

Here the Other's bodily appearance with all manifestations of his spontaneity is an element of the one's surrounding world, and vice versa; further, both participate in the Other's extra-worldly operational acts.

Finally, the partner can be grasped as an undivided self in his bodily presence, whereas I can look at my own self only *modo praeterito* and therefore can grasp only the Me as a partial aspect of my self (myself in this or that role). Definition of the thou as that self which can be grasped in its totality *modo praesenti*. [4091]

Derived social relations:

(i) The gradations of the contemporary world;
(ii) Predecessors;
(iii) Successors;

They are all characterized by the fact that in none of these derived social forms is the Other accessible to the partner as a unity (in his totality): He appears merely as a partial self, as the originator of these or those actions in which I do not participate in a vivid present.

Therefore to each type of derived social relationship belongs a particular type of time-perspective that is derived from the vivid present. E.g. the quasi-present in which I interpret the outcome of the Other's communicative acts without myself having participated in the ongoing performance of this action: the written letter, the printed book.

The time-dimension that links me with "contemporaries" (fellowmen); The historical time, in which I experience the actual present as the outcome of past events, etc., etc. [4092]

IMPORTANT!

All of these time perspectives can be referred to a vivid present: my own actual or former one or the actual or former vivid present of my fellowman, with whom, in turn, I am connected in an originary or derived vivid present; all this in the most varied modes of potentiality or quasi-actuality, each type having its own forms of temporal augmentation and diminution and its appurtenant style of "omissions" ("skippings") in a direct move or a "knight's move."

There are furthermore the different forms of overlapping and interpenetration of these different time-perspectives, their being put into and out of operation by a shift from one to the other or by a transformation of one into the other; finally, different types of synthesizing, combining, isolating, and disentangling them. Manifold as these different time-perspectives and their mutual relations are, they all originate in an intersection of durée and cosmic time. [4093]

(M R 545)

(116) *The social standard time*

In and by our natural attitude in the social life-world, the time-perspectives characterized at the end of (115) are apprehended as one single supposedly homogeneous dimension of time not only embracing all the individual time perspectives of each of us during his wide-awake life but common to all of us. We shall call it the civic or Standard Time. It too originates at the intersection between cosmic time and inner time, though as to the latter, merely a peculiar aspect of inner time enters into the constitution of standard time: namely that aspect in which the wide awake adult experiences his working acts as events in his stream of consciousness. Because standard time partakes of cosmic time, it can be measured with the help of our clocks and calendars.

But because [4094] it also coincides with our sense of time in which, we, if—and only if—we are wide-awake, experience our working acts, standard time also governs the system of our plans, under which we subsume our projects, such as plans for life, for work, and for leisure. Because, finally, it is common to all of us, the standard time makes an intersubjective coordination of the different individual plan systems possible.

As a consequence, to the natural attitude the civic or standard time is the universal temporal structure of the intersubjective world of our everyday life in the same sense as the earth is its universal spatial structure that embraces the spatial environments [of each] of us. [4095]

(117) *Orientation schemata and the strata of reality in the everyday life-world of working*

The wide-awake man, with his natural attitude, is primarily interested in that sector of the world of his everyday life which lies within his scope and is centered in space and time around himself. The place where I am, my actual Here, is the starting point from which I take my bearing in space. It is, so to speak, the center 0 of my system of coordinates.

Relatively to my body, I group the elements of my surroundings under the categories of right, left, above, below, before, behind, near, far, etc. And similarly my actual Now is the origin of all the time perspectives under which I organize the events within the life-world according to the categories of earlier, later, past, future, simultaneity, succession, etc.

Within this basic scheme of orientation, however, the world of working is structurized in various strata of reality. G. H. Mead [4096] has the merit of having analyzed the reality structure at least of physical objects in its relationship to human action, especially to the manipulation of these objects with the hands. What he called the *manipulatory area* constitutes the core of the reality of the life-world. This area includes those objects that can be both seen and handled, in contradistinction to the area of distant objects that cannot be experienced by contact but still lie in the visual field. Only experiences of physical things within the manipulatory area permit the "basic test of reality," namely the experience of resistance; only they define what Mead called the "standard size" of things that appear outside the manipulatory area in the distortions of optical perspectives.
On this: Maine de Biran
      Scheler
      Mead: Philosophy of the Present, pp. 124ff.
          Philosophy of the Act, pp. 103-106, 121ff., 151, 190-192, 196-197, 282-284 [4097]

(M R 546)
(118) *Manipulatory area and distant area in the life-world*

Mead's theory of the manipulatory area as core reality of the life-world coincides with our view that the world of our working, of body movements, of manipulating objects and handling things and men constitutes the specific reality of our life-world. For our purposes, however, the Meadian distinction between manipulatory and distant area (which is important in other respects) should not be overestimated. It can be shown that this dichotomy originates in Mead's behavioristic basic position and in the corresponding application of the stimulus-response scheme.

We, on the other hand, are concerned with the natural attitude of the wide-awake grown-up man in the life-world, who always has at his disposal a stock of previous experiences, among them the notion of distance as such and of the possibility of overcoming distance by acts of working, namely locomotions. In the natural attitude the visual perception [4098] of a distant object implies, therefore, the anticipation that the distant object can be brought into manipulative contact-proximity by locomotions, in which case the distorted perspective of the objects will disappear and their standard size be restored. This anticipation may—like any other—be [confirmed] by supervening actual experience. Its refutation by experience would mean that the distant object does not pertain to the world of our working. A child may [try] to grasp the stars with its hand. To the grown-up with the natural attitude, the shining points lie outside the sphere of his working, even when he uses their position as a means for finding his bearings.

To be considered: the problem of accessibility as essential for reach. In addition empowering; also implementability. Economic commodities and the principle of scarcity. [4099]

(119) *The world within my reach*

For our purposes, the stratum of the world of working that the individual experiences as the core of reality will be called the world within his reach. This includes not only Mead's manipulatory area but all things within the range of sight and hearing, moreover not only the realm of the world open to his actual operation but also adjacent realms open to his potential working. Of course, these realms have no rigid frontiers; rather, they have "halos" and open horizons, and these are subject to modifications of interest (of relevance) and attentional attitudes.

It is clear that the whole system of the world within my reach undergoes changes by any of my locomotions; by displacing my body I shift the center 0 of my system of coordinates, and this alone changes all values of the coordinate numbers pertaining to this system. [4100]

(M R 547)

(120) *Modifications of reach: their time-character*

We may say that the world within my actual reach belongs essentially to the present tense. The world within my potential reach shows a far more complicated time-structure. At least two zones of such potentiality have to be distinguished:

(1) The first refers to the past: what was formerly within my reach can, so I assume, be brought back into my actual reach again *(the world within my restorable reach)*. This assumption is based upon the general idealizations of "And so on" and "I can always do it again," the latter being a correlate of the former. (Although Husserl states this in this way, it must still be examined whether "I can always do it again" is not an independent idealization and the only one of the two that is required for the constitution of the world within my restorable reach, whereas on the contrary the "And so on" at least horizonwise points to a reach to be achieved in the future. [4101]

Example: The shifting of the center 0 of my system of coordinates has turned my former Here to a There. But under the idealization of "I can always do it again" I assume that I can retransform the actual There into a new Here. My past world within my reach has under this idealization the character of a world that can be brought back again within my reach. Thus, for instance, my former manipulatory area continues to function in my present as a potential manipulatory area in the mode of There and has now as such a specific chance of restoration (restorability).

(2) As the first zone of potentiality is related with the past, so is the second one based on anticipations of the future. Within my potential reach is also the world that neither is nor ever has been within my actual reach but is nevertheless attainable under the idealization of "And so on." [4102] The most important instance of this second zone of potentiality is the world within the actual reach of my contemporaneous fellowman. For example, his manipulatory area does not coincide with mine, or at least does so only partly, because it is to him a manipulatory area only in the Here-mode, while for me it is one in the There-mode. Nonetheless it is my attainable manipulatory area that would become my actual one if I were in his place, which by appropriate locomotion actually does happen. G. H. Mead in the essay "The Objective Reality of Perspectives" (*Philosophy of the Present*), p. 173, comes a similar conclusion: "Present reality is a possibility. It is what would be if I were there instead of here."[31]

For the face-to-face relation it is characteristic that the world within my reach [4103] and the world within that of my partner but not necessarily within his manipulatory area and mine overlap, and that at least a sector of the world lies within our common reach.

What has just been said applies, accordingly, quite generally to the world within your, within their, within someone's reach. This encompasses not just the world within the Other's actual reach, but also worlds within restorable and attainable reach. The system thus extended over all the different strata of the social world shows all the shades prearranged in the perspectives of sociality such as intimacy and anonymity, strangeness and familiarity, social proximity and distance, etc., perspectives that govern my relations with consociates, contemporaries, predecessors, successors. [4104] It is enough for our purposes to state that the (contemporary!) social world is a world within attainable reach and has a specific chance of attainment.

But the chances of restoration, peculiar to the first potential zone of reach, and of attainment, peculiar to the second one, are by no means equal. As to the former we have to consider that what is now to me a mere chance of restorable reach was previously experienced as located within my actual reach. My past working acts performed, and even merely projected, belonged to the world within my reach. On the other hand, they are related with my present state of mind, which is what it is only because the now-past reality was once my present one. The anticipated possible [4105] actualization of the once-actual world within my reach is, therefore, founded upon retentions and reproductions of my own past experiences of fulfillment. The chance of restoring the once-actual reach is, then, a maximal one.

The second zone of potentiality refers anticipatorily to future states of my mind. It is not connected with my past experiences, except by the fact that its anticipations (like all anticipations) originate in the stock of experiences sedimented out of past experiences and actually at hand. These prior experiences enable me to weigh the likelihood of carrying out my plans and to estimate my powers. It is clear that this second zone is not at all homogeneous but is subdivided into sectors of different chances of attainment. These chances diminish in proportion with the increasing spatial, temporal, and social distance of the respective sector from the actual center of my world of working. The greater the distance, the more uncertain are my anticipations of the attainable actuality, until finally they become entirely empty and unrealizable.

Fifth Notebook

from New York City

November 9 – 14, 1958

Contains: pp. 5001 – 5049

(M R 549)
[5001]
(120) *The world of working as paramount (main) reality*

It is the world of physical things;
> the area of my bodily operations and locomotions;
> it offers resistance, to overcome which requires effort;
> it places tasks before me, permits me to carry through my plans,
>> enables me to succeed or to fail in my attempts to attain my
>> purposes.

By my working acts I gear into this world; I change it; I can test these
> changes and have others test them, namely as occurrences within
> this objective, intersubjective world, independently of the circum-
> stance that they were produced through my working acts.

I share this world and its objects with others, with whom I have ends and
> means in common.

I work with others with whom I am bound in manifold social relations; I
> act upon them and they upon me.

The world of working is that unique reality which makes communication
> possible and becomes effective in the interplay of mutual motivation
> (my in-order-to, his because-motives, and vice versa).

Therefore it can be experienced under a dual scheme of references: the
> causality of motives and the teleology of purposes. [5002]

(121) *Interest in the world of working and its relevance structure*

To the natural attitude, the world of working is in the first place not an
object of our thought but a field of domination, in which we have an eminently practical interest, caused by the necessity of complying with the
basic requirements of our life. But we are not *equally* interested in all the
strata of the world of working.

The selective function of our interest organizes the world [both] in
temporal [and] in a spatial respect of major or minor *relevance*. From the
world within my actual or potential reach, [elements] that either are actual
ends or means for the realization of my projects or could become so in

the future are selected as particularly important, further such as are dangerous or enjoyable or otherwise relevant to me or could become so. I am constantly anticipating the future repercussions I may expect from these objects and the future changes that my projected working will bring about in and on these objects. [5003]

(122) What "relevance" means in this context

I am, for instance, with the natural attitude, passionately interested in the results of my action and especially in the question: which of my anticipations will stand the practical test. Now, however, all anticipations and plans refer to the stock of experience now at hand, which results from previous experiences and thus enables me to weigh my chances. But that is only half the story. What I am anticipating is one thing; another is why I anticipate certain occurrences at all. What may happen under certain conditions and circumstances is one problem; another is why I am interested in these happenings at all and passionately await the outcome of my prophecies. Only the first element of these dichotomies can be answered by reference to the stock of experiences at hand as the sediment of previous experiences. The second element refers to the system of relevances that governs the individual with his natural attitude in the everyday life-world. [5004]

(M R 550)

(123) Fundamental anxiety as supreme motive of the relevance system

The whole system of relevances that governs us with the natural attitude is founded upon the basic experience of every single one of us: I know that I shall die, and I fear to die. We will call this basic experience the fundamental anxiety. It is the primordial anticipation from which the others originate. From the fundamental anxiety spring the many interrelated systems of hopes and fears, of wants and satisfactions, of chances and risks that incite man with the natural attitude to attempt to master the world, to overcome obstacles, to design and realize projects.

But the fundamental anxiety itself is merely a correlate of our existence as human beings within the main reality of the world of our daily life, and, therefore, our hopes and fears and their correlated satisfactions and disappointments are grounded upon and possible only within the world of working. They are essential elements of its reality but they do not refer to [5005] our belief in it. On the contrary, it is characteristic of the natural attitude that it takes the existence of the world and the objects in it for granted until a counterproof [imposes itself]. As long as the once-established scheme of reference, the system of our and other people's warranted experiences, works, i.e. as long as the actions and operations performed under its guidance yield the desired result, we trust these experiences. We are not interested in finding out whether the world really does exist or whether it is merely a coherent system of consistent appearances. We have no reason to cast any doubt upon our warranted experiences that, so we believe, represent things to us as they really are. It needs a special motivation, such as the upshooting of a strange experience not subsumable under the stock of experience at hand or inconsistent with it, to make us revise our former beliefs. [5006]

(124) The epochē of the natural attitude

The natural attitude thus also knows a specific form of epochē, of course not that of phenomenological suspension of belief in the reality of the world. Man in his natural attitude does not suspend belief in the outer world and its objects but on the contrary: he suspends doubt in its existence. What he puts in brackets is the doubt that the world and its objects might be otherwise than they appear to him. This epochē shall be called the epochē of the natural attitude.

> (To be examined: Spiegelberg's essay in Husserl's memorial volume: The Reality Phenomenon and Reality[32] with his analysis of the dubitability and dubiousness of reality. According to Spiegelberg, reality-criteria are the phenomena of readiness, persistence, perceptual periphery, boundaries in concrete objects, independence, resistance, and agreement.) [5007]

(M R 551)
(125) The many realities and their constitution

In contrast to William James, who speaks of subuniverses of reality, we prefer to speak of finite provinces of meaning, upon each of which we may bestow the accent of reality. For it is the meaning of our experiences and not the ontological structure of its objects that constitutes reality.

> (Cf. Husserl Ideen (Chap.) I, 3, §55 p. 106:
> "In a certain sense and with proper care in the use of words we may say that *all real unities* are *'unities of meaning'* . . . An *absolute reality has as much validity as a round square.* Reality and world are here precisely titles for certain valid *unities of meaning*, namely unities of 'meaning' related to certain contexts of absolute pure consciousness which by their *nature* display meaningful and sensory validity precisely so and not otherwise." (Husserl's [italics])

Hence, we call a certain set of our experiences a finite province of meaning if all of them show a specific cognitive style and are—*with respect to this style*—not only consistent in themselves but also compatible with one another. The italicized restriction is important because inconsistencies and incompatibilities of *some* experiences, all of them partaking of the same cognitive style, do not necessarily [5008] entail the withdrawal of the accent of reality from the respective province of meaning as a whole but merely the invalidation of the particular experiences within that province.

(M R 552)
(126) What is the meaning of the "specific cognitive style" and "accent of reality"?

If we take an example of a finite province of meaning let us consider the paramount reality of the world of everyday life; then we find that the following characteristics constitute its specific cognitive style:

(1) A specific tension of consciousness, namely wide-awakeness, originating in full attention to life;

(2) A specific epoché, namely suspension of doubt;

(3) A prevalent form of spontaneity, namely working (a meaningful spontaneity based upon a project and characterized by the intention to bring about the projected state of affairs by bodily movements gearing into the outer world).

(4) A specific form of experiencing one's self (the working self as the total-self);

(5) A specific form of sociality (the common intersubjective world of communication and social action).

(6) A specific time-perspective (the standard time originating in an intersection between *durée* and cosmic time as the universal temporal structure of the intersubjective world). [5009]

These are at least some of the features of the cognitive style belonging to this particular province of meaning. As long as our valid as well as invalidated experiences partake of this style we may consider this province of meaning to be real: We may bestow upon it the accent of reality. And with respect to the paramount reality of everyday life we, with our natural attitude, are induced to do so because our practical experiences prove the unity and congruity of the world of working as valid and the hypothesis of its reality as irrefutable. Even more, this reality seems to us to be the natural one, and we are not ready to abandon our attitude toward it without having experienced a specific shock that compels us to break through the limits of this finite province of meaning and to shift the accent of reality to another one. [5010]

(M R 553)
(127) *Shock experiences*

There are as many innumerable kinds of shock experiences as there are finite provinces of meaning that can receive the accent of reality.
Examples: falling asleep (cf. Linschoten) as a leap into dream,
　　　　　the theater curtain rises;
　　　　　picture frame;
　　　　　laughter as reaction to wit and involved shift of reality;
　　　　　toys;
　　　　　Kierkegaard's "instant";
　　　　　the scientist's decision for the theoretical attitude.

[5011]

(128) *Examples of finite provinces of meaning; characterization of their nature*

The world of dreams, various worlds of fantasy, especially the world of art, the world of religious experience, of scientific contemplation, the play-world of the child, the world of the insane.

I. Each of the same has

　(a) its specific cognitive style (although not that of the life-world);

(b) all experiences within this field of meaning are consistent in themselves and compatible with one another (although not compatible with the meaning-structure of the life-world);

(c) each of these provinces of meaning can receive a specific accent of reality (although not that of the life-world).

II. Consistency and compatibility with respect to cognitive style subsist merely within the borders of the respective finite province of meaning to which these experiences belong. By no means will that which is compatible within the finite province of meaning P also be compatible within the finite province of meaning Q. On the contrary, seen from P, supposed to be real, Q and all experiences belonging to it appear as merely fictitious, inconsistent, and incompatible, and vice versa.

III. For this very reason we are entitled to talk of *finite* provinces of meaning. This finiteness implies [5012] that there is no possibility of referring one finite province of meaning to another by introducing a formula of transformation. The passing from one to the other can be performed only by a "leap," as Kierkegaard calls it, whose subjective correlate is the shock experience.

IV. What has just been called a "leap" or a "shock" is nothing else than a radical modification of the tension of consciousness that results from a different *attention à la vie*.

V. To the cognitive style peculiar to each of these finite provinces of meaning belongs, thus, a specific tension of consciousness and, consequently, also a specific epoché, a prevalent form of spontaneity, a specific form of self experience, a specific form of sociality, and a specific time-perspective.

VI. The life-world of working is the archetype of our experience of reality. All the other provinces of meaning may be considered as its modifications.

Footnote 19 p. 554
The concept of finite provinces of meaning must not be interpreted statically as if we were to regard one of the same as our home to live in, to start from or to return to. Within a single day, even a single hour, we may run through a whole series of these provinces by modifying the tension of consciousness. There is, furthermore, the problem [5013] of "enclaves"; e.g. any projecting of working within the life-world is a fantasying and involves in addition a kind of theoretical, though not scientific, contemplation.

(M R 554)
(129) *Tasks of a typology of provinces of meaning*
A systematic analysis of groupings of the finite provinces of meaning according to the constitutive principle of diminishing tension of consciousness and diminishing attention to life would show that the more the mind turns away from life, the larger the slabs of the everyday world of working are put in doubt; the epoché of the natural attitude that suspends doubt in the existence of the life-world is replaced by other forms of epoché that

suspend belief in more and more layers of the reality of daily life, "putting them in brackets." In other words a typology of the different finite provinces of meaning could start from an analysis of those factors of the world of daily life from which the accent of reality has been withdrawn because they no longer stand within the focus of our attention to life. What then remains outside the brackets can be defined as the quintessence of the constituent elements of the cognitive style of experience belonging to the province of meaning thus delimited. It may then obtain another accent of reality, or, in the language of the archetype of all reality, namely the world of our daily life—the accent of a quasi-reality. [5014]

(M R 555)
(130) *Language as Belonging to the Reality of Daily Life*

The last remark reveals a specific difficulty for all attempts at describing these quasi-realities. It consists in the fact that language—any language—pertains as communication *kat' exochen* to the intersubjective world of working and, therefore, obstinately resists every effort to [make it] serve as vehicle for meaning relations that transcend its own presuppositions. This fact leads to the manifold forms of indirect communication some of which still need to be discussed. Scientific terminology is one example of a special device to overcome the outlined difficulty within a limited field. (Here insert the Kierkegaard passage from the "Mozart" essay.) [5015]

(131) *Fantasy Worlds*

Their multiplicity; their heterogenous character; their reciprocal irreduceability; examples: daydreams, play, poetry, fairy tale, myths, jokes.

Living in one of the many worlds of fantasy we need no longer master the outer world and overcome the resistance of its objects. We are free from the pragmatic motive that governs our natural attitude to the world of daily life, free also from the bondage of "interobjective" [*trans. note:* German notebook version has "inter*sub*jective"; correction is made here based on M R] space and intersubjective standard time. No longer are we confined within the limits of the world within our actual restorable and attainable reach. Events of the outer world no longer impose on us alternatives between which we have to choose; they put no limits on our possible accomplishments.

However, there are also no "possible accomplishments" in the world of phantasms if we take this term as a synonym of "performable." The self living within its imagination neither works nor performs within the meaning of the aforegiven definitions. Imagining may be projected inasmuch as it is conceived in advance, and it may even be included in a hierarchy of plans. But this meaning of the term [5016] "project" is not exactly the same meaning used when we defined action as projected conduct. Strictly speaking, the opposite holds good, namely, that the projected action is always the imagined performed act, imagined in the "future perfect tense" (*modo futuri exacti*). It remains to be seen whether all or merely some or no form of our imaginative life may be qualified as "action" or whether fancying belongs exclusively to the category of "mere thinking." Yet it is important to understand that all imagining as such lacks the intention to realize the phantasm; it lacks, in other words, the decision of the purposive "fiat." In Husserl's language *Ideas* I (§111) it may be said that all fantasying is "neutral," i.e., it lacks the specific positionality of the thetic consciousness.

However a sharp distinction must be made between imagining as a manifestation of our spontaneous conscious life and the imageries imagined. Acting may be imagined as true acting and even working within the meaning of our definitions; it may be imagined as referring to a preconceived project, as related to specific in-order-to and because-motives [5017], as occupying a particular place in the hierarchy of plans. Indeed, even more: it may be imagined as endowed with an intention to realize the project, to carry it through, and it may even be fancied as gearing into the outer world. All this, however, belongs to the imageries produced within and by the imagining act. The "performances" and "working acts" are merely imagined *as* performances and working acts, and they themselves and the correlated categories bear, to use Husserl's expression, quotation marks. Imagining itself is, however, necessarily inefficient and stays under all circumstances outside the hierarchies of plans and purposes valid within the world of working. The imagining self does not transform the outer world.

> Example: Analysis of Don Quixote and the windmills. (Here insert, perhaps as a supplement, some passages from the Spanish Don Quixote essay.) [5018]

(M R 558)

(132) *Husserl's doctrine of predications of existence and predications of reality in Experience and Judgment (§74a)*

W. James's doctrine of the uncontradicted reality posited as absolute (Vol. II p. 289) (Maggie in her stall) is cited, and it is stated that Husserl came to the same result.

The opposites to the predications of existence: predications of non-existence.

The opposites to the predications of reality: predications of non-reality, of fiction.

EU p. 360 "With the natural attitude there is at the outset (before reflection) no predicate 'real' and no category 'reality.' Only if we fantasy and pass from the attitude of living in the fantasy (that is the attitude of quasi-experiencing in all its forms) to the given realities, and if we, thus, transgress the single casual fantasying and its phantasm, taking both as examples for possible fantasying as such and fiction as such, then we obtain on the one hand the concepts fiction (respectively, fantasying) and on the other hand the concepts 'possible experience as such' and 'reality.' [5019]

We cannot say that he who fantasies and lives in the world of phantasms (the 'dreamer'), posits fictions *qua* fictions, but he has modified realities, 'realities as if,'. . . . Only he who lives in experiences and reaches from there into the world of phantasms can, provided that the phantasm contrasts with the experienced, have the concepts fiction and reality" (Husserl's italics). [5020]

(133) Boundaries of fantasying.

From our analysis of Don Quixote and the Husserl quotation (132) follows:

The compatibilities of experiences that belong to the world of working in everyday life do not subsist within the realm of fantasy; however, the logical structure of consistency or, in Husserl's terms, the predications of existence and non-existence, however, remain valid. I can imagine giants, magicians, winged horses, centaurs, even a *perpetuum mobile;* but not a regular decahedron, unless I stop—as I would have to do in full-awakeness—at a blind juxtaposition of empty terms. But otherwise: within the realm of fantasy merely factual, but not logical, incompatibilities can be overcome.

The corollary of this last statement is the insight that the chances of attaining and restoring factual situations do not exist in the same sense within the world of phantasms or within the world of working. What is a chance in the latter is in the former a *conditio potestiva*, that is, a circumstance which to bring or not to bring about is under the control of the party involved. The imagining individual masters, so to speak, his chances: he can fill empty anticipations of his fantasy with any content he pleases. [5021] The anticipation of imagined future events stands within his free discretion.

(M R 559)

(134) Time perspectives of the fantasy worlds

Husserl on the time of the phantasms: *Erf. Urteil*, §§39-42: Phantasms have no fixed position in objective time; therefore, they are not individualized and the category of sameness is not applicable to them. The "same" phantasm may recur within the uninterrupted continuity of one single fantasying activity the unity of which is warranted by the continuity of inner time within which this action occurs. But phantasms pertaining to different strands of fantasy or—in our terminology—pertaining to different finite provinces of meaning—cannot be compared as to their sameness or likeness. It is meaningless to ask whether the witch of one fairy tale is the same as the witch of another.

For our purposes it is not necessary to follow Husserl into the depth of the problems of constitutional analysis here involved. Yet it is important to point out that the imagining self, in his fantasies, can remodel all the features of standard time except its irreversability. I may, so to speak, imagine the course of events in slow motion or accelerated time. Irreversability, [5022] however, eludes any variation by the fantasy because it originates within the *durée* that itself is constitutive for all our fantasying and the phantasms produced therein. Imagining, and even dreaming, I continue to grow old. The fact that I can in a present fantasy remodel my past is not a counterevidence against this statement.

(135) *The self as object of fantasying*

In my imageries I may fancy myself any role I wish to assume. But doing so I have no doubt that the imagined self is merely a part of my total personality, one possible role I may take, a Me existing only by my grace. In my fantasies I may even vary my bodily appearance but this freedom of discretion has its barrier at the primordial experience of the boundaries of my body. They subsist whether I imagine myself as giant or dwarf. (Here insert reference to Scheler's idols of self-knowledge (On the fall of values)) [5023]

(136) *Social structure of the fantasy world*

Imagining can be practiced in solitude or in society and the latter both in the pure we-relation as well as in all its modifications and derivations. An instance of the first is daydreaming; of the second the mutually oriented intersubjective make-believe play of children or some phenomena studied by mass psychology. On the other hand the others, and also any kind of social relationships, social actions, and reactions, may become objects (contents) of imagining. The freedom of the imagining self has a wide latitude here. It is, for example, possible that the phantasm excludes the imagined cooperation of an imagined fellowman to such an extent that the latter's imagined reactions may corroborate or annihilate my own phantasm. [5024]

(M R 560)
(137) *The world of dreams*

Sleep as complete relaxation of consciousness, complete turning away from life. The sleeping self has no pragmatic interest whatsoever in transforming its confused perceptions into clarity and distinctness, in other words transforming them into apperceptions. But it continues to perceive, to recollect, to think: Somatic perceptions of its own body, its position, its weight, its boundaries; perceptions of light, sound, warmth, without any activity of regarding, listening, attending to them, which alone would make perceptions into apperceptions. The "small perceptions" remain perceived; they escape censorship by the attention to life and gain high importance in the world of dreams. Although they do not become clear and distinct, but remain in a state of confusion, they are no longer concealed and disturbed by the interference of *active*, pragmatically conditioned attention. It is, on the contrary, passive attention—and that is the total effect exercised by the small perceptions upon the intimate center of the personality— that alone determines the interest of the dreamer and the topics that become themes of his dreams.
Cf. Freud. [5025]

The dreaming self neither works nor acts. This is not the case also for the fantasying self. But the worlds of fantasies are characterized by the freedom of discretion, whereas the world of dreams lacks such a freedom. The fantasying self can "arbitrarily" fill its empty protentions and anticipations with any content and, strictly speaking, it is the cases upon which the fantasying self bestows the accent of reality. It may, as it pleases, interpret its chances as lying within its mastery. The dreamer, however, has no such freedom, neither his own discretion nor arbitrary choice in mastering the chances, nor the possibility of filling in empty anticipations. The nightmare, for instance, shows clearly the inescapableness of the happening in the world of dream and the powerlessness of the dreamer to influence it.

This does not, however, mean that the life of dreams is confined exclusively to passive consciousness. On the contrary, most of activities of intentionality, as Husserl calls them, subsist, but without being directed toward objects of the outer world of working and without being steered by active attention. Yet among these activities there are none of apperceiving or of volition. The life of dream is without purpose and project.

But does this not contradict Freud's doctrine of the predominant role of volitions and instincts within the world of dreams? I do not think that there is any contradiction. [5026] Actual volitions, actual projects, actual purposes etc. do not exist in the life of dreams. Whatever volitions, projects, purposes are found in dreams do not originate in the dreaming self. What is involved are presentiations (recollections), retentions, and reproductions of volitive experience that originated within the world of awakeness. Now they reappear, although modified and reinterpreted according to the scheme of reference prevailing in the particular type of dream. We may consider the whole psychoanalytic technique of dream interpretation as an attempt to refer the contents of the dream to the originary experiences in the world of awakeness in which and by which they were constituted.

Generally speaking, the world of working or at least fragments of it are preserved within the world of dreams as recollections and retentions. In this sense we may say that *attention à la vie* of the dreamer is directed to the past of his self. It is an attention in the tense of the past. The contents of dream life consist primarily in past or past perfect experiences that are re-interpreted by transforming previously confused experiences into distinctness, by explicating their implied horizons and looking at their anticipations in terms of the past and their reproductions in terms of the future. The sedimented experiences of the world of awakeness are, thus, so to speak, broken down and otherwise reconstructed, [5027] the self no longer having any pragmatic interest in keeping together its stock of experience as a consistently and coherently unified scheme of reference. But the postulates of the consistency, coherence, and unity of experience originate in pragmatic motives insofar as they presuppose clear and distinct apperceptions. These, and even certain logical axioms, such as the principle of identity, do not, for this very reason, hold good in the sphere of dreams. The dreamer is frequently astonished to see now as compatible what he remembers as having been incompatible in the world of his awake life, and vice versa. Freud and his school saw all this.

I may dream myself as working or acting and this dream may be accompanied frequently by the knowledge that, "in reality," I am not working or acting. Then my dreamed working has its quasi-projects, quasi-plans, and their hierarchies, all of them originating in sedimented pre-experiences I had originating in the world of daily life. It happens frequently that the dreamed *I* (rather *Me*) performs his work without any intention of doing so, without any voluntative fiat, and that this *I (Me)* obtains results with either disproportionately great or small effort. [5028]

(M R 562)
(138) *Time structure of the world of dreams*

Its complex character: earlier and later, present, past, future seem to be intermingled; there are future events observed as if they were past; past and past-perfect events, as open and modifiable and, therefore, as showing a clear character of futurity; successions are transformed into simultaneities, and so forth. Seemingly—but only seemingly—the dream events occur separately and independently of the stream of inner *durée*. They are, however, merely detached from the arrangement of standard time; they have no position in the order of objective time. They roll on within the subjective inner time, although fragments of the standard time, which had been experienced by the past self of the dreamer and has fallen to pieces, are snatched into the world of dreams. The irreversability of *durée* subsists also in the dream-world. Only the awakened person, who remembers his dream, has sometimes the illusion of a possible reversibility. [5029]

(139) *Only the awake person can communicate.*

This last remark (138) reveals a serious difficulty for all dealing with the phenomena of the dream and also of the fantasy. As soon as I turn to them and think of them I am no longer dreaming or fantasying. I am wide-awake and, speaking and thinking, use the implements of the world of awakeness, namely concepts that are subject to the principles of consistency and compatibilty. Are we sure that the awakened person really can tell his dreams, he who no longer dreams? It will probably make an important difference whether he recollects his dream in vivid retention or whether he has to reproduce it. Whatever the case may be, we encounter the eminent dialectical difficulty that there exists for dreams no possibility of communication that would not transcend the sphere to which it refers. We can, therefore, grasp the province of dreams and imageries only by way of "indirect communication," to borrow this term from Kierkegaard. The poet and the artist are thus far closer to an adequate interpretation of the worlds of dreams and phantasms than the scientist and the philosopher, because their categories of communication themselves refer to the world of fantasy. They can, if not overcome, at least make transparent the underlying dialectical conflict. We will discuss a similar difficulty in the analysis of scientific contemplation. [5030]

(M R 563)

(140) *On the solitude of the dreamer*

The state of dreaming—in contrast with fantasying—is essentially lonely. We cannot dream together and the alter ego remains always an object of my dreams, incapable of sharing them. Even the alter ego of which I dream does not appear in common vivid present but in an empty, fictitious quasi-we-relation. The other of whom I dream is always typified, and this holds true even if I dream him to be in the closest relationship to my intimate self. He is an alter ego only by my grace. Thus, the monad, with all its mirrorings of the universe, is indeed lonely, while it dreams. [5031]

(141) *The world as object of scientific contemplation*

The theoretical attitude in the midst of life-world praxis. To "sit down" and think over the problem. This kind of contemplation, however, serves practical purposes. It is a kind of enclave within life-praxis and still governed by the scheme of pragmatic relevancy. This kind of contemplative thinking, as well as that of pure meditation based on no project, has been disregarded here. The theme is, exclusively, scientific theorizing.

Scientific theorizing serves no practical purpose. Its aim is not to master the world but to observe and possibly to understand it. Difference between the scientifically theoretical attitude and the application of science within the world of working. Our topic is the first one, but also the question of how it is possible that the life-world of all of us can be made the object of scientific contemplation and that the outcome of such contemplation can in turn be applied to the world of working. [5032]

(M R 564)

(142) *The nature of scientific contemplation*

It is, within the meaning of our definitions, an action and even a performance—an "action," i.e., an emanation of our spontaneous life carried out according to a project, and a "performance" because the intention to carry through the project is added.

Thus, scientific theorizing has its own in-order-to and because-motives; it is planned, and planned within the hierarchy of a system of plans based on the decision to pursue science. (This action-character of theorizing alone would suffice to distinguish it from dreaming.) Scientific thinking is, furthermore, purposive thinking (and this purposiveness alone would suffice to distinguish it from fantasying). The purpose of scientific thinking is the intention to solve the problem at hand.

Yet scientific action is not as such working, i.e. it does not gear into the outer world. To be sure, scientific theorizing is based upon working (measuring, handling instruments, conducting experiments) and it can be communicated only by [5033] working acts (delivering lectures, writing papers, etc.). All these activities are the precondition or the consequence of theorizing but they do not belong to the theoretical attitude as such.

Further, we have to distinguish between the scientist *qua* human being who lives his daily life among his fellowmen and the theoretical thinker who is not interested in the mastery of the world but in observing it. [5034]

(M R 565)
(143) *The scientist as "disinterested observer"*

A peculiar attention to life [is] the prerequisite of all theorizing. It consists in the abandoning of the system of relevances that prevails within the practical sphere of the natural attitude. Of course, the whole universe of life is pregiven even to the theorizing thinker. But whereas for man with the natural attitude the system of relevancy is determined by his fundamental anxiety, the theoretical thinker, once having made the "leap" into the disinterested attitude, is free from fundamental anxiety and all hopes and fears arising from it.

(Of course, making the leap is itself motivated by fundamental anxiety. Philosophy [is] a time-tested means of overcoming anxiety. An immortal being—say an angel of St. Thomas's—would not need to turn philosopher. The "leap" into the theoretical attitude can be considered as the assumption of a peculiar epochē from the fundamental anxiety, putting it and all its implications in brackets. [5035] Certainly, even the theorizing thinker has a system of anticipations, which, on the one hand, refers back to his stock of sedimented knowledge, on the other to its special system of relevances, which will be discussed later. However, unlike man in the natural attitude of the life-world, the thinker is not passionately interested in the question, whether his anticipations are fulfilled in the sense that they will prove helpful for the solution of his *practical* problems, but merely in whether they will stand the test of verification by supervening experiences. Rightly understood this involves a certain turning away from life and from the state of wide-awakeness.) [5036]

(M R 566)
(144) *Characteristics of theoretical thinking*

(a) As mere performance (in contrast with working), it is revocable; it can be "crossed out."
(b) It is independent of the world within the reach of thinking; this refers not to the inaccessibility of data, but to the fact that the thinker "puts in brackets" his physical existence (the body as center of the system of coordinates) and thus the entire system of orientation formed around his body; his personal psycho-physical existence within the world and this environment. Theoretical problems and their solution have validity not only for him, but for everyone, everywhere, at all times, wherever certain acceptable conditions prevail. The leap to the theoretical attitude involves the resolution of the individual to suspend his subjective point of view.

(c) In the theoretical attitude, not the complete self "acts" but only a partial aspect of the same, a "Me," a taker of a social role, namely the theoretician. He has no "essentially actual" experiences, also none connected with his own body, its movements, and its limits. [5037]

(M R 567)
(145) *Epochē of the theoretical attitude*
In this epochē are "bracketed" (suspended) the following:

(1) the subjectivity of the thinker as a man among his fellowmen, including his bodily existence within the life-world. (But this epochē is made within the "natural" attitude; in phenomenological reduction even the *world* of the epochē is lacking.)

(2) the system of orientation, by which the world of everyday life seems to be grouped (around my body as center 0) in zones of actual, restorable, attainable reach, etc.;

(3) the fundamental anxiety and the system of pragmatic relevances originating therein.

But within this sphere, modified in this way (1-3), the life-world of all of us is preserved as the reality of theoretical contemplation—although not of practical interest. With the shift of the system of relevances from the practical to the theoretical field all terms referring action and performance within the world of working, such as 'plan,' 'motive,' 'project,' change their meaning and receive 'quotation marks.' [5038]

(146) *The system of relevances within the theoretical attitude*
originates in a voluntary act of the scientist: the *stating of the problem*. Therewith the more or less empty anticipation of its solution is set up as the supreme goal of the scientific activity, but simultaneously also that sector or those elements of the world are defined which are actually or potentially related to it or relevant to its solution. Henceforth, the field thus circumscribed as relevant will guide the process of inquiry: it will, first of all, determine the level of the research. (The term 'level' [*Tiefenschicht*] is just another expression for the demarcation line between all that does and does not pertain to the problem under consideration. The former are the topics to be investigated, explicated, clarified; the latter the other elements of the stock of knowledge at the scientist's disposal, which he decides to accept in their unexamined givenness [—] as irrelevant to his problem [—]: the so-called "data." In other words, the demarcation line is the [—] geometrical [—] locus of all points which are of current interest to the scientist and at which he has decided to stop or break off further research.) [5039] Second, the stating of the problem, once done, determines its open horizons, the outer horizon of the other related problems, which will have to be stated later, and the inner horizon of all the implications hidden within the problem itself, which have to be explicated in order to solve it.
    This decision of the scientist that leads to the stating of the problem is, however, by no means an arbitrary one, and he by no means has the

same "freedom of discretion" in choosing and solving his problems as the fantasizing self has in filling out its empty anticipations. Of course, the scientist may freely choose which field he wants to take interest in, and possibly also the level at which he wants to carry on his investigations. But as soon as he has made up his mind in this respect, the scientist has entered a preconstituted world of scientific inquiry handed down to him by the historical tradition of his science. Henceforth, he has to participate in a "universe of discourse" embracing the postulates received from others, problems stated by others, solutions suggested by others, [5040] methods worked out by others. This theoretical universe of the special science is itself a finite province of meaning, having its peculiar cognitive style and its peculiar implications of problem[s] and horizons to be explicated. The regulative principle of the constitution of such a province of meaning, called a special branch of science, can be formulated as follows: Any problem emerging within the scientific field has to partake of the universal style peculiar to this field and has to be compatible with the preconstituted problems of this field and their solutions by either accepting or refuting them.

Accordingly, the latitude of discretion left to the individual scientist is in reality very small.

(Open question: the Aristotelian [—] and also Nicolai Hartmann's [—] problem of the aporias; that is the coherent system of questions and answers that form the horizon of the problem. Further, the notion of key concepts, that is, concepts whose introduction shatters the previously homogeneous field into sectors relevant or irrelevant to the topic under inquiry.) [5041]

(M R 569)
(147) *The scientific method*

But as soon as the problem itself is stated, the latitude of discretion vanishes completely. This insight has been concealed by the static character of our depiction of the process of theoretical thinking. It is, in fact, a process that goes on according to the strict rules of scientific procedure, which it is the task of methodology and epistemology to describe. A few of these rules are, for example:

(1) the postulate of consistency and compatibility of all propositions not only within the field of that special branch of science, but also with all other scientific propositions and even with the experiences of the life-world acquired in the natural attitude, insofar as precisely this life-world, although modified, is preserved within the finite province of meaning of theoretical contemplation;

(2) the postulate that all scientific thought has to be derived, directly or indirectly, from verifiable observations, that is, from immediate self-given experiences of facts within the world;

(3) the postulating of the highest possible clarity and distinctness of all

terms and notions used, which includes especially the transformation of confused prescientific thought into distinctness by explicating its hidden implications, etc. [5042]

The total of these rules sets forth the conditions under which scientific propositions and, in particular, the system of those propositions that form the respective special branch of science can be considered as warranted— or, in our language, the conditions under which an accent of reality can be bestowed upon the finite province of meaning in question. [5043]

(148) *Distinction between theoretical cogitations and the intentional cogitata of such a theorizing*

This distinction corresponds to the one previously made between the world of imagining and the imageries imagined. By their intentionality, the cogitata generated in theorizing refer to the one objective world, the universe within which we all live as psycho-physical human beings, within which we work and think, the intersubjective life-world that is pregiven to all of us, as the paramount reality from which all the other forms of reality are derived.

"With the theoretical attitude," says Farber[33] (p. 525) ". . . the objects become theoretical objects, [objects] of an actual positing of *being*, in which the ego apprehends them as *existent*. This makes possible a comprehensive and systematic view of *all* objects as possible substrates of the theoretical attitude."

But unlike the world of phantasms, which, according to Husserl, lack any fixed position in the order of objective time, the intentional objects of theoretical contemplation (insofar as [5044] they are not ideal objects of a higher order) have their well-defined place within the order of objective, cosmic time; however, insofar as they are objects of a higher order, they are founded upon objects having such a place in objective time.

(Here I cite Farber pp. 457-460 and Husserl VI Log. Untersuchungen § § 47-48, but the whole line of thinking now seems extremely suspicious to me.)

This statement (so Multiple Realities continues), however, covers merely the *objects* of theoretical thought and does not refer to the perspective of time peculiar to the *process* of theoretical thinking. The theoretical thinker too lives within his inner *durée*; he also grows old; his stock of experience also changes permanently by the emergence and sedimentation of new experiences. The theorizing self, therefore, has its specific form of past, namely the history of its pre-experiences and their sedimentations, and its specific form of the future, namely, the open horizons of the problem in need of solution (the project of its on-going theorizing) which refer to other [5045] problems to be stated afterwards and to the methods that could lead to their solution. But this time perspective, which the theorizing self lacks is the vivid present constituted with the natural attitude by the bodily movements as an intersection of inner *durée* and cosmic time.

Consequently, the theoretizing self cannot share a vivid present with others in a pure we-relation; it stays even outside the different time-perspectives of sociality originating in the vivid present of the we-relation. It does not, for this reason, partake of the standard time, which as we have seen, is nothing else than the intersubjective form of all the individual time-perspectives including the vivid present and its derivations. Insofar as scientific activity goes on within the standard time (in working hours, time-table, Husserl's professional times, etc.), it consists of acts of working within the world of everyday life [—] which [deal] with science—but not in acts of pure theorizing.

Nonetheless, the theorizing self has a particular form of specious present, within which it lives and acts. This specious present is defined at any moment by the span of the project conceived. Its "fore" embraces the problems previously stated as tasks the solution of which is just in progress; its "aft" consists in the anticipated outcome of the ongoing theorizing designed to bring about the solution of the problem in hand. [5046]

(M R 571)

(149) *The theorizing self is solitary; how, then, is social science possible?*

The theorizing self has put its physical existence and, thus, also its body in brackets. It has no physical environment, absolutely no world within reach. The "actor" within theoretical activity is never the undivided "I" of the personality of the scientist, but just a partial self, a "Me." The vivid present and the possibility of establishing a pure we-relation and its derivations are inaccessible to the theorizing self. It can therefore never grasp the other as an unbroken unity.

In summary: the theorizing self is solitary; it has no social environment; it stands outside all social relationships.

How can the solitary theorizing self find access to reality and make it the object of its theoretical contemplation?

This dialectical problem—it has a certain similarity to that of the dreamer treated above—does not become fully visible in the case of (mathematical) natural science (although—Heisenberg—"foundational crises" occur when the scientific observer is included in the field of observation). But the whole [5047] intersubjective world of working in the standard time (including the working self of the theoretical thinker as a human being, his fellowmen and their working) and even the problem of how the existence of fellowmen and their consciousness is experienced in the natural attitude, can be a topic of theoretical contemplation. This is even the principal subject matter of all social sciences.

We have to face the difficulty here involved (p. 571/572) in its full earnestness. The theoretical thinker who remains in his solitude cannot experience originarily or grasp in immediacy the world of everyday life, the life-world within which I and You, Peter and Paul, each and all have confused and ineffable perceptions, act, work, plan, suffer, hope, have been born, grow up, and will die—in a word: live their life as unbroken selves in their full humanity.

This world eludes the grasp of the theoretical scientist. He has to build up an artificial device, in order to bring the intersubjective life-world into view, a likeness of the same, in which the human life-world recurs, but deprived of its liveliness, and in which man recurs, but deprived of his unbroken full humanity. This artificial device, [5048] called the method of the social sciences, overcomes the outlined dialectical difficulty by substituting for the intersubjective life-world a model of this life-world. This model, however, is not peopled with human beings in their full humanity, but with puppets, with types, which are constructed as if they could perform actions and reactions. However, these acts are merely fictitious. They are not manifestations of the spontaneous consciousness of the actor, but assigned and ascribed to the puppets by the grace of the scientist.

But if according to certain definite operational rules (described by the methodology of the social sciences) these types are constructed in such a way that their fictitious working acts and performances remain not only consistent in themselves but compatible with all the pre-experiences of the world of daily life that the observer acquired before he made the leap into the theoretical province of meaning—then, and only then, does this model of the social world become a theoretical object, [an object of an actual positing of being]. It receives an accent of reality although not that of the natural attitude. [5049]

(M R 573)

(150) *Dialectics of communication: How can theoretical thinking be communicated, and how is theorizing in intersubjectivity possible?*

Scientific theorizing is possible only within a "universe of discourse" that is pregiven to the scientist as the outcome of other people's theorizing acts. It is, second, founded upon the assumption that the subject matter of my theoretical thought can also become the topic of the theoretical thinking of other poeple, who will verify or falsify my own results (Husserl, *Formale und transcendentale Logik* pp. 172-173, 200-201, 205-215, esp. 209, 212 [§§61, 77, 80-85, esp. 81 and 83]) as I will theirs. But the communication required for this presupposes acts of working within the life-world, i.e. the abandoning of the theoretical attitude. This paradoxical situation [is] similar to that in the case of dreaming.—This is just a special case of the age-old problem that recurs in any type of pure meditation: the problem of indirect communication. This has recently been dealt with as the first of three phenomenological paradoxes so formulated by Fink in his essay on Kant study[33] (1933) pp. 319-383. After having performed the phenomeno-logical reduction, how can the self communicate with the "dogmatist" who remains in the natural attitude? Fink's answer: He [the phenomenologist] remains in the transcendental attitude but he places himself "*in*" the natural attitude as a transcendental situation that is seen through by him. The second paradox consists in the fact that the phenomenologist must use the mundane world-concepts and language ("paradox of the phenomenological proposition"), therefore all phenomenological reports are necessarily inadequate [5049a] because they attempt to give a mundane expression to a non-worldly meaning. The problem is not specific to the transcendental sphere alone; it is just more complicated there because of the question of the plurality of transcendental egos, a community of nomads, which, nevertheless, can communicate directly and immediately merely by the mundane means of bodily gestures including language of any kind. It is, however, a question whether intersubjectivity is possible transcendentally or belongs to the mundane sphere.—But the paradox of communication exists only as long as we take the finite provinces of meaning as ontological static entities, objectively existing outside the stream of individual consciousness within which they originate. Then, of course, the terms and notions, valid within one province, would not only, as is the case, require a complete modification within the others, but would become entirely meaningless, comparable to the coins of a particular country, which cease to be legal tender when we cross the border. But the finite provinces of meaning are not separated states of mental life in the sense that passing from one to the other would require a transmigration of the soul and a complete extinction of memory. They are merely terms for different tensions of one and the same consciousness, unbroken from birth to death, which is attended to in different modifications: All these different experiences belong to my inner time and can be remembered and reproduced. And that is why they can be communicated. See conclusion, p. 575.

List of
Abbreviations

The page references occasionally given by Schutz refer to the following works.

Cart. Med.
Husserl, E. *Cartesianische Meditationen und Pariser Vorträge.* Ed. S. Strasser. *Husserliana,* vol. 1. The Hague, 1963². *Cartesian Meditations.* Translated by Dorion Cairns. The Hague: Martinus Nijhoff, 1960.

Choosing
Schutz, A. "Choosing among Projects of Action." *Philosophy and Phenomenological Research* 12, no. 2 (1951): 161–185.

Common Sense
Schutz, A. "Common Sense and Scientific Interpretation of Human Action." *Philosophy and Phenomenological Research* 14, no. 1 (1953): 1–37.

Concept and Theory
Schutz, A. "Concept and Theory Formation in the Social Sciences." *Journal of Philosophy* 51, no. 9 (1954): 257–273.

Erfahrung und Urteil, EU, Erf. Urteil
Husserl, E. *Erfahrung und Urteil.* Ed. L. Landgrebe. Hamburg, 1954. *Experience and Judgment.* Trans. James S. Churchill and Karl Ameriks. Evanston, Ill.: Northwestern University Press, 1973.

Farber
Farber, Marvin, ed. *Philosophical Essays in Memory of Edmund Husserl.* Cambridge, Mass.: Harvard University Press, 1940.

F. U. T. Logik
Husserl, E. *Formale und Transcendentale Logik, (Versuch einer Kritik der logischen Vernunft).* Ed. Paul Janssen. *Husserliana,* vol. 17. The Hague, 1974. *Formal and Transcendental Logic.* Translated by Dorion Cairns. The Hague: Martinus Nijhoff, 1969.

Ideas (Ideen)
Husserl, E. *Ideen zu einer reinen Phänomenologie und phänomenologischen Psychologie.* Bk. 1, parts 1 & 2, ed. Karl Schuhmann. Bk. 2, ed. Mary Biemel. *Husserliana,* vols. 3–5. The Hague, ²1976/1952/1953.

Krisis

Husserl, E. *Die Krisis der europäischen Wissenschaften und die transcendentale Phänomenologie (Eine Einleitung in die phäno-menologiesche Philosophie)*. Ed. Walter Biemel. *Husserliana*, vol. 6. The Hague, 1962². *The Crisis of European Sciences and Transcendental Phenomenology*. Translated by David Carr. Evanston, Ill.: Northwestern University Press, 1970.

Language, Language Disturbances

Schutz, A. "Language, Language Disturbances and the Texture of Consciousness." *Social Research* 17, no. 3 (1950): 365–394.

Log. Unt.

Husserl, E. *Logische Untersuchungen*. Vol. 1, Prolegomena zur reinen Logik. Ed. Elmar Holenstein. *Husserliana*, vol. 18. The Hague, 1975; also, *Logische Untersuchungen*, 3 vols. Tübingen, 1968⁵. *Logical Investigations*. Translated by J. N. Findley. New York: Humanities Press, 1970.

Multiple Realities M. R., M R

Schutz, A. "On Multiple Realities." *Philosophy and Phenomenological Research* 5, no. 34 (1945): 533–576.

Symbol, Symb., S., Sym.

Schutz, A. "Symbol, Reality and Society." *Symbol and Society: Fourteenth Symposium of the Conference on Science, Philosophy and Religion*, ed. L. Bryson et al. New York, 1955. Pp. 135–202.

Notes

Translators' Preface

[1]Alfred Schutz and Thomas Luckmann, *The Structures of the Life-World,* vol. 1, trans. Richard M. Zaner and H. Tristram Engelhardt, Jr. (Evanston, Ill.: Northwestern University Press, 1973).

[2]This was subsequently published by Luckmann: "On the Boundaries of the Social World," in *Phenomenology and Social Reality: Essays in Memory of Alfred Schutz,* ed. M. Natanson (The Hague: Martinus Nijhoff, 1970), pp. 73–100.

[3]Preface, vol. I, p. xxvi.

[4]This constitutes the core of Luckmann's essay, "The Constitution of Language in the World of Everyday Life," in *Life-World and Consciousness: Essays for Aron Gurwitsch,* ed. Lester E. Embree (Evanston: Northwestern University Press, 1972), pp. 469–88.

[5]In particular, "Common-Sense and Scientific Interpretation of Human Action," in Alfred Schutz, *Collected Papers: The Problem of Social Reality,* vol. 1, ed. M. Natanson (The Hague: Martinus Nijhof) Phaenomenologica 11, pp. 3–47. Others of Schutz's reflections on this issue might be mentioned, in particular: "Concept and Theory Formation in the Social Science," ibid., pp. 48–66; "Phenomonology and the Social Sciences," ibid., pp. 118–39; "Husserl's Importance for the Social Sciences," ibid., pp. 140–49; and "On Multiple Realities," ibid., pp. 207–59.

[6]Preface, vol. 1, p. xxiii.

[7]Ibid., p. xxi.

[8]Ibid., p. xxiv.

[9]Ibid., p. xxv.

[10]Ibid., p. xviii.

Chapter 5

[1]Cf. esp. Chap. 2, A 2; 2, B 4 c; 3, A 2 c. (Chapter references refer to Vol. 1 (Chaps. 1–4) or Vol. 2 (Chaps. 5 & 6).

[2]Aron Gurwitsch, *Théorie du champ de la conscience* (Bruges, 1957).

[3]Chap. 3, B.

[4]More on appresentation in the next chapter.

[5]Chap. 3, B & C.

[6]Chap. 6, C.

[7]Chap. 5, A 5.

[8]Cf. Chap. 2, B 5, as well as Thomas Luckmann, "On the Boundaries of the Social World," in *Phenomenology and Social Reality: Essays in Memory of Alfred Schutz,* ed. Maurice Natanson (The Hague, Nijhoff, 1970), pp. 73–100.

[9]Chap. 6, B.

[10]Chap. 5, B.

[11]Esp. Chap. 3, C.

[12]Cf. Chap. 2, B 4.

[13]Cf. Chap. 2, esp. B 2, 3, & 4.

[14]Chap. 3, B 4 b.

[15]Chap. 3 B 4.

[16]Chap. 3, B 4 a.

[17]Chap. 3, B 2 c.

[18]Chap 1, A; B 2; Chap. 2, 4 c.

[19]Chap. 3, A 1 c.

[20]Chap. 2, B 2; and Chap. 2, B 4 b.

[21]Chap. 2, B 3.

[22]Chap. 3, A 1 c.

[23]Cf. esp. Chap. 3, B 2 c and C 4.

[24]Cf. Chap. 3, B 4.

[25]See note 24.

[26]Chap. 3, B, esp. 2 a.

[27]Cf. esp. Chap. 3, B 1.

[28]Edmund Husserl, *Erfahrung und Urteil,* ed. Ludwig Landgrebe (Hamburg: Claasen, 1954), § 21. English translation: *Experience and Judgment,* trans. James S. Churchill and Karl Ameriks (Evanston, Ill.: Northwestern University Press, 1973).

[29]Cf. Chap. 3, A 2; and Chap. 3, B 1, 2, 3, and 4.

[30]Cf. Chap. 3, A 3.

[31]A few more things would have to be said on the reasonable founding of action. Cf. Chap. 5, D.

[32]Cf. Chap. 4, B 2.

[33]Cf. Chap. 4, D.

[34]Cf. Chap. 4, A 2.

[35]Cf. Chap. 6, C.

[36]Cf. Chap. 5, A 5.

[37]Cf. Chap. 5, A 2 a.

[38]Cf. Chap. 2, B 4.

[39]Chap. 3, B 2 c.

[40]Cf. Chap. 5, A 5.

[41]Cf. Chap. 5, B 4 c.

[42]Cf. Luckmann, "On the Boundaries of the Social World."

[43]Cf. Chap. 2, B 5.

[44]Cf. Chap. 2, B 2, and 2, B 4 b.

[45]Cf. Chap. 2, B 5.
[46]Cf. Chap. 5, A 5.
[47]Cf. Chap. 2, B 5 b ii.
[48]Cf. Chap. 6 B.
[49]We have studied in detail the social stratifications of the life-world. Cf. Chap. 2, B 5.
[50]Max Weber is the one who pointed this out. Cf. Max Weber, *Wirtschaft und Gesellschaft*, ed. Johannes Winckelmann (Tübingen: Mohr, 1976[5]), 1st half-volume, pp. 13ff. Translated as *Economy and Society*, vol. 3, ed. Guenther Roth and Claus Wittich (New York: Bedminster Press, 1968), pp. 11ff.
[51]Cf. on this topic the analysis of the secondary zone of operation, Chap. 2, B 3.

Chapter 6

[1]Cf. Chap. 3, A 1 a and Chap. 3, A 3.
[2]Cf. chap. 6, B 2 & 3.
[3]Cf. Chap. 6, B 4.
[4]Cf. Chap. 6, C 1.
[5]Cf. Chap. 6, B 5.
[6]Cf. Chap. 2, B 2 a and b.
[7]Cf. Chap. 3, A.
[8]Cf. Chap. 6, B 1.
[9]Cf. Chap. 2, B 2, 3, and 4 b.
[10]Cf. Chap. 2, B 2 b iii.
[11]Cf. Chap. 3, B 2 and 3.
[12]Cf., however, Luckmann, "On the Boundaries of the Social World."
[13]Here we are touching upon a basic motif of philosophical anthropology. Cf. on this especially Helmuth Plessner, *Conditio humana* (Pfullingen: Neske, 1964) and *Lachen und Weinen* (Bern and Munich: Franke, 1961[3]). Translated as *Laughing and Crying*, trans. James S. Churchill and Marjorie Grene (Evanston, Ill: Northwestern University Press, 1970).
[14]Cf. Chap. 2, B 5 a.
[15]Cf. Chap. 2, B 5 c i.
[16]Cf. Chap. 2, B 5 c, Chaps. 5 and 6.
[17]Cf. Chap. 3, B 2 a and b, and 3.
[18]Cf. Chap. 3, A 2 c and d.
[19]Cf. Chap. 2, A 4.
[20]Most recently there have been significant signs (in the sociology of knowledge and of religion) of a tremendous increase of interest in the scientific study and semi-scientific exploitation of this field.
[21]Cf. Chap. 2, B 4 2 a i, and Chap. 6, A 4 b.
[22]Cf. Chap. 3, A 3 a.
[23]Cf. also section B of this chapter.
[24]Cf. Chap. 4, B 3 c and C 3.

²⁵In Chap. 6, A 1.

²⁶The illumination of the structure of appresentation begins in the Husserlian analyses, already in his *Logische Untersuchungen* (Tübingen, 1968⁵, 1900¹), especially vol. 2, part 2, where it is still formulated in the terminology of "components of intuition and meaning" but is already recognized in its function of significative relations. Later it is arranged into the general analysis of passive syntheses and active cogitations, into perception, judgments, and in the constitution of intersubjectivity. Cf. Edmund Husserl, *Erfahrung und Urteil* (Hamburg, 1948²), esp. p. 79; E. Husserl, *Ideen zu einer reinen Phänomenologie und phänomenologischen Philosophie*, book 2 (The Hague: Nijoff, 1952), pp. 162ff. (*Husserliana*, vol. 4, ed. M. Biemel); but esp. E. Husserl, *Cartesianische Meditationen* and *Pariser Vorträge* (The Hague: Nijhoff, 1950), esp. pp. 138–149 (*Husserliana*, vol. 1, ed. S. Strasser).

²⁷Husserl, *Cartesianische Meditationen*, § 51, *Husserliana*, vol. 1, p. 142. Translated as *Cartesian Meditations* by Dorion Cairns (The Hague: Martinus Nijhoff, 1969), p. 112.

²⁸Husserl, *Erfahrung und Urteil*, p. 214.

²⁹Husserl, *Cartesianische Meditationen*, § 51, p. 142.

³⁰Ibid., p. 142 (p. 112 of English translation).

³¹Husserl, *Erfahrung und Urteil*, p. 79 (p. 113 of English translation).

³²Husserl, *Cartesianische Meditationen*, § 55, p. 150 (p. 122 of English translation).

³³Cf. Chap. 4, B 2 a, b, and d.

³⁴According to Husserl (*Cartesianische Meditationen*, § 50ff.; *Ideen* §§ 43–50), this constitutes a particularly remarkable case of appresentation. The Other is from the outset given as a material object in space and time and as a subject with his mental life. His body is given within immediate perception (Husserl: originary presence), his life only co-given, appresented (in co-presence).

³⁵Cf. Chap. 4, B 2 d.

³⁶Ibid.

³⁷Cf. Luckmann, "On the Boundaries of the Social World."

³⁸Cf. Chap. 6, C 1.

³⁹Cf. Chap. 4, B 2 d.

⁴⁰E.g. Chap. 2, B 5 c; Chaps. 3, A 2 d, and 6, A 5.

⁴¹The traditions of this quest in the science of religion, cultural anthropology, and political theory are well known. Among their outstanding contemporary representatives we will name only Eric Voegelin and Claude Lévi-Strauss.

⁴²I have already dealt with the problem of the constitution of language in Vol. I. The results of the investigation would have exceeded the framework of the statements of the problem in the chapters of Vol. I, so I have kept them for Vol. II. It was published as an essay under the title "The Constitution of Language in Everyday Life," in *Essays for Aron Gurwitsch*, ed. Lester Embree (Evanston, Ill., Northwestern University Press, 1972), pp. 469–488. The findings of this study also were incorporated, among other things, in my

article "Aspekte einer Theorie der Sozialkommunikation," in *Lexikon der Germanistischen Linguistik*, ed. H. P. Althaus, H. Henne, H. E. Weigand (Tübingen: Niemeyer, 1973), pp. 1–13; second revised edition: (Tübingen, 1979), pp. 28–41. The formulations in the first two sections are in part taken over from my essay "Kommunikation und die Reflexivität der Sozialwissenschaften," in *Sprache und Welterfahrung*, ed. Jörg Zimmermann (Munich: Wilhelm Fink, 1978), pp. 177–191. I have studied the social conditions of language use in a series of publications. The last two sections (C 3 and 4) I have taken mostly from the essay "Gesellschaft und Sprache" in *Dialektologie—Ein Handbuch zur deutschen und allgemeinen Dialektforschung*, ed. W. Besch, U. Knoop, H. E. Wiegand (Berlin: de Gruyter) (in print).

[43]Cf. Chap. 2, B 5 b 1; Chap. 5, E 2 c and Chap. 6, B 1.

[44]In anticipation of constitutional analysis, we have already studied this in connection with the investigation of the social stock of knowledge and its appropriation by the child. Cf. Chap. 4, A 1 b.

Notebooks

[1]Felik Kaufmann, *Methodenlehre der Sozialwissenschaften* (Vienna, 1936).

[2]A. Whitehead, *Process and Reality: An Essay in Cosmology* (New York, 1941).

[3]In the translation by J. L. Achrill, it reads: "Now spoken sounds are symbols of affections in the soul, and written marks symbols of spoken sounds. And just as written marks are not the same for all men, neither are spoken sounds. But what these are in the first place signs of—affections of the soul—are the same for all; and what these affections are likenesses of—actual things—are also the same." Cf. J. L. Achrill, ed., *Aristotle's Categories and De Interpretatione* (Oxford, 1963), p. 43 (16a3ff.)

[4]Schutz's translation. "A *name* as spoken sound significant by conventions" in Achrill translation of Aristotle's *Categories*.

[5]Henri Bergson, *L'évolution créatrice* (Paris, 1930).

[6]G. H. Mead, *The Philosophy of the Present*, ed. A. E. Murphy, (La Salle, Ill., 1959).

[7]G. H. Mead, *The Philosophy of the Act*, ed. Ch. W. Morris (Chicago, 1964).

[8]Schutz, *Gesammelte Aufsätze* III, pp. 86–126.

[9](Not only that, but the indication-relation mediates by my intransparency various levels of clarity of the stock of knowledge at hand.)

[10]Cf. *Husserliana*, vol. 6, Supplement III to § 9 a, pp. 365–386.

[11]Bruno Snell, *Aufbau der Sprache* (Hamburg, 1952).

[12]Susanne K. Langer, *Problems of Art: Ten Philosophical Lectures* (New York, 1957).

[13]Ernst Benz, *Die Ostkirche—im Lichte der protestantischen Geschichtsschreibung von der Reformation bis zur Gegenwart* (Freiburg, 1952).

[14]Curt Sachs, *World History of the Dance* (New York, 1965).

[15]John Dewey, *Logic: The Theory of Inquiry* (New York and Chicago, 1964).

[16]Cf. the 'Comment by Charles Morris,' "Symbol, Reality and Society," in Lyman Bryson, ed., *Symbols and Society* (New York and London, 1955), p. 202.

[17]J. Linschoten, "Über das Einschlafen," part I: Einschlafen und Erleben, *Psychol. Beiträge* II, 1; part II: Einschlafen und Tun, *Psychol. Beiträge* II, 2 (1955/56).

[18]German version, G. E. Moore, *Eine Verteidigung des common sense. Fünf Aufsätze aus den Jahren 1903-1941*, introduction by H. Delius (Frankfurt a. M., 1969).

[19]Karl Jaspers, *Philosophie*, vol. 3 (*Metaphysik*) (Berlin, 1956), pp. 15f. Translated as *Philosophy*, vol. 3, by E. B. Ashton (Chicago: University of Chicago Press, 1971), pp. 15 and 16.

[20]Bruno Snell, pp. 150 f.

[21]Eric Voegelin, *Die neue Wissenschaft der Politik* (Munich, 1956²).

[22]William James, *The Principles of Psychology* (New York, 1950), vol. 2, p. 293.

[23] Ibid., p. 290.

[24]Cf. T. S. Eliot, *Werke*, vol. 3 (Essays 2) (Frankfurt a. M., 1965), pp. 47ff.

[25]Cf. Ludwig Geiger, ed., *Goethes Briefwechsel mit Wilhelm und Alexander von Humboldt* (Berlin, 1909), p. 16.

[26]Ibid.

[27]Cf. G. C. Homans, *Theorie der sozialen Gruppe* (Opladen, 1969⁴), p. 29.

[28]Cf. Eric Voegelin, *The New Science of Politics* (Chicago, 1952), p. 54 (German version: *Die neue Wissenschaft der Politik*, 1965²).

[29]Sources: *[Essai sur les] Données immediates [de la conscience]* 20ff., 94-106; *Matière et mémoire*, 189-195, 224-233; *L'énergie spirituelle: Rêve*, 164-171; *La fausse reconnaisance*, 129-137, *La conscience*, 80-84; *Pensée et le mouvant*: Intro[duction à la] mét[aphysique], 223-228; *La perception du changement*, 171-175, 190-193, *De la position du changement*, 171-175, 190-193; *De la position des problèmes*, 91ff.

[30]To be checked: what according to the present state of my theory of relevance shall be understood by pragmatic relevances: motivational, thematic, interpretational relevance? Are all of them together?

In addition, an interesting reference to the reaches, ranges, horizons of the actual and potential stock of experience determined by (pragmatic) relevances.

[31]G. H. Mead, *Philosophy of the Present* (La Salle, Ill., 1959), p. 173.

[32]H. Spiegelberg, "The 'Reality-Phenomenon' and Reality," in M. Farber, ed., *Philosophical Essays in Memory of Edmund Husserl* (New York, 1968), pp. 84-105.

[33]Eugen Fink, "Die phänomenologische Philosophie Edmund Husserls in der gegenwärtigen Kritik (mit einem Vorwort von E. Husserl)," in *Kantstudien* vol. 38 (1933), pp. 319-384.

Index

Accountability, 4–6

Achrill, J. L., 331

Act, 4, 9, 14, 19–23, 26, 30–37, 46, 50, 53–57, 61–69, 71–77, 80–84, 87–96, 125, 136, 139, 152, 215, 219, 221, 225, 229, 240, 258, 294–97, 299, 301, 304, 311, 317, 322

Action, 1, 4–20, 28–31, 46–75, 101, 114, 124, 205, 207, 211, 213–15, 218, 221, 223, 225–30, 235, 238, 240, 258, 296–99, 307, 311, 317; habitual, 23, 39, 41, 46, 54, 148; plan of, 17, 46, 75, 109; rational, 23, 57–62; social, 68–77, 85, 88, 94, 152; reciprocal immediate, 76–87; reciprocal mediate, 87–91; unilateral, 70, 75; unilateral mediate, 73–76, 91–94

Aging, 25, 100, 118, 126, 210, 256, 300

Alter ego, 136, 141

Althaus, H. P., 331

Ambiguity, 204

Ameriks, Karl, 325, 328

"And so forth," 25, 89, 107, 109, 118, 127, 208, 213, 303

Anonymity, 52, 114

Anonymization, 94, 130, 152, 211, 255

"Answer," 71, 82, 86, 88, 91–94

Anxiety, 124, 129, 272, 307, 318

Apperception, 196, 244, 251

Appresentation, 2, 131–45, 147, 244–47, 250–53, 257, 260, 262–65, 268–71, 275, 279, 284, 287–92, 327

Aquinas, Thomas, 318

Aristotle, 197, 242, 320, 331

Ashton, E. B., 332

Attention, 2, 118, 121, 123, 137, 217, 296, 309, 314

Attitude, 18–21, 30, 43, 48, 69, 115, 202, 211, 286, 294, 296, 320; natural, 2, 4, 7, 28, 57, 66, 72, 99, 101, 105, 112, 118, 120, 123, 126, 129, 133, 136, 142, 145, 246, 293, 301, 306–12, 318–21, 323; theoretical, 47, 129, 146; scientific, 133, 233. *See also* Orientation

"Atypical," 200, 204, 215

Awake(ness), 1–4, 47, 51, 74, 78, 79–83, 118, 121, 131, 146, 191, 283, 293, 295, 301, 309, 313, 315; half-awake, 121, 145

Bayle, Pierre, 222

Because-motive, 18–21, 31, 37, 43, 58, 84, 142, 198, 224, 228, 234, 299, 306, 312

Belief, 196, 233, 238, 307

Berdyaev, Nicolai, 172, 213, 256

Bergson, Henri, 17, 173, 175, 182, 189

Besch, W., 331

Biemel, Mary, 325, 330

Biemel, Walter, 326

Biography, 19, 31, 43, 62, 197, 201, 207, 214, 218, 224, 229, 232–34, 243, 249, 252, 255, 260, 264, 277, 287, 300

Biron, Maine de, 284, 302

Body, 10, 110–13, 194, 203, 238, 255, 257, 284, 300, 302, 314, 318; movements, 10, 16, 79, 253, 257, 262, 265, 281, 291, 295, 297, 306, 309, 319

Boundary, 12, 16, 18, 24, 57, 62, 79, 99–104, 109, 118, 121, 125, 131,